FROM THE LIBRARY OF:

MARTHA'S ENTERTAINING

MARTHA'S ENTERTAINING

MARTHA STEWART

PHOTOGRAPHS BY FRÉDÉRIC LAGRANGE
AND OTHERS

Clarkson Potter/Publishers
New York

Clarkson Potter/Publishers, an imprint of the Crown Publishing Group, a division of Random House, Inc., New York.
www.clarksonpotter.com | www.marthastewart.com. CLARKSON POTTER is a trademark and POTTER with colophon is
a registered trademark of Random House, Inc. Library of Congress Catalog Number: TX731.S7322 2011, 642'.4—dc22;
2010042736. ISBN 978-0-307-36946-4; eISBN 978-0-307-95329-2. Printed in China. Design by William van Roden.
Photograph credits appear on page 432. Some of the recipes and photographs have appeared in Martha Stewart
Living Omnimedia publications. 10 9 8 7 6 5 4 3 2 1 First Edition.

Contents

To my daughter, Alexis,
and her daughter, Jude—may they
continue the family traditions of
entertaining in their own unique ways

To Kevin Sharkey,
for his indefatigable assistance in
the creation of the
parties photographed for this book

To Pierre Schaedelin,
for his expertise in my kitchens and
for sharing so many of his
delicious recipes with all of us

To Frédéric Lagrange,
for his keen eye for beauty—whether
that beauty is found in nature,
in people, or in food and flowers

Introduction

More than thirty years have passed since I wrote my first book, *Entertaining,* and a great deal has transpired in that time. The basic tenets of good entertaining remain the same, but the interest in global cuisine and its preparation, in so-called exotic ingredients, and in distinctive table settings and lush flower arrangements has flourished. Everyone wants secrets and shortcuts, tips and hints, easy instructions, fabulous recipes they can trust, and above all, new inspiration, so their own adventures in entertaining can be ever more unique, more extraordinary, and more innovative.

I really enjoy creating great dinners, holiday gatherings, lovely cocktail parties, and big outdoor or indoor events for which I try hard to make the food and drink served extra-special and extra-delicious, and the presentation extra-beautiful. This book contains examples of some of those parties and events. None of the parties were fabricated for the book—they are shown just as they happened, with friends and colleagues, family members and children, all of whom I hope enjoyed the experiences.

Entertaining family and friends is always challenging; setting a lovely table, always fascinating. Choosing doable recipes that will be appreciated by all is fun but can pose some puzzling problems. In this book, I have tried to focus on new ideas, and to share trusted techniques and solutions I have developed. The book is divided into mornings, afternoons, and evenings, concentrating on a a variety of celebrations, holidays, and gatherings anyone might encounter during the year.

Morning is the time of day when I enjoy entertaining the most. I like setting the table the night before, getting up early, preparing everything, and then going on an early morning escapade with guests. It doesn't matter if I am in Maine, climbing the Beehive; in East Hampton, walking the beach; or in Bedford, hiking in the Reservation. With our appetites formed, we can all sit down to a sumptuous feast of many of my favorite foods: Fresh-squeezed juice, eggs, pastries, popovers, waffles and pancakes, and even good crispy bacon are typically included in our special breakfasts. Selfishly, I like cleaning up after breakfast, or brunch, and then having the rest of the day to garden, ride, bike, or do whatever I please.

In the afternoon, lunch can be hearty or more simple, and it can be extremely varied in terms of food. I love soup and sandwiches, and I also love delicious composed salads, or vegetable tarts, or simply grilled meats and fish. Afternoons can also be a great time to serve a formal tea, throw a cocktail party, or host an ice cream social. I like to invite friends for lunch during the winter months or when I am in a more relaxed location such as Maine or East Hampton. At the farm, it is hard to stop work during the day to sit down and really enjoy a meal.

Evenings offer lots of opportunities to the avid host or hostess. A meal of substantial finger foods with ingenious cocktails, a sit-down formal dinner, a buffet supper, or something more relaxed such as a backyard barbecue—each is a welcome and inviting way to entertain. I have included many such menus that I think will inspire you to create your own original party. Chef Pierre Schaedelin and I thought a lot about the many ways to serve dinner, and the menus we developed are interesting and beautiful. Whether indoors or out, tables can be set with a theme in mind or more simply and effortlessly. Whichever type of menu you choose, make sure there is sufficient illumination, plenty of good beverages, and a scrumptious dessert.

I have used plants, flowers, vegetables, and fruit grown at home, whenever possible, and I seek out the the best meats, fish, dairy, and other ingredients as well, preferably organically grown and produced. All of the dishes and other tableware and linens are from my own collections. We prepared everything for the book in my own kitchens, and tested all the recipes several times to ensure that you will have success preparing delectable food that you will love as much as your guests.

Entertaining guests is not really about "shortcuts," and while some of the recipes and techniques may appear time consuming, many others are really quite easy and contain few ingredients. Menus can be used in their entirety or broken up as you wish. Some of the recipes will certainly become family favorites, and hopefully you will return to them time and again.

ABOVE Each property has a simple logo, which we print on menus, place cards, maps, and welcome messages. In Bedford, we use this lovely woodcut of a sycamore tree (left). French chef Pierre Schaedelin (right) worked with me for more than three years on this book. We had a wonderful time composing menus and serving many memorable dishes to my guests.

PAGE 2 On this antique faux bois table at Skylands, I have arranged glassware, ice buckets, drink garnishes, and silver martini shakers to permit guests to "mix their own."

PAGE 4 The property on Lily Pond Lane in East Hampton is just one acre, but the large circular lawn in front makes it seems much larger. A monumental terra-cotta Italian pot sits year round in the center of the lawn, and roses, hydrangeas, lilies, and wisteria vines are the main features of the gardens.

PAGE 5 'Cardinal de Richelieu', violetta, and 'Constance Spry' are just a few of the many "old" roses I grow in East Hampton. This generous arrangement shows off these and others, interspersed with pink yarrow. Cast-iron urns (lined with plastic to prevent rust) make very good containers for roses.

PAGE 6 Just as much care is given to one guest as to many in my home. This is a cozy spot in the "green" parlor, an area dominated by the Swedish clock, the very heavy green marble Empire table, and the Kyoto green walls, which are "wood-grained" with paint.

PAGE 8 Because I generally entertain fourteen to sixteen people at a time, I like to keep adequate numbers of glasses, service plates, and side dishes on hand.

PAGE 9 This oversized pink lustre bowl, holding more roses from the Lily Pond garden, rests on an ebonized stand.

Mornings

BLUEBERRY BREAKFAST

OPPOSITE A crowded but happy table is the essence of a fun and friendly weekend in Maine. The table seats eighteen, so if I have only fourteen, I invite a few local friends to fill the empty stools. On this weekend we had quite a large group of friends sleeping over at the house in Seal Harbor. Every minute of the weekend was planned, the meals were designed to take place when people were hungry, and the food was home-made and mouthwateringly great.

The kitchen at Skylands is really the hub of the household, just as it is in so many homes. Everything happens there, and no matter how hard I try to move some of the action elsewhere, it all invariably ends up at the kitchen table or the counter. When the house was built, the kitchen, with its great stoves, heavy sinks, large center worktables, and multiple pantries and refrigerators, was off bounds to the family and guests. It was the "back of the house," the domain of the staff only. Meals were eaten in the dining room, at the breakfast table by the window, or at the great table in front of the fireplace.

When I bought the house, I changed the ebb and flow of the traffic, and almost immediately the kitchen became a hub of activity. Casual meals could be eaten at the new giant table. Stools at different heights were purchased to accommodate up to eighteen people. The surface of the table was covered with two large sheets of indestructible, zinc-coated tin, which helps it double as work space (pastry dough, for example, rolls out very well on this material). The cappuccino machine, capable of producing four cups at a time, was positioned on a new long serving table under the wall of windows. The stoves were replaced with a bank of commercial-grade ranges with eighteen burners. One wall was lined with shelves for open storage of everyday dishes, and a long fishmongers' table was placed underneath to hold trays of flatware and serving pieces.

We have at least one big breakfast and one big lunch in the kitchen on weekends. On this October morning, the blueberries were abundant, frozen in August in the big chest freezer in the basement. So a blueberry breakfast it was! Pancakes, waffles, muffins, and smoothies—all were made with the local fruit. Of course, there were other delights: yogurts from the Smith Family Farm, croissants from Petrossian in New York, coffee from Italy, and maple syrup from western Maine.

Menu

BLUEBERRY PANCAKES

DONN'S BLUEBERRY BELGIAN WAFFLES

BLUEBERRY MUFFINS

BLUEBERRY SMOOTHIES

SMITH FAMILY FARM YOGURT

CAPPUCCINO AND CAFÉ AU LAIT

ABOVE White Martha Stewart Wedgwood plates, Christofle silverplate flatware, and café au lait bowls from the Martha Stewart Collection were combined to set a rustic and easy breakfast table; the blueberry theme was carried further with the blue napkins. OPPOSITE Golden moose maple leaves still hanging on to their branches, sumac reddening in the cold air—October is one of the prettiest times of year in Maine or anywhere. This view shows part of the back of the house.

I think this was Kevin Sharkey's plate of blueberry pancakes—his favorite breakfast. I never heat my maple syrup, preferring it cold on hot pancakes. OPPOSITE Along the center of the table we stacked three pedestals and topped them with freshly baked blueberry muffins and warm croissants. The unripe blueberries used as a garnish were found on the big bushes in one of my gardens.

ABOVE (clockwise from left) Skylands is full of great architectural surprises and unusual discoveries; these magnificent stairs descend from the upper terrace to the woodland path. Moss and Irish baby's tears have grown wild in the cracks and corners. A stack of the best waffles you could ever eat; the original recipe comes from my friend Donn Chappellet from Napa Valley, California. This manual calendar came with the house, and it is religiously changed each and every day. An empty café au lait bowl. OPPOSITE It is always a good idea to photograph the table right after everyone has gotten up from it; here there's not much of anything left to consume. This is either good or bad, depending on how you look at it!

A VISIT TO THE DAIRY FARM

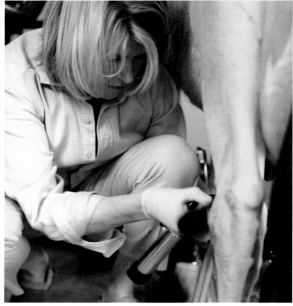

Seventy-five years ago, there were two dozen or so dairy farms on Mount Desert Island. Today there is only one, the Smith Family Farm, on the north side. Because Mount Desert went from an agricultural island in the 19th and very early 20th centuries to a primarily tourist-centric vacationland after 1925, the distance from farm to table increased dramatically. Land appropriate for farming and raising livestock became exceedingly scarce. Maggie and Lucian Smith started their farm several years ago, to provide milk, yogurt, and other organically produced products to the local population. Their mission sounds simple, but in reality, it is highly complex and of utmost importance to those of us who care about sustainable farming; about good, clean food; and about preserving and improving our agricultural practices. Maggie sells her milk and other products, from a small herd of gentle Jersey cows, at the local farmers' markets and at her farm, a verdant 64 acres of green grass and apple trees; Lucian grows and sells lovely produce. I am especially enamored of the yogurts (plain, lemon, and maple), the buttermilk, and the whole milk. On weekends, I often stop in and see how the farm is doing. My guests like to get up early and go with me to the farm or to one of the three markets to talk to the farmers, learn about the business, and buy some products to take home. On this particular weekend, it was so pleasant to make our purchases directly at the farm, walk around a bit, and even milk a couple of the beautiful cows. The dairy is very small, but everything is automated and I learned how to use Maggie's equipment.

ABOVE The Skylands van, an old gray Ford twelve-passenger, is extremely useful and reliable (left). With blue rubber gloves on, I learn the fine points of mechanized milking from Maggie Smith in Bar Harbor, Maine (right). OPPOSITE Maggie Smith's cows, registered Jerseys, are friendly, gently handled, and obedient. They live well on their small farm with the Smiths and their three children and giant dog. I always feel like the camp counselor in Maine because I am the designated driver for my friends when we visit the farm or go on any adventure.

favorite ideas for
BREAKFAST TRAYS

OPPOSITE This French-made, pale yellow china breakfast set, with its covered deep plate, is just the right vessel for a service of perfectly poached eggs on toast. The tiny pullet eggs (from my flock of Bantams) are served on top of lightly buttered crustless whole-wheat toast. Serve with salt and pepper and the guest's choice of coffee in a small pot. Provide a rack with more toast, and butter and jam on the side.

It's pretty old-fashioned to serve guests breakfast in bed or in their bedrooms. This practice was once common in fancy country homes and in other homes with lots of domestic help. Skylands was built in 1925–26 by Edsel Ford as a summer residence for his family. Designed by Duncan Candler, the house was fabricated primarily from local materials: pink granite and first-growth oak. With leaded windows, steel framing, closets and cupboards fashioned from common railroad wood of the time, pink cypress, and lots of galvanized copper inside and out, the house is well lit, beautifully ventilated, and roomy enough for twenty or so weekend guests in the main structure alone!

When the Fords were in residence I understand that "Cook" made delicious tray breakfasts that were sent to the various guests in the main house as well as in the guesthouses. There are lots of breakfast trays and breakfast sets in the china closets, which is good evidence that guests could choose where they ate the first meal of the day. Here are some suggestions for breakfast tray meals that could be served anywhere—on the terrace, at the dining room table, or even in the office. Having the trays, which sit over the knees, and the charming old china sets makes the job easier. Don't forget to include a tiny flower arrangement and the daily newspaper or a printout of the headlines from the Internet.

ABOVE A few years ago I designed a line of dishes for Burleigh Ware (Staffordshire) decorated with faux bois. I now use this set in Maine because faux bois has become the design motif for much of the decoration there. OPPOSITE Well-made porridge is an art, and steel-cut Irish oats are essential for texture and crunch. The additions of honey or maple syrup, dried fruits, nuts, and milk or cream is a personal choice and all should be offered as options. Personally, I like porridge very plain, with just milk and brown sugar. A big cup of café au lait or cappuccino is the only necessary accompaniment.

ABOVE I started a collection of silver "heated" plates when I bought Skylands. Because the rooms are large, I feared that food would cool off too quickly if the plates were not sufficiently warmed. Each of these pieces has a hot-water reservoir, filled through a small opening beneath the top plates, very similar to old-fashioned baby's plates. They are perfect for serving fresh-out-of-the-pan French toast, another of my favorite breakfast treats, sprinkled with powdered or granulated sugar and served with maple syrup. OPPOSITE Another charming breakfast set on one of the many antique trays that were in the house when I purchased Skylands. This is a very simple "calorie counter's" breakfast—puffed whole-grain cereal, skim milk, fresh garden berries, and honeycomb from the Bedford beehives.

ABOVE Sometimes a light eater will be perfectly satisfied with nothing more than coffee or tea and cinnamon toast. This is the same delicious cinnamon toast my mother taught me how to make when I was a child. Use good, old-fashioned white bread, such as pain de mie, or even good-quality commercial white bread for the toast (left). Skylands is a treasure trove of old silver, linens, and china, and we try to use all of it for entertaining throughout the year. I think most of us now realize that if we own these things, they should be put to good use; silver, for example, looks better if it's used often than if it's stored away in a drawer. And storing freshly laundered linens in an accessible place encourages us to use them rather than to rely on the ordinary, everyday (right).

OPPOSITE I keep a supply of frozen croissants from my favorite sources in New York in the big chest freezers in the basement at Skylands or in the flower room at my farm in Bedford. With home-made jams, fresh creamery butter, possibly a platter of scrambled eggs, fresh-squeezed orange juice, and a great cup of tea or coffee, breakfast is always a delicious meal.

HOLIDAY OPEN HOUSE BRUNCH

The tradition of the open house dates back in the United States to the 17th century, when the Dutch settlers commonly opened their homes on January 1 to celebrate the New Year. Now open houses take place anytime one desires to invite friends and neighbors for something a bit out of the ordinary. For this party, I wanted to include a special tribute and thank-you to my longtime editors for the superb job they've done over the past twenty years in the creation of *Martha Stewart Living* magazine. My editors work so hard all year, creating stories that will inspire memorable celebrations, meals, and holiday festivities. Generally they decorate for the holidays out of season, sometimes crafting for Christmas in June and Hanukkah in April. For this get-together, I insisted we have a real holiday meal at the real time, with snow on the ground and my decorations everywhere.

Colleagues were invited with their families because I love to have kids in the house playing with the dogs and searching for the five cats, which is a challenging game since my cats are very good at hiding, anywhere from the darkest basement corner to under the desks in the crafts room on the third floor. And parents are so thoughtful; it often seems that they have prompted the children to respect Martha's house and its contents—be careful! I had food in the kitchen, in the servery, and in the small dining room. People ate with plates on their laps or in the large dining room, where the red canaries sang merrily in their cage. There was at least one trimmed tree in every room, each decorated in a new way to delight my creative staffers, who must always be surprised. Most fun of all was the snowball fight (instigated by collecting editor Fritz Karch) and riding the Kawasaki all-terrain vehicle in the snow, which even the youngest of the guests loved, despite snowballs being pelted at the riders! As a party favor, I gave each guest a bread board cut to resemble a slice of bread, plus a jar of homemade preserves wrapped in a kitchen towel. They were very well liked gifts, I think.

Menu

CANDIED–KUMQUAT CHAMPAGNE
COCKTAILS

POMEGRANATE–APRICOT PUNCH

CARAMEL–TOPPED BRIE
WITH PECANS

BLINI WITH CRÈME FRAÎCHE
AND CAVIAR

POPOVERS WITH FRIED EGGS AND
CREAMED SPINACH

HAM WITH CURRANT–
ROSEMARY GLAZE

BUTTERMILK–CHIVE BISCUITS

SLICED CITRUS FRUITS

MINI HONEY FRUITCAKES

SPRITZ COOKIES

NOAH'S ARK COOKIE
CUTOUTS

ABOVE I am the self-appointed barista at all my parties. I love manning the cappuccino machine and trying to equal the fine cup of cappuccino served at Via Quadronno, for me the best example in New York City. Everything I need for the process is right at hand—either in a drawer, on a shelf, or on top of the machine. OPPOSITE The buffet was very simple and the favorite dish of all was the popover split and filled with creamed spinach and fried eggs. The ham was tender and juicy, glazed with a mixture of red currant jelly and fresh sprigs of rosemary. Citrus slices, buttermilk country biscuits, and a big salad of hothouse greens rounded out the plate in this very satisfying menu.

ABOVE I had not served caramel-topped Brie for a long time and it was a huge success (left); everyone loved the crunchy caramel coating that tasted so good with the perfectly ripe cheese. I made a lot of very tender small blinis and served them with salmon roe caviar and crème fraîche (right). To make light and tender blini, it's best to allow the batter to stand for at least thirty minutes once the yeast is added, before adding the beaten egg whites. Cook blini on a hot griddle that has been brushed with melted clarified butter. Buy your caviar (salmon roe eggs) from the best-quality purveyor; I always get mine at Russ & Daughters in New York City.

Gruyère popovers, cut in half lengthwise, are each filled with creamed spinach, a fried egg, and a strip of bacon, making a most wonderful concoction. The baked ham was lean and tender and the buttermilk-chive biscuits flaky and flavorful.

OVERLEAF A prelit artificial tree was erected in the smaller of my two dining rooms at the farm. Every room boasts at least one tree—some real, some artificial, some vintage. The prelit feature saves a great deal of time and looks really good. This was my Noah's Ark tree—cookie ornaments representing the animals were decorated with great care using royal icing. Polar bear figures, each with a star headdress, were everywhere. The tree stand was really a Noah's Ark barge, fabricated at Martha Stewart Living. The dessert buffet was on display in the servery off the main kitchen. Stacked antique glass pedestals held the homey fruitcakes, spritz cookies were stacked in antique Swedish glasses, and more Noah's Ark animal cookies stood upright in antique wine "rinsers."

ABOVE (clockwise from upper left) James Dunlinson and Lucinda Scala Quinn had lots to chat about while they sipped the Candied-Kumquat Champagne cocktails. Amy Conway's children, Luca and Virginia, did not feel the cold at all while they participated in a very fun snowball fight. Kevin Sharkey always enjoys visiting the stable to pet and cuddle the miniature Sicilian donkeys, the chow chow puppy, and the horses and sheep. Who would have thought that Daisy, Darcy Miller Nussbaum's daughter, would ever even consider throwing a snowball? She had a gleeful time!

Everywhere one looked on that Sunday morning there was pristine white snow. The fence sent extraordinary shadows across the snow as the day wore on. The old corn crib has been restored to its former glory—someday I will use it for a dinner party.

One of the best features of the farm is the well-pruned and shapely ancient apple trees. We dress up these treasures every Christmas with lights and giant ornaments. OPPOSITE Our "family" portrait: Most of us have worked together for years and there is a camaraderie that comes with time. It was such fun to get together for this lovely celebration. Even the dogs were content, but where, oh where, are the children? Throwing snowballs?

an elegant
BREAKFAST AT SKYLANDS

OPPOSITE When I moved into Skylands, I found drawers and racks full of incredibly beautiful household linens. This pink linen set has intricate openwork and goes very well with the set of hand-painted Limoges breakfast/ luncheon dishes left at Skylands by Mrs. Edsel Ford. The oversized pink cappuccino cups and saucers are Limoges, but contemporary. All the pink looks great on the pink granite terrazzo top of the faux bois dining table. OVERLEAF Six place settings are set on the smaller of two faux bois dining tables in the large dining room, which has three window exposures. The glass-domed flower arrangements are actually constructed from fresh flowers that have been coated with melted parrafin and arranged in small silver cups. Waxed flowers will last five or six days. The glass-ware is Venetian.

Oftentimes I will have a small breakfast at Skylands. When I visit I plan business meetings in the morning, generally after a sporting activity such as hiking or kayaking or an early tennis game.

This is a simple menu, very easy to make, but especially luxurious in its look and tastes. Everyone seems to like grapefruit, and this preparation is so tasty and unexpected. Halves of pink grapefruits are broiled, cut side up, until the fruit is warmed and the rind slightly darkened. The sections can be cut prior to warming, but if you use pointy grapefruit spoons, the fruit is actually very easy to extricate, warm, from the rind. I love to use thin slices of orange or grapefruit, dusted with powdered sugar and dried in the oven, as a decorative and delicious garnish. Choose seedless blood or navel oranges, or ruby grapefruits. For thinly slicing the fruit, a very sharp serrated knife works well, as does an extra-sharp carbon-steel Japanese vegetable cleaver.

I found another magical tool, an egg topper, in a chef's supply catalog. It works amazingly well and you can get perfect cuts every time. I use eggs from my own hens or farm-fresh organic eggs whenever I can; the bright yellow of the yolks contrasts very well with the bright orangy red of the salmon roe. I also use pain de seigle from Balthazar Bakery in New York City. I always have several rounds of this extraordinary bread in the freezer and on a weekend it is indeed the bread of the house. Thinly sliced, warmed in the salamander, or toasted, it is perfect with eggs, no matter how they are prepared.

Make sure to have unsalted butter, coarse salt, and plenty of coffee and organic whole milk for making cappuccinos and lattes.

ABOVE Half a loaf of pain de seigle was used as a backdrop for the egg-in-a-shell photo (left). The surface of the table appears to be marble, but it is really waxed butchers' paper crumpled and then spread flat. I use this waxed paper for wrapping food for boat picnics, and also for covering tabletops when we have lobster roasts and other casual feeding frenzies. Cut poppies are really a wonderful flower for arranging; these are arranged in a basket frog set in a low bronze Japanese bowl (right). OPPOSITE The egg shells filled with soft scrambled eggs and topped with caviar look great served in the silver egg holders and caddy, a gift from a friend years ago. Of course, any egg cups will do.

EASTER BRUNCH

OPPOSITE My veterinarian Marty Goldstein has three beautiful young daughters; pictured are ten-year-old Emma and her nine-year-old sister, Hana, with their Easter baskets, full of special candies, stuffed toys, and colored eggs. I spray-painted ordinary baskets a rich chocolate brown enamel—they looked more like real chocolate than the foil-wrapped eggs!

For as long as I can remember I have loved entertaining on Easter Sunday. Whether it's an egg hunt with lots of children, a sit-down breakfast for family, or a brunch for friends, Easter, and the hope it represents for a new season of rebirth and change, is one of my favorite days of the year. Plus, I really like rabbits, bunnies, eggs, and jelly beans! Every year I try to reinvent the menu—adding new things to the list, but never eliminating kielbasa with beet horseradish (Kevin Sharkey's favorite), paska (my favorite), molded butter in the shapes of rabbits or chickens (my friend Jane Heller's favorite), or Easter ham in one of its many variations. I try to have a small hunt for the children who are attending—the golden egg (with a surface of applied gold leaf) is more sought after than the head of the giant chocolate bunny. The buffet is a tasty assortment. This menu featured giant artichoke hearts with poached eggs and hollandaise sauce, and buckwheat crêpes with smoked salmon.

I keep a very organized basement in Bedford where all of my Easter and other holiday decorations are safely stored. Of course, every season I run around to my favorite stores in New York and elsewhere and peruse my favorite catalogs, looking for new and clever ideas to incorporate into my overall setup. My friend Steve Gerard found a chocolate maker in Cleveland, Ohio, called Malley's, and has been sending me something from that old-fashioned store every year in return for an invitation to the Easter festivities. When you see the giant bunny, you will know why I love Steve! Our television crafts department is another very important source of new ideas and decorations. Art Director Anduin Havens and her team never fail to inspire and delight me with clever ways to change the look and feel of this special day. And most important, Kevin has been Mr. Easter for me, every year designing the most unbelievably beautiful and creative Easter baskets. His designs are always a focal point of whatever we do.

Menu

CUCUMBER AND PUMPERNICKEL
CANAPÉS

ARTICHOKES WITH POACHED EGGS AND
"BÉARNAISE" SAUCE

BOURBON— AND BROWN SUGAR—
GLAZED HAM

ROASTED KIELBASA WITH
FRESH HORSERADISH

BUCKWHEAT CRÊPES WITH GRAVLAX
AND SOUR CREAM

PASKA

ABOVE For several years we sold a Martha Stewart ham at Costco. It was delicious, and the brining and smoking process was modeled on the same methods used by my friends at Kurowycky's, a famous, now-defunct Polish butcher shop on the Lower East Side of Manhattan. The ham was scored and glazed with bourbon and brown sugar before roasting, then stood on the cut side for slicing. OPPOSITE I used the servery next to my kitchen for the hearty buffet. Antique glass domes make wonderfully whimsical bell jars for Easter collectibles—assorted blown-out eggs, flocked papier-mâché rabbits, and vintage red-combed felted chickens. The food is served from giant pedestals, platters, and bowls. In one of Tolstoy's novels, he describes what has become one of my favorite sandwiches—thinly sliced cucumber on sweet buttered black bread served with dollops of thick honey. We made lots of them for brunch. The ladies of a Ukrainian church in Stamford, Connecticut, create these incredibly beautiful paskas every Easter. I always order a few to serve at the party.

I keep many tropical and subtropical plants in a large greenhouse and when I entertain I always embellish the rooms with unusual specimens. This large, hairy rhipsalis sits cozily on top of a marble column, and a small mound of decorated eggs sits on top of that. OPPOSITE My seal point Himalayan cat, Bartok, surveys the contents of the parlor coffee table. There are fern and scented geranium arrangements, another flock of baby chicks, and an antique basket filled with moss and topped with faux bois eggs.

I have collected glass eggs, papier-mâché eggs, marble eggs, stone eggs, Ukrainian painted eggs, and foil-covered Styrofoam eggs and they all find their way into table decorations and baskets and compotes displayed around the house. This year Kevin bestowed on me a few glittered chicks he found. They were perfect for small arrangements of the early-blooming narcissus.

OPPOSITE Some years we are really lucky and Easter coincides with the blooming of my daffodil borders. Even before most of the trees have "leafed out," the ground is covered with thousands of many different varieties of daffodils and narcissus. I have been planting about 15,000 per year for six or seven years and the display is both impressive and interesting. Some of the better "naturalizing types" are 'Cheerfulness', 'Erlicheer', 'Sir Winston Churchill', and 'Quail', to name just a few of the hundreds of varieties available now.

ABOVE Each year I take out my tin rabbit chocolate molds and try to make my own molded rabbits in milk, white, and tinted white chocolate. The rabbits are posed in many different stances and are very cute. OPPOSITE The youngest of Marty's daughters, seven-year-old Ayla, bedecked in her Easter finery with her charming Easter bonnet, fell in love with the giant chocolate Easter rabbit from Malley's in Cleveland, and obviously enjoyed posing with it.

I found the deep purple artichokes ('Violetto') in the wholesale flower market in New York City. The great magenta 'Miss Saigon' hyacinths are a fabulous variety to grow for cutting, and they complement the almost-black tulips and purple foil-wrapped chocolate eggs arranged on the desk in the green room. OPPOSITE A tableau featuring a hand-painted giant rabbit, gorgeous flowers, and a charming rustic wood and wire fence becomes a focal point of the green room and something for children and adults alike to admire.

THE APPEAL OF FARM—FRESH EGGS

All of the recipes in this book were cooked with eggs from my farm. Indeed the color is better than most store-bought eggs, and the richness and flavor are deeper, whether the eggs are used in frittatas, omelettes, scrambled eggs, coddled eggs, or even cakes and custards. And the albumen—the white—is thicker, so meringues whip up a lot loftier.

I have been keeping hens for more than forty years. I first got a dozen "egg layers" for our rustic country cottage in Middlefield, Massachusetts. The henhouse was a renovated plywood playhouse we had built for our daughter, Alexis, who had outgrown it. The yard was a chicken-wire fence, 5 feet tall. We lost all of the chickens to varmints over a period of about four months, but I quickly figured out what I had done wrong. I boned up on backyard animal husbandry, and I read a few catalogs of chicken suppliers so I would do better the next time around.

Now I have about two hundred hens of different breeds—all healthy and all good layers. I raise Araucanas for green and blue eggs, French Marans for chocolate-colored eggs, Jersey giants for great white eggs, and others for brown and tan and speckled varieties. The chickens are fed organic corn, organic pellets, and many, many vegetable scraps from the garden and the fields, as well as daily scraps from the magazine and television test kitchens at Martha Stewart Living. The cooks, in return, receive regular deliveries of fresh eggs from the farm.

ABOVE My laying hens (and a few roosters) come in many shapes and sizes and breeds (left). Ranging free in large wire-covered yards, the happy hens lay many eggs a week. The recipes we make using these wonderful eggs are always quite perfect. I make many different types of frittatas, adding vegetables and cheeses and potatoes (right). OPPOSITE Coddled eggs have always been a favorite breakfast or brunch food. These old-fashioned custard cups each hold two eggs, herbs, cheese, and other flavorings that can be added to order.

BREAKFAST ON THE PORCH

OPPOSITE I made two types of scones—a buttermilk version and a cream scone with raisins, currants, and dried cherries. I love stacked pedestals, and these square white ones look especially pretty one on top of another. The glorious yellow flowers are Japanese tree peonies.

I have many good friends who work at Martha Stewart Living, and it is so nice to see them occasionally out of the office, in a social setting. A few of them had heard about the peonies in my garden and wanted to see them in person, so I hosted an impromptu late morning brunch that incorporated tasty cocktails, flaky scones, a variety of frittatas, a tomato tart, and yogurt parfaits with rhubarb.

For the last few years I have had a "peony party," scheduling the date to coincide with what I thought would be the apex of the blooming of the hundreds of peony plants. Unfortunately global warming has played havoc with such "schedules" and it is now almost impossible to judge accurately when a plant is going to bloom. Two years ago the peonies bloomed on June 8. One year ago, they bloomed on May 28. This past year they bloomed closer to May 20. I am now trying to find more varieties with longer blooming periods, and more with early, midseason, and late-blooming properties.

For this breakfast we set two rectangular tables of eight on the front porch. I used blues and greens for dishes and linens, and my turquoise painted metal Windsor chairs for seating, to contrast with the yellows and pinks of the peonies. Many tree peonies as well as herbaceous peonies were in bloom and the colors everywhere were superb. The brightly hued foods provided a striking contrast to the overall color scheme. I tried to use as much from the garden and farm as possible—the eggs, of course, the rhubarb, the early asparagus, the tiny peas, and the spring lettuces and spinach.

Menu

RHUBARB SPARKLERS

FRESH GREEN JUICE

FRESH GRAPE JUICE

BUTTERMILK SCONES

CREAM SCONES WITH DRIED FRUIT

ROASTED TOMATO TART

ZUCCHINI, BELL PEPPER, AND
SCALLION FRITTATA

ARTICHOKE HEART AND
FAVA BEAN FRITTATA

CHORIZO, POTATO, AND
RED ONION FRITTATA

SPINACH AND POTATO FRITTATA

YOGURT, HONEY, AND RHUBARB
PARFAITS

ABOVE (clockwise, from upper left) The porch looks down onto the stone terraces and the parterre herb gardens, and into the fields beyond. Boxwood, allium, *Teucrium*, and various herbs are planted in the beds. Paul Costello is a very talented photographer who came with his wife, Sara Ruffin Costello, a former *Martha Stewart Living* editor. Rhubarb syrup with sparkling water and wedges of orange make very refreshing "sparklers." They can be spiked with vodka for a stronger cocktail. OPPOSITE I love tomato tarts, and even though this one is not made from my own homegrown varieties, it is very delectable—the oven-dried tomatoes are dense and tasty.

ABOVE Another of the frittatas featured zucchini, bell pepper, and scallion. Whipped Greek yogurt is easy to pipe into small dessert glasses or goblets; here it is topped with rhubarb purée and honey. OPPOSITE (clockwise from left) We offered three different frittate—each was unique and full of flavor; this one is made with spinach and potato. It was unseasonably warm that morning and everyone welcomed the soft breezes from the reservoir beyond the fields. Small goblets were filled with freshly squeezed grape juice (from organic red and green grapes). Chorizo, potato, and red onion frittata, fresh from the oven.

Afternoons

PÂTÉ CAMPAGNARD LUNCH

Columbus Day weekend is traditionally the most spectacular on Mount Desert Island, in Maine. It is the last weekend that the "summer folk" visit their homes before closing them up for the long, cold winter ahead. There is a true change that occurs in the landscape: The hardwood trees take on the incredible shades of autumn right before they drop their vibrant leaves. The perennial beds wane, the vegetable gardens decline, the nightly frosts finish off the growing season. There is a rush to cut back, pull out, cover up, and turn over. Storm windows are installed, screens stored, water faucets turned off, and equipment cataloged and requisitioned. Last-minute repairs are completed and a giant quiet descends over the island. But not before the last parties and gatherings take place—celebrations of change and onset, of hesitation and halting. The last great hikes, the last ascents up the mountains, the final boat ride, the last warm rays of the sun, which is falling lower and lower in the sky.

We always try to plan a weekend of parties and this was no exception. A very lively group flew up to Bar Harbor and descended upon Skylands for a busy weekend full of activity. The house has large bedrooms, large living rooms and halls, a spacious, well-equipped kitchen, and a huge terrace for relaxing after hikes and mountain climbs, games of tennis, bike rides or runs, and kayak trips and picnic boat rides to outlying islands. For this weekend, meals were planned to be robust, varied, interesting, and unusual. The lunch, in particular, was an opportunity for Pierre to show us his French training in the art of pâté making. His terrines, rillettes, and pâtés were so delicious. And the new faux bois table in the living hall was the perfect backdrop for an incredible array of delectable offerings.

OPPOSITE It is hard to believe that the tabletop is not grayish wood, or that the metal braces on the corners are not iron, but cement. That is the art of faux bois. The rustic, old-fashioned food was set on platters painted in faux bois, or on vrai bois—slices of real wood—or in wicker baskets.

PREVIOUS There is a trapdoor from the attic of Skylands to a great flat rooftop where this photo was taken. The view is to the south, east, and west, overlooking Seal Harbor to the islands beyond. The terrace on the left is off of Bedroom #1; it is bordered by a knee wall of planters, where I cultivate scented geraniums and ferns.

Menu

VARIETY OF IMPORTED AND
DOMESTIC CHEESES

FOCACCIA ROLLS AND
HERBED FLATBREADS

BUCKWHEAT ROLLS AND FLATBREADS

BERAWEKA

VEGATABLES À LA GRECQUE

TERRINE OF DUCK BREAST AND
LEG CONFIT

TERRINE DE FOIE GRAS

PÂTÉ DE CAMPAGNE

PÂTÉ EN CROÛTE

PORK RILLETES

VEGETABLE TERRINE

FIG CROSTATA

PEAR CROSTATA

ABOVE Years ago, when I was catering, I started a collection of pâté and terrine molds (left). Most of them were made by the old French porcelain maker Pillivuyt (est. 1818). These molds have fanciful but extraordinarily realistic renderings of game birds and beasts on the lids: hare, quail, partridge, grouse, duck, pheasant. This was the first time I could use almost the entire collection for one party. Skylands has a naturalistic landscape designed by Jens Jensen. Stairs and walls made from lichen-covered granite stones were built in place in the mid-1920s (right).

OPPOSITE Kevin Sharkey constructed the autumnal arrangement in the Han Dynasty iron pot: The monumental arrangement is held in place in the pot by wire mesh. Kevin used maple leaves, ferns, love-lies-bleeding, goldenrod, and whatever else he could find in the pastures and woodland. This is a good view of the benches, which fit nicely alongside the table. Despite their weight, the table and benches are easy to slide across the floor whenever we need to move them—thanks to the EZ Glide protectors on the feet.

ABOVE Pierre shared his family's recipe for beraweka, a dense, fruit-studded spiced "pudding" cake that is sliced thinly and served with cheeses and pâtés (left). I found "plates" made from crosscut slabs of wood set on small round feet. Reusable, they are perfect for a rustic meal of this sort (right). OPPOSITE Traditional at such a table of pâtés and terrines are nutmeats (we included Marcona almonds and walnuts), dried and fresh fruits such as figs, fruit preserves, cornichons, artisanal cheeses, and homemade breads. Along with the Pillivuyt, I used Bennington pottery and the wood slices from a downed tree.

ABOVE (clockwise from top left) Free-flowing wine and cozy fires and seating arrangements made it easy for guests to relax and linger over the buffet and its bounty. A few of the cheeses were less well known than others, but all were clearly labeled and accompanied by a wooden spreader for cutting and serving. We made a variety of focaccia, rolls, and toasts to serve with the terrines and cheeses. The Italian fruit condiment known as mostarda was served with the pâtés and cheeses. In Cremona, Italy, home of the most celebrated mostarda, cherries, quince, citron, kumquats, figs, apple, pear, and clementines are simmered in sugar syrup flavored with the essential oil of yellow mustard.

Several of the pâtés were cooked "en croute" in a crust of brioche. These were baked in a type of springform mold that allows one to "release" the pâté by loosening it once it has cooled. The space between the meat filling and the crust is filled with a liquid gelatin consommé that hardens.

RIGHT We continued to eat indoors and outdoors on the large terrace that faces south over the ocean. Most of the terrace plants had been removed because of the threat of frosty nights, but some things still remain lush and colorful even in the autumn, including the *Actinidia*, the kiwi vines which ultimately all turn golden yellow.

ABOVE For dessert after lunch, I baked two types of crostata, which we served together—fresh and dried fig, and fresh pear. The crust for the fig version was liberally sprinkled with coarse sanding sugar before baking, for a sparkling effect (left). Cutting and plating a slice of each crostata on a green antique Cauldon dessert plate (right). OPPOSITE On the lower terrace lies one of Aristide Maillol's masterpieces, *La Rivière*. The very heavy sculpture needed to be handled by a large crew of men. They used elaborate pulleys and cranes to lower this big lady to her place of repose.

Setting up the Faux Bois Table

A few years ago I heard about an artist who specializes in faux bois, or "false wood," construction. His name is Carlos Cortes, and he is a fourth-generation sculptor of this artisanal art form, which was popular in France, Italy, Japan, and Mexico in the early part of the 20th century. Essentially, a metal shape is covered with concrete and then sculpted with primitive tools to resemble wood. This was an inexpensive and long-lasting method to produce practical yet fanciful structures and furniture for backyards, parks, botanical gardens, and even zoos—wherever natural but sturdy wooden-looking objects were desired. In his outdoor studio in San Antonio, Texas, Carlos has created some of that city's most memorable outdoor pieces, including park fixtures, bridges, riverfront benches, and arbors. I commissioned Carlos to make a very large faux bois table for the living hall at Skylands, along with four benches. I have been collecting vintage faux bois for quite some time, and such large tables are nearly impossible to find. Carlos made an absolutely stunning group of furniture, and it was shipped from Texas to Maine by truck. Installation was almost as complicated as placing a major piece of bronze sculpture.

1. The crew used the Skylands tractor with its bucket to position the tabletop on edge in a wood "cradle" for lifting and carrying.
2. The wide front door allowed passage of the many men and the tabletop.
3. Plywood ramps were constructed down the stairs, for easier navigation.
4. The base is slightly lighter than the concrete top, yet still required nine men to lift and carry it down the ramp.
5. While the base was being positioned, the top stood securely in its cradle off to the side. Like a piece of stone or glass, a massive concrete top like this has to travel on edge to prevent cracking or breaking.
6. This is a good view of the extraordinary base of the table; the concrete looks exactly like rough aged wood cleverly fitted together.
7. The guys centered the table base so that it was equally positioned between the stairs and the exterior terrace door. Then, it was time to take a breather.
8. Now for more heavy lifting: Twelve men were required to lift the very heavy top and position it atop the base.
9. The crew was pretty pleased with itself—no chips, no nicks, no breaks. And the table, well, it was perfect and beautiful in its place. Its estimated weight: 3,000 pounds.

EASTER EGG HUNT

I remember clearly the Easter egg hunts that were held on Good Saturday every year in Nutley, New Jersey, when I was a child. There was something fascinating to me about them—the hunt itself, designed so children of all ages would have an opportunity to find some eggs, the giant costumed bunnies prancing around, and the decorated Easter baskets—always festive and beautiful. When Alexis was old enough to understand the concept of a hunt, I started to have one each Easter at Turkey Hill in Westport, Connecticut. When my nieces and nephews were small, they were invited to hunt, and one year we had about forty children looking for hundreds of cleverly hidden eggs on my property in Greenfield Hill in nearby Fairfield.

Bedford is a great place for a hunt; each year I choose a different location on the farm. We hide a lot of eggs—at least twenty per hunter—for it is sad to see any child with an empty basket. I do not have the hunt on Easter Sunday—too distracting. But the day before is actually a very good time, or even the Sunday prior to Easter. Always hoping for a good, sunny day, the hunt is called for a specific time, and an invitation for brunch or lunch is always included. For children, the menu choices can differ widely from those for adults. For this hunt we planned a pretty spectacular menu, and the hunt itself had staggered start times. There were about twenty children, all with very aggressive and spirited attitudes.

The day could not have been better, and cotton dresses and shirtsleeves were enough for the balmy weather. The uncut grass, the long white cedar post-and-rail fences, and the many shrubs and spring blooming flowers in the early spring landscape made the hunt challenging and the hiding of eggs very easy.

OPPOSITE Chocolate bunnies in all sizes, shapes, and poses are always part of the decorations. Pure milk chocolate rabbits are given out as prizes; those that are artificial remain year to year as sentinels of the hunt.

PREVIOUS The group of seriously intentioned kids that came to hunt: Children of colleagues and friends, most had been to a hunt before, and each was primed for a fast and furious egg hunt that would yield good results—namely a basketful of colored eggs. From left to right: John, Annika, Alexandra, Isabella, Aiden, Daisy, Janet, Alessandro, Emma (in back), Mickayla, Hayden, Annika, Jackie, Tabitha, and Jasper.

Menu

CHICKEN SKEWERS

MINI BEEF BURGERS

MINI BLTs

EGG- AND BUNNY-SHAPED GRILLED CHEESE SANDWICHES

SALMON AND VEGETABLE MINI CAKES

PIGS IN A BLANKET

DEVILED EGGS

SPRING GARDEN CAKE

CITRUS-CORNMEAL SHORTBREAD

TEA AND FRUIT PUNCH

ABOVE Running like lightning, Mickayla, daughter of Sarah Carey and Mary Ann Vanderventer, really wanted a golden egg (left). All the urns were filled with moss on which we photographed the golden eggs (right). There was a grand prize for the hunter who found the most eggs plus a golden; a runner-up prize for finding the most eggs; another prize for multiple golden eggs; and a prize for the fewest eggs.
OPPOSITE One of the many baskets of beautiful eggs ready to be hidden. Every year I choose a new color scheme. This particular year featured purple, yellow, orange, and green. The golden eggs are covered with real gold leaf.

PREVIOUS Muscari (grape hyacinths) grow in profusion under the allée of ancient espaliered apple trees, not far from the donkey paddock (left). The milk chocolate–painted baskets were filled with different colors of artificial grass and tied with contrasting ribbons (right). Each egg hunter was given a basket. I set up the childrens' buffet in the sunken garden next to my house. It is conveniently located directly off the kitchen, for easy access. I used florist flowers as well as spring flowers from the garden, and the many different polymer bunnies were happy to be confused with the milk chocolate interlopers.

Ella Bea, a bit too young to hunt, ran around nevertheless, actively engaged with the other children and very happy to be part of the festivities. The courtyard is right next to the sunken garden; it is great for parties and gatherings. In the spring and summer this is my tropical garden. OPPOSITE The food was created with the children's likes and dislikes in mind. I inquired ahead of time about allergies—luckily there were none. We made everything miniature and tasty: homemade versions of favorites like pigs in a blanket, grilled cheese, hamburgers, and deviled eggs. The brown-and-white checked tablecloth really set off the food and the flowers.

OPPOSITE AND ABOVE (from left to right) The chicken skewers tasted like "chicken nuggets" and were gobbled up! The mini BLTs were also a big hit—I think I ate six! The charming deviled eggs were simply prepared but adorned with bunny shapes cut from thinly sliced carrots and zucchini; the tiny rabbit cutter was one I discovered in Japan and had never used before. The salmon and vegetable cakes were so well seasoned that the children ate them up, thinking, certainly, that they were some normally forbidden fast-food item.

Served with lettuce and tomato on miniature sesame buns, the burgers were divine. OPPOSITE Pan-toasted grilled cheese sandwiches were cut using mini egg and bunny cutters—very charming and very, very good.

Pure pleasure showed on Annika's face just before she dug into her piece of the Peter Rabbit cake, decorated with marzipan miniatures of all the vegetables from Mr. McGregor's garden. OPPOSITE The marzipan vegetables take a long time to create, but baking, assembling, and decorating the cake is not a difficult process once marzipan veggies are formed. The result is utterly spectacular—and unforgettable.

A LUNCHEON FOR BEDFORD FARMERS

OPPOSITE For this occasion, we transformed the big carport into a pristine dining room. The walls and floors were scrubbed and the windows washed. We decided on a grange-like setup: Long tables covered with oilcloth, wicker chairs, and enameled tin plates and cups. The food was served semi–family style: cups of creamy vichyssoise, long colorful grissini in old canning jars, fragrant iced teas and lemonades, and baskets of great breads and toasts.

On June 18, 1885, the *New York Times* published an article describing the Bedford Farmers Club's thirtieth annual exhibition of fruits and flowers. That year the show, plus a delicious and abundant meal, was held at the home of Mrs. Jared Holly Green, a prominent member of the oldest agricultural club in New York State. The Hon. John Jay, grandson of one of America's Founding Fathers, gave an address to the crowd gathered about the state of local farming and, in particular, about the state of local dairy farmers and milk sales.

When the Bedford Farmers Club approached me to host one of their monthly lunch meetings, I was delighted at the opportunity to learn more about this illustrious group of active citizens who still care so strongly about farming, about the sustainability of food production, and about local growers. The club, founded in 1852, seeks to foster "an awareness of Bedford's remarkable agricultural heritage" and a knowledge of animal husbandry, horticulture, and backyard farming. Its main objective, of course, is to foster respect for the land, the soil, and the water of the area and to engender a deep understanding of how we can and must protect the environment.

I was told that the group would be about thirty in number, and I heartily agreed to serve lunch to the members who came. Within a few days I was informed that almost every member had responded "yes" to the invitation, and that the guest list would now be closer to one hundred. We got busy planning what I hoped would be an informative tour of my farm, a true "work in progress," followed by a lunch fashioned from as many ingredients from the early summer garden as possible. I wanted the lunch to be tasty, and casual, and comfortable for the members, many of whom are elderly. Everything turned out wonderfully. I learned a great deal and was feted with a one-year membership to the club, which made me so proud.

GRISSINI

GARDEN CRUDITÉS WITH
VINAIGRETTE AND HERB BUTTER

VICHYSSOISE

GARDEN SALAD WITH
ARTICHOKES AND TUNA

ASSORTED COOKIES

ABOVE (clockwise from top left) I was able to take the day off from work in the city, and I led the
garden and farm tour with some of my garden crew. The shade garden surrounding the Tenant
House was of great interest to the club members. It was lush and very advanced for the time of year.
Clive and Rufus, two of my three Sicilian miniature donkeys, were especially inquisitive. Indicative
of the breed is the obvious cross of dark fur across the withers. Everyone loved the vegetable
garden, which was quite full for early June. By the way, hosting a big party is the best incentive to
"clean up" a property quickly, to get it in shape for such a visit.

The blue-mauve clematis arbor was in bloom with climbing as well as shrub clematis, nepeta, and standard wisteria trees. This pergola is constructed from Chinese hand-hewn granite grape stakes and a cedar top. It stretches several hundred feet along the driveway.

ABOVE (clockwise from top left) I had a very good time entertaining the farmers at what turned out to be my first Bedford Farmers meeting. Long French-style radishes, tender leaves intact, were served cold, with sea salt. Yellow and white cauliflower florets were lightly blanched, sprinkled with thyme leaves, and included as part of the offering of crudités. Roasted young red and yellow pepper strips were served in small canning jars. OPPOSITE Bedford is a great climate for growing most produce. In my very large enclosed garden, we get an early start on the many varieties of vegetables and other produce I grow.

I have been making salade niçoise in various incarnations ever since I read about it in Julia Child's *Mastering the Art of French Cooking*. It is always best made early in the summer, with the smallest and most tender string beans, young peas, freshly dug new potatoes, tiny eggs from the Bantam hens, and small, sweet cherry tomatoes. I prefer oil-cured tuna and capers in my salad, but many people love seared fresh tuna and salt- or oil-cured anchovies. This salad is said to have come from the seaside city of Nice, on the Côte d'Azur, where seafood and fresh vegetables abound. OPPOSITE *Grissini* are long, usually thin breadsticks rumored to have originated in Turin, Italy, in the 14th century. These are baked from a delicious recipe for subtly flavored vegetable doughs that are rolled, pulled, and baked into very long, thin sticks.

TEA IN THE AFTERNOON

Although the custom of serving guests breakfast in bed is not at all common these days, tea in the afternoon is still a simple and civilized way of saying, "Let's take a break from the rigors of the day and have a little something to tide us over until dinner." (Tea can also be a healthy "in-between" meal for those with glycemic irregularities; for those who have been advised to partake of smaller, more frequent meals, tea is almost essential.)

English Tea is a formal affair where the service of tea and tea sandwiches and tea cakes and scones with heavy cream and butter and jams actually is very filling (and high in calories). I am not a snacker and a good cup of steaming tea is generally enough for me, but if presented with a delicate and tasty assortment of small tea sandwiches or an especially delicate cookie or biscuit, I will most certainly accept the offer. At Skylands the days are very active—hiking, boating, swimming, kayaking, cycling, tennis, yoga—and by four o'clock in the afternoon this ritual of tea is better than a cocktail, and it's relaxing before we all get ready for dinner. I serve tea in the living room or on the terrace. If perchance we are really splurging and having popovers, we will eat them with tea in the dining room where there is lots of room to enjoy the food and we don't have to worry about dripping jam and melted butter on the sofas.

The canapés were very simple: pickled daikon radish atop softened goat cheese on thinly sliced rectangles of raisin bread, and fine smoked salmon on very thinly sliced pain de mie. I serve Japanese or Chinese teas and prefer not to strain the leaves. The flowers are hellebores floating in water in an antique Japanese pewter-clad bowl. OPPOSITE These cookies are called lemon meltaways and they do just that—melt away in your mouth. Dusted with confectioners' sugar, they are so delicate and ephemeral. You can see how very complex the hammered copper sheathing on the table is.

PEONY GARDEN PARTY

OPPOSITE There are many different peonies on my property blooming in a wide range of flower forms, from simple singles and Japanese types to semi-doubles, doubles, and bombs that resemble large, fat snowballs. This is a two-tone Japanese variety called 'Do Tell'. Since I grow so many peonies, I do a lot of "de-budding" in the month before the flowers bloom—removing lateral buds encourages the main bud to grow larger, producing a much bigger main bloom. Use very sharp scissors to do this.

Coinciding with the blooming of the peonies in my Bedford garden is my annual peony party. For the past several years, ever since the hundreds of herbaceous shrub peonies started putting on the May/June spectacle, each blooming with dozens of plump and luscious blooms, I have been hosting some sort of event to celebrate their beauty. For this particular party, I planned a garden fête—a walk around the farm with various drinks stations, culminating in a buffet of finger foods and desserts in the tropical garden adjacent to the house. The afternoon party, called for four until seven o'clock, attracted almost two hundred guests on a warm and sunny day in early June.

Planning a party of this size in advance, a party that is totally dependent on the weather, is nerve-racking for any hostess, and each year I take a chance that several things will happen: that the weather will be clear, that the peonies will be blooming perfectly (not too closed or too open), and that guests will be able to attend en masse on a particular afternoon. I try to choose a Friday, which allows many friends to stop by on their way out of New York City for the weekend. I have to make it late enough so those guests do not have to leave the city too early.

We were so lucky with this party—the weather cooperated, nature obliged (the peonies were in perfect condition and in full bloom), and the amenable guests were in a wonderful state of mind, happy to partake of beauty for a few hours.

ABOVE The peony garden contains twenty-two varieties growing in eleven long rectangular beds— one type to a single row. They were planted with some regard to their growing and blooming habits, but the vagaries of our weather patterns have played havoc with traditional blooming schedules. Here you can see that not all of the peonies had even begun to open the week of the party, but those that did were in their prime and totally lush. OPPOSITE Here I am with one of my antique flower-picking baskets, cutting enough peonies for a large arrangement. I try to pick early or late in the day, when it is cool. On the right is a very robust blooming of 'Elsa Sass' and on the left, a pink peony called 'Beautiful Señorita'.

Menu

RHUBARB–ORANGE COCKTAILS

GORGONZOLA PALMIERS

RED SNAPPER AND CITRUS SEVICHE

GAZPACHO

CHILLED CAULIFLOWER COCONUT
CURRY

PETITE SALADE NIÇOISE

CHICKEN SALPICÓN

COQUILLES ST. JACQUES

BARBAGIUAN MONEGASQUE

PEA AND HAM QUICHE

SPICY LAMB MEATBALLS WITH
YOGURT–CUCUMBER SAUCE

CHOCOLATE BROWNIES WITH
GANACHE TOPPING

RHUBARB CRUMBLES

STRAWBERRY SORBET

SHORTBREAD WITH LEMON CURD
AND MERINGUE

MINI TIRAMISÙ

BAKED MERINGUES WITH
RASPBERRIES AND PASTRY CREAM

Setting up the buffet table

Because I entertain frequently, and because guests are often invited to parties several times a year, I try to vary the setting, the location, the theme, and the menus so as to surprise my guests every time they come. Doing this does require different furniture, linens, dishes, and glassware, and I am fortunate that after years of collecting and experimenting, I have a variety of tables I can use, various locations on the properties where I can set up dining tables or buffets, and loads of tableware from which to choose interesting settings.

A buffet table is perhaps the most challenging kind of table to set up—it has to be impressive; there has to be lots of food and variety so platters never look empty; and there has to be much thought paid to the decorations. Below is a step-by-step description of setting up the buffet table for the peony garden party.

1. It took several men to carry the antique French mahogany table from its storage location in the carriage house to the tropical garden. I purchased this very beautiful long oval table in Blue Hill, Maine, and restored it with a serious French polishing. I use it for formal dinners and for larger events such as the annual peony party.

2. Setting up such a long table (17 feet, 10 inches) requires careful leveling in an outdoor area such as the gravel garden in back of the Winter House. Small 3-inch squares of wood buried in the gravel serve as invisible "feet" under the table legs.

3. The table divides into two long tables, which must be fitted together very carefully. Built in the 19th century, the table most likely came from a prosperous convent or rectory.

4. The table is so very beautiful that I was reluctant to cover it entirely, so we placed three bright pink linen runners crosswise on the lovely grained wood.

5. Kevin and I spent almost half a day arranging flowers—masses of peonies in giant clear vases.

6. Kevin (hidden from view) and I carrying one of the larger arrangements from the front porch to the tropical garden to place on the table.

7. Stylist Tom Borgese came to help Kevin with the flowers. There was a lot of picking, cleaning, and arranging to do. We used lots of highly polished copper trays (they are pinkish), pink glass cake stands, and silver trays for the food and flowers.

8. Ayesha Patel helped me with a lot of the styling. She is incredibly organized and fastidious in her choice of table settings, cloths, vases, and serving pieces. We all kept in touch with walkie-talkies and mobile devices.

9. Vivaldi spent most of the day in the peony beds. The cats love the smell of the flowers and they just hang out there until dusk falls.

ABOVE A bowl of 'Brother Chuck' peonies behind one of the bronze screened windows (left). Kevin set up "flower shop" on the front porch. Buckets and buckets of peonies—most from my gardens, but some from the market—were groomed and primed for arranging (right). OPPOSITE We used scented geraniums, *Cotinus*, and Solomon's seal as well as assorted peonies in the arrangements. Peonies will last in arrangements for four to five days if picked when just opening and kept in cool, clean water. I always add a spoonful of bleach to the water.

ABOVE (clockwise from left) Charles Koppelman, nattily dressed, and I enjoying the party and the guests. A little bowl of chilled cauliflower coconut curry was garnished with shiso leaves, salty peanuts, and raisins. One of the cocktails was orange juice with rhubarb and vodka. Very tasty little servings of salad niçoise were served with wooden "sporks." I tried to use as much from the spring garden as possible. *OPPOSITE* Pierre and I devised a menu that was perfect for the time of year and the time of day. Because everyone had to travel a distance to get to the farm, we wanted the food to seem as if it was a meal, and not just a snack. Small scallop shells were filled with a delectable mixture of bay scallops, carrots, celery root, dill, and parsley.

ABOVE (clockwise from left) Red snapper and citrus seviche was served in small leaf-shaped bowls. I made sure we had several hundred of these small bowls and plates and glasses for serving. My longtime friend and colleague Susan Magrino Dunning with her stepson, James Dunning, his fiancée, Katherine Stuhlemmer, and Susan's mother, Mary Cross. I first learned how to make salpicón from Necy Fernandez, my former cook and television show set stylist, in Connecticut. This is a great party dish served in small quantities with a fork on a tiny plate. Shaped from puff pastry with a filling of gorgonzola, the palmiers were delicious. They are one of Chef Pierre's favorite hors d'oeuvres. OPPOSITE We served chilled tomato gazpacho in tiny glasses, keeping them cold in a bed of crushed ice.

ABOVE (clockwise from top left) The brownies were extra moist and rich, each finished with a piped rosette of chocolate ganache. Sugary shortbread wafers topped with coins of lemon curd and baked meringue caps were really tasty. The little rhubarb crisps baked in tiny leaf dishes (part of the Martha Stewart Collection for Macy's) could be made with blueberries, apples, pears, or strawberries. These are really tiny meringue cups piped with a small star tip. They are very, very good topped with pastry cream and a raspberry or strawberry. OPPOSITE The dessert buffet was nothing short of spectacular. Guests were delighted with tray after tray of pretty, homemade, bite-sized desserts: shortbread with lemon curd, rhubarb crumbles, mini tiramisù, ganache-topped brownies, strawberry sorbet, and meringues filled with crème pâtissière and topped with raspberries.

This was indeed a beautiful buffet table and by the end of the party there were very few things left on it. Because we arranged the desserts neatly and offered one dessert per platter or pedestal, it was very easy to keep the table looking organized and pretty. OPPOSITE Inexpensive votive candleholders were used for the mini tiramisù confections; we served them with tiny wooden spoons.

A Glossary of Peonies

There are so many, many types of herbaceous peonies to choose from today, and they should be an integral part of any perennial garden. I wanted a large display of peonies in one place, so I created eleven double beds, each planted with two rows of peonies. There are twenty-one different peonies, chosen because I liked their growing habits, their blooming schedules, their colors (they had to range from white to deep rose), their lush foliage before and after bloom, and their intensely fragrant and particularly abundant flowering proclivities.

	NAME	BLOSSOM STYLE	BLOOM SEASON	HEIGHT
1.	'Elsa Sass'	double	late	28 inches
2.	'Victorian Blush'	semidouble	late	27 inches
3.	'Fringed Ivory'	double	midseason to late	36 inches
4.	'Martha'	double	midseason	28 inches
5.	'Pink Charmer'	single	midseason	26 inches
6.	'Madylone'	double	late	32 inches
7.	'Lullaby Coos'	semidouble	midseason	28 inches
8.	'Vivid Glow'	single	early	36 inches
9.	'Star Power'	semidouble	midseason	28 inches
10.	'Prairie Moon'	semidouble	midseason	32 inches
11.	'Angel Cheeks'	bomb	midseason	26 inches
12.	'Miss America'	semidouble	early	36 inches
13.	'Abalone Pearl'	semidouble	early	32 inches
14.	'Cora Stubbs'	Japanese	midseason	32 inches
15.	'Top Brass'	bomb	midseason	36 inches
16.	'Reine Supreme'	double	midseason	34 inches
17.	'Moon River'	double	midseason	28 inches
18.	'Mischief'	single	late	30 inches
19.	'Brother Chuck'	double	midseason	28 inches
20.	'Flying Pink Saucers'	semidouble	midseason	34 inches
21.	'Beautiful Señorita'	Japanese	midseason	30 inches

I purchased the entire collection from Roy Klehm's Song Sparrow Nursery, and I have been thrilled with the results. Not only has each peony plant thrived (there are 770 in all), they have grown so large that it is almost time to dig them up to divide them.

JULY 4TH
BARBECUE

My farm, Cantitoe Corners, is close to the John Jay Homestead in Bedford, New York. I thought it was very fitting to celebrate Independence Day, the Fourth of July, there, since one of our country's Founding Fathers had lived and died right down the street. John Jay was president of the Continental Congress, a staunch supporter of independence, our first chi ef justice of the United States, and the second governor of New York. He was also the state's leading opponent of slavery and he cowrote *The Federalist Papers* with Alexander Hamilton and James Madison. Before the party, I read up on local and national history so that I could be well informed and prepared to have a lively discussion with my neighbors.

My farm in Bedford is a really pleasant place to entertain. There are two convenient kitchens to use: one in the main house, and the other in what was once the "flower room." Essential when hosting lots of people is sufficient refrigeration. If you can, put extra refrigerators in your basement or garage, and establish enough storage space for extra dishware, glassware, linens, and even a few additional tables and chairs.

For this Fourth of July, our most patriotic holiday, I wanted to make a "splash" in the daytime, without fireworks, so we stretched a giant blue and white–striped shade banner across the terrace, as much for effect as for the sun protection it provided. We had an adult table as well as a children's table, both covered in navy cloths printed with white stars. There were flags everywhere—on tables, on porches, on top of swagged banners, and over doorways. The terrace furniture is all painted the same "Bedford Gray" as the buildings and fences and gates. The excellent monotone color does not compete with the colorful gardens and flowering trees. We used the powder-coated metal Windsor chairs that I designed years ago for Bernhardt Furniture.

The food was simple, straightforward barbecue—delicious and desirable. It happened to be a very, very hot day, and luckily I had asked all the guests to dress in summer whites. With the red, white, and blue theme, we looked "picture perfect."

OPPOSITE I don't recall where I first tasted a cherry mojito, but wow! This is one of the very best drinks for the summer. Try to get the biggest, best Bing cherries available; I get mine each Fourth of July from my friend Deborah Olsen, who owns C. J. Olsen Cherries in Sunnyvale, California. I serve a big batch from a punch bowl or glass cylinder container like the one pictured. Ladle the mixture over ice and top with sparkling mineral water.

Menu

BING CHERRY MOJITOS

LEMONADE

RADISHES WITH HERBED RICOTTA DIP,
SWEET BUTTER, AND FLEUR DE SEL

BARBECUED CHICKEN WINGS

BARBECUED BABY-BACK RIBS

GRILLED VEGETABLES

TWICE-BAKED POTATOES WITH BROCCOLI

SUMMERY SALAD WITH VEGETABLES

CUSTARD-FILLED CORNBREAD

RED, WHITE, AND BLUE PARFAITS

The centerpieces were made from flowers on the property: several varieties of allium, which remind me of fireworks, as well as agapanthus blossoms from planters in the greenhouse. OPPOSITE When I first moved to Bedford, I built a very long pergola that I had always planned to plant with blue and lavender clematis, lavender nepeta, and blue hibiscus (rose of Sharon). After I widened the garden a bit to accommodate the spreading nepeta, I added approximately 400 alliums of various sorts—all bluish and purplish—and the blooms created a wonderful display.

ABOVE The porches were swagged and bedecked with flags. Here, Andrew, Peter, and Kianna join me for a photo op (left). Almost all vegetables taste great simply grilled. Tomatoes, summer squash, fennel, carrots, and radicchio were brushed with a bit of herbed olive oil, liberally seasoned with salt and pepper, carefully tended so they did not burn, then served right off the grill (right).

OPPOSITE The real secret to very tender, tasty ribs is to cook them in water for at least an hour before they are basted in barbecue sauce and grilled. The chicken wings are also carefully grilled, then basted with Pierre's secret barbecue sauce when nearly finished.

Layers of red currant gelatin, vanilla panna cotta, and blueberries and currants create a striking and delicious parfait. We served them in the short, thin glass tumblers in which they were prepared. OPPOSITE We could barely get the kids to look at the camera for their portrait, so excited were they to dig into the red, white, and blue dessert.

THE ART OF GRILLING

I might be the last person on earth to be associated with a grill, and yet, for just that reason, I have made it a priority to learn to grill everything to perfection. We all love expertly grilled shell steak, and with the price of quality beef so high, it is imperative to know exactly how to grill it to each person's liking. Hamburgers, too, are so often cooked badly—charred, raw, overdone—yet this does not have to be the case. I think it all has to do with the grill, the fuel, and of course, the heat. I prefer a large, flat grill with a cooking surface that can be raised or lowered. An Argentine polo player made my grill for me, and I have used it for fifteen years with great success. I build a very hot fire in two-thirds of the bottom, using a bit of kindling and high-heat anthracite charcoal specially produced for metal smelts. I found such a foundry nearby by accident and loved their charcoal. A few things to keep in mind: Do not burn anything that has been prepared with chemicals, and do not use fire starters. Get the fire white-hot; the coals should be evenly heated and level. Start cooking over the hottest coals, and move the meat as it cooks to a cooler spot on the grill. Use a digital thermometer for accurate readings of internal temperatures and keep a temperature chart handy. Also keep a strong spray bottle filled with water nearby—at the first sign of a flare-up, spray sparingly with water to reduce the flame. Use long metal tongs to move the meat around. Don't poke, pierce, or squash foods while grilling. Fires must be kept hot; add more charcoal whenever necessary, and stop grilling until the proper heat resumes.

ABOVE Kebabs and chicken wings taste so delectable if properly grilled and flavored. Herb skewers made from branches of woody herbs like rosemary or summer savory impart additional subtle flavors to ground meat (left). Shellfish, such as lobster, langoustines, shrimp, and crab, need very careful attention when put on the grill, as shells tend to burn quickly and flesh toughens rapidly over high heat (right). Basting often is a good practice, and maintaining an even heat is all-important. OPPOSITE I love one- or two-bite hors d'oeuvres, and these tiny tuna burgers are delicate and small enough to fit in that category. Crispy soft brioche, crunchy lettuce and cucumber, tender tuna, rich rémoulade, and thin slices of cherry tomato are the perfect combination of tastes.

SUMMER COCKTAIL PARTY

OPPOSITE I learned long ago that the very best drinks are made from superior liquors, wines, and liqueurs, as well as fresh fruit juices and garnishes. There are no good "drink mixes" that can compare to fresh, and no good premixed bottled drinks that are better than "just made." These margaritas are made with fresh raspberries, freshly squeezed lime juice, and silver tequila; as for the orange-flavored liqueur, I like Cointreau best. In East Hampton, I have many sets of beautiful old glasses and dishes—Venetian, Depression, French, and even old Steuben—that I use all the time.

There are many wonderful organizations in East Hampton, Bedford, and Seal Harbor that hold fund-raisers, benefits, and other events to encourage charitable contributions for their operations and special programs. As an involved and concerned citizen, I try to do what I can, locally, to help many good causes. I open my gardens to tours for fund-raisers, and I host dinners and luncheons and even horseback rides. Last year, I hosted a summer cocktail party for Guild Hall in East Hampton, a wonderful performing arts center in town where theatrical productions, musical concerts, film festivals, and movie premieres take place. It is a fine cultural institution, a gift to the community established in 1931, and like many such places, it is often in need of charitable gifts and patronage.

I agreed to host this particular fund-raiser, a thank-you to patrons, and developed a lovely menu of drinks and hors d'oeuvres. I attempt to hold such parties when the gardens are at their best; we keep a year-to-year calendar of each of my gardens so we can try to judge when the optimum time would be for ultimate bloom. Of course, the weather does not always cooperate and this party was almost rained out, but the house has giant porches, a spacious ground floor, and lots of umbrellas near the pool where guests can and did congregate. Also, I find it is good practice to reserve twenty umbrellas at each house for garden tours in case of rain; hardy souls will still wander around the yard in the rain if they have coverage. Even with uncooperative weather, as long as you make plenty of good drinks and serve lots of delicious food, the party will be a success.

Prosecco, a sparkling white wine from Italy, pairs extremely well with a purée of frozen lychees to make a delicious drink for sipping. Alongside, we served curried crabmeat on crisp fried fresh mini pappadams. OPPOSITE Dried salt cod is the basis for savory croquettes; the drinks are fresh pineapple piña coladas with oven-dried pineapple garnishes.

I first learned about the cocktail known as Sazerac on a trip to New Orleans; this very strong concoction of rye or bourbon (my preference), Herbsaint, lemon and orange juices, and bitters goes especially well with spicy shrimp and other seafood hors d'oeuvres. OPPOSITE The pool garden was such a resounding success this particular year. Planted in gargantuan turquoise blue pots, the *Alocasias* were gigantic. Underplanted with *Lysimachia* 'Aureum' and a feathery blue ground cover (*Lotus berthelotti*), each pot was indeed a spectacle.

ABOVE Small tortilla chips topped with fresh corn and cheddar complement lemon whiskey sours or honeydew mojitos (left). Another plate of spicy shrimp; this was a very popular offering and went well with a Tom Collins (right). OPPOSITE Hornbeams, carefully pruned twice a year, stand tall and square in the backyard—a contrast to the *Alocasia* plants with their huge elephant-ear leaves and the large, round-domed boxwoods.

Martha's drink—making tips

- Keep a stock of good beverages on hand. Buy the very best brands you can. Choose a wide variety as you build your repertoire of drinks recipes. I prefer Russian and Polish vodka to domestic brands, for example, and I love American bourbon but not blended whiskeys. Likewise, stock your pantry with all kinds of mixers: club soda, mineral water, tonic water, ginger ale, and the like.

- Spend a little time getting acquainted with different tastes and choosing what you like. If you taste a drink you love, ask the bartender or maker for the recipe. Make a little notebook of drinks recipes to keep in your liquor closet or bar, and be sure to stock any special ingredients and liqueurs the recipes call for, such as cachaça, St. Germain, Cointreau, Grand Marnier, Herbsaint, or bitters.

- Consider the ice: Make good cubes, round balls of ice, and other shapes for certain drinks and punches.

- Always use freshly squeezed lemon, lime, and orange juices, and fresh purées when necessary. Use fresh fruit and berries for garnishes.

- Start a collection of glasses so you have the appropriate vessels for your drinks. Tag sales, consignment shops, and end-of-season sales are all good places to start.

- Accumulate a variety of useful bar tools: a very good corkscrew; measuring jiggers; long stirrers; citrus reamers, zesters, and presses; a good blender; and a juicer. If you like martinis, invest in a shaker.

- Take a wine-tasting course and start a small collection of your favorite wines. You can build on this as you gain experience and confidence.

OPPOSITE I learned to make traditional caipirinhas from my Brazilian friends and colleagues. The limes must be pressed with a wooden reamer to release the juice and oils. Fresh mint, cane sugar, and cachaça are added to taste. The little round balls are made from yucca and Parmesan cheese.

PICNIC AT SEA

One of the major attractions of owning a house in Maine is the glorious sea and the intriguing coastline. The Atlantic Ocean, clear and cold, with warmer currents coursing up and down the coast, the myriad islands—some inhabited, others forested or barren—the bird life, the aquatic life: All of this draws us out in boats to enjoy the wonders of nature.

When I purchased my home more than a decade ago, it was imperative that I also buy a boat of some sort, and that I obtain a mooring or two at a local yacht club where that boat and its dingy could be safely tethered. I shopped for the right boat, knowing that there would be at least a year's wait for delivery. I chose a very well made, sturdy, traditional Maine boat called a Picnic Boat, made by Hinckley, in Southwest Harbor. I was instructed in its use and since then have become quite adept at navigating it and "parking" it at crowded docks. Nevertheless, I always take a "captain" with me, someone who knows the waters and the weather, and is an expert in navigation and safety. The ocean is the master in Maine and it is not to be taken for granted.

We manage to take one or two trips every weekend, no matter the temperature. Once out on the sea, traveling at about 17 to 20 knots, with the spectacular coastline to gaze at and seals and birds around us, it is like nowhere else on earth. And we usually take a picnic with us to serve, weather permitting, in the stern of the boat on a console that doubles as a table. We have the procedure pretty much down pat; the meal consists of delicious sandwiches, hot soup, and possibly a salad or "finger food" like the Scotch eggs in this menu. We usually include cookies and fresh fruit, and maybe even a cake. The galley is complete with stove and microwave, so anything is possible. I have furnished the boat simply but ele-gantly and it works well for entertaining, time and time again.

Menu

RASPBERRY-VINEGAR CORDIAL

LEMONADE

BOILED LOBSTER TAILS WITH
ENGLISH SALAD CREAM
AND CILANTRO-PARSLEY PESTO

SCOTCH EGGS

ROAST BEEF SANDWICHES WITH
AVOCADO AND HORSERADISH

POTTED CRAB WITH MELBA TOAST

BLUEBERRY JAM TARTLETS

FUDGY BROWNIES

SPICED HOT TEA

CHEWY CHOCOLATE
GINGERBREAD COOKIES

CHOCOLATE CHIP COOKIES

ABOVE When the tide is out, it is quite challenging to walk up the ramps to shore. Even Paw Paw had a hard time on this steep slope. My boat, *Skylands II,* is on the left tied to the dock. OPPOSITE We try to keep the menu for boat picnics very tasty but simple. Another thing to keep in mind is the mess factor, something no boat owner wants. So we take care not to include anything messy—nothing dripping or "crumb-y." I have some large wicker serving trays, which I lined with charts of local waters under Plexiglas. Food is set out on the trays, and everyone can grab what they want. This menu was extra-good—lobster tails, roast beef sandwiches, Scotch eggs, fudgy brownies, blueberry tartlets, and two types of cookies. I use nonbreakable dishes (these are white Hellerware) and plastic glasses. I did splurge on the teakwood-handled stainless steel flatware from Moss.

One of my favorite spots directly south of my home is this barren tip of Big Cranberry Island. The lighthouse is one of many that you can see on a day trip through the islands.

ABOVE (clockwise from top left) Potted crab on melba toast was another favorite offering on this afternoon. The crab is hand-picked on the island by lobstermen's families. The sweet, hard-shelled blue crab is considered a by-product of the lobster industry, and before it became a popular, edible delicacy, it was usually thrown away. We have many sets of linens for the boat—cocktail napkins as well as oversize "lapkins" for the plated food. Even the dogs come along for the day trips. They love being out on the water. The sea was very calm and the air quite warm on this particular day. Although it's only 36 feet long, the boat is quite spacious and does not feel crowded even with fifteen people aboard. There are always cookies—and lemonade—on hand. The fresh Maine air just increases one's appetite so much that a nibble of a chocolate-ginger spice cookie or a chocolate chip cookie is necessary.

ABOVE As we approached Little Duck Island, the sea was extremely calm. But that is not meant to fool you—the temperature of the water is less than 50 degrees at this time of year. Pictured, left to right: Isabella Feigen, Kevin Sharkey, Sheila Berger, Jill Dienst, me, and Ayesha Patel.
OPPOSITE The fudgy brownies are rich and dense; the blueberry jam tartlets are baked in almond short crusts with sliced almonds on top. We use lots of big linen dishcloths for napkins or place mats.

Trust the gentlemen to find the best spot on the boat. Michael Rips and Dan Dienst took an after-lunch snooze in the sun while we explored one of the islands on foot. OPPOSITE Paw Paw loved going on boat rides. His successor, Ghenghis Khan, is not as sure of himself out on the water—not yet anyway.

JAPANESE LUNCH

OPPOSITE In the big dining room at Skylands, there are three or four small round tavern tables that we use for lunch or for serving when we have guests for tea. The 19th-century Japanese trays are perfect for a luncheon, holding the entire meal. Hijiki salad (reconstituted seaweed in a mild vinegar dressing) is served in French porcelain scallop shells, wooden coasters protect the trays, and the hot soup rests on a copper wire trivet, which can double as a steamer insert. Don't forget to serve very good green tea or barley tea, both of which are robust and invigorating.

I have been very lucky to travel to Japan many times in the past few years. Each time I go I discover new and different things: a food I have never tasted, a dish I have never seen, a type of pottery I have never held. I meet new artisans, artists and chefs, gardeners and designers, and I am guided to visit special monuments and unique fabricators. In Kyoto, I have been fortunate to have met antiquarians and linen weavers, and stayed at traditional *ryokans* that have no equal in the hotel realm. My friend Momoko Sano has been my guide all these years, introducing me everywhere and translating in every shop, museum, or sacred place. Momoko took me to Aritsugu, a family cutlery business in Kyoto's Nishiki Market, and I wanted one of everything they made. Originally swordmakers for the Imperial family, Aritsugu now supplies a wide audience with the finest culinary implements, knives, and utensils. The current owner is Shinichiro Terakubo, an 18th-generation blade maker, cooking teacher, and knife sharpener. On each visit to Kyoto I make a pilgrimage to this ancient store and buy more of the handmade equipment: copper soup pots, silver-lined copper cups, chopsticks, steamers, copper teapots, and finely wrought racks and wire trays and wooden-handled spoons and ladles. I have also visited the antiques shops in Kyoto, buying lacquer and wood and silver tableware, including the beautiful wooden trays on which I serve Japanese lunches at Skylands. Each of the trays is embellished with paintings of fir trees and pine trees.

If I had to choose one cuisine to eat the rest of my life, I think it would be Japanese. I love the simplicity of the food yet admire the complexity of the ingredients. Miso soup takes just a few minutes to prepare, but the ingredients—kombu for the dashi, soybeans for the miso, seaweed for the salad—actually take more than one year to create. Other cooked Japanese foods that I like to serve are tomago (omelette), chawanmushi (egg custard), and tempura of all sorts.

Shishito peppers are a favorite part of many Japanese meals. Deep-fried, they are tender and tasty; coarse sea salt sprinkled on top is a must. The plate is new lacquer; the golden spoon is Tiffany's Clinton pattern in vermeil. OPPOSITE An alternative spot for a Japanese lunch is the faux bois lunch table and stools located next to the lost pools on the highest point of the property. The mossy floor and the towering pines are very similar to the northern part of Japan.

ICE CREAM SOCIAL

When I think back on my favorite desserts or sweets, several flavors come to mind: lemon, root beer, cream, and hot fudge. And when asked what I remember most about a meal, my answer is often "the dessert," especially if it incorporated one or more of those flavors.

One summer day, in East Hampton, we decided it was time to make some of my favorite ice creams, sauces, and drinks, and to invite friends over to taste and test. Pierre and I figured out how we would make many flavors of ice cream and how to store them. I have just one upright freezer in the kitchen and a smaller one in the basement. Some of the ice creams were made traditionally, with a custard of egg yolks and milk or cream, but some were more simple and made with just milk, sugar, and fruit.

It helps if you have one of the newer models of ice cream machines; these work quickly and efficiently to produce well-textured ice cream that is smooth and creamy. Store the ice creams in clear glass loaf pans, which will permit you to form elegant scoops when serving. Any of these ice creams would be a very acceptable option for a dinner party; you might consider offering a tasting of small scoops of each. Putting together all of the components for a sundae is easier than making a pie or tart, and guests will appreciate it just as much.

OPPOSITE A very good bowl of ice cream—in this case, cherry-chocolate chunk topped with real hot fudge sauce—is about as perfect a dessert as one can find. One large scoop of ice cream is served in an amber-colored, vintage Venetian glass bowl. The majolica plate embellished with gold is one of a large set, and the silver ice cream spoon is bright-cut with a vermeil bowl.

PREVIOUS Lily Pond is a great old house with a mature, formally planned garden. The pool terrace is a lovely place to relax while sipping a root beer float or enjoying spoonfuls of hot fudge sundae. The garden roses, hundreds of old-fashioned varieties, are in full bloom in June, and the shade garden to the east of the house is lush and verdant and shady— often a full ten degrees cooler than the rest of the property. To the rear of the pool are tall fastigi- ated hornbeam trees planted in fern and lily gardens. Brick paths are designed to take one through the property, which seems larger than just an acre in size. I collected a lot of Lloyd Loom furniture when I first purchased Lily Pond in 1990. The trim color, indeed the main accent color of the house, is teal blue. This color goes well with the landscape and can be found in many of the fabrics used throughout; shades of it also appear in the straws and long soda spoons used for the ice cream social. Here, two root beer floats await sipping.

ABOVE Pictured are some of the cherished old roses that grow in my garden at Lily Pond; 'Reine des Violettes', 'Cardinal de Richelieu', and others look great arranged in a bowl or vase. These types of old-fashioned shrub roses are at once blooming, hardy, and ancient (left). Another Venetian goblet, pale lavender in color, is filled with a generous scoop of chocolate-honey ice cream. A dollop of whipped cream and a spoonful of butterscotch sauce on top add up to a very desirable dessert. The dessert plate is a vintage majolica (right). OPPOSITE Long Island is famous for its June strawberries. There are lots of farms where one can pick quarts of these sweet, red, field-ripened berries, which make the very best ice cream, jams, and toppings for shortcakes. Two scoops of delicious strawberry ice cream with rhubarb compote and whipped cream are served on a Wedgwood embossed plate.

I love homemade ice cream cones; they taste so much better than the store-bought kind. Filling them with small scoops is a nice way to sample each of the ice cream flavors. The rack we set the cones in is actually an egg holder. OPPOSITE I have some unusual and old garden furniture and ornaments at Lily Pond. This is one of a pair of cast-iron garden benches in the fern pattern. Like the rest of the furniture, it is painted with a teal enamel. The roses are from the garden; the peach and yellow examples are David Austin blooms.

During the prolific era of Depression glass production, many dessert cups such as these were made. This one is perfect for a scoop of mint chocolate chip ice cream. OPPOSITE Lily Pond was constructed in the dunes of East Hampton in the 1870s. It is the oldest house on Lily Pond Lane. Over the last 140 years or so, roads have been built, many more houses erected, and the dunes have been transformed into landscaped yards and gardens.

ABOVE Iced coffee with espresso ice cream and whipped cream is served in an old-fashioned ice cream soda glass (left). I found this relic (six of them) at Sage Street in Sag Harbor on Long Island—a tiny, interesting antiques shop run by Liza Werner. Specializing in the vintage, the old, and the not so old, Liza always has something of interest. The Bakelite-handled ice cream spoons are just right for ice cream sodas. When I was a child, I tasted lemon ice cream in Buffalo one summer while visiting my grandmother. I never forgot the taste—tart, creamy, sweet, and sour. This buttermilk ice cream studded with fine shards of lemon peel is the closest I've come to that wonderful memory (right). Candied lemon peel is an added plus. OPPOSITE This lead putto, grasping a large fish, is a charming garden ornament I bought in Birmingham, Alabama, many years ago. The roses make a playful addition.

BRIDAL SHOWER IN MAINE

When my beloved crafts editor, Hannah Milman, told me she was getting married to her longtime boyfriend, James, I suggested we throw her a bridal shower in one of her favorite locales, Mount Desert Island. Hannah has been visiting me and working with me in Maine ever since I bought Skylands. She has edited many stories about Maine industries and Maine crafts, reflecting her appreciation for nature, farming, the seaside, and aquatic life. We planned her shower at the end of a long work week in Seal Harbor, in an old-fashioned boathouse that sits right on the edge of this quiet, sparkling harbor very near the incredible Acadia National Park.

There were several of us involved in the planning of the décor and the menu. What we agreed upon in advance was that everything should reflect or be reminiscent of Hannah's intense love of nature. Her interest in blueberries was evident in the blueberry lemonade and the blueberry parfaits. Lavender and purple are among her favorite colors and we used them throughout the party—for the flowers, the linens, the candied pansies, the purple cauliflower, and even the outfits we chose to wear. A shell collector, and an expert in wampum, Hannah's passions were visibly incorporated—shell wreaths, shell dishes for the lobster shepherd's pies, rare shells arranged artfully as the luncheon centerpiece, and even pearl necklace "favors" artfully displayed at each place setting. The shower was held in September, and the harbor was very quiet and still. The light was gorgeous, the weather mild, and the close friendships of all the guests were very obvious as stories were told, memories recounted, gifts opened, and delicious foods devoured.

Menu

BLUEBERRY LEMONADE

COMPOSED VEGETABLE SALAD WITH
BEET VINAIGRETTE

LOBSTER SHEPHERD'S PIES

VANILLA CUPCAKES WITH SUGARED
PANSIES

BLUEBERRY PARFAITS

MADELEINES

ABOVE On bases of foam core, we hot-glued small shells and starfish, making an *H* for Hannah and a *J* for James. Late-summer flowers from the garden—ageratum, dahlias, and 'Tardiva' hydrangeas— were arranged in a faux bois vase. OPPOSITE The composed salad of locally grown vegetables was very colorful. I used red lettuces, purple caulifower, fingerling potatoes, several types of cherry tomatoes, and fresh herbs for additional flavor; the vinaigrette is made with puréed beets.

ABOVE (clockwise from left) Served on an old diner plate featuring an S monogram in a shell, the lobster shepherd's pie was very well liked as a main course. Jodi, Ayesha, Sarah, Darcy, Hannah, and Lisa (facing away), chatting on the covered porch. Hannah had always admired my St. Barth's pearls strung on leather, and she, the ultimate crafter, copied the method and made a necklace for each of us. The shower's nature theme was pervasive—green mosses were used to bring the woodland to the waterfront. We simply mounded up large cushions of moss; afterward, each mound was carefully returned to its rightful place in the woodland. OPPOSITE Over the mantel we hung a clamshell wreath. Hannah described in detail how one must boil the shells to whiten and clean them before using them.

ABOVE Jodi Levine has been working with Hannah for more than a decade (left). Darcy Miller, of all-things-weddings fame, even decorated my Picnic Boat, a classic 36-foot Hinckley (right). OPPOSITE We put the dessert buffet on the porch, open to the view of the harbor. Thinly crosscut pieces of local fallen trees served as platters. Shells and faux bois vases held flowers and garnishes, while lavender cupcake liners were flattened to use under the parfaits served in glasses.

A new but very rustic-looking faux bois cake stand was covered in moss and lichen; it was the perfect stand for the nature-themed cupcakes. OPPOSITE I found my vintage fish molds and baked madeleines in them as well as in traditional scallop-shaped tins.

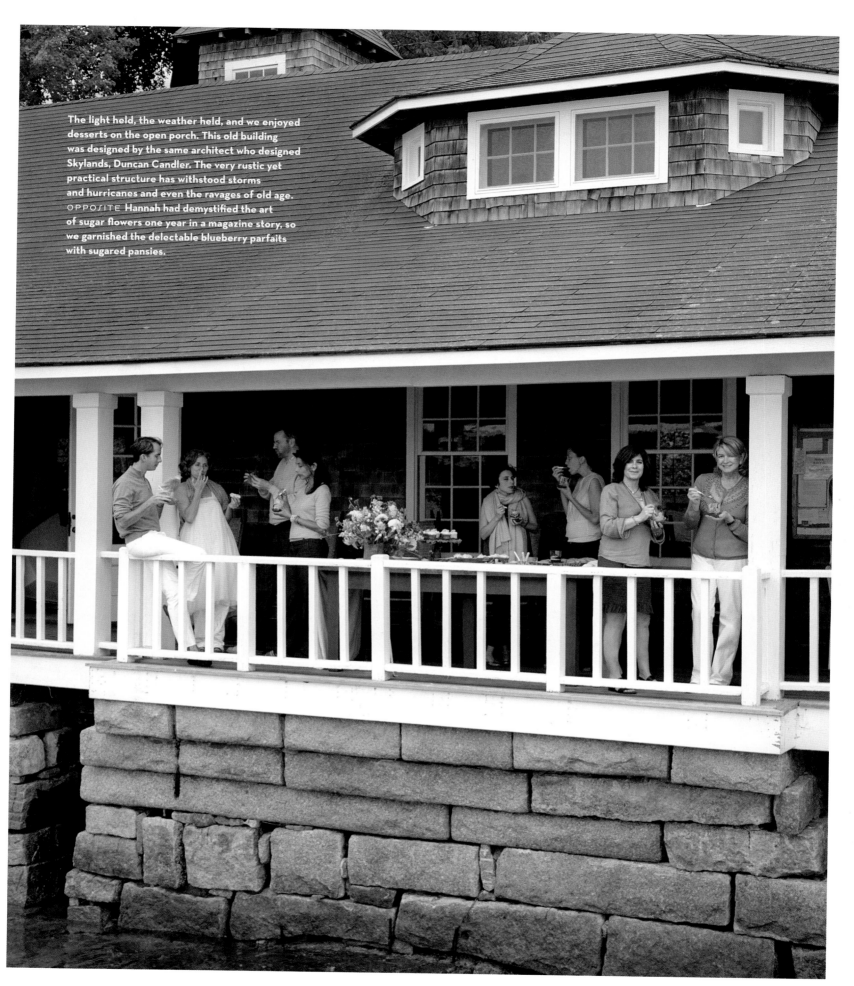

The light held, the weather held, and we enjoyed desserts on the open porch. This old building was designed by the same architect who designed Skylands, Duncan Candler. The very rustic yet practical structure has withstood storms and hurricanes and even the ravages of old age. OPPOSITE Hannah had demystified the art of sugar flowers one year in a magazine story, so we garnished the delectable blueberry parfaits with sugared pansies.

Evenings

CELEBRATING A MASTER GARDENER

OPPOSITE After setting the table—a stretch of four long rental tables placed end to end—and arranging the wicker dining chairs around it, I was challenged to seat the guests carefully—there were so many interesting people and so many requests to sit near or next to a friend or acquaintance that I had to be extra-clever. Wicker floor lamps, wall sconces, and votive candles on the table provided lovely illumination for the dinner.

Dan Hinkley, founder of Heronswood, a preeminent source of unusual perennials for the serious gardener, and famous plant explorer, is such a good friend and stimulating guest that I love to fête him when he travels east from his home and garden in Indianola, Washington. I planned a late summer dinner on the porch of my house in East Hampton. The porch stretches the width of the old 1878 shingle cottage and was designed as a place to hold dinners for up to a hundred guests. This dinner was for thirty people, and Pierre and I were quite busy planning and cooking for two days prior to the party.

The August evening was a bit misty, and the covered porch was a perfect place to sit and enjoy the balmy weather. Hundreds of votive candles lit the garden, the pool, and the porch and some unusual potted plants and epiphytes were used on the table as low but interesting green enigmas that only Dan, our celebrated plantsman, could identify with 100 percent accuracy. I used white linen cloths (a cotton flannel pad—made from "bump"—placed underneath the linen made the wooden-topped rental tables seem as if they had their own custom padded tops), white linen hemstiched napkins, a mix of gold-rimmed and Venetian goblets, and my own silver flatware.

Menu

SUMMER FIGS WITH PROSCIUTTO

MINI CRAB CAKES WITH
TARRAGON TARTAR SAUCE

SMOKED SALMON AND PUMPERNICKEL
MILLEFEUILLES

RISOTTO WITH CANTITOE FARM
TOMATOES AND SAUTÉED SHRIMP

SAUTÉED DAURADE WITH
MEDITERRANEAN VEGETABLES
AND BOUILLABAISSE JUS

BAKED LOCAL PLUM AND
NECTARINE "PITHIVIERS"

PALMIERS

TORRONE

ABOVE Years ago I found a pair of these monumental terra-cotta urns (c. 1900) at an estate sale in Connecticut. They are marked "Impruneta" (a Tuscan town famous for its production of terra-cotta since the 13th century) and are very elaborately decorated and finely finished. They are the focal point of the front staircase to the porch, and each year I plant them with something a bit unusual—this year, giant prickly *Aloe ferox* and an underplanting of echeveria succulents.
OPPOSITE The small backyard is almost entirely occupied by a 60-foot-long swimming pool, made from unpainted concrete, coped in pale slate, and edged in thick bluestone. Brick and bluestone walks and patios surround the pool, and there are several seating areas that allow guests to converse and mingle. We surrounded the pool with scores of votives, which burned for the duration of the party. I keep several hundred votive glasses in large plastic tubs in the basement; the candles I buy at the supermarket are labeled "kosher" for holiday use.

ABOVE Dan Hinkley and I posed for our portrait prior to the evening party (left). Despite the humidity, the linens remained crisp and the plants stayed fresh looking (Irish moss, epiphytes, staghorn ferns, and fancy-leaved begonias were in the mix). The place cards were handwritten. OPPOSITE For houseguests and dinner guests who arrived early, I set out large galvanized trays lined with fig leaves and covered with appetizers. I brought the leaves and figs from my trees in Bedford, which were especially productive this particular year. Several great soft cheeses, a ramekin of honey, and crisp baked artichokes and fig wedges looked pretty all together, and staved off guests' hunger until everyone else had arrived for dinner.

ABOVE We served a few hors d'oeuvres once the guests had all arrived, including tiny, plump crab cakes (left) arranged on a crisscross grid of fresh chive flower stems from the garden, and millefeuilles of pumpernickel filled with smoked salmon and herbed cream cheese (right). OPPOSITE The pool yard is planted with hardy, fast-growing plants like roses, *paniculata* hydrangea standards, and large spheres of boxwood. Teal blue pots are filled with contrasting tropical foliage plants such as *Alocasia*, palms, and kalanchoe.

A first course should always be colorful and fresh. On this evening, the starter was simply sautéed shrimp, garden tomatoes (slow-roasted to concentrate their flavor), and freshly snipped garden herbs served on a bed of tomato-infused risotto.

ABOVE The main course was daurade, the fillet very quickly sautéed and then plated atop an assortment of summer garden vegetables simmered in a flavorful bouillabaisse type of broth. At each of my dinners, I make a toast, elaborating on the accomplishments of the guest of honor, making introductions of other honored guests and friends, and welcoming remarks from others at the table.

OVERLEAF The main dessert was a scored round of pâte feuilletée atop a scoop of homemade vanilla ice cream set on a baked plum. The garnish was candied sage leaves. As an accompaniment, I offered plates of other amazing confections; I had been in Turin earlier that year and had brought home torrone with pistachios and hazelnuts, and great chocolate bars with gianduja and toasted hazelnuts. With the puff pastry left over from the main dessert I made caramelized "papillons," or palmiers.

SETTING THE BANQUET TABLE

There are tomes written about the proper way to set a table: Every royal household has a staff dedicated to preserving and continuing their fine traditions for every occasion. On a recent trip to Sweden I was treated to an afternoon of demonstrations in the Royal Palace in preparation for a state dinner; this included a very interesting practice session on napkin folding. Our White House has a staff devoted to the proper etiquette for setting, decorating, and seating tables for presidential entertaining. For the rest of us, setting a beautiful table can be simple or complex, but a few basic rules apply.

For a dinner that requires a table larger than the one in your dining room, the option to rent is very easy. Tables come in a variety of sizes and the experts at any rental company can help you decide which choices are the best for your particular needs: one long, several shorter rectangles, squares, rounds, tables of different dimensions, or multiples of the same. When I was a caterer I learned how many could fit comfortably at a 60-inch round (ten to twelve), or an 6-foot rectangle (six to eight). I learned to estimate the correct size for tablecloths so the cloth would reach to the floor or cover just the tops as an overlay.

Chairs, too, are another consideration when hosting a large dinner. There are folding chairs, banquet chairs, upholstered seats, and so on. If you have adequate storage space and entertain often (more than four times a year), it makes sense to invest in sets of chairs that can be used multiple times. It is also a good idea to buy 12 to 24 chairs of one kind that fit within the décor of your own home.

In East Hampton I keep thirty-five pretty wicker chairs in the basement. I painted them the color of my porch floor to use for all dinner parties outside. I also have twenty "grange" chairs—wooden hoop-back chairs that fit nicely around my kitchen table for informal meals or breakfasts. In Maine I have lots of the same wicker chairs, which I have painted to match the gray of the house. If you have the room, it might also be wise to purchase a couple of 60-inch round tables, three or four 8-foot-long tables, and possibly a few 36-inch round tables (each seating four to five).

I line rental tables, which can have beaten-up tops, with flannel cloth (or "bump") or special foamy plastic liners. When placed under the fancy linens, they give the tables a finished look. When dressing tables for formal entertaining, most of the rental tables look much better if the cloths skim the ground; round cloths should touch the floor, and rectangles should be placed so that corners are boxed and the cloths touch the ground all the way around. The chart below provides suggested linen measurements for the most common rental table sizes, which have a standard height of 30 inches.

TABLE SIZE	LINEN SIZE	NUMBER OF GUESTS
36-inch round or square	96 inches	4
72-by-36-inch rectangle	132 by 96 inches	6 to 8
54-inch round or square	114 inches	8
84-by-36-inch rectangle	156 by 96 inches	8 to 10
60-inch round or square	120 inches	10 to 12
72-inch round or square	132 inches	12
84-inch round or square	144 inches	14

OPPOSITE I can easily place eight 54-inch round tables or up to seven 8-foot rectangular tables on the porch for festive lunches or dinners. The wicker chairs are all fitted with EZ Glides on the feet so they slide nicely on the wooden porch floor (left). The tables are carefully leveled with wooden shims before they are clothed. The front of the house looks over the rose garden and circle lawn (right). The porch is shady and cool most evenings and it is a lovely place to entertain, even in misty or foggy weather. One thing to remember when dining outdoors is to provide enough light for the guests—candles, hurricanes, electric fixtures with dimmers—all essential for successful entertaining.

FRIDAY NIGHT WELCOME DINNER

Hosting a weekend party for any size group is a big responsibility for the hosts: Beds must be prepared, foodstuffs bought, and menus planned and carefully orchestrated. There must be plenty to drink, lots of activities arranged, and enough help lined up to make the weekend run smoothly and well. Lists are good. Trained helpers are good. It is all about organization and planning and high levels of energy.

Skylands is the perfect place to host a house party. It has many bedrooms and an experienced staff of three, with others available for serving dinners and lunches. The great grounds crew drives to and from the airport, readies the boat and the kayaks and the hiking gear, and keeps the vehicles clean and the gas tanks full. And of course there's Chef Pierre, who travels with us to Skylands and whose wonderful cooking and genial personality make everyone very happy all the time. Sounds a lot like paradise—the paradise that it truly is.

Living on or visiting an island off the coast of Maine educates one quickly as to what is available or not, and what is deemed necessary for a pleasant sojourn. The weekend really starts at home in Bedford right before we go to the airport for the flight to Bar Harbor. The "outside" refrigerator has been loaded with carefully packaged food, arranged neatly in red soft coolers: eggs from the hens, fresh garden veggies and fruits that are not available in Maine, favorite New York City specialties (Balthazar breads, Petrossian croissants, cheeses from Murray's), and of course, any food that has been prepared in advance by me or Pierre.

The house staff always has the house ready for our arrival. We come in like a tornado—bags of food, cases of wine, suitcases, people—and what we find is a tranquil and heavenly home with fires blazing in the giant fireplaces, music playing on the sound system, the table set, and dinner started.

After everyone is shown to the preplanned allocated bedrooms, drinks are served in the living hall. Depending on what follows, or how long or difficult a trip it has been, drinks can be simple—wine or Champagne—or heartier, like martinis or margaritas.

OPPOSITE The living hall is the first room guests enter after the main entrance, so we treat it as a focal point. The book-covered table always has some sort of monumental arrangement on it. For this weekend, Kevin raided the autumn garden and supplemented with material from the woods and fields. It took him quite a while but the result was utterly, astonishingly beautiful. The books, by the way, are publications that have to do with Maine, the area, or the house and its gardens.

PREVIOUS The House That Edsel Built had to have an Edsel car, and my daughter, Alexis, found this vintage two-door station wagon (1958) in original condition. It is used whenever I visit to drive into Bar Harbor or Northeast Harbor for a shopping expedition. There is no power steering, so it is a little difficult to maneuver, but the positives in its avant-garde design certainly outweigh any negatives. It is always parked in the round turn in the front of the house when I am at Skylands.

Menu

PASTA WITH BOLOGNESE SAUCE

WILD-MUSHROOM LASAGNA

MIXED BABY GREENS AND HERBS WITH CANDIED PECANS AND DRIED CRANBERRIES

S'MORES

OPPOSITE In the living room, Kevin and I decided to take advantage of all the artichokes that were about to be hit by frost in the garden. An ancient faux bois container on a faux bois table was the perfect receptacle for the artichokes, which we supplemented with kalanchoe leaves. Small gourds and squash filled faux bois baskets and urns around the house. In one part of the living hall, there is a seating area with this old tufted sofa, reading lamps, and a massive brass tray table. ABOVE The last greens from the garden and the cold frames were picked for the weekend. This green salad is composed of baby spinach, frisée, basil leaves, soft lettuces, herb flowers, and oven-roasted pecans. The Bolognese was chunky and delicious served atop rigatoni with parsley and Parmesan cheese.

The last of the garden's dahlias were salvaged and combined with autumn leaves and Chinese lanterns for a spectacular arrangement in the living hall. OPPOSITE Pierre made a wonderful vegetarian lasagna for the group, featuring wild mushrooms, cheeses, and a fine béchamel sauce.

ABOVE Homemade graham crackers were cut out in the shape of pine trees and imprinted with a wood-graining tool, to mimic faux bois, for the very popular s'mores. Even the marshmallows were homemade. Once roasted and combined with the grahams and fine chocolate, they served as the perfect dessert for a Friday night supper (left). We toasted the marshmallows and assembled the s'mores at the council circle, which is right behind the house. Meant as a place for conversation and contemplation, the circle was part of the original Skylands landscape plan but had never been built. I followed the plans pretty accurately and had it constructed a few years ago; it is a wonderful addition to the property (right). OPPOSITE You can see how scrumptious the assembled s'mores are!

STYLISH DINNER IN THE CLERESTORY

OPPOSITE We served dinner on Martha Stewart reproduction Wedgwood Drabware: This collection was sold a few years ago through the Martha by Mail catalog. It is a favorite tableware, and we all think food looks very good on the tannish hue. The dishes also work well in the very spare environment of our company headquarters.

Not all of the parties I give are at home. In fact, I often like to entertain in other venues, and one of my favorite places on earth is the giant "clerestory" in our offices in the 1925 Starrett-Lehigh Building on West 26th Street and the Hudson River. This is an impressive space where we display our retail products, stage our art and crafts fairs, and hold our company meetings.

When the designer Jasper Conran told me he was coming to New York with Lord Wedgwood, I immediately planned a festive dinner for him, inviting his friends and colleagues from the Wedgwood companies and New Yorkers I thought he would enjoy meeting.

We designed the dinner to reflect the simple New World elegance our company epitomizes, and we used what we could of our company-designed dinnerware for Wedgwood. Our Drabware tableware was so perfect for the delicious menu that Pierre and I created for this very fun dinner party, which began with a cocktail hour, where we served a fine white wine, Champagne, and minimal canapés.

Menu

TOMATO AND GRUYÈRE TOASTS

LEEK AND PORCINI RISOTTO

JOHN DORY WITH RED WINE SAUCE
AND WINTER VEGETABLES

INDIVIDUAL DIABLO CAKES WITH
SUGARED FRUIT

ABOVE (clockwise from top) A single place setting for the dinner in the spare style we prefer for all events held here in the headquarters. Of course, we had printed menus and place cards; these are so easy to design and print using any one of the many programs available on the Internet, good-quality paper, and a good printer. Because this dinner was on a worknight and I had promised it would be an early evening, we had light hors d'oeuvres and cocktails and then promptly sat down to dinner. My daughter came to the dinner looking her usual smashing self; she liked talking to Jasper about design and to Dan Dienst about recycling, his business.

ABOVE (clockwise from left) The main course was light but beautifully balanced: a filet of John Dory with an array of winter vegetables, including cauliflower, brussels sprouts, and fennel. Robin Marino, our president of merchandising, sat beside Thom Browne, a powerful and influential clothing designer. I met Lord Wedgwood when we first forged our partnership with this old and illustrious company to make Martha Stewart designs in England. Years later, Lord Wedgwood is still working as hard as ever to keep the brand vibrant and strong. Jasper Conran is a significant design force in England and, like me, designs for Wedgwood.

OPPOSITE Dessert was excellent: I used an old favorite recipe for Diablo cake, baked for this event in small ring molds. It was then glazed with ganache and decorated with sugared tiny Champagne grapes, little pink macarons, and fresh figs.

BURGUNDY DINNER

Great company, great food, a great location, and a luxuriously comfortable home on a hill on an island off the coast of northern Maine—all set the tone for a dinner party to remember. The weather was ideal: cool, crisp, and clear, with foliage color at its peak. Autumn had done its job and the mountains were ablaze—vivid yellows, brilliant oranges, deep crimsons, and bright reds contrasted with the deep azure of the icy water of the coastal ocean surrounding Mount Desert Island and the deep greens of the firs and spruce and hemlocks of the forest. Saturday dinner was planned as a special occasion with a specific purpose—to taste and hopefully drink the older Burgundies (1980s) that were still intact in the wine cave under the 1925 pink granite house called Skylands. Acadia National Park surrounds the property, and it is congenial at all times of year, even though most people will tell you the season is really July, August, September, and the beginning of October.

In fact, for me, fall is the time of year I love best here in Acadia—I try to plan at least two long weekends at the house with friends who love the outdoors, good food and wine, and exploring the area as much as I do. We arrive, generally, on a Friday late in the afternoon, and return home late Sunday or Monday. Activities are planned, a flexible schedule is set, and the enjoyment begins with a simple supper, followed by a game of Scrabble, cards, or pool. Some of us might watch a movie or decide to retire early to read a book, but everyone rises early for the "morning hike." There is yoga, there is lunch, there are boat rides, bike rides, and cocktails. And on Saturday night there is invariably a sit-down dinner of some significance. The Burgundy Dinner was that sort of dining experience. I planned the menu in advance after I was told by a wine expert friend that many of my "important," inherited, prized bottles of French Burgundy were reaching or had reached "maturity" and that some should at least be opened and drunk. What fun to design the menu, set the table, and sit down to a great and tasty feast, prepared in large part by chef Pierre Schaedelin and in small part by me.

PREVIOUS The terrace permits us to see the incredible views of the ocean and coastal islands from outside, and the large windows allow framed views of the landscape from within. In October the gardens are still green, but the evenings can be quite chilly and sometimes damp. Great fires of white birch logs warm the rooms (almost all have large fireplaces), and candles and numerous lamps and sconces combine to brighten the spaces.

Menu

BAKED STUFFED CLAMS

BRAISED SHORT RIBS

CELERY ROOT PURÉE

BRAISED SALSIFY

CHINESE LONG BEANS

APPLE TART

The large dining room tables are set. Two of them can be joined for large parties, or kept separate. The faux bois concrete furniture was made specially for this room and the pink granite terrazo tabletops were covered with a dark red and brown faux bois–printed linen cloth. We used silvered brass service plates, Russian silver flatware decorated with boars' heads, and grapes on the vine (from my few grape vines in the Skylands vegetable garden) amid the myriad bottles of Burgundy wine that had reached maturity. This dinner and this festive autumnal weekend provided the perfect opportunity to drink them. Small silver saucers served as wine bottle "coasters." The grapes used in the centerpieces are different varietals that I had planted a couple years prior in the Skylands gardens. They were actually productive and delicious as table grapes— nothing like the seedless grapes we get at the supermarket.

Carly Blake, who works as a graphic artist at Martha Stewart Living Omnimedia, helped design the menu covers for each of my homes. For Skylands we used a portion of an old map of Mount Desert Island depicting Seal Harbor and the islands to the south. It's quite fanciful in its illustration. We made the oversized napkins from coordinating cotton cloth and we used small cut and scored birch logs for place card holders. The wineglasses we used were Riedel—appropriate for fine vintage burgundy.

Boned and sauced braised short ribs are one of Pierre's specialties, and we are very fortunate to have this glorious recipe in our collection. The menu was complete with parsnip purée, from my garden-grown parsnips, touched and sweetened by the frost; Chinese long beans cooked just until tender; and braised salsify—another autumn root vegetable.

ABOVE (clockwise from left) I love baked clams, and the local quahogs are extra meaty and delicious. Served on a bed of seaweed we collected on Seal Harbor Beach that day, the clams looked as good as they tasted. Pierre concocted two different fillings, both extraordinary. We sipped, we drank, we ate, we tasted, and everyone participated in lively and spirited conversations— some political, some less so. Chambertin was one of the most delicious of the Burgundies. Paw Paw and the two Frenchies stayed close by, enjoying the hubbub, the crackling fire, and the joie de vivre. OPPOSITE The flat apple tart on a puff pastry crust was well caramelized, crisp and yummy with dollops of whipped crème fraîche; unsweetened whipped heavy cream would also be delicious. The Wedgwood lustre plate is decorated with grapes and vines.

We were so very happy by the end of the evening, having finished all of the wines—and eaten all the food—that I decided to go to bed without totally clearing the table. I did dilute whatever dregs of wine were left in the glasses with water to prevent staining of the glass, but when dawn came the bacchanal remains made for an unusually evocative photo in the morning light.

OPPOSITE One thing I've learned over the years is that linens should be collected at the end of a party and put to soak in tubs of cold water—separate colors, of course. If you have upholstered chairs as I do, someone should check each for stains and crumbs—a quick brush-off or light sponging can very easily avoid staining. My chairs are copies of an original Georgian side chair I purchased at the Ellsworth Antiques Show. A local craftsman made eighteen of them from identical woods and I had them upholstered in silk velvet. They were a very good investment.

halloween
PUMPKIN BLAZE

On the 31st of October, if I am not out trick-or-treating, I am at home, handing out treats to the neighborhood urchins. Or, I am at a party in New York City, dressed in whatever wonderful costume we have dreamed up for my television program or for the cover of our special Halloween issue of *Martha Stewart Living*. But on this particular year, for the benefit of the Historic Hudson Valley and the Van Cortlandt Manor, I threw a festive Halloween dinner at the farm. The manor raises substantial funds with an annual holiday spectacle called the Blaze. Literally thousands of pumpkins are carved and decorated, and many scary tableaux are created—all in celebration of one of America's most beloved holidays, Halloween. It is a blaze of historic proportions, and we sought to honor its importance by making our dinner simultaneously frightening, festive, and ghoulish. It was a good season for pumpkins and squash, and we carved wonderful images on the giant pumpkins we grew on the farm. The large, flat surfaces of the 'Big Max' variety are excellent for a type of carving that is layered into the pale flesh while leaving some of the skin intact.

Long tables were set up in a cruciform shape in the aisles of the stable, the perfect location for our Halloween feast. The black horses in residence, my five Friesians, were very intrigued by the preparations. Live owls housed in large cages were on loan as part of the decorations.

The evening was clear, and the weather pleasantly cool. Pierre did most of the preparations in the main house and outside kitchen, but we cranked up the heat on the Aga stove in the stable kitchen, and there assembled the pumpkin soup served in hollowed-out pumpkins and the choucroute on long oval platters. None of us had to dress in costume—a relief for many—but the spirit of Halloween was pervasive.

OPPOSITE I had a wonderful crew from my television show working with me on the transformation of the stable into an appropriately scary woodland setting of owls and ghouls for the dinner party. Moss- and lichen-covered branches—filled with perched white owls, bats, and small black crows—towered over the netting-covered tables. There were also lots of glittered spiders and bugs.

PREVIOUS You can see how effective a simple image—in this instance, a silly owl—can be, as the translucent windows on paper-bag luminaries are illuminated from within by long-burning candles. The linden tree allée, which leads to the stable, served as the entrance to the party.

Menu

POPPY SEED–CHEESE STRAWS

PUMPKIN SOUP

CHOUCROUTE GARNI

BAKED STUFFED APPLES

POMEGRANATE COSMOPOLITANS

The set tables looked fantastic. We rented black bamboo chairs from Party Rental, hung lanterns overhead, and used faux bois plates and spiderweb votive candle jars. The floor of the stable is embossed in a concrete faux bois pattern, which added to the overall ambience. And, by the way, even though my stable houses five horses and three donkeys and an occasional sheep or two, it is very clean and, because it is extremely well ventilated, fresh-smelling. OPPOSITE Years ago, I bought two of these large American "folk art" wrought-iron wall plant stands. There have been inexpensive, much smaller copies made, but the originals are quite extraordinary. Depending on the season, I place appropriate plants, greenery, or in this case gourds, on the rings, which are really meant for pots.

ABOVE (clockwise from top left) Many pumpkins were lined up on the tops of the stable yard walls, and torches were inserted into the ground for eerie illumination. The chickens were very happy later on in the fall because they ate all of the pumpkins. A friend who had raised several wounded owls loaned them to me for the evening. The chicken wire of the birdcages was fine for a few hours, but the owls would have broken through if they were confined much longer. The sign-in guest book was tea stained and bug ridden. Green glitter embellished the plume. As a trompe l'oeil, we also placed artificial owls here and there, and guests were indeed confused.

A **MENACING** MENU

TUREEN OF TERROR
Pumpkin Soup with chestnuts and crispy herbed crouton

CADAVER'S CHOUCROUTE
Sauerkraut with double-smoked bacon,
wiener sausage, veal sausage, andouille sausage
with smoked pork butt and potatoes "vapeur"

FATAL FINALE
Baked Apple with Torched Meringue and Creme Anglaise

barry levinson

ABOVE The stable kitchen is a good staging area for parties—its focal points are a gray Aga gas-fired stove and a vast collection of antique copper cookware. All the counters are Vermont soapstone supported by architectural brackets from old Victorian houses. Late in the afternoon, we captured this lovely woodland scene on the farm. OPPOSITE The second-floor hayloft proved a great vantage point for photographing the dinner. Covered and brought to the table piping hot, the pumpkin soup retains its warmth in the thick-skinned, small sugar pumpkin "bowls."

PREVIOUS The tables were topped with oilcloth in a faux bois pattern, then covered with spider-like cotton netting. Cheesecloth, dyed black and purple, was draped about. Menu cards were printed, and place cards were made from photocopied spiderwebs cut out with scalloping shears and placed in the center of the wonderful faux bois plastic plates. We rented the black-handled flatware and the stemless glassware (a precautionary measure—we wanted to reduce the risk of stemmed glasses tipping over and breaking in the stable).

OPPOSITE We served a variety of puff pastry cheese straws with the drink of the evening—pomegranate cosmopolitans. My sister Laura Plimpton attended the dinner with her husband, Randy. We all wore shawls or jackets to ward off the autumn chill, but it was very comfortable. ABOVE A close-up view of the soup in a pumpkin; the garnishes were sautéed chestnuts, diced celery root (celeriac), and roasted pumpkin seeds, for crunch. For me, the hit of the evening was the choucroute. Pierre is from Alsace and he certainly knows how to make the very best version of this amazing dish. Schaller & Weber, the German sausage makers and purveyors in New York City, donated the meats and sauerkraut, and Pierre did the rest of the magic. We placed huge oval trays, heaped with the main course, on each table so that guests could serve themselves.

The dessert was a baked apple (from the farm) filled with brandied raisins and nuts and topped with meringue. We created spiderwebs of crème anglaise and chocolate on all the plates before placing a meringue-topped apple in the center of each.

OPPOSITE Party favors are always appreciated, and these paper "coffins" were filled with Halloween candy treats and tied with twine. They are printed with warning signs, of course.

THANKSGIVING AT BEDFORD

I approach each holiday during the year as a pleasant challenge. I certainly am not of the "do it the same exact way" school of entertaining, like some of my friends, whereby every Thanksgiving is identical to the last and the one before that. Their reasoning? "Everyone expects the same things; they will miss my sweet potatoes with marshmallows, they need their oyster stuffing." Sound familiar? Well, as I have admitted, I am an enthusiast for change, for subtly altering the traditional to make it more interesting, more creative, more inventive. I am a firm believer that there are almost infinite choices for a single thing, such as the turkey. We now have access not only to the supermarket varieties and to frozen, factory-raised birds but also to many heritage breeds, including Bourbon Red, Black Spanish, Narragansett, and others, as well as to wild turkeys, hybrid turkeys with extra-broad breasts, organically raised birds, and free-ranging specialty breeds. This opens up so many different ways of preparing a bird, including oven-roasting, smoking, deep-frying, spit-roasting, grilling, poaching, steaming, "turduckening," and so on. And as for the sides, as everyone calls the accompanying vegetables, sauces, relishes, and stuffings: Should the stuffing be in or out of the bird? Baked in a dish or in a giant squash? Should the cranberries be used in a sauce, jelly, or tart filling, or should dried cranberries appear in the stuffing? And for dessert, should the pumpkin pie be fresh pumpkin, canned pumpkin, or squash?

I take notes during the year and tear out pictures of ideas that could possibly be used; we call these tearsheets at the magazine. I search farmstands for unusual pumpkins, gourds, and squash, looking for centerpiece inspiration. I also study the seed catalogs in hopes of discovering heirloom varieties to grow in my own garden in time for the holiday. I engage my crafters at television and at the magazine to think of new ways to "think turkey," in unexpected materials: Wood? Metal? Chocolate? Gilt? Glass? Pottery?

For this Thanksgiving, I set a rustic table using some of my Spode turkey plates and platters and a fine antique rag runner down the center. Warty squash, pomegranates, Amy Goldman's cast bronze squashes, and some old copper birds all made a wild and natural landscape down the middle of the long marble dining table. The food was superb and very Dutch "Vermeer" in appearance on the sideboard.

OPPOSITE The place settings were set directly on the indestructible marble tabletop. I used early flatware and hand-blown, early glassware. The wide-bottomed goblets were originally designed for use on sailing ships—the broad base prevents the glasses from tipping over. The plates are part of a set of early English Staffordshire.

PREVIOUS The brown dining room was once the tractor garage of the farm. Attached to the winter house, it is somewhat adjacent to the kitchen, but removed from the rest of the house. With one wall devoted to cupboards for silver, glass, and serving pieces; shelves containing some of my antique glass collection; two walls of floor-to-ceiling, Thomas Jefferson-inspired, triple-hung windows; and a fireplace wall, this large space is actually quite cozy and comfortable. The room also houses a very large wooden cage full of red canaries who sing while we eat, sometimes a bit too vociferously. I designed the dining room tables—there are two—and the chairs, which were made by the same carpenter as my Skylands chairs. Upholstered in greige linen, they make very nice seating.

Menu

ROASTED TURKEY BREAST WITH
SAGE BUTTER

ROAST TURKEY WITH CORNBREAD
STUFFING

BRAISED TURKEY LEGS

STUFFED PUMPKIN

GLAZED CARROTS AND
RED PEARL ONIONS

ROOT VEGETABLE BOULANGÈRE

BABY BRUSSELS SPROUTS WITH WILD
RICE AND PECANS

SAUTÉED PORCINI MUSHROOMS AND
CHESTNUTS

CORNBREAD "TURKEYS"

CRANBERRY–POMEGRANATE
GELATIN

MERINGUE WITH QUINCE SORBET AND
CRÈME ANGLAISE

PUMPKIN MOUSSE

MAPLE–PUMPKIN PIE

DOUBLE–CRUST APPLE PIE

PECAN–CARAMEL TART

LEFT The buffet was set up in the smaller dining room on the English sideboard. The heritage turkey, a Bourbon Red, was raised in Connecticut and slaughtered by the farmer. The shape of the breed is elongated, unlike hybrid birds, which are much rounder. Roasted, the bird has lots of mahogany skin and tender, tasty meat. The bird photographs are by Carsten Höller, a Danish artist, and beautifully framed by Eli Wilner.

OVERLEAF I always stuff the bird, but since my daughter, Alexis, and other guests are vegetarian, we also try to make a stuffing that is a meal unto itself. This particular year, we baked it in the large potiron *d'estampe* pumpkin from my garden; it was exceptionally flavorful. Once dressed, the bird weighed twenty pounds. It carved well—lots of light meat, lots of dark. In addition, we roasted a brined turkey breast and braised extra turkey legs, which we served on the large silver tray to the seated guests, who had already helped themselves to vegetables and the other "trimmings."

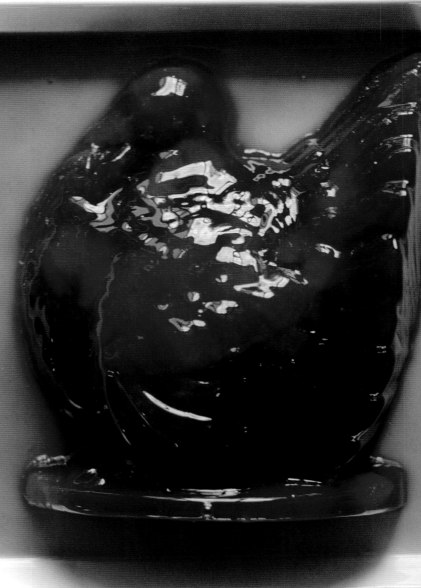

ABOVE Something inspired me to bake the cornbread in the plump turkey cake mold we designed for Macy's. The cast metal mold baked the batter perfectly (left). I used the same mold for the cranberry-pomegranate jelly, which was wonderfully flavored with orange juice, spices, lemon peel, and clementines (right). OPPOSITE All around the house were some autumnal arrangements created by Kevin Sharkey. Here he lined a very old, fine cast-iron container with plastic, then filled it with chrysanthemums, begonia leaves, scented geraniums, Bupleurum, and eucalyptus. The gilded turkeys were made of a composite material covered with gold leaf.

The counters in the servery, just off the kitchen, have several large decorative marble urns and ornaments on them. We filled one urn with Chinese lanterns (*Physalis alkekengi*), and set more gilded turkeys—originally crafted for the magazine—to rest nearby. OPPOSITE I made lots of desserts, as usual: pecan-caramel tart, double-crust apple pie, and maple-pumpkin pie. I baked the pies in old pottery pie plates, which enable the crust to turn perfectly golden brown on the bottom.

The delicately spiced pumpkin mousse was spooned into an assortment of goblets and served with a dollop of whipped cream and a puff pastry maple leaf. OPPOSITE We also had meringue with quince sorbet. I grow fragrant quinces on trees that I brought with me from my house on Turkey Hill in Westport, Connecticut. I love the taste and color of the sorbet.

CHRISTMAS AT CANTITOE CORNERS

Christmas at the farm in Bedford, known as Cantitoe Corners, gets better and better as the farm matures as a place and I identify more and more with it as my primary home and the base of operations for all I do and create. Each year, we do a little bit more with the exterior decorations: lights in the trees, ornaments on the pergola and in the old apple trees, garlands around doorways and along porch railings and fences, shooting stars in the roof peaks and flickering lights under the eaves. Great evergreen trees—cut at a friend's tree farm, set into tree trunk stands in front of my buildings, and illuminated with hundreds of electric lights—bring a new brightness and aura to the place.

Inside, Laura Acuna (she has worked in my homes for twenty-seven years) and I decorate like crazy. We decide which artificial trees go where, and which kinds to display. If last year it was all feather trees, this year it may be all tinsel. Other decorative details vary as well—if last year it was polar bears, this year it is moose. And each room has a color scheme—green in the small dining room, gold accents in the green room, white and turquoise details in the brown room.

This particular year, I hosted a dinner for friends in the small dining room right before Christmas. I wanted a festive but utterly delicious small dinner. Our special guest was a former American poet laureate, Billy Collins, who has written some of my favorite poems—emotionally charged and witty yet deeply heartfelt pieces, including "The Lanyard." Billy read for us that evening during the dinner and it was just wonderful. And the food was delectable.

OPPOSITE While I was incarcerated in West Virginia, I was able to attend a ceramics class. Having studied pottery and ceramics as a child, I understood how to pour molds, shape, paint, glaze, and fire the pieces. I chose to make a set of Nativity figures. In an old storeroom, I uncovered the entire Nativity scene, including the wise men, the animals, the camels, and the family of Christ. I mixed the drab paint color from primary colors—it took a while to perfect all my techniques with very little to work with, but the Nativity set is beautiful.

PREVIOUS I am lucky to have some beautifully shaped, ancient, unnamed but productive apple trees on the property. We illuminated this tree with small white lights and giant silver kugel balls. In the snow, the tree stood out majestically.

Menu

WASABI CAVIAR AND DAIKON CANAPÉS

PHEASANT POTPIES WITH BLACK TRUFFLES AND ROOT VEGETABLES

BUCATINI WITH BROWN BUTTER, CAPERS, AND ANCHOVIES

SEARED PHEASANT BREASTS WITH ENDIVE MEUNIÉRE

CREAM PUFFS WITH WARM CHOCOLATE SAUCE

The table was beautifully set with green dishes, Peking glass, Limoges, Depression glassware, and pearl-handled flatware. OPPOSITE Pale green tinsel trees were placed in each corner of my small dining room. We decorated them with silver, nickel, and bronze ornaments. The glass balls in the center of the table are vintage hand-blown buoys from the North Atlantic fishing industry, which were used to keep fishing nets afloat.

ABOVE We decorate every door and most windows of the houses with wreaths for the holiday season. Here, the Summer House front door is hung with a wreath of greenery sprayed bronzy gold, suspended from a golden ribbon (left). Knowing that we were having a filling menu, the only hors d'oeuvres I served that evening were half-moons of bread topped with wasabi-flavored caviar, pickled daikon, and salmon roe caviar (right). OPPOSITE The green living room in the Winter House at Bedford looks beautiful when decorated for Christmas. Each year the theme is different; this year, it was gold and silver and glass. The windows were hung inside as well as outside with wreaths.

The savory potpie was studded with diced vegetables and tender pheasant. The golden, crisp puff pastry crust was scored with the point of a very sharp knife before baking. It's important to cut through only half the layers of the pastry so that it can rise properly when baked. OPPOSITE Prior to Christmas, with the house in full "decoration," I try to entertain at a series of small dinners. A night of poetry with Poet Laureate Emeritus Billy Collins was a great deal of lighthearted fun, and the food was delicious.

A 19th-century clear glass epergne, tulip vases, and cut-glass hurricanes serve as glistening objects on which to display mercury glass spheres and tinsel ornaments.

ABOVE (clockwise from top left) One tinsel tree had decorations of glass balls and icicles. The bucatini was incredibly flavorful, mixed with brown butter, capers, anchovies, breadcrumbs, and herbs. Billy Collins kept me and my guests entertained all evening, regaling us with stories and poems. We all enjoyed the dinner so very much. The breast of roasted pheasant was sliced and served upon a bed of braised endive and topped with sliced black truffles and fresh endive spears.

I was happy to present a simpler version of the classic croquembouche. We had cream puffs baked with pearl sugar for extra crunchiness on the crust, then filled with pastry cream. There was no caramel holding the puffs together, as there is in the traditional dessert. They were served profiterole-style, with warm chocolate sauce. OPPOSITE I have always loved beautiful linens for tables and beds. These ecru place mats have elaborate embroidery, drawnwork, and crocheted edges and borders. Salt can be placed with pepper in silver dishes, but it is important not to leave it too long or the salt will start to corrode the metal.

DINNER PARTY DESSERTS

OPPOSITE Meringues are miraculous. They can be soft and chewy, or crisp and crunchy all the way through, or soft on the inside and crunchy on the exterior. They can be snow white, creamy, flavored with coconut or chocolate or raspberry, or just touched with a hint of vanilla bean. The popular dessert known as Pavlova was developed in honor of the great ballerina Anna Pavlova while she was dancing in Australia and New Zealand. Both countries claim ownership of this featherlight, pillowy dessert. "Down under," the Pavlova is served with passionfruit, bananas, and whipped cream. For this Pavlova, I filled the two disks of baked meringue with whipped cream and assorted raspberries from my berry patch— golden, brandywine, red, and black. Pavlova is easy to cut with a serrated knife; each guest should receive a generous helping.

I could write an entire book on desserts for dinner parties. For me, a great dessert is essential as an ending to a great dinner. There are many options to choose from and to prepare: meringue desserts, fruit desserts, cold desserts (mousses, ice creams, sorbets), hot desserts (soufflés), pastry desserts (pies, tarts, puff pastry), and, of course, jelly desserts.

I have tried to be inclusive in this book, including many recipes for desserts I have served over the years to my friends, who request them again and again once they have tasted them. My desserts are not perfect: They are not sharply molded, fancifully iced, or laser-cut as many bakery desserts are these days. The flavors are fresh and pure, and only natural, unprocessed ingredients are used: juices from ripe fruit; just-picked, unblemished berries; the finest vanilla beans; the best heavy cream; the finest butter.

I try to make desserts that are so delicious there will not be any leftovers, with nothing pushed off to the side of the plates when people leave the table. Many of the desserts need last-minute attention and must be served straight from the freezer, the oven, the stove, or the refrigerator. This requires a bit of skill and planning, but it is all doable. There are some desserts in this chapter that will go with any menu, and many more throughout the book that you will want to try.

ABOVE This ice cream bombe was formed in one of my antique copper molds. It is garnished with fraises de bois from the garden, or any other berries (left). It is a spectacular end to any meal. To make the bombe, we layered pistachio ice cream, black-currant sorbet, and then strawberry-lavender sorbet in the mold. Many different combinations can be used; I also like vanilla ice cream with black raspberry sorbet and red raspberry sorbet. We sliced and served the bombe with a dark, rich chocolate fudge sauce (right).

OPPOSITE Another very easy but utterly wonderful dessert is a fruit crostata. Batches of pâte brisée can be kept frozen in flat, round disks, ready to thaw and transform into an open-faced tart with little notice. This particular crostata is filled with ripe, sweet, fragrant slices of white nectarines. The folded-over pastry border is sprinkled with coarse sanding sugar, which adds glamour as well as crunch. It's delicious served with whipped crème fraîche or cream.

I think homemade fruit jelly desserts fell out of favor when Jell-O made from a box became so popular in the mid-20th century, but I have always loved the clean, fresh flavors of homemade gelatin desserts. When we had an excess of pomegranates, I squeezed the juice from them and Pierre and I made this magnificent domed "jelly." If you use the correct proportion of gelatin to juice, the jelly will be neither too soft nor too hard; it should shake, but it should also be firm enough to unmold and to slice. The pomegranate juice worked very well, and in combination with the sugared currants made a most wonderful and refreshing dessert. I served it without any accompaniment, but, in fact, it is even better with thick, unsweetened heavy cream.

This cake is made from pure semolina, which is derived from the kernel of the wheat and separated from the bran or germ of yellow durum wheat. It is the same flour traditionally used to make couscous. It has a slightly rough, "gritty," yet ultimately pleasant texture; the cake itself is similar to a British steamed pudding—moist, dense, and delicious. OPPOSITE Pears poached in Riesling wine syrup are garnished with chocolate leaves made by painting melted chocolate on the backs of pear leaves. The soft green leaves can be peeled off the hardened chocolate, leaving an exact replica. Firm, ripe pears are crucial to the success of this dessert; I find Comice very flavorful, as well as yellow Bartletts.

One of my most memorable desserts was served to me in Jacksonville, Florida, at a lovely woman's home. It is a giant île flottante, or a floating island or boule de neige. Generally floating islands are poached in water or milk, but here the stiffly beaten egg whites are baked in a Bundt pan, to simplify the process. The baked meringue is then inverted and served with caramel and crème anglaise. OPPOSITE For Christmas or another special occasion, try making this mound of cream puffs. It is a true croquembouche, formed from pâte à choux puffs filled with crème patissière and "glued" together with caramel syrup. Everyone enjoys pulling apart the glorious mound, either with spoons or their fingers.

EASTER DINNER

OPPOSITE The dining table was quite whimsical, set in a spring garden theme. I always attempt to use different dishes, silver, and glassware during the year so friends who have dined previously don't see the same things very often. I put "gilded" eggs in small "cabbage leaf" baskets. The eggs were dyed in pastel colors, stickered with Avery "dots," and then spray-painted in metallic shades. When the dots are removed, they leave pastel polka dots behind. They were placed here and there among the faience cabbage bowls of daffodils, the cardboard velour rabbits, and the foil-covered chocolate bunnies I used as place cards. The antique Wedgwood "basket weave" embossed bread and butter plates and the green-bordered Wedgwood plates date from the late 19th and early 20th centuries. The English silver and Swedish hand-blown glasses all combined to make an eclectic but pleasing table arrangement. I use tiny silver plates for salt and pepper.

I have hosted Easter breakfasts, brunches, lunches, and even dinners at my house in Westport, and now at my home in Bedford. If we have had an Easter egg hunt on Saturday, I will most likely have a more formal meal on Sunday. This year it was dinner set on the marble tables in the brown dining room. My bulbs were in full bloom, so I was able to pick many different narcissi and daffodils and arrange bunches in my leafy French faience bowls. Usually by Easter, I have already picked and arranged the many different kinds of *Salix* I have growing on the property, including pussy willows, which can help fill up the empty spaces in any room.

Easter is a holiday associated with bunnies, baby chicks, eggs, and lambs. In my house, bunnies were everywhere for this dinner: on the table, on the buffet, in baskets, and peeping out from behind flower arrangements. Tiny bunnies were even in the aspic and on the mantels. Jelly beans and chocolate rabbits abounded, as did marshmallow chicks, or "peeps," Kevin's must-haves. I set tableware in pastel colors for dinner: peach-rimmed Limoges dessert plates, Wedgwood embossed green-rimmed dinner plates, pale green and blue majolica asparagus platters, and Paris porcelain.

The dinner was very different from the Easter-ham-and-kielbasa feasts I had as a child in Nutley, but just as memorable, I hope, for my guests. We prepared a choice of appetizers: charming and delicious oeufs en gelée and two puréed spring soups. The vegetables were organically grown, the asparagus fresh from my garden. More guests came after dinner to partake of the elaborate dessert buffet. Most of the sweets were homemade, but a couple were gifts—fanciful sugar cookies and a bunny-shaped cake iced beautifully in a Beatrix Potter sort of style. Of course, the annual giant chocolate rabbit made his appearance and stood sentrylike over the dinner until he was broken into pieces for guests to take home.

ABOVE This tilt-top pie crust table was "hopping" with rabbits at Easter. The two tallest bunnies are actually artificial acrylic shapes painted to look exactly like milk chocolate. The other molded rabbits are edible, delicious chocolate. Parrot tulips from the garden are arranged in an epergnelike way in flip glasses on cake pedestals. OPPOSITE I don't remember where I found this agate enamelware tub, but I knew instantly that it would find its way as a "prop" in many of my photographs. This multihued enamel was filled with golden straw (borrowed from the horse barn) and topped with dozens of eggs—hard-boiled, colored, and natural. The compotes alongside are filled with stone eggs I purchased in South America. The jadeite baskets on the mantel are from our collection produced for the Martha by Mail catalog business; they are filled with a mix of hellebore flowers, fern fronds, and philodendron leaves.

Menu

OEUFS EN GELÉE

TURNOVERS WITH CHANTERELLES
AND FRESH HERBS

PURÉED CARROT SOUP

WHITE ASPARAGUS SOUP

LEEK TERRINE

BRAISED LEG OF LAMB WITH
MINT JELLY

RAGOUT OF SPRING VEGETABLES

ASPARAGUS WITH MUSTARD
VINAIGRETTE

RICOTTA GNOCCHI

PASKA

LEMON TART

RHUBARB TART

ORANGE EASTER–EGG CAKE
WITH TINY MERINGUE NESTS

OPPOSITE Pierre loves interesting small cups and dishes in which to serve all manner of delicious things. He chose these pottery jars from the china closet (I found five hundred of them in a French flea market) to hold the two types of soup: white asparagus purée garnished with tiny spears of fresh white asparagus, and a purée of carrot. One of Pierre's specialties—and a recipe I will never tire of—is the leek terrine made in a triangular metal terrine mold. The cooked leeks are so tender and the flavoring of the gelatin so delicate that guests always ask for seconds. ABOVE I have always loved oeufs en gelée, and these, with finely minced vegetables and a gelatinous beef broth, are utterly memorable. The tiny rabbits are formed with my Japanese cutters (the same ones I used to garnish the deviled eggs for the Easter Egg Hunt). I don't often get to use my French majolica asparagus service set, but when my own asparagus are served, fresh from the garden, I arrange the green spears, with a topping of mustard vinaigrette or warm hollandaise, on top of the colorful patterned plates and platters.

The leg of lamb with mint jelly was tender and very flavorful, cooked exactly as it should be. It was basted with the pan juices during the long, slow roast (more than three hours), until it just started to fall off the bone. OPPOSITE Velour-covered cardboard rabbits with egg baskets on their backs are reproductions of antique toys that we found while shopping in the flower district in Manhattan. The glass epergne is a wonderful display item; here it holds different marbleized blown-out eggs. The round glass containers are antique American leech bowls, and were filled with tulips, hyacinths, ranunculus, and peonies.

The giant *Salix* arrangement (this is a form of curly willow) was supported in one of several pottery stands known as sewer art because it was made from the same clay in the same pottery in Ohio where clay sewer pipes were fabricated. These unusual pots are collectors' items. I used the arrangement as a tree for Easter egg ornaments. OPPOSITE I baked a golden sponge cake, formed it into an egg shape, filled it with a citrus curd, and "iced" it with Italian meringue. Set in a bed of slivered almonds on a silver tray, it looked like a present from the Easter Bunny. The little white cups are baked meringue "nests" filled with jelly beans.

ABOVE (clockwise from top left) My friend Susan Magrino Dunning sips a cappuccino after dinner. A tart made from fresh spring rhubarb is another specialty of the house. I grow a lot of rhubarb and use it often while the stalks are young and tender. My nephew Christopher Herbert joined us. An assortment of eggs dyed with botanical motifs. OPPOSITE The dessert buffet was varied and abundant. In the window is another of the large pussy willow arrangements I make early each spring, before the velvety buds turn into green leaves. Candy eggs, marshmallow chicks, cakes, cookies, and tarts, interspersed with fresh-cut flowers, fill the festive table where guests can serve themselves.

For this citrus tart, a rich lemon filling is baked into a pâte sucrée crust flavored with ground almonds. It is dusted with powdered sugar and topped with oven-dried, sugared slices of Meyer lemon. OPPOSITE A good view of the *Salix* tree hung with some of the egg ornaments I have collected over the years. Each has a story—some are homemade, others were given to me by friends—and this is a great way to display them in the round for all to see.

danish
SMØRREBRØD *in*
NEW YORK CITY

OPPOSITE I stood in the bow
of the SKAT, a 232-foot-long
Lürssen-made ship, as we passed
by the Statue of Liberty on our
way around the tip of Manhattan.
The boat's tender carried the
photographer, affording her an
opportunity to get this amazing
composition.

I have entertained on land and on sea, but one of the best parties I ever hosted was aboard a friend's yacht right in New York Harbor. It is incredible how different New York City looks from the Hudson River, or in the harbor near the Statue of Liberty.

The boat was docked for two weeks at the end of Chelsea Piers near 23rd street on the Hudson River. I lived on the boat, enjoying the commute to 26th Street where my corporate offices and TV studios are located. I invited many of my New York friends to come to the boat for cocktails and a cruise around the tip of Lower Manhattan and up the East River a bit. Many of us had been on smaller boats that cruise the river, but none of us had been on such a mammoth, powerful yacht so high up over the water. It was very exciting.

The chef on the boat was Danish, and he suggested we serve Danish open-faced sandwiches and provide an open bar with lots of white wine and Champagne. The sandwiches were hearty enough for dinner, and guests were thrilled with the evening's cruise. A Scandinavian open sandwich is made with one piece of buttered bread (white, whole grain, rye, or black) topped with an assortment of ingredients, ranging from sliced cucumber and tomato wedges to liver pâté, shrimp, hard-boiled eggs, and even small meatballs. Rendered lard, or pig fat, might be substituted for butter if herring is used for the topping.

I find the art of sandwich making very interesting and it was fun to choose the different toppings for the menu. The first time I sampled Danish sandwiches, even before I had been to Denmark, was in a small café in the Museum of Modern Art in New York City. Those sandwiches were made by an artist and I could eat two or three servings of them for lunch. When I did finally travel to Denmark, I discovered that cafés like the one in New York were common and the sandwiches just as beautiful and tasty as I remembered.

ABOVE Captain Brad is standing to my left as I await the arrival of my guests. The crew of the SKAT is amazingly friendly and accommodating and such fun to travel with. Notice the crew each has a Danish sandwich, which for them was not so special—it is part of their common fare. OPPOSITE I made beautiful wooden trays for the party and painted them in red, white, blue, and yellow nautical letters spelling SKAT when they were placed side by side. They were perfect for the display of the food. From top to bottom: cured ham with cucumber, sour cream, and parsley; red lettuce, shrimp, hard-boiled quail eggs, and caviar with dill; beef tongue with vegetable mayonnaise and white asparagus.

Menu

ASSORTED DANISH SANDWICHES:

CORNED BEEF WITH HORSERADISH CREAM

BOILED FINGERLING POTATO WITH FRIED ONIONS

HARD-COOKED EGGS WITH TOMATOES AND RADISHES

HERB PORK ROLL WITH VEAL ASPIC

SALAMI WITH QUICK RÉMOULADE

LIVER PÂTÉ WITH CHANTERELLES AND BACON

SHRIMP AND EGGS WITH CAVIAR

ROAST BEEF WITH CAPERBERRIES AND PICCALILLI

BEEF TONGUE WITH VEGETABLE MAYONNAISE AND WHITE ASPARAGUS

PICKLED HERRING WITH CAPERS AND DILL

The minimal furniture on the
boat is primarily Danish
and Italian design, with artworks
by Victor Vasarely. The simple
color scheme of red, gray, blue,
and black is minimal as well.
The boat's interiors were designed
by Marco Zanini.

ABOVE (clockwise from top left) My friends Memrie Lewis, Doug Newhouse, and Kevin Sharkey in the bow of the boat as we cruised the river. Here I am with Robin Marino, Gael Towey, and Ayesha Patel. Friends enjoying the New York skyline and the warm and inviting climate. A good shot of the boat under way in the harbor. It is a fine, sleek, planar design by the well-known Swedish naval architect and designer Espen Øino. Painted battleship gray, it is one of the most unique luxury superyachts.

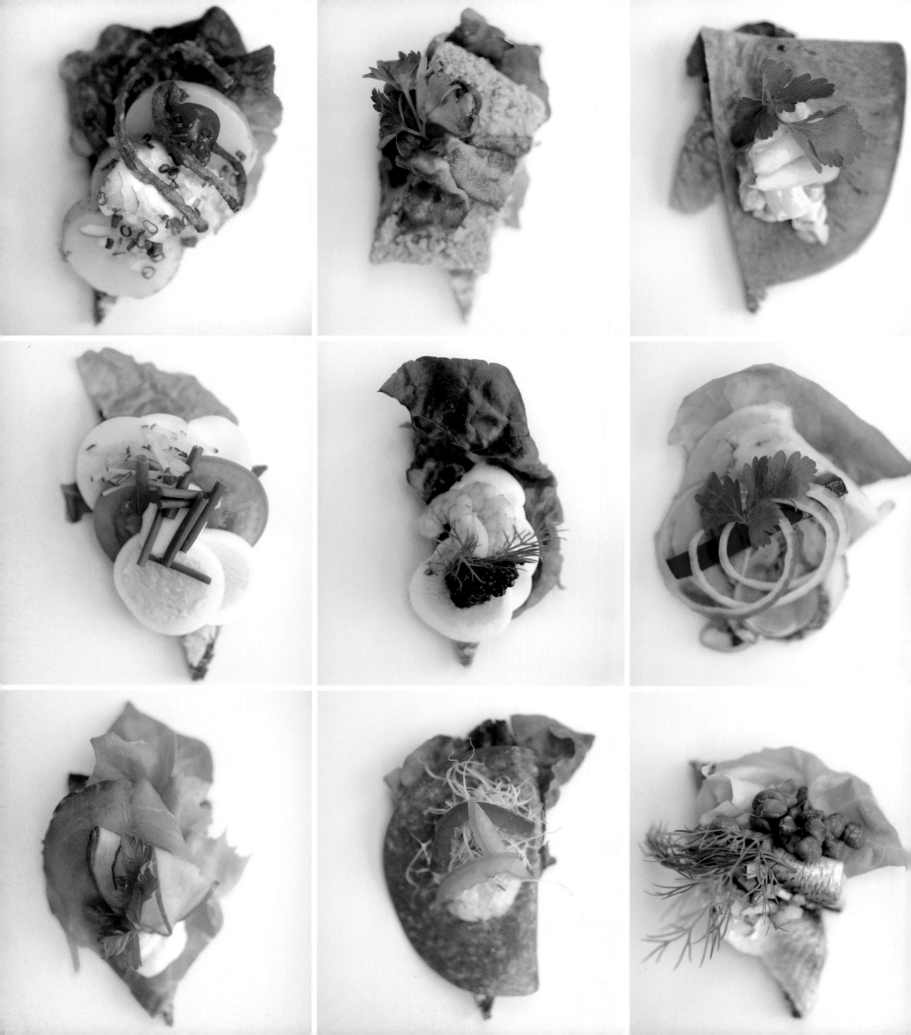

The Jersey City skyline from the boat at twilight. The water was calm and smooth and it was a very nice evening for such a cruise. OPPOSITE More scrumptious Danish sandwiches (left to right, top row to bottom): boiled fingerling potato and fried onion; liver pâté with bacon and chanterelles; beef tongue with white asparagus and vegetable mayonnaise; hard-cooked egg with radish and tomato; shrimp with quail egg and caviar; herb pork roll with veal aspic and red onion; corned beef with horseradish cream and cucumber; salami, rémoulade, and radish sprouts; pickled herring with capers and fresh dill.

VERDANT SPRING DINNER

OPPOSITE The centerpieces were herbaceous peonies and tree peonies from the garden. We made the bright, spring green tablecloths from linen we found in New York City; it very closely matched the green wicker chairs that I use outdoors for dinners and lunches. The round tables of ten looked awesome with the bright pinks and roses of the peonies, the green glass goblets, the shiny silver, and the Wedgwood Drabware dishes.

Sometimes it is nice to have a dinner party just for the fun of it. I try to entertain friends, colleagues, new acquaintances, and business partners on a regular basis, hosting at least one big dinner a month and several smaller fêtes such as lunches or informal breakfasts. Recently, I hosted my first Christmas open house at the farm and because it went very well, I am now planning a second. But a dinner party, just to gather interesting people together and serve them delicious food and great wines, can be a refreshing way to hone your entertaining skills, try new recipes, and even set a fresh new table.

To usher in the month of May, I bottled up white wine (a fine Riesling) with sweet woodruff flowers a couple weeks before this dinner. It's easy to do: You merely insert a handful of sprigs of sweet woodruff in a newly opened bottle of wine, recork the bottle, and refrigerate for at least two weeks to get an infusion. The wine will last for six weeks or more like this.

Some friends in Maine informed me that the fresh crab was extra-good and plentiful at the time, so I planned on serving crab cakes as a first course (my friends kindly shipped the crab to me overnight). I love lamb, so we settled on that as a main course, accompanied by spring vegetables. For hors d'oeuvres, we made fresh gravlax with wild salmon, and placed thin slices atop crispy potato skins and potato purée. We served spicy tuna tartare on thinly sliced and toasted French bread. And we served small glasses of chilled asparagus soup.

We gathered while it was still light out in the garden for cocktails. I designed a new cocktail—the elderflower martini—for the party, and served those along with the May wine, which everyone liked. Friends came from as far away as the Yucatán and California and we ate in the carport, transformed for the evening into a cordial dining room with great flowers, colorful linens, and romantic music.

Menu

MAY WINE

ELDERFLOWER MARTINIS

STUFFED POTATO CRISPS WITH
GRAVLAX

GRILLED SHRIMP WITH
GUACAMOLE AND CHIPOTLE
RÉMOULADE

SPICY TUNA TARTARE CROSTINI

TOMATO MOUSSE WITH GARDEN BASIL

CHILLED ASPARAGUS SOUP WITH
PROSCIUTTO–WRAPPED
ASPARAGUS

JUMBO LUMP CRAB CAKES WITH
CUCUMBER SALAD AND DILL SAUCE

ROASTED LAMB SADDLE WITH
LEMON–THYME JUS

FAVA BEAN RAGOUT

MACARONS

RHUBARB AND RASPBERRY SORBETS
WITH FRUIT COMPOTE

ABOVE There were five tables of ten, and I needed at least eight spectacular blossoms for each table. I picked the flowers late in the afternoon and they were in very good condition, as the weather was not too hot. I had to mix and match the silverware, but I have been collecting old sets of silver for a long time and have plenty to accommodate fifty or sixty for a sit-down dinner. We used all antique white damask napkins for dinner. I find that the older the napkins get, the more times they are laundered and ironed, the more absorbent, softer, and nicer they become. OPPOSITE We cut some peonies with extra-long stems so they could be amassed in tall vases and placed on the sideboard. Because I knew I would want to use the carport for meals and parties, I covered the walls in beadboard, painted everything Bedford Gray, and added a giant sideboard, supported on architectural salvage brackets, for serving or display. A vintage French mirror was painted the same gray and hung in the space.

ABOVE My friend Paula Cussi from Mexico, Joel Motley, and Earl Nemser (left). Garnished with mint leaves, the elderflower martini is a tasty mix of lemon juice, St. Germain liqueur, and pomegranate juice (right). OPPOSITE I have made many different kinds of serving trays over the years and these wooden trays, auto-body painted, are very useful. Several of a few different hors d'oeuvres are passed on the trays at one time; pictured are the tuna, the salmon, the shrimp, the soup, and the tomato mousse served in eggcups.

ABOVE The short-stemmed flowers are positioned in small shot glasses, juice glasses, and tiny tumblers; flowers rest comfortably on the rims and last for several days like this. The saddle of lamb, plated, is a really elegant dinner offering, dressed up with fresh vegetables including baby potatoes, fava beans, spring carrots, and small tomatoes. *OPPOSITE* Here is a better view of the tables and the room, a great kind of space to have on one's property.

Scoops of fresh raspberry and rhubarb sorbets, sitting on top of a serving of compote of rhubarb, were served to each guest. Whipped cream can be formed into a nice oval shape (called a quenelle) by using two sharply pointed tablespoons. OPPOSITE Dessert was really colorful. Macarons such as these have become very popular in the past few years. You can make them—this recipe is excellent—or buy them at many fine bakeries. I presented them to each table on a Fire King green pedestal cake stand surrounded by peonies.

LEFT I do not like very dark dining rooms, so I just barely dimmed the overhead lights in the carport. The dinner was so colorful and the guests so attractive that I wanted to see everything. I planted the birch logs, which we had recycled from a shoot for my television show, across the entrance to the carport. They stood upright on plywood square bases, which I buried under the gravel and covered with some woodland moss.

Recipes

ABOVE A plate of carefully cooked garden asparagus with a buttery, lemony hollandaise appears complex, perfect, "hard to do"—but is in reality a simple first course that can be prepared with very little difficulty.

ABOVE Pierre is like a ballet dancer or orchestra conductor in my kitchen at Bedford. Working at a bank of Jade stoves and ovens, he has everything within easy reach: pots on racks overhead, drawers filled with every imaginable utensil facing the stoves, and a broad marble island that is a perfect serving counter for a buffet lunch or dinner (left). One of my favorite brunch foods is scrambled eggs served in egg shells and topped with salmon roe caviar (right). Soft, warm, buttery biscuits are a perfect accompaniment.

Breakfast and Brunch

BLUEBERRY SMOOTHIES

SERVES 8 *from* **BLUEBERRY BREAKFAST**

1 pint fresh blueberries (2 cups)
2 cups plain yogurt, preferably Greek style
2 cups milk
¼ cup honey
2 cups ice cubes

Combine all ingredients in a blender and purée until smooth. Divide evenly among tall glasses and serve immediately.

BROILED GRAPEFRUIT

SERVES 4 *from* **AN ELEGANT BREAKFAST AT SKYLANDS**

1 blood orange, preferably organic
  Confectioners' sugar, for dusting
2 grapefruits

Preheat oven to 250° F. Wash and dry blood orange, then use a serrated knife to slice off four thin rounds. Arrange on a baking sheet lined with a nonstick baking mat; dust liberally with confectioners' sugar. Cook until completely dry, flipping halfway through, about 45 minutes. Let cool completely.

Heat broiler, with rack 6 inches from heat. Halve grapefruits; loosen segments from membranes with a knife, keeping halves intact. Broil until browned in spots on top, 2 to 3 minutes. Top each half with a blood orange slice, and dust with confectioners' sugar. Serve immediately

PUFFED CEREAL *with* BERRIES *and* HONEYCOMB

SERVES 2 *from* **FAVORITE IDEAS FOR BREAKFAST TRAYS**

Honeycomb is available at many health food stores and farmers' markets or from online sources.

2½ cups mixed puffed cereals, such as rice and kasha
2 cups fresh strawberries, rinsed, hulled, and sliced
4 to 6 pieces (1 to 3 inches each) honeycomb
  Milk, for serving

Divide cereal between serving bowls, top with berries and honeycomb, and serve milk alongside.

PORRIDGE *with* DRIED FRUITS *and* NUTS

SERVES 4 *from* **FAVORITE IDEAS FOR BREAKFAST TRAYS**

¾ cup wheat berries
4 cups water, plus more for cooking wheat berries
½ teaspoon salt
1 cup Irish steel-cut oats
½ cup milk, plus more, warmed, for serving
3 tablespoons unsulfured molasses
3 tablespoons honey
¾ teaspoon ground cinnamon
¾ cup mixed dried fruit, such as cranberries, currants, raisins, and chopped figs or apricots, for serving
¾ cup walnuts or pecans, toasted (page 423) and broken into large pieces, for serving

Fill a large pot with water; cover, and bring to a boil. Add wheat berries, and return to a boil. Cook until grains are al dente, about 1 hour. Drain.

Meanwhile, bring 4 cups of water to a boil in a medium saucepan. Add salt and oats, and cook, stirring, until beginning to thicken, about 3 minutes. Reduce heat to medium low, and simmer until almost all the liquid is absorbed, about 30 minutes. Add ½ cup milk along with the molasses, honey, cinnamon, and drained wheat berries. Cook, stirring constantly, until heated through and thick, about 5 minutes.

Divide porridge among shallow bowls, and pour warm milk over the top. Sprinkle with dried fruits and toasted nuts, dividing evenly, and serve immediately.

MARTHA'S FRENCH TOAST

SERVES 2 *from* **FAVORITE IDEAS FOR BREAKFAST TRAYS**

2 large eggs, lightly beaten
½ cup milk
1 tablespoon light brown sugar
½ teaspoon ground cinnamon
¼ cup Cognac or other brandy
  Finely grated zest of 1 orange
2 slices (1 inch) brioche or challah bread, preferably day-old
2 tablespoons unsalted butter
2 tablespoons neutral-tasting oil, such as safflower
2 tablespoons granulated sugar mixed with 1 teaspoon ground cinnamon, for sprinkling (optional)
  Confectioners' sugar, for dusting (optional)
  Pure maple syrup, for serving

Whisk together eggs, milk, brown sugar, cinnamon, brandy, and orange zest in a shallow dish. Dip bread slices in egg mixture to coat.

Heat butter and oil in a large skillet over medium. Cook bread on both sides until golden brown, about 2 minutes per side. Sprinkle with sugar-cinnamon mixture or dust with confectioners' sugar, as desired. Serve immediately, with syrup on the side.

CINNAMON TOAST

SERVES 2 *from* **FAVORITE IDEAS FOR BREAKFAST TRAYS**

¼ cup sugar
Ground cinnamon
4 slices good-quality white bread, such as pain de mie
Unsalted butter, softened

Heat broiler. Combine sugar with cinnamon to taste. Toast bread under broiler until golden, then turn and spread with butter. Sprinkle with cinnamon sugar, dividing evenly, and broil until golden brown and bubbling on top. Serve hot.

BLUEBERRY MUFFINS

MAKES 12 *from* **BLUEBERRY BREAKFAST**

6 tablespoons unsalted butter, softened, plus more for tin (optional)
3 cups plus 2 tablespoons all-purpose flour
1 tablespoon baking powder
1 teaspoon salt
1¼ cups granulated sugar
1 large whole egg plus 2 large egg yolks
1 teaspoon pure vanilla extract
1 cup milk
1¾ cups fresh blueberries
Sanding sugar, for sprinkling

Preheat oven to 375° F. Butter a standard 12-cup muffin tin (or line with paper liners). Sift together flour, baking powder, and salt into a bowl.

With an electric mixer on medium high, cream butter and granulated sugar until pale and fluffy. Add whole egg, yolks, and vanilla; mix until well combined. Reduce speed to low; alternate adding reserved flour mixture and milk, beginning and ending with flour. Gently fold in berries.

Divide batter evenly among prepared cups; sprinkle generously with sanding sugar. Bake until light golden on top, rotating tin halfway through, about 30 minutes. Cool in tin on a wire rack 15 minutes before turning out muffins. Serve warm or at room temperature.

BLUEBERRY PANCAKES

MAKES 16 TO 18 *from* **BLUEBERRY BREAKFAST**

For pancakes that are especially golden, grease the griddle with rendered bacon fat instead of butter; wipe off excess before cooking batter.

2 cups all-purpose flour
2 teaspoons baking powder
1 teaspoon baking soda
½ teaspoon coarse salt
3 tablespoons sugar
2 large eggs
3 cups buttermilk
4 tablespoons unsalted butter, melted, plus more for griddle
1¼ cups fresh blueberries
Pure maple syrup, for serving

Preheat oven to 200° F, and heat a griddle (or large cast-iron skillet). Whisk together flour, baking powder, baking soda, salt, and sugar in a large bowl. Add eggs, buttermilk, and melted butter; whisk to combine. Do not overmix; batter should be slightly lumpy.

When griddle is ready (test by sprinkling with a few drops of water; they should instantly sizzle and disappear), brush lightly with melted butter. Working in batches, ladle batter onto griddle (about ¼ cup per pancake), spacing 2 inches apart. Sprinkle some berries evenly over each. Cook until slightly dry around edges and bubbles appear on top, 2 to 3 minutes. Flip pancakes, and cook until golden on bottom and set, about 1 minute more.

Transfer to a heatproof platter and keep warm in the oven. Repeat with remaining batter and berries, brushing griddle with more melted butter between batches. Serve warm, with syrup.

DONN'S BLUEBERRY BELGIAN WAFFLES

MAKES 5 *from* **BLUEBERRY BREAKFAST**

This recipe, which originated in the kitchen of winemakers Donn and Molly Chappellet, in California's Napa Valley, produces the lightest, crunchiest waffles. If you are making more than five waffles, prepare each batch separately; do not double the recipe. Also, whisk the egg whites and fold them into batter just before cooking to prevent them from deflating. The dry ingredients can be measured and combined ahead of time.

2 large egg yolks
¾ cup sour cream
1 cup all-purpose flour
2 tablespoons polenta or coarse-ground cornmeal
1 teaspoon baking soda
1 teaspoon coarse salt
1½ cups buttermilk
5 tablespoons unsalted butter, melted
5 large egg whites
¾ cup fresh blueberries
Blueberry Compote, for serving (optional; recipe follows)
Pure maple syrup, for serving
Vegetable oil cooking spray

Preheat oven to 200° F, and heat a waffle iron. Mix egg yolks, sour cream, flour, polenta, baking soda, and salt. Stir in buttermilk, ¾ cup at a time. Add melted butter, and mix just to combine. Do not overmix; batter should be slightly lumpy.

With an electric mixer on high speed, whisk egg whites until stiff peaks form. Stir half of the whites into the batter, then gently but thoroughly fold in remaining whites.

Once waffle iron is hot, coat lightly with cooking spray. Spoon enough batter onto iron so it just covers in a thin layer, then sprinkle evenly with about 2 tablespoons blueberries. Spoon more batter over the blueberries, filling the iron but not allowing it to overflow. Cook until golden and crisp, about 5 minutes (depending on iron model).

Remove waffle from iron. Quickly and gently flip the waffle back and forth from one hand to the other (to allow any residual moisture to evaporate so waffle won't become soggy). Place on a baking sheet and keep warm in the oven. Repeat with remaining batter and blueberries, adding more cooking spray as needed. Serve warm, with compote and syrup, as desired.

Blueberry Compote MAKES 2½ CUPS

    4   pints fresh blueberries (8 cups)
    3   cups sugar

Combine blueberries and sugar in a small saucepan, and bring to a simmer over medium heat, stirring to dissolve sugar. Continue to simmer, stirring occasionally, until berries soften and liquid is thick enough to coat the back of the spoon, about 30 minutes. Serve warm or at room temperature. (Compote can be cooled completely and refrigerated in an airtight container up to 1 week; reheat over medium, if desired.)

BUCKWHEAT CRÊPES *with* GRAVLAX *and* SOUR CREAM

SERVES 8   *from* EASTER BRUNCH

Look for buckwheat flour at natural-foods stores and many supermarkets. Gravlax, a Scandinavian specialty made by curing salmon in salt and sugar (and usually dill), can be found at specialty food stores and online retailers, or you can make your own using the recipe that follows. Smoked salmon is a good substitute. Don't skip the important step of letting the crêpe batter rest for an hour, as this will help ensure the proper texture.

    ¼   cup plus 2 tablespoons all-purpose flour
    ¼   cup plus 2 tablespoons buckwheat flour
    ¼   teaspoon sugar
    ⅛   teaspoon coarse salt
    1   large egg, lightly beaten
    1   cup milk
    ¼   cup plus 2 tablespoons water
    4½ tablespoons unsalted butter, melted, plus more for pan
    ¼   cup sour cream, plus more for serving
        Gravlax (recipe follows)

Whisk together both flours, sugar, and salt. In another bowl, whisk together egg, milk, and the water. Whisk egg mixture into dry ingredients, then stir in 1½ tablespoons melted butter. Let batter stand 1 hour at room temperature.

Preheat oven to 200° F. Heat an 8-inch skillet over medium high. Brush pan lightly with melted butter, and wipe off excess with a paper towel. Add 2 tablespoons batter to pan, swirling to coat bottom of pan evenly. Cook until dry around edges, 1 to 2 minutes, then flip with a metal spatula and cook until just set, 30 to 60 seconds more. Transfer to a baking sheet and keep warm in the oven. Repeat with remaining batter to make 16 crêpes total, stacking them on the baking sheet. After every few crêpes, brush skillet lightly with more melted butter, and wipe excess with a paper towel. (Crêpes can be prepared up to a day ahead; let cool completely before stacking in an airtight container and refrigerating. When ready to proceed, spread on a baking sheet in a slightly overlapping layer, cover with parchment and then foil, and reheat in a 200° F oven.)

To assemble, spread a crêpe with about ½ teaspoon sour cream. Place a piece of gravlax on one side of crêpe, then fold other side over gravlax to form a half-moon shape. Spread more sour cream on top, then place another piece of salmon on one side of folded crêpe. Fold into a triangle, again enclosing gravlax. Repeat with remaining crêpes, sour cream, and gravlax. Arrange crêpes on a platter, and serve with additional sour cream.

Gravlax MAKES 3 POUNDS

    1   side of salmon, skin on (about 3 pounds)
    3   tablespoons extra-virgin olive oil
        Finely grated zest and juice of 1 lemon
    ½   cup coarse salt
    ¼   cup sugar
    1   tablespoon juniper berries
    1   tablespoon whole black peppercorns
    1   tablespoon coriander seeds
    1   tablespoon mustard seeds
    1   bunch dill, leaves coarsely chopped
    1   bunch parsley, leaves coarsely chopped

Place salmon on a parchment-lined rimmed baking sheet. Score skin three or four times with a sharp knife, in even intervals. Rub both sides of salmon with olive oil and lemon juice.

In a bowl, combine salt, sugar, lemon zest, and spices. Press seasoned salt evenly on both sides of salmon, then turn flesh side up, and top with chopped herbs. Cover tightly with plastic wrap. Place another baking sheet on top, and weight with canned goods or other heavy objects. Refrigerate 2 days, flipping salmon over once. Before serving, lightly rinse salmon and pat dry. Slice very thinly on the bias.

SCRAMBLED EGGS *with* SALMON ROE IN EGGSHELL CUPS

SERVES 4   *from* AN ELEGANT BREAKFAST AT SKYLANDS

To create the eggshell cups, you will need a special tool called an egg topper; look for one at specialty stores or from online retailers.

    8   large eggs
    ¼   cup heavy cream
        Coarse salt and freshly ground pepper
    4   tablespoons unsalted butter
    2   to 3 tablespoons salmon roe

To prepare "eggshells," bring a large pot of water to a boil. Holding an egg in one hand, tapered end up, cut off top with an egg topper, squeezing gently and using a scissor motion. Pour the egg into a bowl and repeat with remaining eggs. Boil shells 5 minutes, then gently transfer to a wire rack with a slotted spoon; let dry, cut sides down.

Add cream to eggs and season with salt and pepper. Beat with a fork until frothy. Melt butter in a large skillet over medium heat. Pour in egg mixture. Cook, using a heatproof flexible spatula to gently pull eggs to center of pan and letting liquid parts run underneath, until just set, 2 to 3 minutes.

Transfer eggs to a pastry bag fitted with a ½-inch plain round tip. Place shells in egg cups, then pipe scrambled eggs into the shells. Top with salmon roe (about 1 teaspoon per shell), and serve immediately.

BLINI *with* CRÈME FRAÎCHE *and* SALMON CAVIAR

MAKES ABOUT 48   *from* **HOLIDAY OPEN HOUSE BRUNCH**

At the holiday brunch, the blini were served with two types of caviar— salmon roe and trout roe—from Russ & Daughters, a wonderful family-owned shop on the Lower East Side of Manhattan. You can cook the blini up to two days ahead; let cool completely before refrigerating in an airtight container, and reheat in a 250-degree oven before serving.

- 1 envelope active dry yeast (2¼ teaspoons)
- ½ cup warm water (110° F)
- 1 cup all-purpose flour
- ½ teaspoon coarse salt, plus a pinch
- ½ cup buttermilk
- 1 tablespoon unsalted butter, melted
- ½ teaspoon sugar
- 2 large eggs, separated
  Crème fraîche, for serving
  Caviar, such as salmon and trout roe, for serving

Sprinkle yeast over the warm water in a small bowl; let stand in a warm place until foamy, about 7 minutes (if mixture doesn't foam, discard and start over with new yeast and water). Whisk together flour and salt in a small bowl. In a large bowl, stir together buttermilk, melted butter, sugar, and egg yolks; whisk in yeast mixture and then the flour mixture. Let batter stand, covered, in a warm place 30 minutes.

Beat egg whites until stiff peaks form; fold into batter. Let stand 10 minutes. Heat a crêpe pan or nonstick skillet over medium. Working in batches, add a tablespoon of batter for each blini; cook, flipping as soon as bubbles appear on the surface, until golden on both sides, 1½ to 2 minutes per side. Transfer to a parchment-lined baking sheet. Let cool at least 30 minutes. Serve warm or at room temperature, with crème fraîche and caviar.

PERFECT POACHED EGGS

SERVES 4   *from* **FAVORITE IDEAS FOR BREAKFAST TRAYS**

Eggs can be poached up to a day ahead of serving. After poaching, immediately place eggs in an ice-water bath to quickly cool, then transfer them to a bowl of cool water. If storing longer than an hour, cover bowl and refrigerate. Reheat by placing eggs in a pan of barely simmering water, just until warmed through.

- 12 medium or large eggs
- 4 thin slices rustic bread, trimmed of crusts and toasted
  Unsalted butter
  Coarse salt and freshly ground pepper

Fill a wide, deep saucepan with about 2 inches of water, and bring to a boil. Reduce heat to a bare simmer. Break 1 egg into a small heatproof bowl or cup. Placing lip of bowl in the water, gently tip bowl to slide egg carefully into pan. Use a small spoon to "fold" the edges of the white over the egg for a neater appearance. Repeat with 3 more eggs.

Cook until whites are just set but yolks are still soft, 2 to 3 minutes. With a small mesh sieve or slotted spoon, carefully lift out eggs and let drain briefly on paper towels. Repeat with remaining 8 eggs in two batches. (To keep eggs warm while finishing batches, place them in a baking dish or large bowl filled with warm—under 120° F—water; drain before serving.) Trim edges of cooked eggs with a paring knife or kitchen shears if desired.

To serve, halve each slice of toast into rectangles; spread butter on one side, and top each with 3 poached eggs. Season with salt and pepper.

POTATO *and* ONION FRITTATA

SERVES 8   *from* **THE APPEAL OF FARM-FRESH EGGS**

- 7 small red potatoes, scrubbed and quartered
  Coarse salt and freshly ground pepper
- 18 large eggs
- ⅓ cup olive oil
- 3 large red onions, diced

Preheat oven to 400° F. Place potatoes in a saucepan and add enough water to cover by 1 inch. Bring to a boil, and add 1 tablespoon salt. Reduce heat, and simmer until tender, 10 to 15 minutes. Drain well. Combine eggs in a bowl, season with salt and pepper, and beat with a fork until frothy.

Heat an 11-inch straight-sided skillet over medium high. Add olive oil. When hot, add onions, and sauté, stirring occasionally, until translucent, about 5 minutes. Add potatoes, and cook 3 minutes without stirring. Pour eggs into pan. Cook for 1 minute without stirring, then run a heatproof flexible spatula around edge of pan to allow egg from the center to flow underneath.

Transfer pan to oven. Bake until center is set and top is slightly puffed, 20 to 25 minutes. Cut into wedges; serve hot, warm, or at room temperature.

ZUCCHINI, BELL PEPPER, *and* SCALLION FRITTATA

SERVES 6   *from* **FROM BREAKFAST ON THE PORCH**

The filling for this frittata can be replaced with virtually any precooked vegetables, including those in the three variations that follow.

for the filling

- 1 tablespoon extra-virgin olive oil
- 6 scallions, trimmed and sliced into ½-inch lengths (½ cup)
- 2 small zucchini, halved lengthwise and sliced crosswise ¼ inch thick (3 cups)
- 1 red bell pepper, ribs and seeds removed, cut into 1-inch pieces (1 cup)

for the egg mixture

- 6 large eggs
- ¼ cup heavy cream
- ¾ cup finely grated Parmigiano Reggiano or pecorino Romano cheese (3 ounces)
- 4 fresh basil leaves, sliced into chiffonade
- 2 tablespoons finely chopped fresh chives
  Coarse salt and freshly ground pepper
  Unsalted butter, for baking dish or skillet

Sauté the filling: Heat olive oil in a large skillet over medium. Cook scallions until soft, stirring occasionally, 2 to 3 minutes. Add zucchini and bell pepper and sauté, stirring occasionally, until beginning to turn golden brown, about 6 minutes. Set aside to cool.

Prepare the egg mixture: Preheat oven to 375° F. Use a whisk to lightly beat eggs in a large bowl, then whisk in cream, ½ cup cheese, the basil, and chives; season with salt and pepper. Stir in filling mixture.

Butter an 8-inch baking dish or ovenproof skillet. Add egg mixture and sprinkle with remaining ¼ cup cheese. Bake until center is set and top is slightly puffed, 20 to 25 minutes. Gently run an offset spatula around the edges and underneath the frittata to loosen before slicing into wedges. Serve hot, warm, or at room temperature.

Variations

Artichoke Heart and Fava Bean: Follow above recipe for making the egg mixture, whisking 1 minced garlic clove; 6 cooked artichoke hearts, quartered (see recipe for artichokes with Béarnaise sauce, this page, or substitute 6 thawed frozen artichoke hearts); and 1½ cups blanched and peeled fava beans (page 360, from 1 pound pods) into egg mixture along with the cream, cheese, herbs, salt, and pepper. Proceed with above recipe.

Chorizo, Potato, and Red Onion: In a medium saucepan, cover ¾ pound Yukon Gold potatoes, peeled and cut into ¾-inch pieces, with 1 inch of water. Bring to a boil; add salt. Reduce heat and simmer until just tender, 6 to 8 minutes. Drain; return potatoes to pan (off heat) to dry. Heat 2 tablespoons extra-virgin olive oil in a large skillet over medium high. Cook 9 ounces chorizo, sliced into ¼-inch rounds, until beginning to brown on one side, about 3 minutes. Add 1 small red onion, cut into ½-inch wedges; cook, stirring occasionally, until just translucent, about 8 minutes. Remove from heat; let cool slightly. Prepare the egg mixture, omitting cheese and replacing basil and chives with ¼ cup coarsely chopped fresh flat-leaf parsley; stir in the potatoes and chorizo. Proceed with above recipe.

Spinach and Potato: In a medium saucepan, cover 1½ pounds Yukon Gold potatoes, peeled and cut into ½-inch pieces, with 1 inch of water. Bring to a boil; add salt. Reduce heat and simmer until just tender, 4 to 6 minutes. Drain; return potatoes to pan (off heat) to dry. In a pot of boiling salted water, blanch 20 ounces baby spinach until bright green, about 1 minute, then plunge into an ice-water bath to stop the cooking. Drain, squeeze out as much liquid as possible, and finely chop (to yield about 1 cup). Prepare the egg mixture, omitting herbs, and stir in potatoes and spinach. Proceed with above recipe.

BAKED EGGS *with* BACON, CHEESE, *and* HERBS

SERVES 6 *from* **THE APPEAL OF FARM-FRESH EGGS**

- 4 ounces bacon (4 strips), diced
- 1 tablespoon snipped fresh chives
- 1 tablespoon chopped fresh flat-leaf parsley
- 2 tablespoons unsalted butter, softened
- 12 large eggs
- 2 tablespoons crumbled fresh goat cheese
- 2 tablespoons grated fontina, Gruyère, or mild white cheddar cheese
  Coarse salt and freshly ground pepper

Preheat oven to 375° F. Cook bacon in a medium sauté pan over medium heat, stirring occasionally, until crisp, 6 to 8 minutes. Drain on a paper towel–lined plate. In a small bowl, combine chives and parsley.

Butter six 8-ounce ramekins, and add bacon to each, dividing evenly. Crack two eggs into each ramekin, being careful not to break the yolks. Place ramekins in a roasting pan, and pour in enough steaming hot water to reach halfway up sides of ramekins. Cover pan tightly with foil; bake 20 minutes.

Carefully remove pan from oven. Dividing evenly, sprinkle two ramekins with goat cheese; sprinkle another two ramekins with fontina. Top each of remaining two ramekins with 1 tablespoon mixed herbs. Cover pan again and continue baking for another 10 minutes. Remove pan from oven.

Using tongs, carefully remove ramekins from water bath. Season eggs with salt and pepper, and serve immediately.

ARTICHOKES *with* POACHED EGGS *and* "BÉARNAISE" SAUCE

SERVES 8 *from* **EASTER BRUNCH**

Unlike in most recipes, the eggs called for here are medium, as this size happens to fit best in the artichoke hearts once cooked. If you use large eggs, you may need to trim the edges after poaching.

- 1 lemon, halved
- 8 medium-to-large artichokes (8 to 12 ounces each)
  Coarse salt
- 8 Perfect Poached Eggs (page 328; use medium eggs)
  "Bérnaise" Sauce (recipe follows)

Squeeze juice from lemon halves into a large bowl of cold water, then add lemon halves. Working with one artichoke at a time, snap off tough outer leaves until leaves that are half yellow, half green are exposed. Using a serrated knife, cut off and discard top half of artichoke, leaving pale part intact. With a paring knife, trim off stem and all green from bottom of artichoke. With a small spoon or a melon baller, scrape out and discard sharp leaves and fuzzy choke from center of artichokes. Drop artichoke hearts into lemon water as soon as they are trimmed.

Transfer lemon water to a saucepan, and bring to a boil. Add salt and artichokes, and return to a boil; reduce heat and simmer, partially covered, until artichokes are tender when pierced on the bottom with the tip of a sharp knife, 30 to 35 minutes. Remove from heat. Artichokes can be kept warm in their cooking liquid for up to 15 minutes; remove with a slotted spoon. (To store longer, remove from liquid and let cool completely, then refrigerate in an airtight container up to 1 day; reheat by simmering in a large skillet with 1 tablespoon butter and ½ cup water, about 2 minutes.)

Just before serving, arrange artichoke hearts on a platter. Top each with a poached egg, and spoon sauce over eggs, dividing evenly.

"Béarnaise" Sauce MAKES ¾ CUP

In its classic form, Béarnaise sauce is simply a variation of hollandaise that is flavored with tarragon and a shallot-and-wine reduction. This easy and verdant version skips the egg yolks and is puréed with fresh herbs at the end.

- ½ cup (1 stick) plus 1 tablespoon unsalted butter, cut into ½-inch pieces
- 2 shallots, minced (about ⅓ cup)
- 2 tablespoons cider vinegar
- ¼ cup dry white wine
- 1 cup lightly packed fresh tarragon leaves, coarsely chopped
- 1 cup firmly packed fresh dill
  Coarse salt and freshly ground pepper

Melt 1 tablespoon butter in a small saucepan over medium heat. Add shallots, and cook, stirring occasionally, until translucent but not taking on any color, about 5 minutes. Add vinegar, and raise heat to high. Cook until almost all liquid has evaporated, about 1 minute. Add wine and half of the chopped tarragon; cook until liquid has almost evaporated, 1 to 2 minutes. Remove pan from heat. Whisk in remaining ½ cup butter, a few pieces at a time, whisking to incorporate before adding more. (If butter is not melting, briefly return pan to low heat while stirring.)

Transfer to a blender, and purée with dill and remaining tarragon, scraping down sides with a flexible spatula as needed. If sauce is too thick, add water, a tablespoon at a time, until it reaches the desired consistency. Season with salt and pepper. Keep warm by placing pan in a hot-water bath until ready to serve; if the sauce "breaks," or separates, add 2 teaspoons water, and place saucepan over low heat, whisking until smooth again.

POPOVERS *with* FRIED EGGS *and* CREAMED SPINACH

SERVES 12 *from* **HOLIDAY OPEN HOUSE BRUNCH**

- 2½ cups milk
- 2½ cups all-purpose flour
- 1 teaspoon coarse salt, plus more for seasoning
- 18 large eggs
  Unsalted butter, softened, for pans
- 1 cup grated Gruyère cheese (4 ounces)
- 12 to 24 slices bacon
  Creamed Spinach (recipe follows)

Preheat oven to 425° F. Whisk together milk, flour, and salt to combine, then whisk in 6 eggs. Do not overmix; batter should be slightly lumpy.

Heat two 6-cup popover pans in oven 5 minutes, then brush cups generously with butter. Fill each cup a little more than halfway with batter, then sprinkle with cheese, dividing evenly. Bake 20 minutes. Reduce oven to 350° F, and continue baking until golden brown, about 25 minutes. Let stand 5 minutes before turning out popovers.

Meanwhile, heat a large skillet over medium. Cook bacon, turning occasionally, until the slices begin to turn crisp; use tongs to transfer them to paper towels to drain.

Pour off all but 1 tablespoon rendered fat, reserving the rest in a heatproof bowl. Working in batches, crack one of the remaining 12 eggs into a cup, then slip into pan; repeat with as many eggs as will fit without crowding. Season with salt and pepper. Cook, covered, until whites are set and yolks are still runny, 1 to 2 minutes. Remove with a spatula. Repeat with remaining uncooked eggs, adding some of the reserved bacon fat as necessary.

To serve, split popovers in half (and toast under a broiler, if desired). Fill one half with creamed spinach, then top with fried eggs and bacon slices.

Creamed Spinach MAKES ABOUT 4 CUPS

- 5 pounds fresh spinach, trimmed and washed, water clinging to leaves
- 2 tablespoons unsalted butter
- 2 shallots, minced
- ¼ cup all-purpose flour
- 3 cups milk
  Coarse salt and freshly ground pepper
  Pinch of freshly grated nutmeg

Working in batches, place spinach in a large pot over medium-high heat. Cover and steam until wilted and bright green, stirring occasionally, 2 to 4 minutes. Drain in a colander. Let cool, then squeeze out as much liquid as possible into a bowl, reserving liquid. Coarsely chop spinach.

In a medium skillet, melt butter over medium heat. Add shallots, and cook, stirring occasionally, until translucent, about 5 minutes. Add flour, and cook, whisking, 1 to 2 minutes. Gradually add milk, whisking until fully incorporated. Bring to a simmer, then cook 2 minutes. Season with salt and pepper.

Add spinach and nutmeg, and stir to combine. Thin with reserved spinach liquid, as necessary, and cook just to heat through. Serve immediately.

ROASTED TOMATO TART

MAKES ONE 9-INCH TART *from* **BREAKFAST ON THE PORCH**

A layer of mashed roasted garlic adds flavor to this savory tart; the tomatoes are roasted before being baked in the tart shell to bring out their natural sweetness. For step-by-step instructions on assembling the tart, see the how-to photographs on page 375.

- 3½ pounds ripe but firm beefsteak tomatoes
- 3 tablespoons unsalted butter, melted
  Coarse salt and freshly ground pepper
- 1 head garlic
- 1 tablespoon extra-virgin olive oil
  All-purpose flour, for dusting
- ½ recipe Pâte Brisée (page 421)
- ¾ cup grated fontina cheese (about 3 ounces)
  Fresh parsley leaves, for garnish

Preheat oven to 375° F. Bring a large pot of water to a boil, and prepare a large ice-water bath. Working in batches, blanch tomatoes until skins are loosened, 5 to 30 seconds, depending on ripeness. Using a mesh spider or a slotted spoon, transfer tomatoes to the ice bath. When cool, slip off skins, cut tomatoes in half crosswise, and squeeze out seeds (discard).

Arrange tomatoes cut side down in a 9-inch baking dish (it should be just large enough to hold them in a single, snug layer). Drizzle with 2 tablespoons melted butter, and sprinkle with salt and pepper. Cook until tomatoes are very soft, about 45 minutes. Remove from oven and let cool.

Meanwhile, slice off top of garlic head and place on a piece of parchment; drizzle with the olive oil. Fold parchment to encase garlic; wrap in foil. Roast until golden brown and the tip of a sharp paring knife easily pierces the flesh, about 45 minutes. When garlic is cool enough to handle, squeeze out cloves into a small bowl (discard skins); mash with a fork.

On a lightly floured work surface, roll out the dough to a 13-inch round, about ⅛ inch thick. With a dry pastry brush, remove excess flour. Fit the dough into a 9-inch fluted tart pan with a removable bottom, pressing into the edges. Using a rolling pin, trim dough flush with the top edge of the tart pan. Pierce bottom of dough all over with a fork. Chill tart shell until firm, about 30 minutes. Reduce oven to 350° F.

Line shell with parchment, leaving a 1-inch overhang; fill with pie weights or dried beans. Bake until crust is just beginning to turn golden, 20 to 25 minutes. Remove parchment and weights; bake until crust is golden brown, 15 to 20 minutes more. Let cool completely on a wire rack. Raise oven to 425° F.

Spread roasted garlic evenly on the bottom of baked tart shell. Sprinkle with half the cheese. Arrange tomatoes in a single layer on top of the cheese. Season with salt and pepper. Sprinkle with remaining cheese, and drizzle with remaining 1 tablespoon melted butter.

Bake tart until cheese is melted and golden on top, and filling is heated through, about 20 minutes. Let cool on a wire rack 20 minutes. Serve garnished with parsley.

ROASTED KIELBASA *with* FRESH HORSERADISH

SERVES 8 TO 12 *from* **EASTER BRUNCH**

Prepared horseradish is available in every grocery store, but when the fresh root is available in the spring and fall, it's worth grating your own. First, wash and peel the root, cutting out and discarding any green areas under the skin, which will be bitter. (You may want to wear gloves while handling horseradish, just as you would with chiles.) If the root is large, the heart should be discarded. Grate with a stainless-steel grater (a Microplane-style rasp grater works best). If you do this ahead of time, keep the grated root from turning brown by sprinkling it with lemon juice. If using prepared horseradish, buy both plain and beet varieties for a colorful presentation.

- 1 pound kielbasa
- ½ cup water
  Spicy mustard, for serving
  Finely grated horseradish, for serving

Preheat oven to 400° F. Pierce kielbasa all over with the tip of a sharp knife. Place in a roasting pan or baking dish, and add the water. Cover with parchment, then foil. Roast until heated through, about 20 minutes. Remove parchment and foil, and continue to cook until crisp and blistering a bit on the outside, flipping halfway through, about 15 minutes more.

Transfer to a cutting board and slice kielbasa on the diagonal, ¾ to 1 inch thick. Serve with mustard and horseradish.

BOURBON- *and* BROWN SUGAR– GLAZED HAM

SERVES 8 TO 12, WITH LEFTOVERS *from* **EASTER BRUNCH**

You can use either light or dark brown sugar, or a combination of the two, depending on the type of glaze you prefer. Dark brown sugar will result in a rich glaze with a molasses-like flavor, while light brown sugar yields a glaze that is slightly sweeter and less pronounced.

- 1 bone-in, fully cooked smoked half ham (about 10 pounds)
- 1½ cups packed brown sugar
- ½ cup bourbon

Preheat oven to 300° F. Trim fat on ham to ¼ inch thick. Wrap ham with parchment, then foil, and place on a rimmed baking sheet or in a roasting pan. Bake 1 hour.

Meanwhile, heat brown sugar and bourbon in a small saucepan over low, stirring, until sugar has dissolved, 3 to 5 minutes.

Remove ham from oven, and unwrap. Use a sharp knife to score fat layer in a diamond pattern, being careful not to cut into the meat. Brush some glaze all over ham, making sure to thoroughly coat the top. Bake 30 minutes, basting with more glaze once or twice. Continue baking, again basting once or twice, until a crust has formed, about 1 hour more.

Transfer ham to a cutting board; cut into thin slices with a slicing knife.

HAM *with* CURRANT-ROSEMARY GLAZE

SERVES 8 TO 12, WITH LEFTOVERS *from* **HOLIDAY OPEN HOUSE BRUNCH**

For the brunch, the ham was garnished with flowers from the greenhouse at Bedford, and served with a salad of mixed pale greens, including Boston lettuce, frisée, endive, and escarole. A simple platter of mixed sliced citrus, garnished with orange blossoms, is the perfect accompaniment.

- 1 bone-in, fully cooked smoked half ham (about 10 pounds)
- 1 cup currant (black or red) jelly or jam
- 3 sprigs rosemary
- 2 teaspoons fresh lemon juice, plus more to taste

Preheat oven to 325° F. Trim fat on ham to ¼ inch thick. Wrap ham with parchment, then foil; place in a roasting pan. Bake 1 hour.

Meanwhile, bring currant jelly and rosemary to a simmer in a saucepan over medium-high heat. Reduce heat, and simmer until thick and syrupy, about 3 minutes. Remove from heat, and stir in lemon juice.

Remove ham from oven, and unwrap. Raise oven to 375° F. Use a sharp knife to score fat layer in a diamond pattern, being careful not to cut into the meat. Brush some glaze all over ham, coating evenly. Bake 30 minutes, then brush with more glaze, and continue cooking 10 minutes more. Remove from oven, and brush again with glaze.

Transfer ham to a cutting board; cut into thin slices with a slicing knife. If desired, reheat remaining glaze, and serve alongside.

Breads

BUTTERMILK-CHIVE BISCUITS

MAKES 2 DOZEN *from* **HOLIDAY OPEN HOUSE BRUNCH**

- 4   cups all-purpose flour, plus more for dusting
- 1   tablespoon baking powder
- ½   teaspoon baking soda
- 2   teaspoons freshly ground pepper
- 1   teaspoon salt
- 1   teaspoon sugar
- 3   tablespoons finely chopped fresh chives
- 1   cup (2 sticks) unsalted butter, cut into small pieces, well chilled
- 1½ cups buttermilk

Preheat oven to 375° F. In a large bowl, whisk together flour, baking powder, baking soda, pepper, salt, sugar, and chives. With a pastry blender or two knives, cut butter into flour mixture until it resembles coarse crumbs with a few large clumps remaining. Using a flexible spatula, fold buttermilk into mixture, incorporating crumbs at the bottom of bowl, until dough just comes together. Do not overmix; the dough should be slightly sticky.

Transfer to a lightly floured work surface, and, with floured fingers, gently pat dough into a round about 1½ inches thick, pressing in any loose bits. Do not overwork dough. With a lightly floured 2-inch biscuit or cookie cutter, cut out rounds as close together as possible (to minimize scraps). Place rounds about 2 inches apart on parchment-lined baking sheets. Bake until golden and flecked with brown spots, rotating sheet halfway through, 20 to 22 minutes. Let biscuits cool slightly on a wire rack. Serve warm.

BUTTERMILK SCONES

MAKES 12 TO 16 *from* **BREAKFAST ON THE PORCH**

- 4   cups all-purpose flour, plus more for dusting
- 2   tablespoons granulated sugar
- 2   tablespoons baking powder
- 1   teaspoon baking soda
- 1½ teaspoons salt
- 1   cup (2 sticks) cold unsalted butter, cut into small pieces
- 1¼ cups buttermilk
- 1   large egg, lightly beaten
     Sanding sugar, for sprinkling

Preheat oven to 350° F. Whisk together flour, granulated sugar, baking powder, baking soda, and salt in a large bowl. Using a pastry blender or two forks, cut butter into flour mixture until it resembles coarse meal. Add buttermilk; stir to combine.

On a lightly floured surface, roll out dough to about 1 inch thick. Using a 2¼-inch biscuit cutter, cut out as many rounds as possible, and place on a parchment-lined baking sheet. Reroll scraps once; cut out more rounds.

Lightly brush top of scones with beaten egg; sprinkle with sanding sugar. Bake until golden, rotating sheet halfway through, 20 to 25 minutes. Let cool on a wire rack. Serve warm or at room temperature.

CREAM SCONES *with* DRIED FRUIT

MAKES ABOUT 2 DOZEN *from* **BREAKFAST ON THE PORCH**

This recipe makes scones that are perfectly crisp and golden on the outside, light and flaky on the inside (thanks to the folding and turning method used in making the dough). For the step-by-step how-to photographs, see page 373. The dried fruit needs to soak overnight, so plan accordingly.

- 1   cup dried cherries, currants, or raisins (or a combination)
- 2   teaspoons finely grated orange zest
- ¼   cup Grand Marnier or other orange-flavored liqueur
- 2   cups cake flour (not self-rising), sifted
- 1½ cups all-purpose flour, plus more for dusting
- ½   cup (1 stick) unsalted butter, cut into small pieces, well chilled
- ¼   cup plus 2 tablespoons granulated sugar
- 1   tablespoon plus 2 teaspoons baking powder
- 1   teaspoon coarse salt
- 1   cup heavy cream
- 1   large whole egg plus 1 large egg, separated
     Sanding sugar, for sprinkling

In a small bowl, toss to combine dried fruit, zest, and liqueur. Cover with plastic wrap, and refrigerate 1 day.

Preheat oven to 350° F. Whisk together both flours in a large bowl. Transfer half to a food processor; add the butter, and pulse several times to combine, leaving some butter pieces the size of large peas. Add sugar, baking powder, and salt to remaining flour in bowl; whisk to combine. Add butter mixture and, using a pastry blender or your fingertips, work in butter pieces until mixture resembles coarse crumbs.

In a small bowl, whisk to combine cream, whole egg, and yolk. Create a well in middle of flour mixture, and pour in half of cream mixture. Using a large flexible spatula, draw dry ingredients over wet ingredients, scraping bottom of bowl to incorporate all dry crumbs. Add remaining cream mixture and gently mix just until incorporated; do not overwork dough.

Turn out dough onto a lightly floured surface; gently roll into a rectangle, about 1 inch thick. Sprinkle dried fruit mixture evenly over dough. With a short side facing you, fold rectangle into thirds like a business letter. Rotate dough a quarter-turn clockwise, so the flap is on the right, like a book.

With a rolling pin or your hands, gently roll or pat into another rectangle. Repeat folding and rotating process to complete a second turn.

Using lightly floured hands, pat dough into a 1¼-inch-thick rectangle. With a floured 2-inch round biscuit or cookie cutter, cut out rounds as close together as possible. Place rounds about 2 inches apart on a baking sheet. Gather together scraps and reroll once, cutting out more rounds.

Lightly beat egg white and brush over top of dough; sprinkle with sanding sugar. Bake until golden brown, rotating sheet halfway through, 20 to 25 minutes. Let cool on a wire rack. Serve warm or at room temperature.

CUSTARD-FILLED CORNBREAD

SERVES 12 TO 16 *from* **JULY 4TH BARBECUE**

This cornbread recipe has been adapted from one by Marion Cunningham, author of Lost Recipes.

- 3 tablespoons unsalted butter, melted, plus more for pan
- 2 cups all-purpose flour
- ¾ cup yellow cornmeal, preferably stone-ground
- 1 teaspoon baking powder
- ½ teaspoon baking soda
- 2 large eggs
- ¼ cup sugar
- 1¼ teaspoons salt
- 2 cups milk
- 1 tablespoon plus 1½ teaspoons white vinegar
- 1 cup fresh (from 1 to 2 ears) or thawed frozen corn kernels
- 1 cup heavy cream

Preheat oven to 350° F. Butter a 9-by-2-inch round baking pan, and place in the oven. Whisk together flour, cornmeal, baking powder, and baking soda in a bowl. Whisk eggs and melted butter in a large bowl to combine, then whisk in sugar, salt, milk, and vinegar. Add flour mixture, and whisk just until smooth. Stir in corn kernels.

Remove pan from oven, and transfer batter to pan. Pour cream into center of batter; do not stir. Bake until cornbread is just set in the middle and pale golden brown, about 50 minutes. Let cool on a wire rack 15 minutes before removing from pan. Serve warm.

CORNBREAD "TURKEYS"

SERVES 10 TO 12 *from* **THANKSGIVING AT BEDFORD**

These loaves were baked in a pan with two turkey molds (such as one made by Nordic Ware). You can also use individual turkey-shaped Bundt pans.

- ½ cup plus 2 tablespoons (1¼ sticks) unsalted butter
- 2 cups fresh (from about 3 ears) or thawed frozen corn kernels
- 3 jalapeño chiles, minced (ribs and seeds removed for less heat, if desired)
- 2 shallots, minced
- 1 cup plus 2 tablespoons all-purpose flour
- 2¼ cups yellow cornmeal
- 1 tablespoon plus 1 teaspoon coarse salt
- ¾ teaspoon freshly ground pepper
- 3 tablespoons sugar
- 1 tablespoon plus 1½ teaspoons baking powder
- ¾ teaspoon baking soda
- 3 large eggs
- 2¼ cups buttermilk
- 1½ cups grated cheddar cheese
- Vegetable oil cooking spray

Preheat oven to 350° F. Coat two 5-cup turkey-shaped pans with cooking spray. Melt ½ cup butter and let cool.

Melt remaining 2 tablespoons butter in a skillet over medium-high. Cook corn, jalapeño, and shallots, stirring occasionally, until soft, 4 to 6 minutes.

Whisk together flour, cornmeal, salt, pepper, sugar, baking powder, and baking soda in a large bowl. Make a well in the center of the mixture and add eggs; whisk eggs into flour mixture.

Whisk together melted butter and buttermilk; stir into flour mixture, along with corn mixture and cheddar. Mix until well combined.

Divide the batter evenly between prepared pans; smooth tops. Bake, rotating pan halfway through, until a cake tester inserted into the centers comes out clean, 30 to 35 minutes. Let cool slightly before inverting onto a wire rack. Serve warm or at room temperature.

BUCKWHEAT ROLLS *and* FLATBREADS

MAKES 12 ROLLS AND 2 FLATBREADS *from* **PÂTÉ CAMPAGNARD LUNCH**

Half of the dough is used to make rolls, and the other half to make flatbreads. You could make just one or the other by following the directions using all of the dough.

- 1½ cups buckwheat flour
- 3 cups all-purpose flour, plus more for dusting
- 1 envelope active dry yeast (2¼ teaspoons)
- 1¼ teaspoons coarse salt
- 1 cup hot water (120° F)
- 1 cup hot milk (120° F)
- ¼ cup plus 3 tablespoons olive oil, plus more for bowl
  Large-flake sea salt such as Maldon or sel gris, for sprinkling

In the bowl of a standing electric mixer, stir together buckwheat flour, ½ cup all-purpose flour, the yeast, and salt. Add the hot water and milk along with ¼ cup olive oil. Using the paddle attachment, beat on medium speed until combined. Raise speed to medium high and beat 1 minute. Cover bowl with plastic wrap or a kitchen cloth, and let stand in a warm, draft-free place until dough has doubled in bulk and is bubbly on top, 1½ to 2 hours.

With mixer on low speed, add remaining 2½ cups all-purpose flour, ½ cup at a time, beating until incorporated before adding more, occasionally scraping down side of bowl. Switch to the dough-hook attachment, and knead dough on medium speed 5 minutes. Dough will be quite wet. Transfer to an oiled bowl, cover with plastic wrap, and refrigerate 1 day.

Remove plastic, and punch down dough. Turn out onto a lightly floured surface, and knead with floured hands 5 minutes, working in as little additional flour as necessary to form a slightly soft dough. Divide dough in half, and shape each into a round. Let rest 15 minutes before forming rolls and flatbreads, as instructed below:

Make rolls: Preheat oven to 400° F. Quarter one round of dough with a bench scraper or large knife, then cut each quarter into three equal parts. With your hands, form dough into balls, gently tucking dough under to make them smooth. Arrange on a parchment-lined baking sheet; brush tops with 1 tablespoon olive oil, dividing evenly. Cover rolls loosely with plastic wrap; let rise in a warm place until nearly doubled in bulk, about 1 hour.

(RECIPE CONTINUES)

Sprinkle dough lightly with sea salt. Bake until lightly browned on top, 15 to 18 minutes, rotating sheet halfway through. Transfer to a wire rack to cool. Keep in an airtight container until ready to serve, preferably the same day.

Make flatbreads: Cut parchment to fit two large baking sheets (each about 13 by 18 inches). Place one piece of parchment on work surface, and lightly flour.

Halve remaining dough round. Working with one piece of dough at a time, roll out on floured parchment into a rough rectangle, about ⅛ inch thick. (If dough tears while rolling, pinch it back together.) Cut four or five 2-inch-long slits across middle of dough, spacing them evenly. Gently stretch dough to widen the slits. Repeat. Brush each with 1 tablespoon olive oil.

Preheat oven to 450° F, with racks in upper and lower thirds. Loosely cover dough with plastic wrap, and let rise in a warm place for about 30 minutes.

Sprinkle dough lightly with sea salt. Bake just until beginning to brown on top, 12 to 15 minutes, rotating sheets from top to bottom and front to back halfway through. Transfer breads to wire racks to cool completely (they will turn crisp). Keep breads in an airtight container (you can break them into large pieces to fit) until ready to serve, preferably the same day.

FOCACCIA ROLLS *and* HERBED FLATBREADS

MAKES 12 ROLLS AND 2 FLATBREADS *from* **PÂTÉ CAMPAGNARD LUNCH**

This recipe is used to make twelve rolls and two flatbreads. If you prefer to make only one type of focaccia, follow the directions using all of the dough. For traditional focaccia bread, see the variation that follows.

- 4½ cups all-purpose flour, plus more for dusting
- 1 envelope active dry yeast (2¼ teaspoons)
- 1¼ teaspoons coarse salt
- 1 cup hot water (120° F)
- 1 cup hot milk (120° F)
- ¼ cup plus 3 tablespoons olive oil, plus more for bowl
- 3 tablespoons finely chopped garlic
- 3 tablespoons chopped fresh flat-leaf parsley
  Large-flake sea salt such as Maldon or sel gris, for sprinkling

In the bowl of a standing electric mixer, stir together 2 cups flour, the yeast, and coarse salt. Add the hot water and milk along with ¼ cup olive oil. Using the paddle attachment, beat on medium speed until combined. Raise speed to medium high and beat 1 minute. Cover bowl with plastic wrap or a kitchen cloth, and let stand in a warm, draft-free place until dough has more than doubled in bulk and is bubbly on top, about 2 hours.

With mixer on low speed, add remaining 2½ cups flour, ½ cup at a time, beating until each addition is incorporated before adding the next, and occasionally scraping down side of bowl. Switch to the dough-hook attachment, and knead on medium speed 5 minutes. Dough will be quite wet. Transfer dough to an oiled bowl, turning to coat. Cover bowl with plastic wrap and refrigerate 1 day.

Remove plastic, and punch down dough. Turn out onto a lightly floured surface, and knead with floured hands for 5 minutes, working in as little additional flour as necessary to form a slightly soft dough. Divide dough in half, and shape each into a round. Let rest 15 minutes before forming rolls and flatbreads, as instructed below.

Make rolls: Preheat oven to 400° F. Quarter one round of dough with a bench scraper or large knife, then cut each quarter into three equal parts. With your hands, form dough into balls, gently tucking dough under to make them smooth. Arrange on a parchment-lined baking sheet; brush tops with 1 tablespoon olive oil, dividing evenly. Cover rolls loosely with plastic wrap; let rise in a warm place until nearly doubled in bulk, about 1 hour.

Sprinkle dough with 1 tablespoon each chopped garlic and parsley, dividing evenly, and some sea salt. Bake until lightly browned on top, 15 to 18 minutes, rotating sheet halfway through. Transfer to a wire rack to cool. Keep in an airtight container until ready to serve, preferably the same day.

Make herbed flatbreads: Flatten remaining dough round slightly. Sprinkle evenly with 1 tablespoon each chopped garlic and parsley, and knead for 1 minute to incorporate. Cut dough in half. Cut parchment to fit two baking sheets (each about 13 by 18 inches). Place one piece of parchment on work surface, and lightly flour.

Working with one piece of dough at a time, roll out on floured parchment into a rough rectangle, about ⅛ inch thick. (If dough tears while rolling, pinch it back together.) Cut four or five 2-inch-long slits across middle of dough, spacing them evenly. Gently stretch the dough to widen the slits. Repeat with remaining piece of dough. Brush each with 1 tablespoon olive oil.

Preheat oven to 450° F, with racks in upper and lower thirds. Loosely cover dough with plastic wrap, and let rise in a warm place about 30 minutes.

Sprinkle dough with remaining 1 tablespoon each chopped parsley and garlic, dividing evenly, and some sea salt. Bake until tops are golden brown in spots, 12 to 15 minutes, rotating sheets from top to bottom and front to back halfway through. Transfer breads to wire racks to cool completely (they will turn crisp). Keep breads in an airtight container until ready to serve, preferably the same day.

Variation

Focaccia Bread: Prepare dough as directed above, and let rest 15 minutes. Rub a rimmed baking sheet (about 13 by 18 inches) generously with olive oil. Place dough on sheet and turn to coat with oil. With fingertips, push dough out toward edges of sheet (it will not fill entirely). Cover with plastic wrap and let rest 15 minutes.

Continue pressing dough outward toward edges and allowing it to rest, covered, until it completely fills sheet. Brush dough generously with olive oil. Cover and let rise in a warm place until doubled in bulk, 1 to 1½ hours.

Preheat oven to 400° F, with rack in lower third. Sprinkle dough generously with salt and pepper. Bake until top is golden, about 20 minutes, rotating sheet halfway through. Transfer focaccia to a wire rack to cool. Serve warm or at room temperature. (Focaccia is best eaten the same day it is made, although it will keep for up to 1 day at room temperature, wrapped well in plastic. For best results, reheat in a 250° F oven for about 15 minutes.)

PASKA

MAKES TWO 8- OR 9-INCH ROUND LOAVES
from **EASTER BRUNCH** *and* **EASTER DINNER**

The loaves are best baked in two saucepans that are eight or nine inches wide and at least five inches in height. If your pans are shorter, you will need to form a collar: Cut a piece of parchment about two inches longer than the circumference of the pan. Fold this in half lengthwise to make a double thickness. Wrap paper around the inside of the pan, patting it to adhere to the butter and sealing the flap with more butter. The collar should extend three to four inches above the rim of the pan. For step-by-step how-to photographs on forming the decorative tops, see page 374.

  2   envelopes active dry yeast (each 2¼ teaspoons)
 10   to 12 cups plus 1 tablespoon sifted all-purpose flour
  ⅔   cup plus 1 tablespoon sugar
  3   tablespoons warm water (110° F)
  2   cups warm milk (100° to 110° F)
  5   large whole eggs plus 8 large yolks, room temperature
  ¼   teaspoon salt
  1   teaspoon pure vanilla extract
       Finely grated zest of 1 lemon
       Finely grated zest of 1 orange
  3   tablespoons rum or brandy
  ½   cup neutral-tasting oil, such as safflower, plus more for bowl
  ½   cup (1 stick) unsalted butter, melted, plus more for pans

To make the sponge, combine yeast, 1 tablespoon flour, 1 tablespoon sugar, and the warm water in a large bowl. Mix until smooth, and let stand until mixture is foamy, 10 to 15 minutes. Add 4 cups flour and the warm milk, and mix with a wooden spoon until well combined. Cover with plastic wrap, and let rise in a warm, draft-free place until doubled in bulk, about 30 minutes.

In the bowl of a standing electric mixer fitted with the whisk attachment, beat 3 whole eggs, 8 yolks, and remaining ⅔ cup sugar until pale yellow, about 5 minutes. Switch to the paddle attachment; add the sponge mixture, salt, vanilla, both zests, rum, and oil. Beat on medium speed until combined. With mixer on low, gradually add melted butter; beat until combined.

Switch to the dough hook. With mixer on medium-low speed, gradually add enough of remaining 6 to 8 cups flour until dough just comes together. Turn out dough onto a clean work surface and knead, adding more flour if necessary, until smooth and elastic, 5 to 10 minutes. Transfer dough to a large oiled bowl and cover with a kitchen towel or plastic wrap. Let rise in a warm, draft-free place until doubled in bulk, 1 to 2 hours.

Butter two 8- to 9-inch high-sided saucepans. Punch down dough, and divide into thirds. Transfer one-third of the dough to a medium bowl, and cover with plastic wrap; reserve for making decorations. Shape each of remaining dough pieces into a ball, tucking edges under to make a smooth top, and put dough balls into prepared pans. Let dough in pans rise in a warm, draft-free place until 2 inches from top of pans or collars.

To make the decorative tops, trace two 8- or 9-inch circles onto parchment and turn paper over. When dough in bowl has risen 30 minutes, turn out onto work surface and cut in half. Use one portion of dough for the decoration on one paska, keeping unused portion covered while you work. Form decorations using the instructions and photographs on page 374 as a guide, and arrange on parchment circles.

Preheat oven to 350° F, with rack in lower two-thirds. Separate remaining 2 eggs. Lightly beat egg whites, and brush over risen dough in pans. Attach decorative tops. Let rise until dough almost reaches the top of the pans, 15 to 30 minutes.

Whisk together 2 yolks and remaining 1 tablespoon water. Brush egg wash on surface of loaves. Bake 10 minutes. Lower oven to 325° F and bake 50 minutes more. Remove from oven, and let cool in pans 30 minutes before turning out loaves onto a wire rack to cool completely.

BERAWEKA

MAKES TWO 8-INCH LOAVES   *from* **PÂTÉ CAMPAGNARD LUNCH**

A specialty of the Alsace region of France, this bread is filled with dried fruit and nuts, and is often described as being similar to an English steamed pudding. Be sure to buy good-quality candied fruits for this recipe, as they contribute to the bread's distinctive flavor.

  1   cup dried currants
  ⅔   cup golden raisins
  ½   cup dark raisins
  ½   cup diced dried pear
  ½   cup diced dried figs
  ½   cup diced dried apricots
  ¼   cup plus 2 tablespoons sugar
  ½   cup kirsch (cherry-flavored liqueur)
  1   teaspoon active dry yeast
  ¼   cup warm water (110° F)
  2   to 2¼ cups all-purpose flour, plus more for dusting
  ½   cup milk
  2   tablespoons unsalted butter, melted, plus more for bowl
  ½   teaspoon coarse salt
       Pinch of ground cloves
       Pinch of ground cinnamon
       Pinch of ground anise seed
  ½   cup slivered almonds
  1   cup walnuts (about 4 ounces), very coarsely chopped
  ¼   cup candied lemon peel
  ¼   cup candied orange peel

Combine dried fruits with ¼ cup sugar and the kirsch in a bowl. Cover, and macerate 1 day at room temperature.

In a large mixing bowl, stir yeast into the warm water, and let stand until creamy, about 5 minutes. Add 1 cup flour along with the milk, melted butter, salt, and spices. Beat with an electric mixer on medium speed until well combined, about 2 minutes. Add another 1 cup flour and beat on high speed 2 minutes more, adding just enough additional flour (up to ¼ cup) as necessary to make a soft dough.

Preheat oven to 375° F. Turn out dough onto a lightly floured surface, and knead 2 to 3 minutes. Place dough in a buttered bowl, turning to coat. Cover with plastic wrap or a kitchen cloth, and let rise in a warm, draft-free place until dough is almost doubled in bulk, about 30 minutes.

Punch down dough and transfer to another large bowl. Add dried fruit mixture, nuts, and candied peels; knead until evenly incorporated. (The mixture will be mostly fruits and nuts with a little dough holding them together.) Divide dough in half, and shape each into a log, about 8 inches long and 3½ inches wide. Place logs on a parchment-lined baking sheet.

Bake until bread is very dark and firm to the touch, about 1 hour, rotating sheet halfway through. Transfer to a wire rack to cool completely. (Beraweka will keep up to 3 days at room temperature, wrapped well in plastic.)

Drinks and Cocktails

BLUEBERRY LEMONADE

MAKES ABOUT 3½ QUARTS   *from* **BRIDAL SHOWER IN MAINE**

2 cups Blueberry Purée (recipe follows)
1½ cups fresh lemon juice (from 10 to 12 lemons)
1 cup superfine sugar
3 quarts cold water
Fresh blueberries, for garnish

Stir together blueberry purée, lemon juice, superfine sugar, and the cold water in a large pitcher or punch bowl. Cover and refrigerate until ready to serve, up to 2 days. Serve over ice, garnished with fresh blueberries.

Blueberry Purée MAKES 4 CUPS

This purée is also used to make the parfaits on page 395.

3 pints fresh blueberries (6 cups)
1½ cups granulated sugar
⅔ cup water

Bring all ingredients to a boil in a medium saucepan, stirring occasionally. Reduce heat, and simmer, stirring, until sugar has dissolved, about 2 minutes. Remove from heat, and let cool.

Purée in a blender until smooth, then strain through a fine sieve into a bowl, pressing on solids to remove as much liquid as possible. Discard solids. (Purée can be refrigerated, covered tightly, up to 2 days.)

RASPBERRY-VINEGAR CORDIAL

SERVES 10   *from* **PICNIC AT SEA**

Vinegar not only adds tartness to this old-fashioned drink, it also acts as a preservative; the cordial can be refrigerated in an airtight container for up to four months before serving.

2 pounds fresh raspberries (about 8 cups)
2 cups cider vinegar or white-wine vinegar
4½ cups sugar, or to taste
Seltzer water, for serving

Mash raspberries with a wooden spoon in a large bowl. Stir in vinegar. Cover with plastic wrap; refrigerate 24 to 36 hours.

Pour berry mixture through a fine sieve lined with cheesecloth into a saucepan, pressing to release as much liquid as possible; discard solids. Stir in sugar. Bring to a boil over high heat; cook, stirring occasionally, 10 minutes. Remove from heat and skim foam from surface. Let cordial cool completely before serving or storing.

To serve, fill 10 glasses with ice; add 3 tablespoons cordial to each, and top off with about 1 cup seltzer.

FRESH GREEN JUICE

SERVES 4   *from* **BREAKFAST ON THE PORCH**

2 Kirby cucumbers
¼ pound green Swiss chard or spinach
6 sprigs flat-leaf parsley
1 Granny Smith apple
1½ cups cubed (peeled and seeded) honeydew melon
2 celery stalks
½ fennel bulb
1 piece (2 inches) fresh ginger

Using an electric juicer, extract juice from all ingredients into a small pitcher. Stir until well combined, pour into glasses, and serve.

RHUBARB SPARKLERS

MAKES 6   *from* **BREAKFAST ON THE PORCH**

2 cups coarsely chopped rhubarb
½ cup sugar
½ cup water
Seltzer, for serving
Orange wedges, for garnish

Combine rhubarb, sugar, and the water in a saucepan, and stir to combine. Bring to a boil, then reduce heat, and simmer until rhubarb is soft and liquid has thickened slightly, about 20 minutes. Remove from heat and let cool slightly, then strain through a fine sieve, pressing on solids to extract as much liquid as possible. Discard solids. Let cool completely. (Syrup can be refrigerated in an airtight container up to 1 week.)

To serve, add 2 tablespoons rhubarb syrup to each of 6 glasses. Top off with seltzer, and garnish with orange wedges.

POMEGRANATE-APRICOT PUNCH

SERVES 12   *from* **HOLIDAY OPEN HOUSE BRUNCH**

This punch is fragrant with mint and ginger. You can also spike it with vodka, if desired.

1½ cups sugar
1½ cups water
12 slices (⅛ inch thick) fresh ginger (do not peel)
2¼ cups packed fresh mint (leaves and stems), plus more for garnish
6 cups unsweetened pomegranate juice
¾ cup apricot nectar
2½ cups seltzer

Bring sugar, the water, and ginger to a boil in a saucepan, stirring to dissolve sugar, then remove from heat. Add mint; let steep, covered, 30 minutes. Strain through a fine sieve, and let cool. (You should have 2 cups syrup.)

Stir together syrup, pomegranate juice, and apricot nectar. Transfer to a punch bowl filled with ice. Add seltzer, garnish with mint leaves, and serve.

POMEGRANATE COSMOPOLITANS

SERVES 8 *from* **HALLOWEEN PUMPKIN BLAZE**

To make your own pomegranate juice, split a fruit in half. Holding each half over a bowl, whack the skin with a wooden spoon to release seeds. Crush with a wooden reamer, then strain through a fine sieve, pressing on solids to remove as much liquid as possible. You will need three to four pomegranates to yield two cups of juice.

- 24 ounces (3 cups) vodka
- 2 cups unsweetened pomegranate juice
- 1 cup fresh lime juice (from 8 to 10 limes)
- 8 ounces (1 cup) Cointreau or other citrus-flavored liqueur

Combine all ingredients in a pitcher, then pour 1¾ cups into a cocktail shaker filled with ice. Shake vigorously and strain into 2 martini glasses. Repeat with remaining mixture.

MAY WINE

SERVES 6 *from* **VERDANT SPRING DINNER**

In Germany, this is the traditional drink to celebrate May Day. Sweet woodruff is an aromatic herb that can be found at some nurseries. Other sweet herbs, such as sweet thyme or marjoram, can be used in its place.

- 1 bottle (750 ml) dry Riesling
- 2 sprigs sweet woodruff

Open wine, and add woodruff. Return cork and refrigerate 1 week before straining out woodruff and serving.

CANDIED-KUMQUAT CHAMPAGNE COCKTAILS

SERVES 12 *from* **HOLIDAY OPEN HOUSE BRUNCH**

- 2 pints kumquats
- 3 cups sugar
- 2 cups water, plus more for blanching kumquats
- 2 bottles (each 750 ml) Champagne, well chilled
- 3 tangerines, quartered

Rinse kumquats, and pierce each in a couple of places with a clean straight pin. Place in a large saucepan with enough cold water to cover. Bring to a boil, then drain. Repeat two more times, always starting with cold water.

Combine kumquats, sugar, and 2 cups water in a large saucepan. Bring to a boil, stirring to dissolve sugar. Remove from heat; let cool completely. (Kumquats and syrup can be refrigerated up to 1 month in an airtight container.)

To serve, spoon 3 kumquats into each of 12 flutes, and top with 1 tablespoon syrup; top with Champagne, and add a wedge of tangerine.

PROSECCO *with* LYCHEE SORBET

SERVES 6 *from* **SUMMER COCKTAIL PARTY**

- 1 can (20 ounces) pitted lychees in syrup
- 1 bottle (750 ml) prosecco or other sparkling wine, well chilled

In a blender, purée lychees, with their syrup, until very smooth, about 5 minutes. Pour purée into an ice-cream maker, and freeze according to manufacturer's instructions, until just barely set and slightly slushy.

To serve, add 1 tablespoon lychee sorbet to each of 6 Champagne flutes, then top with prosecco.

CHAMPAGNE-CITRUS COCKTAIL

SERVES 6 *from* **SUMMER COCKTAIL PARTY**

- ½ cup raw sugar, such as turbinado
- ¼ cup fresh orange juice, plus more for rims
- 9 ounces (1 cup plus 2 tablespoons) Grand Marnier or other orange-flavored liqueur
- 2 tablespoons fresh lemon juice
- 1 bottle (750 ml) Champagne, well chilled

Spread sugar on a small plate. Dip the rim of each of 6 flutes in orange juice, and then into the sugar.

Pour 3 tablespoons Grand Marnier, 2 teaspoons orange juice, and 1 teaspoon lemon juice into each flute; top with Champagne and serve.

RHUBARB-ORANGE COCKTAILS

SERVES 12 *from* **PEONY GARDEN PARTY**

The rhubarb syrup can be refrigerated in an airtight container for up to one week; serve any extra syrup warm, over ice cream.

- 4 cups chopped rhubarb
- 1 cup sugar
- 1 cup water
- 4 cups fresh orange juice (from 12 to 15 oranges)
- 24 ounces (3 cups) vodka
- 1 orange, preferably organic, peel removed in strips for garnish

Combine rhubarb, sugar, and the water in a large saucepan, and stir to combine. Bring to a boil, then reduce heat, and simmer until rhubarb is soft and liquid has thickened slightly, about 20 minutes. Remove from heat and let cool slightly, then strain through a fine sieve into an airtight container, pressing on solids with a flexible spatula to remove as much liquid as possible. Discard solids. Let cool completely. (Syrup can be refrigerated in an airtight container up to one week.)

Stir together 2 cups rhubarb syrup, the orange juice, and vodka in a pitcher. Serve over ice; garnish with strips of orange peel.

CAIPIRINHAS

SERVES 6 *from* **SUMMER COCKTAIL PARTY**

Cachaça is a Brazilian sugarcane brandy similar to rum. It is the foundation of the caipirinha, Brazil's national cocktail.

- 5 limes
- 16 ounces (2 cups) cachaça
- ¼ cup plus 1 tablespoon sugar

Cut each lime into four to six wedges. Squeeze juice into a large pitcher, then drop in wedges. Add cachaça and sugar, and stir to combine. Fill pitcher with ice, stir well to chill, and serve drinks in tall glasses.

PIÑA COLADAS

SERVES 6 *from* **SUMMER COCKTAIL PARTY**

- 1 pineapple
- ¼ cup confectioners' sugar, plus more for dusting
- 3 cups ice cubes
- 12 ounces (1½ cups) dark rum
- 12 ounces (1½ cups) canned cream of coconut, such as Coco López

Preheat oven to 250° F. Peel pineapple. Using a mandoline (or other adjustable-blade slicer) or a very sharp chef's knife, slice off 12 very thin rounds. Arrange in a single layer on a baking sheet lined with a nonstick baking mat. Dust liberally with confectioners' sugar, flip slices, and dust again. Cook 30 minutes, turn slices, and cook until dried and starting to turn golden brown on the edges, 10 to 20 minutes more (depending on thickness of slices). Thread slices onto six skewers, dividing evenly.

Cut remaining pineapple into chunks, and purée in a blender. Strain through a fine sieve into a bowl, and return juice to blender; discard solids. Add ice cubes, rum, cream of coconut, and confectioners' sugar; blend on high speed 3 minutes. Divide among 6 glasses; garnish each with a skewered pineapple slice. Serve immediately.

BING CHERRY MOJITOS

SERVES 12 *from* **JULY 4TH BARBECUE**

- 1¼ cups fresh lime juice (from 10 to 12 limes)
- 3 pounds Bing cherries
- 2 cups Simple Syrup (page 422)
- 18 ounces (2¼ cups) best-quality vodka, preferably black cherry–flavored
- 1 bottle (750 ml) sparkling water

Pour lime juice into a nonreactive bowl. Halve and pit cherries; add to lime juice. Stir in simple syrup. Refrigerate at least 1 hour or up to 1 day.

Pour vodka into a large serving bowl; stir in cherry mixture. Fill 12 glasses with ice. Ladle about ½ cup cherry-vodka mixture into each glass. Top off with sparkling water. Serve immediately.

HONEYDEW MOJITOS

SERVES 8 *from* **SUMMER COCKTAIL PARTY**

- Juice of 4 limes (about ½ cup), plus wedges for rims and garnish
- Superfine sugar, for rims
- 1 honeydew melon (about 6 pounds), quartered, peeled, and seeded
- ¼ cup granulated sugar
- ¼ cup water
- ¼ cup packed fresh mint leaves, plus sprigs for garnish
- 4 ounces (½ cup) medium-bodied golden rum
- 3 cups small ice cubes

Rub a lime wedge on rims of 8 glasses, then dip rims in superfine sugar. Cut 3 melon quarters into 1-inch chunks. Purée melon chunks in a food processor until smooth, then strain through a cheesecloth-lined sieve, and discard solids. (You should have about 4 cups.) Using a melon baller, scoop balls from remaining melon quarter, and reserve.

Bring granulated sugar and the water to a boil in a small saucepan, stirring until sugar dissolves. Remove from heat, and add mint. Let steep (uncovered) 10 minutes. Strain through a fine sieve, discarding mint leaves. (You should have a scant ⅓ cup syrup.)

Combine melon purée, mint syrup, rum, and lime juice in a pitcher; refrigerate until cold, about 30 minutes. Add ice to pitcher; divide mixture among glasses. Serve, garnished with melon balls, mint sprigs, and lime wedges.

ELDERFLOWER MARTINI

SERVES 1 *from* **VERDANT SPRING DINNER**

St. Germain, an artisanal French liqueur flavored with handpicked elderflowers, is sold at specialty wine shops.

- 4 fresh mint leaves, plus sprigs for garnish
- 2 ounces (¼ cup) gin
- 2 tablespoons fresh lemon juice
- 1 ounce (2 tablespoons) St. Germain
- 2 tablespoons unsweetened pomegranate juice
- 2 teaspoons Simple Syrup (page 422), or to taste

Muddle mint leaves with gin in a cocktail shaker. Add lemon juice, St. Germain, pomegranate juice, and simple syrup. Fill shaker halfway with ice. Shake; strain into a chilled martini glass. Garnish with a sprig of mint.

BOURBON MILK PUNCH

SERVES 2 *from* **SUMMER COCKTAIL PARTY**

- 1 cup milk
- 4 ounces (½ cup) bourbon, preferably Maker's Mark
- 1 ounce (2 tablespoons) Cognac or other brandy
- 1 teaspoon sugar
- Pinch of freshly grated nutmeg, plus more for garnish

Fill a cocktail shaker three-quarters full with ice, then add all ingredients and shake vigorously. Divide between 2 glasses, and garnish with nutmeg.

RASPBERRY MARGARITAS

SERVES 4 *from* **SUMMER COCKTAIL PARTY**

- 2 tablespoons sugar
- 8 ounces fresh raspberries (about 2 cups), plus more for garnish
- ¼ cup coarse salt
  Lime wedge, for rims
- 4 ounces (½ cup) tequila, preferably blanco (silver)
- 2 ounces (¼ cup) Cointreau or other citrus-flavored liqueur
- 2 teaspoons fresh lime juice
  Small mint sprigs, for garnish

Combine sugar and half the raspberries in a bowl; crush berries with a flexible spatula. Mix well; let stand 5 minutes. Pass through a fine sieve into another bowl, pressing to remove as much liquid as possible. Discard solids.

In a small bowl, mix the salt with 2 teaspoons raspberry purée. Pour onto a small plate. Rub lime wedge around the rims of 4 margarita glasses and then press rims into salt mixture. Fill glasses halfway with ice.

Fill a cocktail shaker halfway with ice, and add tequila, Cointreau, lime juice, and remaining raspberry purée. Shake vigorously, and strain into glasses. Garnish each with a few raspberries and a sprig of mint.

LEMON WHISKEY SOURS

SERVES 8 *from* **SUMMER COCKTAIL PARTY**

- 1 cup fresh lemon juice (from 4 to 5 lemons), plus a lemon wedge for rims and 8 thin strips lemon zest for garnish
- ½ cup superfine sugar, plus more for rims
- 14 ounces (1¾ cups) whiskey
- 6 ounces (¾ cup) kirsch (cherry-flavored liqueur)
- 4 dashes of bitters
- 6 cups small ice cubes, plus more for glasses
- 8 cherries, for garnish

Rub lemon wedge on rims of 8 glasses, then dip rims in superfine sugar. Combine whiskey, kirsch, lemon juice, superfine sugar, bitters, and the ice in a pitcher, stirring until sugar dissolves. Divide among ice-filled glasses, and serve immediately, garnished with cherries and lemon zest.

TOM COLLINS

SERVES 1 *from* **SUMMER COCKTAIL PARTY**

- 2 ounces (¼ cup) gin
- 2 ounces (¼ cup) club soda or tonic water
- 2 teaspoons superfine sugar
- 1 teaspoon fresh lemon juice
- 1 teaspoon fresh lime juice
  Lemon and lime wedges, for garnish

Stir to combine all ingredients except citrus wedges in a pitcher filled with ice. Pour into a tall glass. Garnish with a lemon and lime wedge; serve.

SAZERAC

SERVES 1 *from* **SUMMER COCKTAIL PARTY**

This classic cocktail is made with Herbsaint, a liqueur with a taste similar to absinthe (though without the wormwood). Other anise-flavored liqueurs, such as Pastis and Pernod, are good substitutes.

- 1 sugar cube
- 2 ounces (¼ cup) bourbon or rye
- 4 dashes of orange bitters
- ¼ teaspoon Herbsaint or other anise-flavored liqueur
- 1 strip of lemon peel

Pack an old-fashioned glass with ice to chill. Crush sugar cube in a cocktail shaker with just enough water to moisten. Add bourbon and bitters, stirring to combine. Fill with ice, and stir to chill.

Remove ice from glass. Pour in Herbsaint and swirl to coat, then pour off excess. Strain bourbon mixture into glass. Twist lemon peel and rub around rim (do not add to drink).

SPICED HOT TEA

SERVES 8 *from* **PICNIC AT SEA**

- 6 cups water
- 1 piece (3 inches) fresh ginger (unpeeled), halved lengthwise
- 8 bags black tea
- 2 whole cinnamon sticks, plus more for garnish (optional)
- 12 whole cloves
- ½ teaspoon whole black peppercorns
- 4 cups milk
- ½ cup honey, or to taste

In a large saucepan, bring the water and ginger to a boil. Reduce heat; simmer 8 minutes. Add tea bags, cinnamon, cloves, peppercorns, and milk. Cover and steep over medium-low heat until fragrant, about 6 minutes. Strain through a fine sieve; discard solids. Stir in honey and divide among 8 mugs. Serve hot, garnished with additional cinnamon sticks, if desired.

FRESH GRAPE JUICE

SERVES 4 *from* **BREAKFAST ON THE PORCH**

- 2 cups red or green seedless grapes, preferably organic
- ½ to ¾ cup water

Wash grapes thoroughly and drain well. Remove stems and extract juice with an electric juicer, adding the water as desired. Alternatively, purée grapes with the water in a blender, then strain through a fine sieve, discarding solids. Divide among glasses and serve.

Appetizers

POPPY SEED–CHEESE STRAWS

MAKES ABOUT 30 *from* **HALLOWEEN PUMPKIN BLAZE**

To roll out the dough and form the straws, follow the step-by-step how-to photographs on page 375.

- ½ cup finely grated Parmigiano-Reggiano cheese (2 ounces)
- 3 tablespoons poppy seeds
- ¼ teaspoon cayenne pepper
- 1 package (14 ounces) frozen all-butter puff pastry, such as Dufour, thawed in refrigerator
  All-purpose flour, for dusting

Mix cheese, poppy seeds, and cayenne in a bowl. Unfold pastry dough on a lightly floured surface, then fold sheet of puff pastry crosswise in half. With a floured rolling pin, roll out to a 12-by-16-inch rectangle. Trim edges to make even. Sprinkle cheese mixture evenly over dough, rolling with pin to help it adhere.

Preheat oven to 375° F, with rack in the center. Using a pastry wheel or pizza cutter, cut the pastry into ½-inch strips, and transfer to baking sheets, about 1 inch apart. Twist from one end to another, then press ends gently onto sheet. Chill twists on baking sheets until firm, about 15 minutes.

Bake one sheet at a time, rotating it halfway through, until straws are golden brown and puffed, about 10 minutes. Transfer cheese straws to a wire rack to cool. Straws are best eaten the same day they are baked.

GORGONZOLA PALMIERS

MAKES ABOUT 40 *from* **PEONY GARDEN PARTY**

- 1 package (14 ounces) frozen all-butter puff pastry, such as Dufour, thawed in refrigerator
  All-purpose flour, for dusting
- 6 ounces Gorgonzola cheese, crumbled (⅔ cup)
- 1 large egg beaten with 1 tablespoon water, for egg wash
- ½ cup finely grated Parmigiano-Reggiano cheese (2 ounces)

Unfold puff pastry on a lightly floured surface and gently roll out to a 14-inch square with a lightly floured rolling pin. Trim edges with a pastry wheel or paring knife. Sprinkle evenly with Gorgonzola; gently press into dough. Fold dough into thirds, like a business letter, then fold length-wise in half. Wrap in plastic; chill at least 1 hour or up to 1 day.

Preheat oven to 450° F, with racks in upper and lower thirds. Brush folded dough on all sides with egg wash; sprinkle with Parmesan, pressing gently to adhere. Cut crosswise into ¼-inch-thick slices. Place on parchment-lined baking sheets, spacing 2 inches apart. Bake until golden, rotating sheets from top to bottom and front to back halfway through, about 12 minutes. Let cool on a wire rack. Serve warm or at room temperature. Palmiers are best eaten the same day they are baked.

GRISSINI

MAKES 6 DOZEN *from* **LUNCHEON FOR BEDFORD FARMERS**

You can make an arresting array of colorful breadsticks by using the variations that follow, each tinted with a different vegetable or an herb.

- 2 cups all-purpose flour, plus more for dusting
- ¼ teaspoon coarse salt, plus more for sprinkling
- 1½ teaspoons baking powder
- 3 tablespoons vegetable shortening
- ½ to ¾ cup ice water
- 2 tablespoons extra-virgin olive oil

Preheat oven to 350° F. Pulse flour, salt, and baking powder in a food processor to combine. Add shortening; pulse until mixture resembles coarse meal. With processor running, gradually add ½ cup ice water; process until a dough forms, about 1 minute. If dough is dry, add up to ¼ cup more ice water, 1 tablespoon at a time, pulsing after each addition.

Turn out dough onto a lightly floured surface. Pat into a rectangle, then roll out to an 8-by-10-inch sheet (¼ inch thick). Cut lengthwise into ¼-inch-wide strips. Roll each strip with the palms of your hands to a rope about 16 inches long.

Arrange on baking sheets, spacing ½ inch apart. Brush with olive oil, dividing evenly, then sprinkle with salt. Bake until firm, rotating sheets halfway through, 12 to 14 minutes. Let cool on a wire rack. (Grissini can be stored in airtight containers at room temperature up to 4 days.)

Variations

Beet: Add 2 tablespoons fresh beet juice (from 1 small beet) to the ½ cup ice water; add just enough of this mixture to form a dough.

Carrot: Replace the ½ cup ice water with a mixture of ¼ cup fresh carrot juice (from 3 carrots) and ¼ cup ice water.

Parsley: Replace the ½ cup ice water with a mixture of ¼ cup strained fresh parsley juice and ¼ cup ice water.

Tomato: Replace the ½ cup ice water with a mixture of 2 tablespoons tomato paste and ½ cup plus 2 tablespoons ice water.

CARAMEL-TOPPED BRIE *with* PECANS

SERVES 12 *from* **HOLIDAY OPEN HOUSE BRUNCH**

- 1¼ cups sugar
- ⅓ cup water
- 1 wheel (8-inch diameter) Brie or Camembert cheese
- 20 pecan halves
  Toasted bread or crackers, for serving

Prepare an ice-water bath. Combine sugar and the water in a saucepan; bring to a boil over medium-high heat, swirling to dissolve sugar. Wash down sides of pan with a pastry brush dipped in water to prevent crystals from forming. Continue cooking, without stirring, until mixture is dark amber, swirling pan occasionally to color evenly. Immediately dip bottom of pan in ice bath to stop the cooking.

Place cheese wheel on a small board or serving plate. Using wooden skewers, dip pecans in caramel, allowing excess to drip into pan. Place around outer edge of cheese, spacing evenly. Pour remaining caramel over top of cheese, swirling to cover top, and allowing it to drip down the side. Let stand until caramel is hardened. Crack caramel with a sharp knife, and serve cheese with toasted bread or crackers.

VEGETABLES *à la* GRECQUE

MAKES 3 QUARTS *from* **PÂTÉ CAMPAGNARD LUNCH**

Lightly pickled vegetables provide a refreshing accompaniment to a meal of pâté and assorted breads.

- 1½ cups dry white wine
- 1½ cups white vinegar
- 1½ cups water
- ¾ cup sugar
- 2 sprigs dill, plus 1 tablespoon chopped
- 2 tablespoons coarse salt
- 1 tablespoon coriander seeds
- 2 garlic cloves, halved lengthwise
- 1 dried red chile, such as ancho or pasilla (optional)
- 8 baby artichokes (or 2 large artichokes, trimmed and quartered as directed on page 329)
- 1 pound carrots (about 6 medium), peeled and sliced ½ inch thick on the bias
- 1 bag (10 ounces) white pearl onions, peeled (page 423)
- 8 ounces button mushrooms, cleaned and halved
- 1 red bell pepper, roasted (page 423) and cut into 1-inch pieces

In a large heavy pot, combine wine, vinegar, the water, sugar, dill sprigs, salt, coriander, garlic, and chile (if using). Working with one baby artichoke at a time, pull off tough outer leaves; cut off top third of artichoke with a serrated knife, and discard. Trim stem end, cut artichoke in half, and drop into pot. (If using large artichokes, add quarters to pot.)

Add carrots and pearl onions; bring to a boil. Reduce heat, and simmer until carrots and artichokes are tender, about 20 minutes. Add mushrooms; simmer 5 minutes. Remove from heat, and gently stir in roasted pepper. Allow vegetables to cool completely in liquid before refrigerating, covered, 1 day.

Use a slotted spoon to remove vegetables from pickling liquid; toss with chopped fresh dill just before serving.

RADISHES *with* HERBED RICOTTA DIP, SWEET BUTTER, *and* FLEUR DE SEL

SERVES 12 *from* **JULY 4TH BARBECUE**

A combination of French Breakfast, White Icicle, and Pink Beauty was used at the barbecue, but you can use any variety you'd like. When the weather is hot, sprinkle radishes with crushed ice before serving to keep them crisp.

- 1 pound fresh ricotta cheese
- 2 tablespoons finely chopped fresh flat-leaf parsley
- 1 tablespoon finely chopped fresh dill
- 1 tablespoon finely chopped fresh basil
  Coarse salt and freshly ground pepper
- 4 bunches radishes, trimmed if desired
- 4 tablespoons unsalted butter, softened, for serving
  Fleur de sel, for serving

Stir together ricotta, parsley, dill, and basil in a bowl. Season with salt and pepper. (Dip can be refrigerated in an airtight container up to 2 days.)

Serve radishes on a platter with bowls of dip, butter, and fleur de sel.

GARDEN CRUDITÉS *with* VINAIGRETTE *and* HERB BUTTER

SERVES 12 *from* **LUNCHEON FOR BEDFORD FARMERS**

  Coarse salt and freshly ground pepper
- 1 small head cauliflower, trimmed and cut into large florets
- 1 small head broccoli, trimmed and cut into large florets
- 1 bunch asparagus, ends trimmed
- ⅓ cup white-wine vinegar
- 1 tablespoon plus 1½ teaspoons Dijon mustard
  Pinch of sugar
- 1 shallot, minced
- 1 cup extra-virgin olive oil
  Garlic and Herb Butter, for serving (recipe follows)

Prepare an ice-water bath. Blanch cauliflower in a pot of boiling salted water until bright and crisp-tender, about 1 minute. With a slotted spoon, transfer cauliflower to ice bath to stop the cooking; drain. Repeat with broccoli and then asparagus, blanching each batch about 1 minute. Blot vegetables dry.

Whisk together vinegar, mustard, sugar, and shallot; season with salt and pepper. Slowly add olive oil in a steady stream, whisking until emulsified.

To serve, arrange vegetables on a platter with vinaigrette and herb butter alongside.

Garlic and Herb Butter MAKES ABOUT ½ CUP

- ¼ cup packed chopped fresh flat-leaf parsley
- 2 tablespoons chopped fresh curly parsley
- ½ recipe Garlic Confit and reserved oil (recipe follows)
- ½ cup (1 stick) unsalted butter, softened
  Coarse salt

Blend together both parsleys and the garlic confit and oil in a food processor until finely chopped. Add butter and season with salt; process until incorporated. Transfer to a serving dish. Serve at room temperature. (Herb butter can be refrigerated, tightly covered, 1 day.)

Garlic Confit MAKES ABOUT ½ CUP

2 garlic heads, cloves separated and peeled
⅔ cup extra-virgin olive oil

Cook garlic and oil in a small saucepan over medium-low heat until cloves are very soft, 20 to 35 minutes (cloves will release bubbles until cooked through). Remove from heat and let cool completely in oil. Remove garlic and refrigerate in an airtight container until ready to use, up to 2 days. Refrigerate the oil in a separate airtight container up to 1 week (use for cooking or making vinaigrettes).

HERB-MARINATED GREEN OLIVES

MAKES 4 CUPS   *from* PEONY GARDEN PARTY

4 cups pitted green olives
½ bunch fresh flat-leaf parsley, leaves picked and coarsely chopped
6 to 8 sprigs thyme, leaves picked and finely chopped
2 sprigs rosemary, leaves picked and finely chopped
3 cloves Garlic Confit, halved lengthwise (recipe above)
½ cup extra-virgin olive oil (or reserved oil from Garlic Confit)

Combine all ingredients in a nonreactive bowl; toss well to combine. Cover tightly; let marinate in the refrigerator 1 day. Serve at room temperature.

MARINATED OLIVES *and* PEPPERS

MAKES 4 CUPS   *from* LUNCHEON FOR BEDFORD FARMERS

1 red bell pepper, roasted (page 423)
1 yellow bell pepper, roasted (page 423)
4 cups drained pimiento-stuffed olives
20 anchovy filets, finely chopped
½ cup extra-virgin olive oil
¼ cup balsamic vinegar

Cut roasted peppers into medium dice. Place in a nonreactive bowl with the remaining ingredients, tossing to combine. Cover tightly, and marinate in the refrigerator at least 8 hours or up to 1 day. Serve at room temperature.

ORANGE-MARINATED KALAMATA OLIVES

MAKES 4 CUPS   *from* LUNCHEON FOR BEDFORD FARMERS

4 cups Kalamata olives
Finely grated zest and juice of 2 oranges
¼ cup extra-virgin olive oil

Mix ingredients in a nonreactive bowl. Cover tightly, and marinate in the refrigerator at least 8 hours or up to 2 days, tossing occasionally. Serve at room temperature.

ROASTED–BELL PEPPER CONFIT

MAKES 2 CUPS   *from* LUNCHEON FOR BEDFORD FARMERS

5 red bell peppers, roasted (page 423)
4 yellow bell peppers, roasted (page 423)
¾ cup extra-virgin olive oil
2 garlic cloves, coarsely chopped
1 bunch fresh rosemary, leaves picked
Coarse salt

Cut peppers into large dice. In a saucepan, heat olive oil and garlic over medium until garlic starts to sizzle. Remove from heat; let cool slightly. Stir in peppers and rosemary, and season with salt. Serve at room temperature.

CUCUMBER *and* PUMPERNICKEL CANAPÉS

MAKES 16   *from* EASTER BRUNCH

8 thin slices black pumpernickel bread
3 tablespoons unsalted butter, softened
8 Kirby cucumbers, peeled, halved lengthwise, and seeded
Coarse salt
Best-quality honey, for serving

Spread each slice of bread lightly with butter. Thinly slice cucumbers crosswise and arrange on buttered bread, slightly overlapping slices. Cut bread into two rectangles. Before serving, season with salt and drizzle with honey.

GOAT CHEESE *and* PICKLED DAIKON CANAPÉS

MAKES 8   *from* TEA IN THE AFTERNOON

4 thin slices raisin bread, trimmed of crusts
3 to 4 ounces fresh goat cheese
2 pickled daikon radishes, thinly sliced

Preheat oven to 300° F. Arrange bread on a baking sheet; place in oven to dry out and toast slightly, 5 to 7 minutes per side. Let cool completely.

Cut each bread slice into two rectangles. Stir goat cheese until smooth and fluffy; spread over canapés. Top each with two slices pickled daikon; serve.

GLAZED BACON

MAKES ABOUT 30 PIECES *from* **SUMMER COCKTAIL PARTY**

1 pound thick-cut bacon, room temperature
½ cup raw turbinado sugar

Preheat oven to 350° F. Line a rimmed baking sheet with foil and place a nonstick baking mat on top. Lay bacon slices in a single layer on mat, then sprinkle with sugar, spreading to coat evenly and pressing to adhere. Let rest in a warm place until sugar begins to dissolve, about 10 minutes.

Bake until bacon is crisp and evenly glazed, turning pieces halfway through, 25 to 35 minutes. Cut bacon into 2-inch pieces, and keep in a warm place until ready to serve.

SMOKED SALMON TRIANGLES

MAKES 8 *from* **TEA IN THE AFTERNOON**

2 tablespoons olive oil
1 tablespoon capers, drained and rinsed
4 thin slices white bread, trimmed of crusts
2 tablespoons unsalted butter, softened, or whipped cream cheese
4 ounces smoked salmon

In a small sauté pan, heat the olive oil over medium high until hot but not smoking. Add capers; cook, stirring occasionally, until crisp, about 3 minutes. Using a slotted spoon, transfer to a paper towel–lined plate to drain.

Spread each slice of bread with butter, then top with salmon. Cut in half diagonally to form two triangles. Sprinkle with capers and serve.

WASABI CAVIAR *and* DAIKON CANAPÉS

MAKES 24 *from* **CHRISTMAS AT CANTITOE CORNERS**

These hors d'oeuvres get their festive colors from wasabi caviar, white daikon radishes, and Red Currant tomatoes fresh from the garden. If you can't find wasabi caviar, you can make a similar version at home: In a small bowl, sift a teaspoon of wasabi powder into one ounce of golden caviar; mix well, and let sit for fifteen minutes before using. You can omit the Red Currant tomatoes altogether, or substitute grape tomatoes (use the tiniest ones, or halve larger ones).

24 very thin slices white bread
1 small daikon radish
6 ounces (¾ cup) cream cheese, softened
¼ cup finely chopped fresh chives
3 ounces wasabi caviar
1 cup Red Currant tomatoes

Preheat oven to 300° F. Arrange bread on two baking sheets; place in oven to dry and toast slightly, 5 to 7 minutes per side. Let cool completely.

Using a mandoline (or other adjustable-blade slicer) or a sharp knife, very thinly slice the radish into rounds. Cover with damp paper towels until ready to serve.

Mix cream cheese and chives; spread each bread slice with an even layer. Cut out twenty-four 2¼-inch rounds with a biscuit cutter; cut each round in half. For each canapé, spread 1 teaspoon caviar over cream cheese, add a few tomatoes, then top with two radish slices. Serve immediately.

SMOKED SALMON *and* PUMPERNICKEL MILLEFEUILLES

MAKES 16 *from* **CELEBRATING A MASTER GARDENER**

These hors d'oeuvres make for a supremely easy take on millefeuilles ("a thousand leaves"), a classic French pastry made by stacking layers of puff pastry with either a sweet or savory filling.

12 ounces cream cheese (1½ cups), softened
¼ cup plus 2 tablespoons crème fraîche
¼ cup plus 2 tablespoons finely chopped fresh chives
½ teaspoon finely chopped fresh tarragon
32 slices cocktail pumpernickel or rye bread
12 ounces smoked salmon

Combine cream cheese, crème fraîche, chives, and tarragon in a bowl. For each sandwich, spread top of a bread slice with 1 to 2 teaspoons cream cheese mixture, then top with ¼ ounce salmon. Spread both sides of another piece of bread with cream cheese mixture and stack on the other. Top with salmon, another slice of bread with cream cheese on both sides, and more salmon. Finish by spreading cream cheese on one side of another bread slice and place, coated side down, on stack. Place sandwiches on a baking sheet and freeze, about 30 minutes. Slice off crusts and cut each sandwich in half to make two rectangles (for a total of 16). Serve at room temperature.

PAN-FRIED SHISHITO PEPPERS

SERVES 4 *from* **JAPANESE LUNCH**

Shishito peppers are very popular in Japanese cooking, especially when pan-fried as in this recipe. Spanish Padron peppers are a good substitute.

1 tablespoon sesame or peanut oil, plus more if needed
4 ounces shishito peppers, rinsed and dried, stems left intact
Sea salt

Heat oil in a large cast-iron skillet over medium high. Working in batches, fry peppers until beginning to darken in spots, tossing frequently, about 2 minutes (add more oil between batches as needed). Transfer to a platter, season with salt, and serve hot.

POTTED CRAB *with* MELBA TOAST

MAKES 3 CUPS *from* **PICNIC AT SEA**

1½ cups (3 sticks) unsalted butter
1   pound jumbo lump crabmeat, picked over
1   tablespoon brandy
2   teaspoons minced fresh red chile, such as mirasol or serrano (ribs and seeds removed for less heat, if desired)
½   teaspoon coarse salt
½   teaspoon freshly ground pepper
¼   teaspoon paprika
¼   teaspoon freshly grated nutmeg
    Melba Toast, for serving (recipe follows)

Melt 1 cup butter in a small saucepan over low heat. Simmer 10 minutes. Remove from heat, and let stand 10 minutes. Skim foam from surface with a spoon, then carefully pour clarified butter (the clear liquid) into another saucepan, leaving milk solids behind (discard solids).

Heat clarified butter over medium. Gently stir in crabmeat; heat until just bubbling, then remove from heat. Gently stir in brandy, chile, salt, pepper, paprika, and nutmeg. Divide crab mixture among three 1-cup glass jars. Let cool completely.

Melt remaining ½ cup butter in saucepan over low heat. Let cool completely. Pour over crab mixture in jars. Refrigerate, tightly sealed, up to 1 week. Let stand at room temperature 30 minutes before serving, with melba toast.

Melba Toast MAKES ABOUT 3 DOZEN

You can use any type of loaf bread, such as pullman or whole wheat, for this recipe.

1   small loaf bread (about 8 ounces)

Preheat oven to 250° F. Slice bread very thin; cut into rectangles. Arrange on a baking sheet in a single layer. Toast bread in oven, flipping slices halfway through, until dry, about 2 hours. Transfer to a wire rack to cool. (Toast can be stored in airtight containers at room temperature up to 3 days.)

SPICY TUNA TARTARE CROSTINI

MAKES ABOUT 24 *from* **VERDANT SPRING DINNER**

1   small baguette, thinly sliced
    Extra-virgin olive oil, for brushing
    Coarse salt
2   tablespoons mayonnaise
½   teaspoon Asian hot chili sauce, such as Sriracha
8   ounces fresh yellowfin tuna, cut into ¼-inch dice
2   tablespoons sour cream
2   jalapeño chiles, halved lengthwise and cut thinly crosswise (ribs and seeds removed for less heat, if desired)

Preheat oven to 375° F. Arrange baguette slices on two baking sheets. Brush tops with olive oil; sprinkle with salt. Toast until golden, rotating sheets halfway through, 8 to 10 minutes. Let cool on a wire rack.

Whisk together mayonnaise and chili sauce in a nonreactive bowl. Add tuna, season with salt, and gently combine with a fork. (Tartare can be refrigerated, covered, for up to 2 hours.)

To serve, use two small spoons to form tartare into a quenelle (football shape), and place on top of a toast piece. Repeat with remaining tartare and toasts. Top each with a small dollop of sour cream and a jalapeño slice.

TOMATO *and* GRUYÈRE TOASTS

MAKES ABOUT 24 *from* **STYLISH DINNER IN THE CLERESTORY**

3   to 4 tablespoons Dijon mustard
1   ficelle or small baguette, cut into ¼-inch-thick rounds
1   pint grape tomatoes, halved
3   scallions, trimmed and thinly sliced on the bias (about ¼ cup)
¾   cup grated Gruyère cheese (about 3 ounces)

Preheat oven to 400° F. Dividing evenly, spread mustard over bread rounds. Arrange 2 tomato halves on top, cut sides up; sprinkle with scallions, then cheese. Bake on a large rimmed sheet until cheese is melted and bread is crisp around the edges, about 8 minutes. Serve warm.

MINI CRAB CAKES *with* TARRAGON TARTAR SAUCE

MAKES ABOUT 24 *from* **CELEBRATING A MASTER GARDENER**

¼   cup plus 2 tablespoons yellow cornmeal
2   tablespoons unsalted butter, melted and cooled
2   large eggs
3   tablespoons sour cream
2   tablespoons coarsely chopped fresh flat-leaf parsley
2   tablespoons fresh lemon juice, plus wedges for serving
½   teaspoon Worcestershire sauce
½   teaspoon paprika
    Pinch of cayenne
½   teaspoon coarse salt
1   pound jumbo lump crabmeat, picked over
3   hot pickled peppers, such as Peppadew, coarsely chopped
¾   cup plain dried breadcrumbs
¼   cup neutral-tasting oil, such as safflower, plus more if needed
    Tarragon Tartar Sauce, for serving (recipe follows)

Preheat oven to 250° F. Line a large baking sheet with parchment; sprinkle with 3 tablespoons cornmeal. Whisk together butter, eggs, sour cream, parsley, lemon juice, Worcestershire, paprika, cayenne, and salt in a large bowl. Gently mix in crab, peppers, and breadcrumbs.

Using your hands, shape crab mixture into 1½-inch patties. Place on prepared sheet. Once all patties have been formed, sprinkle evenly with remaining 3 tablespoons cornmeal. Cover with plastic wrap; chill 15 minutes.

Heat the oil in a large skillet over medium high. Working in batches, cook crab cakes until golden brown and cooked through, 4 to 5 minutes per side, adding more oil as needed. Transfer to a baking sheet, and keep warm in the oven. Serve with lemon wedges and tartar sauce.

Tarragon Tartar Sauce MAKES 2½ CUPS

- 2 cups mayonnaise
- ¼ cup plus 1 tablespoon sweet relish
- 2 tablespoons fresh lemon juice
- ¼ cup plus 2 tablespoons capers, drained and rinsed
- 2 tablespoons chopped fresh tarragon
  Coarse salt and freshly ground pepper

Stir together mayonnaise, relish, lemon juice, capers, and tarragon in a medium bowl. Season with salt and pepper. (Sauce can be refrigerated in an airtight container up to 1 week.)

JUMBO LUMP CRAB CAKES *with* CUCUMBER SALAD *and* DILL SAUCE
MAKES 8 *from* VERDANT SPRING DINNER

- 1 tablespoon olive oil
- ½ red bell pepper, ribs and seeds removed, diced
- ½ yellow bell pepper, ribs and seeds removed, diced
- ½ cup plain dried breadcrumbs
- 1 large egg, lightly beaten
- 1 pound jumbo lump crabmeat, picked over
- ¼ cup packed cilantro leaves, coarsely chopped
- 2 scallions, trimmed and coarsely chopped
- 1 jalapeño chile, diced (ribs and seeds removed for less heat, if desired)
- ⅓ cup mayonnaise
  Coarse salt and freshly ground pepper
- ½ cup neutral-tasting oil, such as safflower
  Cucumber Salad (recipe follows)
- 2 cups tender salad greens
- 1½ cups cherry tomatoes, halved
  Dill Dressing (recipe follows)

Preheat oven to 375° F. Heat olive oil in a small sauté pan over medium high. Cook bell peppers until tender, stirring occasionally, about 5 minutes. Transfer to a large bowl along with breadcrumbs, egg, crabmeat, cilantro, scallions, jalapeño, and mayonnaise. Season with salt and pepper, and gently mix to combine.

With your hands, form the mixture into 8 thick cakes, each 2 to 3 inches in diameter. Heat vegetable oil in a large skillet over medium-high. Sear crab cakes until golden brown, about 2 minutes per side. Transfer to a rimmed baking sheet, and bake until cooked through, 8 to 10 minutes.

To assemble, divide cucumber salad among plates, then top each with greens, a few halved tomatoes, and a crab cake. Serve dill dressing alongside.

Cucumber Salad MAKES 2½ CUPS

- 2 cucumbers
  Coarse salt and freshly ground pepper
- ¼ cup sour cream
- 2 tablespoons chopped fresh dill

Peel cucumbers and halve lengthwise, scraping seeds from halves with a small spoon (reserve peels, seeds, and liquid for Dill Dressing; recipe follows). Slice cucumbers thinly crosswise, then transfer to a colander in the sink. Sprinkle generously with salt, and let stand 30 minutes. Squeeze out excess liquid into a bowl (reserve) and transfer cucumbers to a bowl. Stir in sour cream and dill, and season with salt and pepper. Refrigerate, covered, until ready to serve, up to 2 hours.

Dill Dressing MAKES 1⅓ CUPS

- Reserved peels, seeds, and liquid from Cucumber Salad (recipe above), coarsely chopped
- ½ cup fromage blanc or sour cream
- ½ cup fresh dill
  Coarse salt and freshly ground pepper
- ¼ cup extra-virgin olive oil
- 1 tablespoon fresh lemon juice

Place reserved cucumber peels, seeds, and liquid in a saucepan, adding enough water to cover. Bring to a boil, then reduce heat, and simmer until peels are soft, about 15 minutes. Let cool. Purée in a blender until smooth. Add fromage blanc and dill, and season with salt and pepper; purée to combine. With the blender running, slowly add olive oil in a steady stream until emulsified. (Dressing can be refrigerated in an airtight container up to 1 day.) Just before serving, stir in lemon juice.

CURRIED CRAB PAPPADAMS
MAKES ABOUT 36 *from* SUMMER COCKTAIL PARTY

Mini pappadams can be found in Indian food markets and specialty stores. If you can't find the uncooked variety called for here, you can use the pre-cooked ones, but you may want to crisp them as instructed on the package.

- 2 cups neutral-tasting oil, such safflower, for frying
- ¼ package (13 ounces) plain (uncooked) mini pappadams
- 2 scallions, trimmed and finely diced
- 2 tablespoons mayonnaise
- ½ teaspoon curry powder, preferably Madras, toasted just until fragrant in a hot, dry pan
- 1 teaspoon finely grated lemon zest plus 1 teaspoon fresh lemon juice
- ¼ teaspoon coarse salt
- 8 ounces jumbo lump crabmeat, picked over
- ½ cup dessicated coconut, lightly toasted, for garnish

Heat oil in a small pot over medium low until it registers 325° F on a deep-fry thermometer. Fry pappadams in batches of 8 to 10, until they become crisp and the surface blisters, about 30 seconds. With a mesh spider or slotted spoon, remove to a paper towel–lined tray. Repeat with remaining pappadams. (Extra pappadams can be stored in an airtight container at room temperature for up to 6 months before frying.)

Combine scallions, mayonnaise, curry powder, lemon zest and juice, and salt in a bowl; mix well. Gently fold in crabmeat, keeping some large chunks.

To serve, spoon 1 tablespoon crab mixture onto center of each pappadam, and sprinkle with toasted coconut.

SALMON *and* VEGETABLE MINI CAKES

MAKES 24 *from* **EASTER EGG HUNT**

2 large russet potatoes, peeled and cut into 1-inch chunks
   Coarse salt and freshly ground pepper
2 tablespoons unsalted butter
2 carrots, peeled and finely diced
2 celery stalks, finely diced
6 ounces baby spinach (about 6 cups), coarsely chopped
1 pound skinless salmon fillets, cut into small dice
¼ cup plus 3 tablespoons extra-virgin olive oil
⅓ cup chopped fresh chervil (from 1 small bunch)
⅓ cup finely chopped fresh chives
½ cup all-purpose flour
2 large eggs, lightly beaten
1 cup panko (Japanese breadcrumbs)
   Zucchini Ribbons (optional; recipe follows)

Place potatoes in a large saucepan with enough cold water to cover by 1 inch; bring to a boil and add salt. Reduce heat, and simmer until potatoes are fork-tender, about 10 minutes. Drain in a colander; let dry completely.

Melt butter in a medium sauté pan over medium-high heat. Cook carrots and celery, stirring frequently, just until tender, 2 to 3 minutes. Add spinach and salmon, and season with salt and pepper. Cook, stirring occasionally, until fish is opaque throughout, about 5 minutes. Remove from heat.

Transfer potatoes to a large bowl; drizzle with 3 tablespoons olive oil. Mash to combine. Add salmon mixture, chervil, chives, and 1 tablespoon olive oil; season with salt and pepper. Stir well and let cool. Form mixture into 2-inch squares, about 1 inch thick. Place on a parchment-lined baking sheet.

Place flour, eggs, and panko in three separate shallow dishes. Dredge salmon cakes in flour to coat, tapping off excess; return to baking sheet. Dip each square in egg, letting excess drip back into bowl; dip in panko, gently pressing to adhere. Return cakes to baking sheet, reshaping as needed.

Heat remaining 3 tablespoons olive oil in a large skillet over medium high. Fry the salmon cakes in two batches until golden brown, 1 to 2 minutes per side. Transfer salmon cakes to a platter. If desired, wrap each cake in a zucchini ribbon, tucking ends under. Serve warm.

Zucchini Ribbons MAKES 24

1 medium zucchini
   Coarse salt

With a vegetable peeler, remove skin of zucchini in long, 1-inch-wide strips. (Reserve flesh for another use.) Blanch strips in a saucepan of boiling salted water until bright green, about 1 minute. Transfer to a colander to drain, then run under cold water to stop the cooking. Pat dry. Cut strips lengthwise into twenty-four ¼-inch-wide ribbons.

BAKED STUFFED CLAMS

SERVES 8 *from* **BURGUNDY DINNER**

At the Burgundy Dinner, the clams were nestled in a coil of seaweed on each plate, but you could simply serve them on their own.

2 tablespoons olive oil
1 small red onion, coarsely chopped
5 garlic cloves, crushed
1 cup dry white wine
16 cherrystone or littleneck clams (each about 3 inches wide)
   Herbed Breadcrumb Stuffing (recipe follows)
   Chorizo Stuffing (recipe follows)
   Seaweed, for garnish (optional)

Heat olive oil in a pot over medium high. Cook onion until softened but not browned, stirring occasionally, about 5 minutes. Add garlic, and sauté, stirring, just until fragrant, about 1 minute.

Add wine, and bring to a simmer. Add clams, and stir to combine. Cover and steam until clams have opened, 5 to 7 minutes. Remove from heat. Use a slotted spoon to transfer clams to a rimmed baking sheet to cool, discarding any that do not open. Strain clam broth through a fine sieve, and reserve for making stuffings.

When clams are cool enough to handle, remove all meat, and reserve. Remove half of each clam shell, and discard. Arrange the remaining halves on a rimmed baking sheet. Cut each clam into ½-inch pieces; return pieces to shell. (Clams can be prepared to this point up to 1 day ahead. Cover with plastic wrap and refrigerate.)

Preheat oven to 350° F. Dividing evenly, press each type of stuffing into half of the clam shells, smoothing with the back of a spoon. Bake until tops are golden, 25 to 30 minutes. Arrange one of each kind of stuffed clam on individual plates; garnish with seaweed, if desired, and serve immediately.

Herbed Breadcrumb Stuffing

MAKES ENOUGH FOR 8 SERVINGS

2 tablespoons extra-virgin olive oil
½ medium white onion, minced
2 garlic cloves, minced
½ cup almond flour (or finely ground blanched almonds)
1 cup fine fresh breadcrumbs
½ cup chopped fresh flat-leaf parsley
1 teaspoon chopped fresh thyme
1 tablespoon chopped fresh dill
½ teaspoon finely chopped fresh rosemary
4 tablespoons unsalted butter, softened
   Coarse salt and freshly ground pepper
4 to 6 tablespoons clam broth (reserved from steaming clams, recipe above)

Heat olive oil in a sauté pan. Cook onion until beginning to turn translucent, stirring frequently, about 3 minutes. Add garlic; cook until onion is completely translucent, stirring frequently, about 5 minutes more. Remove from heat, and let cool completely.

In a bowl, stir together onion mixture, almond flour, breadcrumbs, herbs, and butter; season with salt and pepper. Stir in just enough clam broth until stuffing is moist. (Stuffing can be refrigerated, covered, up to 1 day.)

Chorizo Stuffing MAKES ENOUGH FOR 8 SERVINGS

- 1 tomato, blanched and peeled (page 423), cut into ¼-inch dice
- 8 ounces Spanish chorizo, cut into ¼-inch dice
- 2 tablespoons olive oil
- ½ medium white onion, minced
- 2 garlic cloves, minced
- 1 cup fine fresh breadcrumbs
- 2 tablespoons chopped fresh flat-leaf parsley
- 1 teaspoon sweet Hungarian paprika
- 4 tablespoons unsalted butter, softened
  Coarse salt and freshly ground pepper
- 2 to 4 tablespoons clam broth (reserved from steaming clams, recipe opposite)

Drain tomato in a colander to remove excess liquid.

Heat a sauté pan over medium high, and cook chorizo until light golden brown and some fat has been rendered, stirring occasionally, 4 to 5 minutes. Remove chorizo with a slotted spoon.

Heat olive oil in same pan over medium high. Cook onion until beginning to turn translucent, stirring frequently, about 3 minutes. Add garlic, and sauté until onion is completely translucent, stirring frequently, about 5 minutes more. Remove from heat. Let cool completely.

In a bowl, stir together chorizo, onion mixture, breadcrumbs, parsley, tomato, paprika, and butter; season with salt and pepper. Stir in just enough clam broth until stuffing is moist but not soggy. (Stuffing can be refrigerated, covered, up to 1 day.)

BACALAO CROQUETTES

MAKES ABOUT 36   *from* SUMMER COCKTAIL PARTY

Aleppo pepper, made by crushing Turkish chiles, is a spicier, smokier alternative to supermarket-variety red-pepper flakes. Look for it at specialty shops and from online sources, such as Penzeys Spices. Pimentón, or smoked Spanish paprika, is another option. The croquette mixture can be made a day ahead and fried just before serving.

- 1 pound russet potatoes
  Coarse salt and freshly ground black pepper
- 10 ounces bacalao (dried salt cod), soaked 24 hours in cold water (changing water once)
- 2 cups milk, plus more if needed
- 5 garlic cloves
- ½ cup olive oil, plus more if needed
- ¼ cup heavy cream
- 1 large egg yolk
- ½ cup finely chopped fresh flat-leaf parsley
  Neutral-tasting oil, such as safflower, for frying
  Aleppo pepper or pimentón, for dusting

Peel potatoes; cut into 2-inch chunks. Combine potatoes with enough water to cover by ½ inch in a large saucepan; bring to a boil and add 1 tablespoon salt. Reduce heat; simmer until potatoes are fork-tender, about 20 minutes. Drain potatoes; pass through a potato ricer while still warm.

Break salt cod into 1-inch chunks. Place in a pot. Add enough milk to cover fish, and bring to a boil. Reduce heat to medium low; simmer 8 minutes. Remove from heat, and let stand 15 minutes. Drain cod, discarding milk.

In a small saucepan, combine garlic cloves and enough olive oil to cover. Cook over medium-low heat until garlic is soft throughout, 20 to 35 minutes. Garlic will bubble until it is cooked through. Remove garlic from oil with a slotted spoon, then crush with a large knife. Reserve garlic oil.

With an electric mixer, mix potatoes, cod, and crushed garlic on medium-low speed to combine. With the mixer running, add heavy cream in a steady stream, then add 3 tablespoons reserved garlic oil, and mix until combined. Season with salt and black pepper. Add egg yolk, and mix until incorporated. Fold in parsley. (Croquettes can be made to this point up to 1 day ahead and kept refrigerated in an airtight container.)

Preheat oven to 250° F. Heat 3 to 4 inches of vegetable oil in a medium pot over medium until a deep-fry thermometer registers 375° F. Gently drop 1 tablespoon cod mixture into oil with your fingertip or another spoon. Fry in batches of 4 until golden brown, about 2 minutes. Transfer to paper towels to drain, then dust with Aleppo pepper. Keep warm on a baking sheet in the oven while frying remaining batches. Serve warm.

SPICY SHRIMP *with* FRESH THYME

MAKES ABOUT 40   *from* SUMMER COCKTAIL PARTY

To butterfly the shrimp, use a paring knife to slice open each shrimp (along where the vein was removed) from head to tail, leaving tail intact; spread open flesh slightly.

- 1½ teaspoons celery seeds
- 1 teaspoon caraway seeds
- ¼ teaspoon crushed red-pepper flakes
- ¼ teaspoon cayenne
- 1 pound medium shrimp (40 to 50 count), peeled, deveined, and butterflied (see headnote)
- 4 garlic cloves, finely chopped
- 3 tablespoons extra-virgin olive oil
- 1 tablespoon finely chopped fresh thyme
- 1 teaspoon coarse salt
- 1 teaspoon Worcestershire sauce

Grind celery seeds, caraway seeds, red-pepper flakes, and cayenne in a spice grinder until finely ground, about 10 seconds.

In a large bowl, toss shrimp with ground spices, garlic, olive oil, thyme, salt, and Worcestershire. Cover, and refrigerate 1 hour to allow flavors to blend.

Preheat oven to 450° F. Arrange shrimp in a single layer on a rimmed baking sheet. Cook until edges are starting to curl and shrimp are opaque throughout, 7 to 10 minutes. Serve hot.

COQUILLES ST. JACQUES
SERVES 12 *from* **PEONY GARDEN PARTY**

For the peony party, the scallops were served in about two dozen three-inch scallop shells (available at craft stores and from online retailers), but larger shells or even small broiler-safe dishes would work as well. Adjust the amount in each vessel according to the size. If you can't find bay scallops, cut sea scallops into half-inch pieces.

- 3 tablespoons olive oil
- 1 pound bay scallops
  Coarse salt and freshly ground pepper
- ⅔ cup water
- ½ celery root, peeled and cut into ¼-inch dice
- 1 celery stalk, cut into ¼-inch dice
- 1 carrot, peeled and cut into ¼-inch dice
- 4 tablespoons unsalted butter
- 2 tablespoons plus 1½ teaspoons all-purpose flour
- 1½ cups milk
- ⅓ cup finely grated Parmigiano-Reggiano cheese (1 to 2 ounces)
- 2 tablespoons finely chopped fresh dill
- 2 tablespoons finely chopped fresh flat-leaf parsley

In a large sauté pan, heat 2 tablespoons olive oil over medium high until shimmering. Pat dry scallops, then season with salt and pepper. Sear until golden brown, turning once, about 3 minutes. Remove with a slotted spoon to a colander set over a bowl. Add ⅓ cup of the water to the sauté pan, stirring to scrape up browned bits. Reserve pan with liquid.

Heat remaining 1 tablespoon oil in a small sauté pan over medium. Cook celery root, celery, and carrot, stirring occasionally, until starting to soften, about 3 minutes. Add the remaining ⅓ cup water, and simmer, covered, until vegetables are tender, about 3 minutes. Uncover; cook until liquid is evaporated. Season with salt. Transfer to colander with scallops.

To make béchamel sauce, melt butter in a small saucepan over medium heat. Whisk in flour; cook, whisking, 1 minute (do not brown). Gradually whisk milk into flour mixture; simmer, whisking constantly, until thickened and smooth. Remove pan from heat. Whisk in Parmesan, then season with salt and pepper. Let béchamel sauce cool slightly.

Bring reserved scallop liquid to a simmer and cook until reduced to 2 to 3 tablespoons. Mixture will be slightly thickened and caramel-colored. Stir into béchamel sauce. In a bowl, stir together scallop-vegetable mixture, béchamel sauce, and herbs. (Scallop filling may be prepared to this point up to 1 day ahead. Let cool completely, then refrigerate, covered.)

Heat broiler, with rack 5 to 6 inches from heat. Arrange 3-inch scallop shells on a large rimmed baking sheet. Spoon 1 slightly heaping tablespoon of filling into each shell. Broil until top is bubbly and golden, rotating sheet halfway through, about 5 minutes (watch carefully toward end of broiling time to prevent burning). Serve immediately.

RED SNAPPER *and* CITRUS CEVICHE
SERVES 12 *from* **PEONY GARDEN PARTY**

The acid in the lime and orange juices "cooks" the fish in this Peruvian-style cold seafood starter. The ceviche was served in scallop shells, which you can find at craft stores and from online retailers.

- 2 limes
- 1 navel orange
- 1 pound red snapper fillets, skin removed, cut into ¼-inch dice
- ½ red onion, cut into ¼-inch dice
- 3 tomatoes (about 1 pound)
- 1 mango, peeled, pitted, and cut into ¼-inch dice
- ¼ cup packed cilantro leaves, finely chopped
- 1 teaspoon hot sauce, such as Tabasco, or to taste
  Coarse salt

Using a rasp-style grater, such as a Microplane, remove 1 teaspoon zest each from 1 lime and the orange into separate bowls. Squeeze juice from limes and orange into separate bowls. In a large nonreactive bowl, combine fish, zests, half the lime juice, and all the orange juice; toss to combine. Cover, and refrigerate for at least 1 hour, or up to 12 hours.

Meanwhile, soak onion in a bowl of cold water 10 minutes; drain well.

Peel tomatoes as described on page 423; when removing the pulp and seeds, work over a sieve set in a bowl. Reserve tomato quarters separately. Mash pulp with back of a spoon to extract as much tomato water as possible. Discard solids left in sieve. Cut tomato quarters into ¼-inch dice.

Add onion, diced tomato and tomato water, mango, cilantro, hot sauce, and remaining lime juice to fish, stirring gently to combine. Cover, and marinate in refrigerator 1 hour. Season with salt just before serving.

GRILLED SHRIMP *with* GUACAMOLE *and* CHIPOTLE RÉMOULADE
SERVES 6 TO 8 *from* **VERDANT SPRING DINNER**

Be sure to soak wooden skewers in water for an hour before grilling to prevent them from scorching.

- 1 pound large shrimp (30 to 40 count), peeled and deveined
  Olive oil
  Coarse salt and freshly ground pepper
  Guacamole, for serving (recipe follows)
  Chipotle Rémoulade, for serving (recipe follows)
  Cilantro leaves, for garnish

Heat grill to medium high (if using a charcoal grill, coals are ready when you can hold your hand 5 inches above grates for just 3 to 4 seconds). Thread one shrimp on each skewer. Drizzle with oil, and season with salt and pepper. Grill shrimp, flipping once, until seared on the outside and opaque throughout, about 2 minutes per side.

Arrange shrimp on a platter. Spoon a small amount of guacamole on top of each; dot with rémoulade. Garnish with cilantro, and serve.

Guacamole MAKES ¾ CUP

1 ripe avocado
1 tablespoon chopped shallot
1 small garlic clove, minced
2 tablespoons chopped cilantro
1 tablespoon plus 1½ teaspoons fresh lime juice
2 tablespoons extra-virgin olive oil
  Coarse salt and freshly ground pepper

Halve avocado lengthwise, remove pit, and scoop flesh into a bowl. Mash with a fork until smooth. Mix in shallot, garlic, cilantro, lime juice, and olive oil. Season with salt and pepper. Use immediately, or cover with plastic wrap, pressing it directly onto surface to prevent discoloration, and refrigerate up to 6 hours.

Chipotle Rémoulade MAKES ¾ CUP

1 to 2 canned chipotle chiles in adobo sauce
½ cup mayonnaise
1 tablespoon chopped shallot
1½ tablespoons fresh lime juice
  Coarse salt

Scrape seeds from chiles, and discard. Mince chiles, and stir together with mayonnaise, shallot, and lime juice in a bowl. Season with salt. (Sauce can be refrigerated, covered, up to 2 days.)

GRILLED PRAWNS with LEMONGRASS MARINADE

SERVES 4   from THE ART OF GRILLING

8 jumbo head-on prawns
1 lemongrass stalk, white and pale yellow parts only, thinly sliced on the diagonal
3 to 4 dried red chiles
1 teaspoon coriander seeds
4 garlic cloves, smashed
½ lime, thinly sliced
½ cup neutral-tasting oil, such as safflower
  Coarse salt and freshly ground pepper

Use a paring knife to cut along back of each prawn shell, leaving shell on and head intact; remove vein. Combine lemongrass, chiles, coriander, garlic, lime, and oil; pour marinade over prawns in a shallow nonreactive dish. Cover; refrigerate overnight.

Heat grill to medium high. (If using a charcoal grill, coals are ready when you can hold your hand 5 inches above grates for just 3 to 4 seconds.) Remove prawns from marinade, wiping off excess, and season with salt and pepper. (Discard marinade.) Grill until shell is slightly charred and prawns are cooked through, 3 to 4 minutes per side. Serve hot.

CHICKEN SKEWERS

MAKES 20   from EASTER EGG HUNT

2 pounds boneless, skinless chicken breast halves, cut into 1-inch strips
  Coarse salt
2 cups plain fresh breadcrumbs
2 large eggs
½ cup neutral-tasting oil, such as safflower

Pat dry chicken strips; season with salt. Stir breadcrumbs with 2 teaspoons salt. In another shallow bowl, lightly beat eggs with a fork. Add chicken to eggs, tossing to coat. Dredge, one strip at a time, in breadcrumbs. Arrange in a single layer on a parchment-lined rimmed baking sheet. (Chicken strips can be refrigerated, covered with plastic wrap, up to 1 day.)

In a large, heavy skillet, heat oil until shimmering. Cook chicken in two batches until golden brown, turning once, about 4 minutes. Transfer chicken to paper towels to drain. Insert skewers lengthwise into chicken, and serve.

STUFFED POTATO CRISPS with GRAVLAX

SERVES 8   from VERDANT SPRING DINNER

In a pinch, you can purchase good-quality gravlax at specialty food stores instead of making your own.

  Coarse salt and freshly ground pepper
1 pound fingerling or other small potatoes (about 1½ inches in diameter)
½ cup sour cream
2 tablespoons finely diced red bell pepper
1 tablespoon minced shallot
1 tablespoon minced fresh chives
1 teaspoon chopped fresh dill, plus sprigs for garnish
  Neutral-tasting oil, such as safflower, for frying
  Gravlax (page 327), thinly sliced

Preheat oven to 375° F. Spread an even layer of coarse salt on a rimmed baking sheet. Place the potatoes on top, and bake until tender when pierced with the tip of a sharp knife, 25 to 30 minutes, depending on their size.

When cool enough to handle, cut potatoes in half crosswise. Use a small melon baller or teaspoon to scoop out the flesh (and reserve), leaving a ⅛-inch border in the shells. Cut a small slice off the bottom of each potato shell so it will stand upright. Pass the flesh through a ricer, food mill, or wide-mesh sieve into a bowl. Stir in sour cream, bell pepper, shallot, chives, and dill. Season with salt and pepper. Place potato mixture in a pastry bag fitted with a medium plain tip (such as #7 or #8).

Heat 2 inches of oil in a medium, heavy-bottomed pot until a deep-fry thermometer registers 375° F. Working in batches, fry potato shells until golden and crisp, 1 to 2 minutes. Use a mesh spider or slotted spoon to transfer shells to paper towels to drain. Immediately season with salt and pepper.

Arrange potato shells on a serving tray. Pipe filling into shells. Top each with a thin slice of gravlax, and garnish with a sprig of dill. Serve immediately.

LAMB KEBABS

MAKES 12 *from* **THE ART OF GRILLING**

Garam masala, an Indian spice blend, and ras el hanout (literally "top of the shop"), a Moroccan mix of more than twenty ingredients, can be found at ethnic food markets and from online retailers, such as penzeys.com.

- 12 long rosemary stems
- 2 pounds ground lamb
- 1 garlic clove, minced
- 1 tablespoon garam masala
- 1 teaspoon ras el hanout
- 1 teaspoon ground cardamom
- ½ teaspoon ground cumin
- 1 tablespoon coarse salt

Heat grill to medium high. (If using a charcoal grill, coals are ready when you can hold your hand 5 inches above grates for just 3 to 4 seconds.) To prepare rosemary skewers, remove leaves from bottom two-thirds of rosemary stalks, leaving only top leaves intact. Finely chop 2 teaspoons removed leaves; discard the rest.

Gently mix lamb, garlic, garam masala, ras el hanout, cardamom, cumin, chopped rosemary, and salt. Form into 12 oblong patties (about 2 inches wide and 3 inches long). Make an indentation in middle of each patty, then place bare end of rosemary stalk on indentation; wrap patty completely around stalk and press to seal.

Grill until patties are cooked through, 4 to 5 minutes per side. Serve hot.

TURNOVERS *with* CHANTERELLES *and* FRESH HERBS

MAKES 8 *from* **EASTER DINNER**

- 2 tablespoons unsalted butter
- 1 shallot, thinly sliced
- 12 ounces fresh chanterelles, trimmed and wiped clean, very coarsely chopped
- 2 tablespoons coarsely chopped fresh flat-leaf parsley
- 1 teaspoon coarsely chopped fresh dill
- ½ teaspoon finely chopped fresh thyme
  Coarse salt and freshly ground pepper
- 1 large egg, lightly beaten
- 1 package (14 ounces) frozen all-butter puff pastry, such as Dufour, thawed in refrigerator
  All-purpose flour, for dusting

Melt butter in a medium sauté pan over medium heat. Sauté shallot until golden brown, stirring frequently, about 8 minutes. Add chanterelles, and cook over medium-high heat until tender and juices have evaporated, stirring occasionally, about 10 minutes. Remove from heat, stir in herbs, and season with salt and pepper. Let cool, then stir in 1 tablespoon beaten egg, reserving remaining for brushing pastry.

Unfold puff pastry on a lightly floured surface. With a floured rolling pin, roll out dough into a 10-by-17-inch rectangle. Trim to form an 8-by-16-inch rectangle. Halve lengthwise; quarter crosswise to make eight 4-inch squares.

Working with one pastry square at a time, brush edges of square with water. Place 1 to 2 tablespoons mushroom filling slightly off center on pastry square, and fold dough over filling, forming a triangle. Press to seal, and flute edges with a fork. Transfer turnover to a parchment-lined baking sheet, then repeat with remaining pastry squares and filling.

Brush turnovers with beaten egg, and refrigerate on a baking sheet 10 minutes. Brush once more with beaten egg, then refrigerate at least 30 minutes more, or up to 4 hours (covered with plastic wrap).

Preheat oven to 400° F. Bake turnovers until puffed and golden, rotating sheet halfway through, 20 to 25 minutes. Serve immediately.

PIGS *in a* BLANKET

MAKES 30 *from* **EASTER EGG HUNT**

- 1 package (14 ounces) frozen all-butter puff pastry, such as Dufour, thawed in refrigerator
  All-purpose flour, for dusting
- 10 all-beef hot dogs, each cut into thirds
- 1 large egg, lightly beaten

Unfold puff pastry on a lightly floured surface, and cut dough crosswise in half. Keep one half covered with a kitchen towel or plastic wrap while you work. With a lightly floured rolling pin, roll out other dough half to a 10-by-10½-inch rectangle. Cut rectangle lengthwise into five 2-inch-wide strips, then cut each strip crosswise into three 3½-inch-long strips (to make 15 strips total). Repeat with remaining dough half.

Preheat oven to 375° F. Roll each hot dog piece in pastry; brush edges with beaten egg to seal. Place on a parchment-lined baking sheet. Refrigerate until dough is firm, about 20 minutes (or up to 1 day, covered with plastic).

Just before baking, brush pastry with remaining egg wash. Bake until pastry is puffed and golden brown, 20 to 30 minutes. Serve warm.

SAGE POTATO CHIPS

MAKES ABOUT 50 *from* **SUMMER COCKTAIL PARTY**

You will need a mandoline (or other adjustable-blade slicer) to slice the potatoes paper-thin; an inexpensive plastic model, such as Benriner, will work just fine.

- 4 russet potatoes (about 1½ pounds)
- 2 large egg yolks
- ¼ cup cornstarch
- 2 teaspoons water
- 1 bunch fresh sage, larger leaves torn
  Neutral-tasting oil, such as safflower, for frying
  Coarse salt

Peel potatoes and slice as thin as possible on a mandoline. Soak briefly in a bowl of cool water, then pat dry.

Whisk together egg yolks, cornstarch, and the water. Lay 10 potato slices on a clean surface, and brush with egg-yolk mixture. Top with a sage leaf and another potato slice, pressing slices together firmly to adhere. Repeat with remaining potato slices and sage leaves.

Heat 2 inches of oil in a medium pot over medium heat until a deep-fry thermometer registers 300° F. Working in batches of 5, gently add potatoes to the hot oil, and cook 30 seconds, just to soften. Using a mesh spider or slotted spoon, transfer chips to paper towels to drain, then repeat with remaining potatoes, maintaining oil at 300° F.

Raise heat so oil reaches 350° F, and fry chips again, in batches of 10, until golden brown. Transfer to paper towels to drain, spreading in a single layer, and immediately season with salt. Serve warm.

TORTILLA CHIPS TOPPED *with* GRILLED CORN *and* CHEDDAR

MAKES 24 *from* **SUMMER COCKTAIL PARTY**

- 2 ears of corn, husked
  Extra-virgin olive oil, for brushing
  Coarse salt and freshly ground pepper
- 1 to 2 jalapeño chiles
- 1 scallion, trimmed and thinly sliced
- 2 tablespoons minced cilantro, plus sprigs for garnish
- 1 tablespoon fresh lime juice
- 4 ounces cheddar cheese, grated (1¾ cups)
- 24 tortilla chips

Heat grill to medium high. (If you are using a charcoal grill, coals are ready when you can hold your hand 5 inches above grates for just 3 to 4 seconds.) Brush corn with oil, and season with salt and pepper. Grill corn and chiles, turning occasionally, until corn is tender and jalapeños are blackened all over, about 10 minutes. Let cool slightly.

Shave corn kernels from cobs, and place in a bowl. Use paper towels to rub off skins from jalapeños, then remove ribs and seeds; cut chiles into fine dice. Add to corn, along with the scallion, minced cilantro, lime juice, and 1¼ cups cheese. Toss to combine.

Heat broiler, with rack 4 inches from heat. Arrange chips in a single layer on a rimmed baking sheet. Top each chip with a tablespoon of corn mixture. Sprinkle remaining ½ cup cheese evenly over chips. Broil until cheese is bubbly, about 30 seconds. Garnish with cilantro sprigs; serve immediately.

SCOTCH EGGS

MAKES 6 *from* **PICNIC AT SEA**

- 1 pound ground pork
- 1¼ cups plain fresh breadcrumbs
- 8 medium eggs; 2 raw, 6 hard-cooked (page 423) and peeled
- 1 teaspoon dried thyme
- 1 teaspoon ground allspice
  Coarse salt and freshly ground pepper
  All-purpose flour, for dusting
- 3 tablespoons milk
- 6 cups neutral-tasting oil, such as safflower, for frying

In a bowl, combine pork, ¼ cup breadcrumbs, 1 raw egg, the thyme, and allspice; season with salt and pepper. Mix gently with your hands to combine. Use dampened hands to form a 2-inch piece (about 3 ounces) of meat mixture, and flatten into a patty. Place a hard-cooked egg in center of patty, and work meat mixture up sides until egg is completely enclosed. Repeat with remaining meat mixture and cooked eggs.

Dust each patty with flour. Whisk together remaining raw egg and the milk in a shallow bowl. Place remaining 1 cup breadcrumbs in another shallow bowl. Roll patty in milk mixture and then in breadcrumbs to coat.

Heat the oil in a large, heavy saucepan until a deep-fry thermometer registers 360° F. Working in two batches, fry eggs until meat mixture is golden and cooked through, about 6 minutes. Use a mesh spider or slotted spoon to transfer to a plate lined with paper towels to drain. Serve warm or at room temperature.

DEVILED EGGS

MAKES 20 *from* **EASTER EGG HUNT**

- 10 large eggs, hard-cooked (page 423)
- ½ cup mayonnaise
- 2 teaspoons Dijon mustard
  Coarse salt and freshly ground pepper
- 5 chives, snipped into 1-inch lengths, for garnish
  Zucchini and Carrot Bunnies (recipe follows)

Peel eggs, cut in half lengthwise, and transfer yolks to a bowl. With a fork, mash yolks with mayonnaise and mustard, and season with salt and pepper. Transfer to a pastry bag fitted with a small star tip (such as #18) and pipe mixture onto egg whites. Garnish with chives and vegetable bunnies.

Zucchini and Carrot Bunnies

MAKES ENOUGH FOR 20 DEVILED EGGS

Animal-shaped aspic cutter sets are available at baking supply stores and online specialty retailers. A Japanese cutter was used to cut out bunny shapes from the blanched vegetables for the Easter Egg Hunt.

- 1 large carrot, peeled
- 1 medium zucchini
  Coarse salt

Cut carrot into ⅛-inch-thick slices on the bias. Cut one 1-inch-wide-by-⅛-inch-thick lengthwise slice from zucchini. Turn cut side down and continue to cut more slices in the same manner, turning after each slice (discard middle portion).

Blanch vegetable slices in a saucepan of boiling salted water just until tender, 2 to 3 minutes. Transfer to paper towels to drain. Use small bunny-shaped aspic cutters to cut out shapes.

OEUFS *en* GELÉE

MAKES 8 *from* **EASTER DINNER**

for the consommé
- 2 onions, peeled and halved
- 2 pounds boneless top round of beef
- 2 celery stalks, halved
- 2 carrots, peeled and halved
- Coarse salt

for the garnishes
- 1 large carrot, peeled
- 1 small zucchini
- 1 tablespoon fresh lemon juice
- ½ small celery root
- Coarse salt

for assembly
- 1 tablespoon plus 1 teaspoon unflavored powdered gelatin
- ¼ cup cold water
- 8 Perfect Poached Eggs (page 328, using medium eggs)

Make the consommé: Heat a cast-iron skillet over high. Add onions, cut side down, and cook, undisturbed, until blackened on cut side, about 10 minutes.

Meanwhile, place beef in a medium pot, and add enough water to cover. Bring to a boil, then drain in a colander. Rinse out pot, and return the meat, along with the onions, celery, carrots, and enough water to cover by 2 inches. Bring almost to a boil over medium-high heat, then reduce to a simmer (a candy thermometer should register between 200° F to 210° F). Cook, skimming off foam frequently, 4 hours.

Remove meat from pot, and pour broth through a fine sieve lined with cheesecloth into a clean pot, discarding vegetables. Cut meat into ¼-inch dice; you will need at least 2 cups.

Prepare the garnishes: Cut carrot into ⅛-inch-thick slices on the bias. Cut one 1-inch-wide-by-⅛-inch-thick lengthwise slice from zucchini. Turn cut side down, and continue to cut more slices in the same manner, turning after every slice (discard middle portion). Add lemon juice to a bowl of water. Peel celery root, and cut into ⅛-inch-thick slices, dropping slices into lemon water to prevent browning. With an aspic cutter, cut eight decorative shapes (such as bunnies) from slices of each vegetable, and cut scraps into ⅛-inch dice. Return celery root to acidulated water after cutting.

Working with one type of vegetable at a time, blanch shapes in a pot of boiling salted water just until tender, about 2 minutes each, using a slotted spoon to transfer them to a kitchen towel or paper towels to drain.

Cook diced vegetables in same pot 1 minute, transferring to a fine sieve to drain well. Transfer to a small bowl, and add diced meat, mixing to combine.

Assemble the dishes: Simmer strained broth until reduced to 3 cups, and season with salt. Stir gelatin into the cold water and let soften for 5 minutes, then stir into hot broth until dissolved.

Place eight 4-ounce ramekins or other small baking dishes on a rimmed baking sheet. Add 1 tablespoon of broth with gelatin to each mold. Refrigerate until set, about 30 minutes.

Add vegetable garnishes to molds; spoon about 1 tablespoon more broth with gelatin over vegetables. Refrigerate again until set, about 30 minutes.

Place a poached egg in each mold, and surround with about 2 tablespoons meat-vegetable mixture. Add enough broth to fill molds to rim. Return to refrigerator until set, at least 4 hours (or up to 1 day, covered with plastic).

To unmold, dip bottoms of ramekins in warm water for several seconds to loosen, then invert onto a serving platter. Serve at room temperature.

CHICKEN DRUMETTES *with* SWEET-*and*-SPICY ORANGE GLAZE

MAKES 36 *from* **SUMMER COCKTAIL PARTY**

Drumettes are the first length of the chicken wing; once prepared, they look like mini drumsticks—just the right size for cocktail nibbles.

- 3 pounds chicken drumettes
- 2 tablespoons olive oil
- 2 teaspoons coarse salt
- Finely grated zest of 1 lime
- Finely grated zest of 1 lemon
- 3 blood oranges
- ⅓ cup sugar
- 1 teaspoon water
- 3 tablespoons light corn syrup
- 1 teaspoon finely chopped peeled fresh ginger
- 2 teaspoons Asian hot chili sauce, such as Sriracha
- ¼ teaspoon cayenne

Preheat oven to 450° F. Using poultry shears or a very sharp, heavy knife, cut off the wing-tip joint of the drumette at the tip of the bone. Pull meat halfway down over the other end to expose the bone.

In a large bowl, toss chicken with the olive oil, salt, and half the lemon and lime zests. Spread evenly on a rimmed baking sheet. Roast until cooked through and golden brown, flipping halfway through, about 30 minutes.

Meanwhile, slice off top and bottom ends of blood oranges with a paring knife. Following the curve of the fruit, and working from top to bottom, remove peel and bitter white pith. Working over a bowl to catch the juices, cut between membranes to remove whole segments. Once segments have been removed, squeeze membranes over bowl to extract juice. Coarsely chop segments; place in a fine sieve set over the bowl to drain, gently pressing down on oranges to release more juice (to yield ½ cup juice).

In a saucepan, bring sugar and the water to a boil over medium-high heat, stirring until sugar is dissolved. Stop stirring, and boil until mixture is light amber, brushing down sides of pan with a pastry brush dipped in water to prevent sugar crystals from forming. Remove from heat, and carefully pour in blood-orange juice (mixture will spatter). Return to heat, and cook until liquid is reduced by half, about 4 minutes. Stir in corn syrup, and continue cooking until mixture is thickened to a glaze, about 3 minutes more. Remove from heat, and add ginger, chili sauce, and cayenne.

Remove chicken from oven, and pour citrus glaze evenly on top. Sprinkle with orange segments and remaining zests, and toss to coat. Return to oven, and cook until glaze has set, 3 to 5 minutes. Serve hot.

CHICKEN SALPICÓN

SERVES 12 *from* **PEONY GARDEN PARTY**

Salpicón, a mixture of vegetables and chicken or seafood, is a popular appetizer in South America and Mexico. This dish can be prepared in stages: The potatoes can be fried two days ahead and refrigerated in a paper towel–lined airtight container; the chicken can be cooked the day before serving, and refrigerated as instructed below; and the haricots verts, carrots, and onion can be cut or grated the morning of the party, then refrigerated in separate covered containers until ready to use.

for the chicken

- 4 large bone-in, skin-on chicken breast halves (about 3 pounds)
  Coarse salt and freshly ground pepper
- 2 tablespoons extra-virgin olive oil, plus more if needed
- 1 large onion, chopped
- 3 garlic cloves, finely chopped
- 1 tablespoon sweet Hungarian paprika
- 2 cups water

for the vegetables

- 4 large boiling potatoes (about 2 pounds)
  Neutral-tasting oil, such as safflower, for frying
  Coarse salt
- ½ pound haricots verts, trimmed and cut into ¼-inch pieces
- 2 large carrots, peeled, coarsely grated, and squeezed of excess moisture
- 1 large white onion, halved lengthwise, then thinly sliced into half-moons
- ¼ cup fresh flat-leaf parsley leaves, finely chopped
- ¼ cup plus 1 tablespoon mayonnaise
  Juice of 1 lemon
  Freshly ground pepper

Cook the chicken: Rinse chicken breasts and pat dry, then season generously on both sides with salt and pepper. Heat 2 tablespoons olive oil in a large, heavy pot over medium high until it shimmers. Sear chicken until golden, about 2 minutes per side. Transfer chicken to a bowl. Add onion and garlic to pot (adding more oil, if necessary), and sauté until tender, stirring frequently, about 3 minutes. Add paprika, and cook, stirring, 1 minute more. Stir in the water, scraping up browned bits from bottom of pot with a wooden spoon. Return chicken and any accumulated juices to pot, and simmer over medium heat, covered, until chicken is cooked through, about 20 minutes. Transfer chicken to a large bowl.

Simmer mixture remaining in pot (uncovered) until reduced by about half, about 10 minutes. Strain through a fine sieve into a bowl, discarding solids.

When chicken is cool enough to handle, discard skin and bones, and shred the meat with your fingers or a fork. In a bowl, toss chicken with strained cooking liquid. Cover; refrigerate until chilled, at least 1 hour or up to 1 day.

Prepare the vegetables: Peel potatoes and grate on the large holes of a box grater. Rinse in cold water, drain well, and squeeze to remove excess moisture. In a medium pot, heat 1½ inches of vegetable oil to 375° F on a deep-fry thermometer. Working in batches, gradually sprinkle one handful of shredded potatoes into hot oil, and fry, stirring occasionally, until golden brown, 3 to 4 minutes. (If you add a handful all at once, the oil may overflow.) With a mesh spider or slotted spoon, transfer fried potatoes

to a paper towel–lined baking sheet to drain. Return oil to 375° F between batches, and add more oil as needed. Season fried potatoes with salt.

Blanch haricots verts in a saucepan of salted boiling water until crisp-tender and bright green, about 1 minute. Transfer to a colander, and rinse with cold water to stop the cooking. Drain well and pat dry.

Toss together chicken, potatoes, haricots verts, carrots, onion, parsley, mayonnaise, and lemon juice in a bowl. Season with salt and pepper. Divide among small plates and serve.

PEA *and* HAM QUICHE

MAKES TWO 8-INCH TARTS OR ONE 10-INCH TART *from* **PEONY GARDEN PARTY**

If you do not have two eight-inch tart pans, you can follow the recipe to make one ten-inch tart. In this case, do not divide the dough in half, and roll it out to a fourteen-inch round.

   Pâte Brisée (page 421)
   All-purpose flour, for dusting
- 1 tablespoon olive oil
- ½ onion, diced
- 2¼ cups fresh shelled or thawed frozen peas (10 ounces)
- ¾ cup milk
- 1 cup heavy cream
   Coarse salt and freshly ground pepper
- 3 large whole eggs plus 2 large yolks
- 4 ounces cooked ham, cut into ¼-inch dice (about ⅔ cup)

Preheat oven to 400° F. Divide dough in half. On a lightly floured surface, roll out one piece of dough into a 10-inch round. Fit into an 8-inch round tart pan with a removable bottom, then trim dough to a 1-inch overhang and fold over to make a double-thick edge. Repeat with remaining piece of dough and another tart pan. Pierce bottom of dough all over with a fork. Freeze until firm, about 15 minutes.

Line tart shells with parchment, and fill with pie weights or dried beans. Bake until crust is firm around the edges, about 20 minutes. Remove parchment and weights. Reduce oven to 375° F, and continue baking until crust is pale golden, 10 to 15 minutes. Let cool on a wire rack.

While tart shells are baking, heat olive oil in a heavy saucepan over medium high. Cook onion, stirring frequently, until tender, about 3 minutes. Reserve ½ cup peas and add remaining peas to pan; cook 2 minutes more. Stir in milk and heavy cream, and simmer over medium-low heat for 10 minutes. Season with salt and pepper, and remove from heat. Let cool slightly before puréeing in a blender, then strain through a fine sieve; discard solids. Whisk together eggs and yolks in a large bowl, and gradually stir in pea purée.

Place tart shells on a rimmed baking sheet. Dividing evenly, sprinkle each with ham and reserved peas; pour in egg mixture. Bake until center is set and top is slighty puffed, 20 to 25 minutes. Transfer to a wire rack to cool before cutting into thin wedges. Serve warm or at room temperature.

BARBAGIUAN MONEGASQUE

MAKES 24 DUMPLINGS *from* **PEONY GARDEN PARTY**

These vegetable-and-sausage dumplings are a specialty in Monaco at Christmastime. They can be assembled and frozen in an airtight container, between sheets of parchment paper, for up to three months. Omit the sausage for a vegetarian version.

- 2 tablespoons olive oil
- 3 pork breakfast sausages (3 ounces), casings removed
- 1 small leek, halved lengthwise, thinly sliced crosswise, washed well and drained
- 1 zucchini, cut into ¼-inch dice
- ½ large bunch spinach, trimmed and washed, water still clinging to leaves
- 1 red bell pepper, roasted (page 423) and cut into ¼-inch dice
- ¼ cup packed fresh flat-leaf parsley leaves, finely chopped
- ¼ cup finely grated Parmigiano-Reggiano cheese (1 ounce)
- 3 tablespoons fresh ricotta cheese
  Coarse salt and freshly ground pepper
  Olive Oil Dough (recipe follows)
  All-purpose flour, for dusting
- 1 large egg, lightly beaten
  Neutral-tasting oil, such as safflower, for frying

Heat the olive oil in a skillet over medium high. Cook sausage, breaking it into small pieces with a spoon, until browned, 3 to 4 minutes. Add leek and zucchini; cook, stirring frequently, until tender, about 4 minutes. Transfer to a bowl. Wipe skillet clean. Add spinach and cook over medium heat until just wilted and water has evaporated. Let cool, then coarsely chop and squeeze to remove excess moisture. Add to sausage mixture, then stir in bell pepper, parsley, Parmesan, and ricotta. Season with salt and pepper.

Divide the dough into quarters. Work with one portion of dough at a time, and keep remaining dough covered with plastic wrap to prevent it from drying out. Roll dough through consecutively smaller settings on a pasta machine, starting with the largest setting and ending with the second finest one. (When finished rolling, dough should be about ¹⁄₁₆ inch thick and about 14 inches long.) If dough begins to stick at any time, dust with flour. Cover and stack dough sheets with plastic wrap as they are rolled out.

Lay one dough sheet on a lightly floured work surface. Drop slightly rounded tablespoons of filling every 2 inches along lower half of dough. Brush beaten egg around filling, then fold top half of dough over filling, pressing to seal. Use a sharp knife to cut around filling on sealed side to create half-moon-shaped dumplings. Place dumplings on a floured rimmed baking sheet, and cover with plastic wrap. Repeat rolling, assembling, and cutting with remaining dough sheets and filling. (Dumplings can be refrigerated, covered with plastic wrap, up to 4 hours. Or freeze until firm, then transfer to a resealable plastic bag, and freeze for up to 3 months; thaw in the refrigerator before frying.)

Heat 2 to 3 inches of vegetable oil in a small heavy-bottomed pot until 375° F on a deep-fry thermometer. Fry dumplings in batches of four or five until golden brown, about 2 minutes, turning halfway through. Return oil to 375° F between batches, and add more oil as needed. Use a mesh spider or slotted spoon to transfer dumplings to paper towels to drain. Serve immediately.

Olive Oil Dough MAKES ENOUGH DOUGH FOR 24 DUMPLINGS

- 1 cup all-purpose flour
- 2 tablespoons olive oil
- 1 large egg
- ½ teaspoon coarse salt
- 1 tablespoon ice water, plus more if needed

Pulse all ingredients in a food processor until dough holds together and is slightly sticky. If dough is too dry, add more water, 1 teaspoon at a time, pulsing to incorporate. Knead 6 times by hand. Wrap in a damp kitchen towel, and place in the refrigerator; let rest 20 minutes before using.

CHILLED CAULIFLOWER COCONUT CURRY

SERVES 12 *from* **PEONY GARDEN PARTY**

At the garden party, the individual serving dishes were lined with shiso leaves (available at Asian markets), but you could use mint leaves instead. Look for unsweetened coconut flakes, such as from Bob's Red Mill, at natural food stores and some supermarkets.

for the cauliflower
- 2 small heads cauliflower (about 1 pound each), trimmed and cut into bite-size florets
- 2 tablespoons extra-virgin olive oil
  Coarse salt and freshly ground pepper

for the curry sauce
- 1 tablespoon extra-virgin olive oil
- 1 onion, cut into 1-inch pieces
- 3 garlic cloves, minced
- 1 piece (1½ inches) fresh ginger, peeled and thinly sliced
- 2 teaspoons curry powder, preferably Madras
- 3 tomatoes (about 1 pound), quartered
- ¼ cup plain Greek-style yogurt
- 2 tablespoons chopped cilantro, plus sprigs for garnish
- 1 cup water
  Coarse salt

for the garnish
- ⅓ cup unsweetened coconut flakes
- ⅓ cup roasted salted peanuts
- ⅓ cup raisins

Roast the cauliflower: Preheat oven to 350° F. On a rimmed baking sheet, toss cauliflower with the olive oil, and season with salt and pepper. Spread in an even layer, and roast until florets are light golden and just tender, 20 to 30 minutes, rotating sheet halfway through. Remove from oven.

Meanwhile, make the curry sauce: Heat olive oil in a saucepan over medium high. Cook onion, garlic, and ginger, stirring frequently, until softened, about 5 minutes. Stir in curry powder; cook, stirring, 1 minute. Add tomatoes, and continue to cook, stirring occasionally, 2 minutes. Stir in yogurt, cilantro, and the water; simmer (uncovered) until slightly thickened, about 15 minutes. Don't worry if yogurt separates during cooking; it will come together again when blended. Let cool slightly, then purée with an immersion blender or a standard blender. Season with salt. You should have about 1¼ cups sauce.

Make the garnish: Pulse coconut and peanuts in a food processor or spice grinder until coarsely ground. Add raisins; pulse until coarsely chopped.

Bake the curry: Reserve ¼ cup curry sauce for garnish, and refrigerate, covered. Pour remaining sauce over cauliflower on the baking sheet, tossing to coat. Bake until florets are very tender when pierced with the tip of a knife, about 20 minutes. Remove from oven, and season with salt. Let cool, then transfer to an airtight container and chill, at least 1 hour or up to 1 day.

To serve, divide cauliflower among plates; drizzle with reserved sauce, and sprinkle with coconut garnish.

SPICY LAMB BALLS *with* YOGURT-CUCUMBER SAUCE

MAKES ABOUT 20 *from* **PEONY GARDEN PARTY**

¼ cup olive oil, plus more if needed
1 onion, finely chopped
2 garlic cloves, minced
1 teaspoon finely chopped fresh oregano
1 pound ground lamb
1 teaspoon finely chopped fresh mint, plus whole leaves for garnish
¼ cup finely chopped fresh flat-leaf parsley
1 teaspoon coarse salt
½ teaspoon toasted sesame oil
1 teaspoon Asian hot chili sauce, such as Sriracha
Yogurt-Cucumber Sauce, for serving (recipe follows)

Heat 2 tablespoons olive oil in a large, heavy skillet over medium high. Add onion, garlic, and oregano; cook, stirring frequently, until onion is translucent, 3 to 5 minutes. Let cool, then transfer to a medium bowl along with the lamb, chopped mint and parsley, salt, sesame oil, and chili sauce. Stir to combine thoroughly, then gently form into 1-inch balls. (Meatballs can be made to this point up to 1 day ahead. Cover tightly with plastic wrap and refrigerate. Bring to room temperature before proceeding.)

Heat remaining 2 tablespoons olive oil in same skillet over medium high. Cook meatballs in batches, turning occasionally, until well browned on all sides and cooked through, 5 to 7 minutes. Transfer to a paper towel–lined plate to drain. Add more oil between batches as needed.

To serve, top each meatball with a dollop of yogurt sauce and a mint leaf.

Yogurt-Cucumber Sauce MAKES ¾ CUP

1 Kirby cucumber, peeled, halved lengthwise, seeded, and finely diced
2 tablespoons finely chopped onion
½ cup plain Greek-style yogurt
1 tablespoon fresh mint leaves, finely chopped
1½ teaspoons fresh lime juice
Coarse salt and freshly ground pepper

Wrap diced cucumber in a clean kitchen towel; squeeze to remove excess liquid. Stir together cucumber, onion, yogurt, mint, and lime juice in a bowl; season with salt and pepper. Serve chilled or at room temperature.

VEGETABLE TERRINE

MAKES ONE 6-CUP TERRINE *from* **PÂTÉ CAMPAGNARD LUNCH**

4 large carrots, trimmed and peeled (trimmings reserved)
3 large parsnips, trimmed and peeled (trimmings reserved)
3 leeks, white and pale green parts only, washed well (trimmings reserved)
1 celery root, trimmed and peeled (trimmings reserved)
4 zucchini, halved lengthwise, seeds scooped out
1½ teaspoons unflavored powdered gelatin
⅓ cup cold water
⅓ cup chopped fresh flat-leaf parsley
Coarse salt and freshly ground pepper

Make a stock by placing vegetable trimmings in a large pot, and covering with water by 3 inches. Bring to a boil, reduce heat, and simmer 1 hour.

Place carrots, parsnips, leeks, and celery root in another pot, and strain stock through a fine sieve into pot (discard trimmings). If necessary, add enough water to just cover vegetables. Cover pot, and bring to a boil, then reduce to a simmer. Cook until vegetables are very tender when pierced with a sharp knife, 35 to 40 minutes.

Meanwhile, line a 6-cup terrine mold with plastic wrap, leaving overhang on all sides. (If necessary, sprinkle mold with water to help plastic adhere.) Cut a piece of cardboard to fit in top of mold and wrap it with foil.

Place zucchini on top of vegetable mixture in pot; cover, and cook until tender, 6 to 7 minutes. Using a slotted spoon, transfer zucchini to a rimmed baking sheet; immediately place in the refrigerator to cool quickly (to set the color). Use tongs to remove remaining vegetables from pot, and let cool on another baking sheet.

Raise heat, and boil cooking liquid until reduced to 2 cups, about 20 minutes. Remove from heat. In a small bowl, mix gelatin with the cold water, and let stand 5 minutes. Remove ¾ cup cooking liquid from pot, and reserve. Add softened gelatin to remaining 1¼ cups liquid in pot, and cook over medium-high heat, stirring, until gelatin has completely dissolved. Remove from heat; stir in parsley and ½ teaspoon salt. Cover to keep warm.

Squeeze vegetables to remove excess moisture. Halve celery root lengthwise, then slice into ¼-inch-thick half-moons. Slice carrots and parsnips lengthwise into ¼-inch-thick strips. Halve leeks crosswise (to fit lengthwise in mold). Working with one kind at a time, layer vegetables lengthwise in terrine, pressing to fill snugly; season each layer with salt, and cover with 2 to 4 tablespoons gelatin mixture (you may not have to use all the liquid).

Wrap plastic overhang from long sides tightly over the top, tucking inside terrine, then wrap short sides of plastic over the top. Use a sharp knife to poke several holes in plastic wrap, and squeeze out additional gelatin mixture. Press foil-wrapped cardboard onto top of terrine, and weight evenly with canned goods. Refrigerate 1 day.

Remove terrine from refrigerator, and remove cardboard and weights; let sit at room temperature 1 hour. Unwrap plastic from top and run a paring knife around the edge of the terrine; unmold onto a serving platter or cutting board and peel off plastic wrap. Slice terrine ¼ to ½ inch thick with a sharp knife, dipping knife in hot water before each slice.

YUCCA CHEESE PUFFS

MAKES ABOUT 24 *from* **SUMMER COCKTAIL PARTY**

Polvilho is a type of yucca (cassava) flour popular in Brazilian cooking; look for it at specialty stores or from online sources, where it may also be called manioc. Tapioca flour can be substituted. These traditional Brazilian snacks are otherwise known as pão de queijo, or cheese bread.

- 2½ to 3 cups polvilho or tapioca flour
- 1½ teaspoons coarse salt
- ½ cup water
- ½ cup olive oil, plus more for hands
- 2 large eggs
- 1½ cups coarsely grated Parmigiano-Reggiano cheese (6 ounces)

Preheat oven to 375° F, with racks in upper and lower thirds. Stir together 2½ cups flour and the salt in a large bowl. Bring the water and olive oil to a boil in a saucepan over medium-high heat, then pour over flour mixture, stirring to combine. Stir in eggs one at a time, mixing well after each addition.

Knead in enough of remaining ½ cup flour to make a soft, slightly sticky dough. Knead until smooth, then knead in Parmesan until incorporated. With lightly oiled hands, roll tablespoons of dough into balls. Arrange 1 inch apart on two baking sheets lined with nonstick baking mats or parchment.

Bake until puffs are golden and cracked, about 25 minutes, rotating sheets from top to bottom and front to back halfway through. Serve immediately.

TOMATO MOUSSE
with GARDEN BASIL

SERVES 20 *from* **VERDANT SPRING DINNER**

The tomato water needs to drain overnight, so plan accordingly. Piping makes fast, easy work of filling the cups with mousse, but you could pour the mousse from a spouted pitcher or measuring cup instead.

for the mousse
- 1¼ pounds (about 4) ripe beefsteak or heirloom tomatoes, cored and cut into quarters
- Coarse salt
- 1½ teaspoons unflavored powdered gelatin

for the tomato relish
- 1 ripe beefsteak or heirloom tomato
- Coarse salt and freshly ground pepper
- 2 tablespoons chopped fresh basil, plus small leaves for garnish

Make the mousse: Line a bowl with a double layer of cheesecloth, leaving ample overhang. Purée tomatoes in a blender until smooth, season with salt, and pour into prepared bowl. Gather ends of cheesecloth together over purée to form a bundle, and tie with kitchen string. Suspend bundle from a large spoon resting across the top of a tall container, with room underneath so the bundle will not sit in accumulated liquid. Let drain overnight in the refrigerator; you should have about 1½ cups tomato water.

Prepare an ice-water bath. In a small saucepan, sprinkle gelatin over ¼ cup of the tomato water, and let soften 5 minutes. Cook over medium heat, swirling pan until gelatin is dissolved. Transfer remaining tomato water to a bowl, and pour in gelatin mixture. Set bowl in ice bath; whisk until mixture is thick and foamy, and there is no more liquid in the bottom of the bowl, 7 to 10 minutes. You should have about 4 cups mousse.

Make the tomato relish: Quarter tomato and remove seeds and pulp; discard. Cut tomato into ¼-inch dice, and place in a bowl. Season with salt and pepper, and stir in chopped basil.

Assemble the dish: Transfer mousse to a large pastry bag fitted with a large plain tip (such as Ateco #806). Arrange 20 egg cups (or other 2-ounce serving cups, such as demitasse or espresso cups) on a rimmed baking sheet. Spoon ½ teaspoon tomato relish in bottom of each cup, then pipe mousse on top, leaving ¼ inch between mousse and rim. Cover lightly with plastic wrap and refrigerate until chilled, at least 1 hour or up to 1 day.

To serve, top each mousse with ¼ teaspoon tomato relish and a basil leaf.

LEEK TERRINE

MAKES ONE 6-CUP TERRINE *from* **EASTER DINNER**

- 12 leeks
- Coarse salt and freshly ground pepper
- 1½ teaspoons unflavored powdered gelatin
- ¼ cup plus 2 tablespoons cold water
- 2 large egg yolks
- ¼ cup plus 1 tablespoon Dijon mustard
- ¼ cup extra-virgin olive oil, plus more for drizzling
- Fresh tarragon leaves, for garnish

Cut off root ends from leeks, and trim leeks to the length of the terrine mold you are using, discarding any dark green leaves. Halve each leek lengthwise to within 2 inches of root end. Swish leeks in a large bowl of water to dislodge any sand; change water as needed. Simmer leeks in a large pot of boiling salted water until very tender, about 20 minutes. Transfer leeks to a platter to cool, then cover and refrigerate until chilled, up to 1 day.

Stir gelatin into 2 tablespoons cold water, and let stand at least 5 minutes to soften.

Squeeze excess liquid from leeks, reserving 1 cup in a saucepan and discarding the rest. Pat leeks dry. Bring reserved leek liquid to a simmer. Add softened gelatin, stirring until dissolved.

Line a 6-cup terrine mold or loaf pan with plastic wrap, leaving a 3-inch overhang on the long sides. (If necessary, sprinkle mold with water to help plastic adhere.) Pour ¼ inch of gelatin mixture into bottom of mold. Add a layer of leeks and a little more gelatin mixture. Repeat until all the leeks are used, then pour remaining gelatin mixture over leeks. Wrap plastic wrap over leeks, pressing lightly to compress. Chill until completely set, at least 4 hours or up to 1 day.

When ready to serve, whisk together egg yolks and mustard; season with salt and pepper. Whisk in ¼ cup water, then the olive oil, until well blended.

Lift terrine out of mold using plastic wrap; place on a cutting board (still wrapped in plastic). Using a serrated knife, slice terrine (through plastic wrap) 1 inch thick. Arrange slices on a platter, discarding plastic wrap. Drizzle with olive oil; garnish with tarragon leaves. Serve sauce on the side.

PÂTÉ en CROÛTE

MAKES ONE 6-CUP TERRINE *from* **PÂTÉ CAMPAGNARD LUNCH**

- 1 onion, sliced ¾ inch thick
- 1 pound boneless veal loin, sliced into ½-inch strips, plus 1 pound veal bones
- 1 leek, quartered, washed well, and drained
- 2 carrots, each quartered
- 3 celery stalks, each quartered
- 4 bay leaves
- ½ cup plus 2 tablespoons port wine
   Coarse salt and freshly ground pepper
- 1 whole chicken breast (12 to 16 ounces), boned, half sliced into ½-inch strips, the rest cut into ¾-inch pieces
- 1¼ pounds boneless pork shoulder, two-thirds sliced into ½-inch strips, the rest cut into ¾-inch pieces
- 1 cup dry white wine
- 2 tablespoons Cognac
- 6 ounces fatback (without rind)
- ½ bunch fresh flat-leaf parsley, leaves stripped from stems
- ¼ teaspoon ground allspice
- ¼ teaspoon ground coriander
   Brioche Dough (recipe follows)
   All-purpose flour, for dusting
- 1 large egg, lightly beaten
- 1 envelope unflavored powdered gelatin (1 scant tablespoon)
- ¼ cup cold water

Bring a pot of water to a boil, and heat a cast-iron skillet over high. Add onion, cut side down, to skillet, and cook, undisturbed, until blackened on cut side, about 10 minutes.

Add veal bones to pot of water, and boil 5 minutes, then drain and rinse thoroughly. Return bones to pot, and add onion along with the leek, carrots, celery, bay leaves, and enough water to cover. Bring to a boil, then reduce heat; simmer, skimming off foam as necessary, 2 hours. Strain through a fine sieve into another pot, and discard solids. You should have about 2 cups stock. Add ½ cup port, and season with salt. Let cool completely. (Stock can be refrigerated in an airtight container up to 1 day.)

Combine the chicken, pork, and veal strips in a nonreactive dish with the wine, Cognac, remaining 2 tablespoons port, 2 teaspoons salt, and ½ teaspoon pepper. Cover, and marinate in the refrigerator 24 hours.

Using the medium die of a meat grinder, grind the diced chicken and pork pieces with the fatback into a large bowl. Add parsley, allspice, coriander, 2 teaspoons salt, and 1 teaspoon pepper, stirring binder well to combine.

Remove meats from marinade, and discard marinade. Pat meats dry with paper towels, then season with salt and pepper, tossing to combine.

Turn out dough onto a lightly floured surface; divide in half. Roll out one piece to ¼ inch thick; stretch to fit into a 6-cup terrine mold, pressing into sides and leaving about ½ inch overhang.

Spread a thin layer of binder mixture in terrine, then layer sliced meats on top, alternating the different types and pressing gently as you go. Repeat to make four more layers of binder and meats, ending with meats. Do not overfill. Stretch dough over the top, then trim to an even ¼-inch border.

Preheat oven to 325° F, with rack in lower third and no rack above it. Pat out remaining half of dough to ½ inch thick and same length and width of top of mold. Moisten edges of dough in mold, then attach other piece of dough, tucking it down around bottom dough and inside mold to seal. Let rise in a warm spot until puffed up (but not quite doubled in bulk), about 20 minutes.

Place terrine on a baking sheet, and brush dough liberally with beaten egg. Bake until an instant-read thermometer inserted into middle registers 160° F, and crust is golden brown, about 80 minutes. Tent with foil if crust is browning too quickly. Transfer to a wire rack to cool completely.

Prepare a large ice-water bath. Stir gelatin into the ¼ cup cold water and let soften 5 minutes. Add softened gelatin to reserved veal stock, and set bowl in the ice bath, stirring just until starting to set and thick enough to coat the back of a spoon. Cut out a small square (½ to 1 inch) from top of brioche, and reserve. Pour gelatin mixture through a funnel into mold, tilting mold to distribute evenly. Replace reserved brioche square. Refrigerate overnight.

To serve, unmold onto a platter or cutting board, and slice ¼ inch thick with a serrated knife.

Brioche Dough MAKES ENOUGH FOR ONE 6-CUP PÂTÉ EN CROUTE

- 1 envelope active dry yeast (2¼ teaspoons)
- ⅓ cup warm water (110° F)
- 1½ cups bread flour, plus more for dusting
- 1 cup pastry flour
- 10 tablespoons (1¼ sticks) cold unsalted butter, cut into pieces
- 4 large eggs
- 3 tablespoons sugar
- 2 tablespoons plus 1 teaspoon nonfat milk powder
- 1 teaspoon salt

In a bowl, sprinkle yeast over the warm water. Stir with a fork until dissolved; let stand until creamy-looking, about 5 minutes. Add ¼ cup bread flour; stir until well combined. Cover with a dry towel; let rise in a warm spot until doubled in bulk and bubbles appear on surface, about 1 hour.

Combine remaining 1¼ cups bread flour with the pastry flour, butter, eggs, sugar, and milk powder in the bowl of an electric mixer fitted with the dough hook. Beat on low speed until well combined, about 5 minutes. Add yeast mixture, and beat on low speed 5 minutes. Increase speed to medium; beat 5 minutes more. Sprinkle in salt; beat on medium speed until dough is smooth, shiny, and elastic, about 5 minutes more. Cover bowl with plastic wrap; immediately place in freezer 30 minutes.

Remove dough from freezer; punch down in bowl. Fold sides into the center, and invert, so dough is smooth side up. Cover with plastic wrap and refrigerate 1 day before using.

THE RECIPES

PÂTÉ *de* CAMPAGNE

MAKES ONE 6-CUP TERRINE *from* **PÂTÉ CAMPAGNARD LUNCH**

You should be able to buy fatback and caul fat from a butcher. Instead of the caul fat, you can use prosciutto or bacon.

- 2½ slices white sandwich bread
- ⅔ cup heavy cream
- ½ pound chicken livers, trimmed
- 12 ounces boneless pork shoulder
- 6 ounces boneless veal breast
- 5 ounces fatback (without rind)
- 1 tablespoon olive oil
- 1 small onion, finely chopped
- 1 garlic clove, minced
- ½ cup shelled pistachios
- 2 teaspoons coarse salt
- ¼ teaspoon freshly ground pepper
- ¼ teaspoon ground allspice
- ¼ teaspoon ground coriander
  Pinch of freshly grated nutmeg
- 1 tablespoon port wine
- 1 tablespoon Cognac
- 2 ounces pork caul fat (or 6 slices prosciutto or 12 slices bacon)
- 3 bay leaves, plus more for topping

Soak bread in cream until liquid is absorbed, about 15 minutes.

Cut chicken livers, pork shoulder, veal breast, and fatback into ¾-inch pieces. Using the medium die of a meat grinder, grind livers, meats, fatback, and soaked bread into a large bowl, alternating them in small batches.

Heat olive oil in a large sauté pan over medium high. Cook onion, stirring occasionally, until softened, 2 to 3 minutes. Add garlic, and cook, stirring, 1 minute more. Cool slightly, and add to ground-meat mixture along with pistachios, salt, pepper, spices, port, and Cognac. Stir well to combine.

Line a 6-cup terrine mold or loaf pan with caul fat, leaving 2 inches of overhang on long sides. Gently fill terrine with meat mixture, pressing as you go to ensure that there are no gaps and being careful not to disturb lining. The mixture can be packed above rim, as it will condense during baking. Arrange bay leaves on top, then fold edges of caul fat over meat mixture, and trim excess, if necessary. Top with more bay leaves. Cover well with plastic wrap, and refrigerate 24 hours.

Preheat oven to 375° F. Remove plastic wrap, and bake terrine on a rimmed baking sheet 1 hour or until an instant-read thermometer inserted in middle registers 160° F. Transfer to a wire rack to cool completely. Wrap well in plastic, and refrigerate at least overnight, or up to 1 week.

Remove terrine from refrigerator and let sit at room temperature 1 hour. To serve, remove plastic wrap, run a paring knife around the edge of the terrine, and unmold onto a serving platter or cutting board. Slice ¼ inch thick with a sharp knife, dipping knife in hot water before each slice.

TERRINE *de* FOIE GRAS

MAKES ONE 6-CUP TERRINE *from* **PÂTÉ CAMPAGNARD LUNCH**

The USDA recommends cooking foie gras to an internal temperature of 160° F. Here, the terrine is removed from the oven when it reaches 130° F, then allowed to sit in the bain-marie (the internal temperature will continue to rise). If you prefer to follow USDA guidelines, allow three to four hours for it to cook. The quatre epices, or "four spices," blend is classically used for making pâtés and terrines. To make your own, use equal parts freshly ground white or black peppercorns, grated nutmeg, and ground ginger and cloves.

- 3 pounds foie gras
- 1 tablespoon plus 1 teaspoon coarse salt
- ½ teaspoon freshly ground white pepper
- ¼ teaspoon quatre epices (see headnote)
- 2 tablespoons port wine
- 1 tablespoon Cognac
- 1 tablespoon Madeira

Let foie gras sit at room temperature about 1 hour. Cut a piece of cardboard to fit into the top of a 6-cup terrine mold, and wrap it with foil.

Gently separate lobes of foie gras, and remove veins with a paring knife, keeping each lobe as intact as possible. In a small bowl, stir together salt, white pepper, and quatre epices. Place foie gras on a rimmed baking sheet, and sprinkle evenly with port, Cognac, Madeira, and salt mixture. Toss gently to combine. Cover tightly with plastic wrap, and refrigerate 24 hours.

Preheat oven to 200° F. Heat a large pot of water (about 4 quarts) until an instant-read thermometer registers 160° F.

Unwrap the foie gras, and press it into terrine, smooth side down, wedging any small pieces into corners and gaps to make a snug fit. Cover foie gras with parchment, then cover terrine with lid (or foil), sealing tightly around edges. Put terrine in a roasting pan, and pour enough of the hot water into roasting pan to reach halfway up side of terrine. Bake until an instant-read thermometer inserted into foie gras registers 130° F, 1 to 1½ hours. Remove from oven; let terrine cool in bain-marie.

Remove terrine from roasting pan; pour off water from pan. Return terrine to pan; remove lid, leaving parchment intact. Press foil-wrapped cardboard onto top of terrine, and weight evenly with canned goods (excess fat will spill out of terrine; reserve in pan). Refrigerate 1 day.

Remove weights, cardboard, and parchment from terrine. Scrape fat from pan into a saucepan; heat just until melted. Spoon a thin layer of fat over terrine to seal. Wrap well in plastic; refrigerate at least 1 day or up to 1 week.

Remove terrine from refrigerator, and let sit at room temperature 1 hour. To serve, remove plastic wrap and run a paring knife around the edge of the terrine, and unmold onto a platter or cutting board. Slice ¼ inch thick with a sharp knife, dipping knife in hot water before each slice.

PORK RILLETTES

MAKES ONE 6-CUP TERRINE *from* **PÂTÉ CAMPAGNARD LUNCH**

Rillettes—or confiture de cochon ("pig jam")—is a rustic pâté made by "poaching" meat in its own fat, similar to a confit. Then the ultra tender meat is blended to a spreadable consistency and most often served with toast points. Pork (and fatback) is the most traditional meat for making rillettes, but duck or goose is also common. Be sure to let the rillettes sit at room temperature sufficiently before serving, to allow its full flavor to shine and for easier spreading.

- 2 tablespoons olive oil
- 3 pounds pork shoulder, cut into 2-inch cubes
- 1½ pounds fatback (without rind), cut into ¾-inch pieces
- 1 large white onion, halved
- 2 carrots, cut into large pieces
- 2 heads garlic, separated into cloves (unpeeled)
  Coarse salt and freshly ground pepper
- 2 bay leaves
- 3 juniper berries
- 3 whole cloves
- 3 to 4 sprigs thyme
- 3 to 4 sprigs rosemary

Preheat oven to 350° F. Heat olive oil in a 5- to 6-quart Dutch oven over medium high. In two batches, cook pork until browned, turning with tongs as necessary. Return first batch to pot, and add fatback, onion, carrots, garlic, 1 tablespoon salt, 1 teaspoon pepper, the bay leaves, juniper berries, and cloves.

Add thyme and rosemary sprigs to pork mixture, cover pot, and transfer to oven. Cook until meat is very tender and most fat has melted, about 1½ to 2 hours. Remove from oven.

Prepare a large ice-water bath. With tongs, transfer meat to the bowl of an electric mixer, and let cool to room temperature. Strain liquid through a fine sieve into another bowl set in the ice bath; discard solids. Once the fat has risen to the top, spoon off fat into a small bowl; reserve both fat and remaining liquid.

Using the paddle attachment, beat pork on medium speed until shredded. With mixer on low speed, gradually add 2½ cups of the strained liquid; raise speed to high, and beat until incorporated. (If you have less than 2½ cups liquid, add some of the reserved fat.) Season with salt and pepper.

Gently fill a 6-cup terrine mold, pressing as you go to make sure there are no gaps. Cover with plastic wrap and refrigerate 1 hour.

In a small saucepan, heat reserved fat just until melted, then pour over terrine, spreading to cover completely. Wrap well in plastic; refrigerate 1 day or up to 2 weeks. Remove from refrigerator and let sit at room temperature 1 hour before serving with a spoon.

TERRINE *of* DUCK BREAST *and* LEG CONFIT

MAKES ONE 6-CUP TERRINE *from* **PÂTÉ CAMPAGNARD LUNCH**

Duck confit and smoked duck breast can be found at specialty shops and from online sources, such as D'Artagnan.

- 14 ounces boneless pork shoulder, cut into ¾-inch cubes, well chilled
- 14 ounces fatback (without rind), cut into ¾-inch cubes, well chilled
- 4 confit duck legs (about 5 ounces each)
- 1 boneless duck breast (about 8 ounces)
- 2 smoked boneless duck breast halves (about 8 ounces each)
- 2 teaspoons coarse salt
- 1 teaspoon freshly ground pepper
- ¼ teaspoon ground allspice
- ¼ teaspoon ground coriander
  Pinch of freshly grated nutmeg
- 2 tablespoons Cognac
- 2 tablespoons port wine
- 2 rosemary sprigs
- 1 tablespoon olive oil

Using the small die of a meat grinder, grind pork shoulder and fatback into a large bowl, alternating them in small batches as you go. Refrigerate, covered with plastic wrap. Discard fat and bones from duck confit, and coarsely chop meat. Cut fresh duck breast, with fat, into 1-inch pieces. Slice smoked duck breasts lengthwise, ⅛ inch thick. Leaving the bottom of a 6-cup terrine mold or loaf pan empty, line the long sides with smoked duck slices, overlapping them slightly to cover completely and leaving about 2 inches of overhang. Cut any remaining smoked duck into 1-inch pieces.

Preheat oven to 325° F. In a large bowl, combine all duck meat (confit, fresh breast, and remaining smoked breast) with ground-meat mixture, salt, pepper, spices, Cognac, and port, mixing with your hands to blend well. Gently fill terrine with meat mixture, pressing as you go to ensure there are no gaps and being careful not to disturb lining. (Mixture can be packed above rim, as it will condense during baking.) Fold smoked duck over filling in a crisscross fashion, and arrange rosemary sprigs on top. Drizzle with olive oil.

Bake on a rimmed baking sheet until an instant-read thermometer inserted in middle registers 160° F, about 1½ hours. Transfer to a wire rack to cool completely. Wrap well in plastic; refrigerate at least 1 day or up to 1 week.

Remove terrine from refrigerator, and let sit at room temperature 1 hour. To serve, remove plastic wrap and run a paring knife around edge of terrine. Unmold onto a platter or cutting board. Slice ¼ inch thick with a sharp knife, dipping knife in hot water before each slice.

Soups, Salads, and Sandwiches

GAZPACHO

SERVES 6 *from* **PEONY GARDEN PARTY**

To allow the flavors to meld, combine all ingredients and refrigerate at least one day before blending.

- 5 tomatoes, cored and cut into quarters
- 1 cucumber, peeled, seeded, and cut into 1-inch pieces
- 3 celery stalks, cut into ½-inch pieces
- 1 red onion, cut into ½-inch dice
- 2 red bell peppers, cored, seeded, and cut into ½-inch dice
- ½ jalapeño chile, minced (ribs and seeds removed for less heat, if desired)
- 2 garlic cloves, minced
- ¼ cup chopped fresh flat-leaf parsley
- ¼ cup chopped cilantro
- ¼ cup red wine vinegar
- 1 teaspoon hot sauce, such as Tabasco, or to taste
- 1 cup water
- ¼ cup extra-virgin olive oil
- ¼ cup ketchup
- 1 tablespoon coarse salt, plus more for seasoning

Stir together all ingredients in a bowl, then cover and let marinate in the refrigerator overnight, or up to 2 days.

Working in batches, process soup in a blender until vegetables are finely chopped. Season with additional salt, and serve chilled.

WHITE ASPARAGUS SOUP

SERVES 8 *from* **EASTER DINNER**

Frozen shelled edamame are a convenient, no-peel substitute for fava beans in this soup; thaw them according to package instructions. For a colorful presentation, blanch some green asparagus tips to use as a garnish, either along with or instead of white asparagus tips.

- 3 pounds white asparagus, tough ends trimmed, spears cut into 2-inch pieces
- 2 tablespoons unsalted butter
- 2 onions, thinly sliced
- 2 quarts Vegetable Stock (page 421) or water
- ¾ pound russet potatoes, peeled and cut into 1-inch pieces
  Coarse salt
- 5 ounces fava beans, shelled (about ¼ cup)

Reserve 12 asparagus tips (3 inches) for garnish. Melt butter in a medium pot over medium-high heat. Cook onions until translucent, stirring

occasionally, about 8 minutes. Add stock, remaining asparagus, and potatoes, and season with salt. Bring to a boil, then reduce heat and simmer, partially covered, until vegetables are very tender, about 30 minutes. Remove from heat, and let soup cool slightly.

Meanwhile, prepare an ice-water bath. Blanch reserved asparagus tips in a pot of boiling salted water until tender, about 3 minutes. Using a slotted spoon, transfer asparagus tips to a plate to cool, then cut lengthwise in half. Boil fava beans for 2 minutes, then transfer to ice bath to stop the cooking. When cool, drain favas, and squeeze gently to pop out of skins.

Working in batches, purée soup in a blender until smooth, being careful not to fill jar more than halfway each time. Strain each batch through a fine sieve into a clean pot, pressing on solids with a flexible spatula to remove as much liquid as possible. Reheat soup over medium before serving; garnish with asparagus tips and fava beans.

CHILLED ASPARAGUS SOUP *with* PROSCIUTTO-WRAPPED ASPARAGUS SPEARS

SERVES 6 *from* **PEONY GARDEN PARTY**

- 2 pounds asparagus, tough ends trimmed
- 2 tablespoons extra-virgin olive oil
- 1 large shallot, thinly sliced
- 2 cups Chicken Stock (page 420) or low-sodium store-bought broth
- ½ cup water
- 1 cup loosely packed spinach leaves (trimmed and washed)
- ¼ cup crème fraîche
  Coarse salt and freshly ground pepper
- 1 or 2 thin slices prosciutto

Reserve 12 asparagus tips (3 inches) for garnish. Coarsely chop remaining asparagus. Heat olive oil in a medium pot over medium high. Cook shallot until softened but not browned, stirring frequently, about 2 minutes. Add chopped asparagus; cook, stirring, 1 minute. Stir in stock and the water, and simmer until asparagus is tender, about 15 minutes. Remove from heat and stir in spinach. Let cool slightly.

Working in batches, purée soup in a blender, being careful not to fill jar more than halfway each time and pouring each batch into a bowl. Stir in crème fraîche; season with salt and pepper. Cover and refrigerate at least 3 hours or up to 1 day.

Preheat oven to 400° F. Prepare an ice-water bath. Blanch reserved asparagus tips in a pot of boiling salted water just until bright green, about 1 minute. Transfer to ice bath to stop the cooking, then drain.

Halve prosciutto crosswise, then cut into twelve 1-inch-wide strips, and wrap a strip around each asparagus tip. Arrange in a single layer on a parchment-lined baking sheet. Roast until prosciutto is golden and crisp, about 10 minutes. Let cool slightly.

Serve soup in small glasses or cups; garnish with prosciutto-wrapped asparagus.

VICHYSSOISE

SERVES 12 *from* **LUNCHEON FOR BEDFORD FARMERS**

- 3 tablespoons unsalted butter
- 5 large leeks, white and pale-green parts only, sliced crosswise ¼ inch thick, washed well, and drained
- ½ large onion, coarsely chopped
- 1½ pounds russet potatoes, peeled and cut into 1-inch pieces
- 2 quarts water, plus more as needed
  Coarse salt and freshly ground white pepper
- 2 tablespoons extra-virgin olive oil
  Flat-leaf parsley sprigs, for garnish

Melt butter in a medium pot over medium heat. Cook leeks and onion until tender but not browned, stirring frequently, about 7 minutes. Add potatoes and the water, and season with salt. Bring to a boil, then reduce heat, and simmer gently, partially covered, until potatoes are very tender, about 20 minutes. Remove from heat and let soup cool slightly.

Working in batches, purée soup in a blender until smooth, being careful not to fill jar more than halfway each time. Strain each batch through a fine sieve into a large bowl, pressing on solids to release as much liquid as possible. Add olive oil, season with salt and white pepper, and thin with water, if needed. Cover and refrigerate at least 3 hours or up to 1 day.

To serve, divide among chilled bowls; garnish each with a sprig of parsley.

PURÉED CARROT SOUP

SERVES 8 *from* **EASTER DINNER**

- 2 tablespoons unsalted butter
- 2 onions, thinly sliced
- 2 quarts Vegetable Stock (page 421) or water
- 2 pounds carrots, peeled and cut into 1-inch pieces
- ¾ pound russet potatoes, peeled and cut into 1-inch pieces
  Coarse salt
  Dill sprigs, for garnish

Melt butter in a medium pot over medium-high heat. Cook onions until translucent, stirring occasionally, about 8 minutes. Add stock, carrots, and potatoes, and season with salt. Bring to a boil, then reduce heat, and simmer, partially covered, until vegetables are very tender, about 30 minutes. Remove from heat, and let soup cool slightly.

Working in batches, purée in a blender until smooth, being careful not to fill jar more than halfway each time. Return to clean pot, and reheat over medium, stirring occasionally. Adjust seasoning; serve, garnished with dill.

MISO SOUP

SERVES 4 *from* **JAPANESE LUNCH**

Dashi, a simple Japanese broth, is the flavorful foundation of this nourishing soup. You can use other types of mushrooms, such as shiitake (stems trimmed) or oyster, in place of matsutake, and other types of baby greens, including tatsoi and mustard greens, instead of the spinach.

- 1 square (4 inch) dried kombu, cleaned with a damp cloth
- 4 cups water
- ⅔ cup bonito flakes
- 6 ounces matsutake mushrooms, cleaned
- 3 tablespoons mild miso
- 6 ounces firm tofu, drained and cut into ½-inch cubes
- 5 ounces (½ package) baby spinach
- 3 scallions, trimmed and sliced 1 inch thick on the bias

Bring kombu and the water to a boil in a pot. Remove kombu; discard. Add bonito flakes, stirring to combine; remove from heat. Let stand until flakes settle at bottom of pot; strain dashi through a fine sieve, discarding bonito.

Return dashi to pot and add mushrooms. Cook over medium heat until mushrooms have softened, about 3 minutes. In a small bowl, dissolve miso in a ladleful of dashi, then stir mixture into soup. Add tofu and spinach; cook just until tofu is heated through and spinach is slightly wilted. Remove from heat and stir in scallions. Serve immediately.

PUMPKIN SOUP

SERVES 8 TO 10 *from* **HALLOWEEN PUMPKIN BLAZE**

For the Halloween Pumpkin Blaze party, this soup was served in individual tureens made from small hollowed-out pumpkins. You could also present the soup in a large tureen carved from a big ten-pound pumpkin, which could double as a centerpiece for a dining or buffet table. Save the seeds from the pumpkin used in the soup recipe to make the garnish.

- 1 small sugar pumpkin (about 4 pounds), skinned, seeded, and cut into 1-inch pieces
- 1 leek, white and pale green parts only, cut into large dice, washed well, and drained
- 1 large red onion, cut into large dice
- 2½ quarts Vegetable Stock (page 421) or low-sodium store-bought broth
  Coarse salt and freshly ground pepper
- 2 tablespoons unsalted butter (optional)
  Sautéed Chestnuts and Celery Root, for garnish (optional; recipe follows)
  Roasted Pumpkin Seeds, for garnish (optional; recipe follows)

Combine pumpkin pieces, leek, onion, and stock in a large pot; add water, if necessary, to just cover vegetables. Bring to a boil, then reduce heat; simmer until pumpkin is tender, about 20 minutes. Let soup cool slightly.

Working in batches, purée soup in a blender, being careful not to fill jar more than halfway each time. Return soup to clean pot, and reheat over medium, stirring occasionally. Season with salt and pepper, then whisk in butter. Serve hot, garnished with chestnuts and pumpkin seeds, as desired.

Sautéed Chestnuts and Celery Root

MAKES ABOUT 1 CUP

- 1 tablespoon unsalted butter
- ½ cup cooked and peeled chestnuts (page 423, or use jarred), broken into bite-size pieces
  Coarse salt and freshly ground pepper
- 2 slices whole wheat bread, trimmed of crusts, cut into ½-inch dice
- 2 tablespoons extra-virgin olive oil
- ½ celery root, peeled and cut into ¼-inch dice

Preheat oven to 375° F. Melt butter in a small sauté pan over medium-high heat. Cook chestnuts until they begin to brown, stirring occasionally, about 5 minutes. Transfer to a plate and season with salt.

On a rimmed baking sheet, toss bread cubes with 1 tablespoon olive oil, and season with salt and pepper. Spread in an even layer, and toast until crisp, tossing once or twice, about 10 minutes.

Heat remaining 1 tablespoon olive oil in a small saucepan over medium. Cook celery root until tender, stirring occasionally, about 5 minutes.

Transfer chestnuts, bread, and celery root to a bowl, then toss well to combine before using as garnish.

Roasted Pumpkin Seeds MAKES ABOUT 1 CUP

- 1 cup pumpkin seeds
- 1 tablespoon extra-virgin olive oil
- ½ teaspoon coarse salt
- ¼ teaspoon freshly ground black pepper
- ⅛ teaspoon cayenne
- ⅛ teaspoon ground ginger

Rinse and dry pumpkin seeds. Spread on a baking sheet in a single layer, and dry at room temperature overnight.

Preheat oven to 375° F. Toss seeds with olive oil, salt, pepper, cayenne, and ginger. Spread in an even layer on a baking sheet lined with a nonstick baking mat. Roast until completely dried and crisp, tossing occasionally, about 15 minutes. Let cool completely. (Pumpkin seeds can be stored in an airtight container at room temperature up to 3 days.)

MIXED BABY GREENS *and* HERBS *with* CANDIED PECANS *and* DRIED CRANBERRIES

SERVES 10 TO 12 *from* **FRIDAY NIGHT WELCOME DINNER**

This salad is made with whatever soft, leafy herbs and baby greens are growing in the Skylands garden. Any herbs and greens will do; toasted pecans can be used in place of the candied ones.

- 4 cups assorted fresh herbs, such as chervil, basil, sorrel, and parsley
- 4 to 6 bunches mixed baby greens, such as tatsoi, arugula, spinach, and romaine
  Mustard Vinaigrette (recipe follows)

- 1 cup dried cranberries
  Candied Pecans (recipe follows)

Combine herbs and greens in a salad bowl. Add vinaigrette, a little at a time, tossing to coat; toss with cranberries and pecans. Serve immediately.

Mustard Vinaigrette MAKES 1⅓ CUPS

- 2 tablespoons Dijon mustard
- ⅓ cup white-wine or sherry vinegar
  Coarse salt and freshly ground pepper
- 1 cup extra-virgin olive oil

Whisk mustard and vinegar together in a small bowl; season with salt and pepper. Slowly add oil in a steady stream, whisking constantly until dressing is emulsified.

Candied Pecans MAKES ABOUT 1½ CUPS

- ½ cup sugar
- ¼ cup water
- 1½ cups raw pecans

Line a rimmed baking sheet with a nonstick baking mat. Bring sugar and the water to a simmer in a heavy saucepan, stirring occasionally, until sugar is dissolved. Stop stirring; cook until syrup comes to a boil, washing down sides of pan with a wet pastry brush to prevent crystals from forming. Boil, gently swirling pan occasionally, until mixture is light amber. Remove from heat. Stir in pecans with a wooden spoon to coat completely. Immediately remove pecans from caramel, and spread in a single layer on prepared baking sheet. Let cool completely; break apart nuts, if necessary. (Candied pecans can be stored in an airtight container at room temperature up to 3 days.)

PETITE SALADE NIÇOISE

SERVES 12 *from* **PEONY GARDEN PARTY**

- 12 quail eggs
  Coarse salt and freshly ground pepper
- ½ pound haricots verts, trimmed
- 1 pound fresh tuna loin, trimmed
- 2 tablespoons olive oil, plus more if needed
- 6 cooked artichoke hearts (page 329), quartered
- 1 red bell pepper, roasted (page 423) and cut into ½-inch strips
- 1 celery stalk, thinly sliced on the bias
- 2 Kirby cucumbers, peeled, quartered lengthwise, seeded, and cut into ¼-inch slices
- 3 tomatoes, cut into ¾-inch chunks
  Balsamic Vinaigrette (recipe follows)
- 12 anchovy fillets, rinsed (optional)
- ½ cup Niçoise or Kalamata olives, pitted
  Parsley sprigs, for garnish

Prepare an ice-water bath. Place quail eggs in a saucepan large enough to hold them in a single layer; add water to cover by 2 inches. Bring to a boil, then reduce heat, and simmer gently 1½ minutes. Using a slotted spoon, transfer eggs to ice bath, and let cool (reserve water in pan). Peel eggs, and cut in half.

Return water in pan to a boil, and season generously with salt. Blanch haricots verts until crisp-tender, about 2 minutes. Transfer to ice bath to stop the cooking. Drain and pat dry.

Cut tuna into 1½-inch-wide strips, and season on both sides with salt and pepper. Heat olive oil in a large sauté pan over medium. Sear tuna in two batches until browned, about 20 seconds per side; transfer to a cutting board, and let rest 5 minutes before slicing crosswise, 1 inch thick.

To assemble, toss vegetables with ¼ cup vinaigrette, and divide among 12 small serving dishes. Arrange anchovy, tuna, and halved quail eggs on top of salad, and garnish with olives and parsley. Drizzle with more vinaigrette, and season with salt, if desired.

Balsamic Vinaigrette MAKES ½ CUP

- 1 tablespoon balsamic vinegar
- 1 tablespoon Dijon mustard
- 1 tablespoon water
  Coarse salt and freshly ground pepper
- ¼ cup extra-virgin olive oil

In a small bowl, whisk together vinegar, mustard, and the water; season with salt and pepper. Add olive oil in a steady stream, whisking until emulsified.

COMPOSED VEGETABLE SALAD *with* BEET VINAIGRETTE

SERVES 8 *from* BRIDAL SHOWER IN MAINE

Follow the recipe for Artichokes with Poached Eggs (page 329) to trim and clean the artichokes, dropping them into lemon water as you work.

- 1½ pounds fingerling potatoes
  Coarse salt and freshly ground pepper
- 8 artichokes, cleaned and trimmed (page 329)
- 1 small head white cauliflower, cut into florets
- 1 small head purple cauliflower, cut into florets
- 1½ pounds baby red beets, stems trimmed to 2 inches
- 3 tablespoons sherry vinegar
- ½ cup extra-virgin olive oil
- 2 pints small mixed heirloom tomatoes, halved or quartered, depending on size
- 2 to 3 bunches mixed baby lettuces, such as mâche, Lollo Rossa, red and green oak-leaf, and deer tongue
- 1 bunch opal or regular basil, leaves picked

Place potatoes in a saucepan large enough to hold them in a single layer, and cover with water by 2 inches. Bring to a boil, and add salt. Reduce heat, and simmer until tender when pierced with the tip of a sharp knife, about 15 minutes. Drain and let cool, then halve crosswise.

Meanwhile, place prepared artichokes in another saucepan, and add water to cover. Bring to a boil, then add salt. Reduce heat, and simmer until artichokes are tender when pierced with the tip of a sharp knife, 8 to 12 minutes (depending on size). Drain well.

Prepare an ice-water bath. Bring a pot of water to a boil; add salt. Blanch both cauliflowers until just tender, about 5 minutes. Use a slotted spoon to transfer to ice bath to stop the cooking, then remove and drain well. Add beets to pot, and boil until tender when pierced with the tip of a sharp knife, 25 to 35 minutes (depending on size). Drain, and let cool slightly, then peel beets using a paring knife or vegetable peeler. Halve or quarter beets.

Purée 3 beet quarters in a blender, then transfer to a bowl. Whisk in the vinegar, and season with salt and pepper. Add ¼ cup plus 2 tablespoons olive oil in a steady stream, whisking until emulsified.

Just before serving, combine cauliflowers, artichoke hearts, tomatoes, lettuces, and basil in a salad bowl. Toss with remaining 2 tablespoons oil to lightly coat. Season with salt, and toss again. Immediately arrange on plates, dividing evenly. Arrange potatoes in center, cut side down. Add beets to same bowl, season with salt, and toss to coat with any residual oil. Divide beets among plates, and drizzle each salad with beet vinaigrette. Serve immediately.

SUMMERY SALAD *with* VEGETABLES

SERVES 12 *from* JULY 4TH BARBECUE

You can use any variety of tender baby lettuces for this salad.

- 4 small carrots (each 3 inches long), peeled and shaved into ribbons with a vegetable peeler
- 3 tablespoons fresh lemon juice
- 1 tablespoon white wine vinegar
  Coarse salt and freshly ground pepper
- ½ cup extra-virgin olive oil
- 2 small heads Boston lettuce, torn into pieces
- 2 heads baby Lollo Rossa lettuce, torn into pieces
- 2 heads baby romaine lettuce, torn into pieces
- 2 heads baby oak-leaf lettuce
- 2 cups baby or wild arugula
- 2 heads red or white endive, leaves separated
- 4 ounces yellow wax beans, trimmed
- 4 ounces Romano beans, trimmed
- 4 ounces haricots verts, trimmed
- 1 pint cherry tomatoes (red, yellow, or a combination of both), halved

In a small bowl, cover carrot ribbons with cold water; let stand 10 minutes. Drain well. Whisk together lemon juice and vinegar in another small bowl, then season with salt and pepper. Gradually whisk in olive oil until emulsified. Toss lettuces, arugula, and endive in a large bowl; cover with a damp towel, and refrigerate until ready to use.

Prepare an ice-water bath. Bring a large pot of water to a boil; add salt. Blanch beans in separate batches, starting with wax beans and ending with haricots verts, just until color is brightened and they are crisp-tender, about 1 minute. When each batch is finished cooking, use a slotted spoon or mesh spider to transfer to ice bath to stop the cooking. Once cool, remove beans and drain well.

Add beans, carrots, and tomatoes to lettuces; toss with some vinaigrette to coat. Serve immediately, with additional vinaigrette on the side.

GARDEN SALAD *with* ARTICHOKES *and* TUNA

SERVES 8 *from* **LUNCHEON FOR BEDFORD FARMERS**

Follow the recipe for Artichokes with Poached Eggs (page 329) to trim and clean the artichokes, dropping them into lemon water as you work.

- ½ pound small Yukon Gold potatoes
  Coarse salt and freshly ground pepper
- 1 tablespoon dry vermouth
- ¾ cup Mustard Vinaigrette (page 362)
- 2 artichoke hearts, cleaned and trimmed (page 329)
- ½ pound haricots verts, trimmed
- 1 pint cherry tomatoes, halved
- ¼ cup packed fresh basil leaves, finely chopped
- 2 teaspoons balsamic vinegar
- ¼ cup plus 1 tablespoon extra-virgin olive oil
- 1 red bell pepper, roasted (see page 423) and cut into ½-inch pieces
- 1 yellow bell pepper, roasted (see page 423) and cut into ½-inch pieces
- ¼ cup finely chopped fresh flat-leaf parsley leaves
- 4 large celery stalks, peeled and sliced ¼ inch thick on the bias
- 1 tablespoon champagne vinegar
- 1 English cucumber, peeled, quartered lengthwise, any seeds removed
- 1 sprig lemon balm or mint, leaves finely chopped
- 2 tablespoons rice vinegar (unseasoned)
- 2 pounds fresh yellowfin tuna steaks (each about 1 inch thick)
- 2 to 3 bunches mixed baby lettuces, such as mâche, Lollo Rossa, red and green oak-leaf, and deer tongue
- 8 medium hard-cooked eggs (page 423), peeled and halved
- ½ bunch French breakfast radishes, thinly sliced crosswise
- 3 cans (5 to 6 ounces) best-quality oil-packed solid white tuna, drained

Place potatoes in a saucepan large enough to hold them in a single layer, and cover with water by 2 inches. Bring to a boil, and add salt. Reduce heat, and simmer until tender when pierced with the tip of a sharp knife, about 15 minutes. Drain and let cool, then halve and place in a bowl. Toss with the vermouth, then toss with 2 tablespoons of the vinaigrette.

Meanwhile, place prepared artichokes in another saucepan, and add water to cover. Bring to a boil, then add salt. Reduce heat, and simmer until artichokes are tender when pierced with the tip of a sharp knife, 8 to 12 minutes (depending on size). Drain well.

Prepare an ice-water bath. Blanch haricots verts in a saucepan of boiling salted water until crisp-tender, about 2 minutes. Transfer to ice bath to stop the cooking, then drain and pat dry. Combine in a bowl with 2 tablespoons vinaigrette, tossing to coat.

In separate bowls, toss together cherry tomatoes, basil, balsamic vinegar, and 1 tablespoon olive oil; toss artichoke hearts with 2 tablespoons mustard vinaigrette; toss bell peppers with chopped parsley and 1 tablespoon olive oil; and toss together celery and champagne vinegar. Slice cucumber crosswise, 1 inch thick on the bias, and toss to combine in a bowl with lemon balm and rice vinegar.

Pat tuna steaks dry, then season on both sides with salt and pepper. Heat remaining 3 tablespoons olive oil in a large skillet over medium. Working in batches if necessary, sear tuna steaks until golden on the outside and cooked to medium rare, about 3 minutes per side. Transfer to a cutting board, and let rest 3 minutes before slicing 1 inch thick on the bias.

To assemble, divide lettuces among serving plates. Starting with the tomatoes, place small clusters of each vegetable on lettuce, then add two hard-cooked egg halves to each, along with some radishes. Divide canned and seared tuna among salads, and serve immediately.

HIJIKI SALAD

SERVES 4 *from* **JAPANESE LUNCH**

- 1 cup dried hijiki (seaweed)
- 3 scallions, green parts only, sliced thinly lengthwise
- 2 tablespoons rice vinegar (unseasoned)
- 2 teaspoons toasted sesame oil
- 1 teaspoon sugar
  Coarse salt
  Tender lettuce leaves, such as Bibb, for serving

Place seaweed in a bowl and cover with warm (not boiling) water. Let soak until tender, about 30 minutes, then drain well and place in another bowl along with scallion greens. Whisk together vinegar, sesame oil, and sugar; season with salt. Toss with seaweed mixture. To serve, line 4 bowls with lettuce leaves, and spoon seaweed salad on top, dividing evenly.

ROAST BEEF SANDWICHES *with* AVOCADO *and* HORSERADISH

SERVES 6 *from* **PICNIC AT SEA**

To make slicing easier and more precise, roast the beef a day ahead of serving, and refrigerate it overnight.

- 2 tablespoons olive oil
- 1 tablespoon unsalted butter
- 1½ pounds beef eye of round
  Coarse salt and freshly ground pepper
- 3 firm, ripe avocados
- 2 medium tomatoes, cut into ¼-inch-thick slices
  Lettuce and radicchio, for serving
- 12 slices rustic bread (½ inch thick each)
  Horseradish Cream (recipe follows)

Preheat oven to 425° F. Heat a large ovenproof skillet over medium high. Add olive oil and butter; heat until oil is hot and butter has melted. Pat dry beef, then season all over with salt and pepper. Cook until beef is well browned on all sides, about 5 minutes.

Transfer skillet to oven. Roast until an instant-read thermometer inserted in middle of meat registers 130° F for medium rare, 18 to 22 minutes. Transfer beef to a cutting board; let rest at least 20 minutes before slicing very thinly crosswise.

To assemble sandwiches, peel and pit avocados; cut into ¼-inch-thick slices. Arrange tomatoes, lettuce and radicchio, avocados, and beef over half the bread. Spread horseradish cream onto each remaining bread slice, and place on top of beef to form sandwiches.

Horseradish Cream MAKES ABOUT 1 CUP

8 ounces cream cheese, softened
¼ cup prepared horseradish, or to taste
Coarse salt and freshly ground pepper

Stir together cream cheese and horseradish in a small bowl until smooth, then season with salt and pepper. (Horseradish cream can be refrigerated, covered, up to 1 week. Bring to room temperature before using.)

DANISH SMØRREBRØD SANDWICHES

ABOUT 2 DOZEN   *from* DANISH SMØRREBRØD IN NYC

Smørrebrød means buttered bread, and all of the following recipes start by spreading good-quality unsalted butter over thin slices of rye or pumpernickel bread. Layer with toppings as instructed, or improvise to make sandwiches featuring your favorite flavor combinations.

½ cup (1 stick) unsalted butter, softened
1 package (16 ounces) rye or pumpernickel bread
10 lettuce leaves, torn into pieces, ribs discarded
Assorted Toppings (recipes follow)

Spread a thin layer of softened butter over one side of each bread slice, then cut each slice into 4 triangles. Cover half of each triangle with a piece of lettuce. Layer with desired toppings.

Corned Beef with Horseradish Cream: Make horseradish cream by whisking 1 cup heavy cream, 1 tablespoon sugar, 2 teaspoons fresh lemon juice, and 1 tablespoon grated fresh or prepared horseradish to medium-stiff peaks. Top each bread triangle with a slice of corned beef folded in half, a dollop of horseradish cream (piped or spooned), and a few dill pickle slices. Garnish with a parsley sprig.

Boiled Fingerling Potatoes with Fried Onions: Prepare fried onions by heating 2 inches neutral-tasting oil such as safflower in a Dutch oven until 320° F on a deep-fry thermometer. Thinly slice 2 yellow onions, then rinse slices and pat dry; toss with flour to lightly coat. Fry in batches until crisp, about 2 minutes, then drain on paper towels. Top each bread triangle with 3 slices boiled fingerling potatoes and season with salt and pepper; add a dollop of mayonnaise and sprinkle with diced red onion and snipped chives. Garnish with fried onions.

Hard-Cooked Eggs with Tomatoes and Radishes: Top each bread triangle with 3 slices hard-cooked egg and season with salt and pepper, then layer with a tomato slice and 2 more slices of egg. Add a dollop of mayonnaise, sprinkle with snipped chives, and garnish with a few radish matchsticks (cut with a mandoline or other adjustable blade slicer).

Herb Pork Roll with Veal Aspic: Top each bread triangle with a slice of pork roll (such as by Taylor or Case) folded in half, a slice of veal aspic (available from online sources), and a few red onion slices. Garnish with a parsley sprig.

Salami with Quick Rémoulade: Mix together equal parts mayonnaise and store-bought piccalilli. Top each bread triangle with a thin slice of salami folded in half, then layer with a dollop of remoulade, a strip of red bell pepper, and a cherry tomato quarter. Garnish with a few radish sprouts.

Liver Pâté with Chanterelles and Bacon: Heat 3 loaves (each 8 ounces) liver pâté in the oven just until warmed through. Meanwhile, sauté 1 pound trimmed chanterelle mushrooms in 3 tablespoons olive oil until tender, then add 3 tablespoons dry white wine and season with salt and pepper, stirring to combine, and remove from heat. Top each bread triangle with a slice of pâté, then layer with mushrooms and a slice of crisped bacon. Garnish with a parsley sprig.

Shrimp and Eggs with Caviar: Cook 28 peeled and deveined small shrimp in a pot of boiling salted water with a thinly sliced lemon added just until bright pink, 1 to 2 minutes. Drain, pat dry, and slice lengthwise in half. Top each bread triangle with 3 slices hard-cooked egg and season with salt and pepper; layer with a dollop of mayonnaise, a halved shrimp, and a tiny spoonful of Osetra caviar. Garnish with a thin wedge of lemon.

Roast Beef with Caperberries and Piccalilli: Leaving stem intact, slice each of 28 caper berries thinly, then fan out in a circle. Top each bread triangle with a slice of roast beef folded in half, then layer with piccalilli, a caperberry, and a cherry tomato quarter. Garnish with a parsley sprig.

Beef Tongue with Vegetable Mayonnaise and White Asparagus: Cut 14 white asparagus spears into 1-inch pieces, leaving tips intact. Blanch ½ cup thawed frozen peas, ½ cup diced carrots, and the asparagus in a pot of boiling salted water until just tender, 1 to 2 minutes, then plunge into an ice-water bath to cool. Drain well. Slice asparagus tips in half lengthwise; mix remaining vegetables with 1 cup mayonnaise. Top each bread triangle with a slice of beef tongue folded in half, then layer with a dollop of vegetable mayonnaise and a halved asparagus tip. Garnish with a parsley sprig.

Pickled Herring with Caper and Dill: Top each bread triangle with three 1-inch pieces pickled herring, then sprinkle with capers and minced red onion. Garnish with a dill sprig.

MINI BEEF BURGERS

MAKES 24   *from* EASTER EGG HUNT

3 tablespoons olive oil
1 onion, cut into ¼-inch dice
3¾ pounds ground beef chuck, preferably not lean
2 tablespoons Worcestershire sauce
⅓ cup finely chopped fresh flat-leaf parsley
1 tablespoon coarse salt
Mini Hamburger Buns (recipe follows)
1 head Boston lettuce, leaves torn into 3-inch pieces
3 plum tomatoes, cut into 24 (¼-inch) slices

Heat 1 tablespoon olive oil in a large sauté pan over medium high. Cook onion, stirring occasionally, until translucent, about 3 minutes. Let cool, then transfer to a bowl and add beef, Worcestershire, parsley, and salt. Mix gently with your hands to combine. Form into 24 equal-size patties.

Wipe pan with paper towels. Heat remaining 2 tablespoons olive oil over medium high. Cook burgers in batches until browned and cooked through, about 3 minutes per side. Serve in buns with lettuce and tomatoes.

Mini Hamburger Buns MAKES 24

1 tablespoon plus ¾ teaspoon active dry yeast
¾ cup warm water (110° F)
1 teaspoon sugar
3 cups all-purpose flour
1¼ teaspoons coarse salt
2 tablespoons unsalted butter, cut into small pieces
2 tablespoons unsulfured molasses
2 large eggs
Olive oil, for hands, work surface, and bowl
1 teaspoon cold water
2 teaspoons poppy or sesame seeds

Stir together yeast and ¼ cup of the warm water in a small bowl until yeast is dissolved. Stir in sugar, and let stand until foamy, about 10 minutes.

In a large bowl, whisk together flour and salt. In a small bowl, stir together remaining ½ cup warm water with the butter and molasses until butter is melted; add to flour mixture. Lightly beat 1 egg, and add to bowl along with the yeast mixture. Stir to make a soft, sticky dough.

Lightly oil hands. Turn out dough onto a lightly oiled work surface. Knead dough until smooth, 3 to 5 minutes, adding more oil to surface and hands if dough begins to stick. Transfer dough to an oiled bowl. Cover and let rise in a warm spot (80° F to 85° F) until doubled in bulk, about 1 hour.

Punch down dough; turn out onto a clean work surface. Knead two times; form into a ball. Cut dough into eight equal pieces, then cut each piece into thirds to make 24 small pieces of dough. Form each piece into a ball by pulling sides down and tucking them under (do not roll into a ball). Arrange balls 2 inches apart on parchment-lined baking sheets. Gently press dough to flatten into ½-inch-thick disks. Cover; let rise in a warm spot 1 hour.

Preheat oven to 375° F, with racks in upper and lower thirds. Lightly beat remaining egg with the cold water for egg wash, then brush over tops of buns. Sprinkle evenly with poppy or sesame seeds. Bake until golden, 10 to 12 minutes, rotating sheets from top to bottom and front to back halfway through. Transfer buns to wire racks to cool before splitting and serving. (Buns are best eaten the day they are baked, but you can store them up to 2 days in an airtight container at room temperature.)

MINI BLTs

MAKES 20 *from* **EASTER EGG HUNT**

14 slices bacon (about 14 ounces)
1 large beefsteak tomato
10 slices firm white sandwich bread, trimmed of crusts
¾ cup mayonnaise
1 head Boston lettuce, leaves torn into 1½-inch pieces

Preheat oven to 400° F. Arrange bacon slices as close together as possible without overlapping on a large parchment-lined rimmed baking sheet. Top with a piece of parchment and another large baking sheet. Cook bacon until browned and crisp, rotating sheet halfway through, 20 to 30 minutes, depending on thickness. Check frequently toward end of cooking. Transfer bacon to paper towels to drain.

Cut bacon slices into thirds. With a serrated knife, cut tomato into ¼-inch-thick slices, and cut each slice into quarters. Cut bread slices into quarters. Spread each piece of bread generously with mayonnaise. Top half the bread with tomato, lettuce, two pieces of bacon, and another piece of bread. Keep covered with plastic wrap until ready to serve, up to 1 hour.

EGG- *and* BUNNY-SHAPED GRILLED CHEESE SANDWICHES

MAKES 20 *from* **EASTER EGG HUNT**

½ cup plus 2 tablespoons (1¼ sticks) unsalted butter, plus more for bread
40 slices (¼ inch thick) brioche or very thin, firm white sandwich bread
40 thin slices melting cheese, such as cheddar or American

Preheat oven to 350° F. Butter one side of each slice of brioche. In a large skillet over medium heat, melt 1 tablespoon butter. Arrange four slices of bread in skillet, buttered side down, and top each with one slice cheese. Cook until bread is golden and cheese is beginning to melt, about 2 minutes. Transfer to a baking sheet as they are cooked, and make sandwiches, putting cheese sides together. Repeat with remaining bread and cheese, adding more butter between batches.

Cut sandwiches into bunny or egg shapes with cookie cutters, discarding crusts. If desired, cut 1-inch rounds from top of egg-shaped sandwiches to expose the "yolks."

Bake sandwiches in oven just long enough to melt cheese, 2 to 3 minutes. Let cool slightly before serving.

TINY TUNA BURGERS *with* CURRY RÉMOULADE

MAKES 12 *from* **THE ART OF GRILLING**

Be sure to soak wooden skewers in water for an hour before grilling to prevent them from scorching.

1½ pounds yellowfin or ahi tuna, chopped
½ teaspoon Chinese five-spice powder
1 to 2 teaspoons coarse salt
½ teaspoon ground coriander
¼ teaspoon cayenne
2 teaspoons black sesame seeds
1 tablespoon finely chopped lemongrass (from white and pale yellow parts of stalk)
2 tablespoons cilantro leaves, chopped
12 brioche slices (1½ inches thick)
3 tablespoons unsalted butter
Vegetable oil, for grill
12 lettuce leaves
1 Japanese or Kirby cucumber, very thinly sliced into 36 rounds
Curry Rémoulade (recipe follows)
2 to 3 tomatoes, thinly sliced

Heat grill to medium. (If using a charcoal grill, coals are ready when you can hold your hand 5 inches above the grates for just 4 to 5 seconds.)

In a large bowl, gently but thoroughly mix together tuna, five-spice powder, salt, coriander, cayenne, sesame seeds, lemongrass, and cilantro. Form into 12 patties, about 2 inches in diameter. Thread 2 wooden skewers, side by side, horizontally through the middle of a patty, then insert same skewers through 2 more patties. Repeat with 6 more skewers and remaining patties, adding 3 patties to each set of skewers. Refrigerate on a plate.

Using a 3-inch cutter, cut rounds from brioche slices. Heat butter in a large skillet until just melted. Toast brioche rounds on each side in melted butter until light brown and crisp, 1 to 2 minutes per side.

Remove tuna skewers from refrigerator. Brush hot grates lightly with oil. Grill tuna until just cooked through, about 3 minutes per side. Remove from grill; carefully slide burgers off skewers. Arrange a lettuce leaf and 3 cucumber slices on each brioche round, then top with a tuna burger; spoon rémoulade over burger, then top with a tomato slice. Serve immediately.

Curry Rémoulade MAKES 1½ CUPS

- 1 cup mayonnaise
- ⅓ cup sour cream
- 1 garlic clove, minced
- 1 tablespoon curry powder, preferably Madras
- 1 tablespoon sweet tomato-based chili sauce
- ⅛ teaspoon ground coriander
- 1 tablespoon finely chopped peeled fresh ginger
- 2 teaspoons chopped cilantro
- 1 teaspoon soy sauce
- ½ teaspoon sesame oil
- 2 teaspoons rice vinegar (unseasoned)
- 2 teaspoons Asian hot chili sauce, such as sambal oelek or Sriracha
- ½ lemon, juiced

Mix together all ingredients until well combined. Cover and refrigerate overnight to allow flavors to develop before serving.

Risotto and Pasta

PASTA with BOLOGNESE SAUCE

SERVES 8; MAKES ABOUT 4 CUPS SAUCE *from* **FRIDAY NIGHT WELCOME DINNER**

The hearty sauce can be doubled to make enough for two pounds of pasta. Serve half now; freeze the rest in an airtight container, up to three months, and thaw in the refrigerator before using.

- 2 tablespoons olive oil
- 1 large white onion, diced
- 2 carrots, peeled and diced
- 3 celery stalks, diced
- 6 ounces ground beef chuck, preferably not lean
- 6 ounces ground pork

- 6 ounces ground veal
  Coarse salt and freshly ground pepper
- 1 cup dry red wine
- 2 tablespoons tomato paste
  Pinch of freshly grated nutmeg
- 1 can (28 ounces) whole peeled tomatoes, chopped, juice reserved
- 2 tablespoons finely chopped fresh thyme
- 1 cup Beef Stock (page 421), Chicken Stock (page 420), or low-sodium store-bought broth
- 1 pound whole-wheat penne
  Finely grated Parmigiano-Reggiano cheese, for serving

Heat olive oil in a Dutch oven or medium pot over medium high. Cook onion, carrots, and celery until tender, stirring occasionally, about 5 minutes. Add all meats, and season with salt; cook, stirring to break up meat with a spoon, until it is no longer pink, about 7 minutes.

Stir in wine, and simmer until almost evaporated, about 10 minutes. Stir in tomato paste and nutmeg, and cook, stirring, 1 minute. Add tomatoes and their juice along with the thyme and stock; cook (uncovered) at a bare simmer, stirring occasionally, until sauce thickens, about 45 minutes. For best flavor, do not skim fat from sauce. Season sauce with salt and pepper.

When sauce is almost finished cooking, cook pasta in a pot of boiling salted water until al dente, according to package instructions. Drain, toss with the sauce in a pasta bowl, and serve, with cheese alongside.

BUCATINI with BROWN BUTTER, CAPERS, and ANCHOVIES

SERVES 8 AS A FIRST COURSE *from* **CHRISTMAS AT CANTITOE CORNERS**

- 1 pound dried bucatini or spaghetti
  Coarse salt
- 2 tablespoons olive oil
- 3 garlic cloves, crushed
- 1 cup coarse fresh breadcrumbs, made from country bread
- 12 anchovy fillets, rinsed and patted dry, finely chopped, plus 24 whole fillets for garnish (optional)
- ¼ cup capers, drained and rinsed
- 2 tablespoons unsalted butter
- 3 tablespoons chopped fresh flat-leaf parsley

Cook pasta in a pot of boiling salted water 1 or 2 minutes less than package instructions. Reserve 1 cup cooking liquid, and drain pasta.

While pasta is cooking, heat olive oil in a medium skillet over medium. Add garlic and breadcrumbs, and cook, stirring, until crumbs are lightly toasted, about 3 minutes. Add chopped anchovies and the capers, and cook, stirring, until heated through, about 3 minutes more.

Heat butter in a large skillet over medium, swirling frequently, until nut brown in color, about 5 minutes. Add drained pasta along with enough cooking water to form a thin sauce to coat the strands. Cook, stirring, until pasta is al dente, then add breadcrumb mixture, and toss to combine and heat through.

Divide among shallow bowls, and garnish each with three whole anchovy fillets, if desired, and parsley. Serve immediately.

RICOTTA GNOCCHI

SERVES 8 *from* **EASTER DINNER**

Unlike the most traditional gnocchi, made with cooked potatoes, this easy version relies on ricotta cheese for its flavor and texture. You do need to let the cheese drain overnight, so plan accordingly.

- 1 pound fresh ricotta cheese
- ⅔ cup all-purpose flour
- 1 large egg
  Coarse salt
- 10 fresh sage leaves, plus more for garnish
- 2 tablespoons unsalted butter
- ⅓ cup water

Place ricotta in a fine sieve set over a bowl, and let drain 1 day in the refrigerator. Discard liquid. Purée ricotta in a food processor until very smooth. Add flour, and pulse to blend, then add egg, and season with salt, pulsing to blend. Mixture will form a very thick batter. Chill, covered, 1 hour.

Bring a pot of water to a simmer, and add salt. Prepare an ice-water bath. Shape quenelles using two wet soup spoons: use one spoon to scoop up a tablespoon of ricotta batter; with one spoon in each hand, and spoons pointing toward each other, scrape batter back and forth from one spoon to the other a few times, mounding it into a small, neat egg shape. Drop quenelles into simmering water as they are formed, working in batches of eight. Cook until quenelles float to the top and surface springs back when lightly pressed, about 8 minutes. Using a slotted spoon, gently transfer gnocchi to the ice bath as they are cooked. Drain gnocchi, and chill, covered, until ready to serve, up to overnight.

Stack sage leaves, and slice thin to make a chiffonade. Melt butter in a large sauté pan over medium heat, then add gnocchi and the ⅓ cup water. Cook until water evaporates, butter is browned, and gnocchi are heated through, about 5 minutes. Add sage chiffonade, tossing to mix, and season with salt. Serve immediately in shallow bowls, garnished with sage.

WILD-MUSHROOM LASAGNA

SERVES 8 TO 10 *from* **FRIDAY NIGHT WELCOME DINNER**

For step-by-step how-to photographs on making the pasta sheets and assembling the lasagna, see pages 376–77.

- Fresh Pasta Dough (recipe follows)
  Italian "00" flour (or all-purpose flour), for dusting
- ¼ cup plus 1 tablespoon extra-virgin olive oil
  Mushroom Béchamel (recipe follows)
  Wild-Mushroom Filling and Mushroom Broth (recipe follows)
- 1¼ cups finely grated Parmigiano-Reggiano cheese (5 ounces)
  Freshly ground pepper
  Unsalted butter, well chilled, for topping

Shape one piece of dough into a flattened rectangle, and lightly flour dough and pasta rollers. Keep remaining dough pieces covered with a kitchen towel or plastic wrap to prevent them from drying while you work.

Roll dough through machine twice on widest setting. (If pasta pulls or tears when passing through machine, sprinkle a little more flour over dough; use a dry pastry brush to remove excess flour.) As pasta sheet emerges, gently support it with your palm and guide it onto the work surface. Fold dough into thirds, turn dough 90 degrees, and then feed through machine at widest setting. Repeat folding and turning with pasta machine at widest setting.

Thin dough by passing it through ever finer settings of the pasta machine, twice on each setting, until dough is about 1⁄16 inch thick (second or third setting from the finest, depending on machine). Drape pasta sheets over a drying rack as they are rolled out and let stand until almost dry, about 20 minutes. Cut pasta sheets into 8-by-4-inch rectangles, reserving scraps.

Preheat oven to 350° F. Coat a 9-by-13-inch baking dish with 2 tablespoons olive oil, and spread one-fourth of the béchamel sauce over bottom of dish. Arrange four pasta strips on top, overlapping them slightly; fill in any gaps with reserved pasta scraps, as needed. Spread one-half of mushroom filling over pasta, then layer with another one-fourth béchamel. Repeat layering with pasta sheets, remaining mushroom filling, and more béchamel.

Add remaining pasta sheets, tucking edges down around side of dish. Spread remaining béchamel evenly on top, then sprinkle evenly with Parmesan and season with pepper. Using a vegetable peeler or very sharp knife, very thinly slice butter (or cut into small pieces) and arrange on top.

Bake lasagna until bubbling and top is golden brown, 35 to 40 minutes. Let cool 5 minutes before cutting and serving.

Fresh Pasta Dough

MAKES ENOUGH FOR ONE 9-BY-13-INCH LASAGNA

Look for Italian "00" flour at specialty food stores or from online retailers. You can substitute a combination of semolina flour (one-half cup) and all-purpose flour (one-and-a-half cups) for two cups of Italian "00" flour.

- 2 cups Italian "00" flour
- 3 large eggs
- ¼ teaspoon coarse salt
- 1 tablespoon olive oil

Mound flour on a clean work surface or in a large wide bowl, and make a well in the middle. Crack eggs into well, then add the salt and olive oil; using a fork, whisk to combine, then begin to work the flour into the eggs. Use your hands and a bench scraper to work in rest of flour mixture just until a sticky dough forms. (Alternatively, pulse flour, salt, eggs, and olive oil in a food processor until mixture begins to form a ball.)

Divide dough in half, form each into a rounded mass, and knead until smooth, about 10 minutes. Wrap in plastic, and let rest at room temperature for 1 hour. (Dough can be refrigerated at this point up to 1 day; let come to room temperature before proceeding.)

When ready to roll dough in pasta machine, divide each dough half into equal pieces (six for lasagna; four for ravioli or other filled pasta shapes; four for long-strand pasta such as fettuccine or linguine).

Wild-Mushroom Filling and Mushroom Broth

MAKES ABOUT 4 CUPS FILLING AND 1⅔ CUPS BROTH

If wild mushrooms are unavailable, substitute button or cremini mushrooms; for a more pronounced flavor, add some dried mushrooms to the filling: Soak two to three ounces of dried porcini mushrooms in three cups of hot water for thirty minutes, then lift mushrooms from soaking water, leaving any sandy grit behind, and coarsely chop. Then skip the first step of the recipe and use 1¾ cups strained soaking liquid for the broth.

- 2¼ cups water
- 1 pound fresh chanterelle mushrooms, cleaned, trimmed, and coarsely chopped (trimmings reserved)
- 1 pound fresh porcini mushrooms, cleaned, trimmed, and coarsely chopped (trimmings reserved)
- 2 pounds fresh oyster mushrooms, cleaned, trimmed, and coarsely chopped (trimmings reserved)
- 1 pound fresh button mushrooms, cleaned and coarsely chopped
- ¼ cup plus 2 tablespoons olive oil
- 3 large leeks, white and pale green parts only, halved lengthwise and thinly sliced crosswise, washed well, and drained
- Coarse salt and freshly ground pepper
- 5 garlic cloves, minced
- 1 large bunch parsley, leaves coarsely chopped

In a saucepan, bring the water and reserved mushroom trimmings to a boil, then reduce heat and simmer 30 minutes. Remove from heat, and steep mushroom trimmings 30 minutes longer. Strain liquid through a fine sieve, pressing on solids. Discard solids. You should have about 1⅔ cups mushroom broth (add water, if necessary).

Heat 2 tablespoons olive oil in a large sauté pan over medium high until shimmering. Sauté half of the mushrooms over medium-high heat, stirring occasionally, until mushrooms release all juices and begin to turn golden brown, about 15 minutes. Transfer mushrooms to a bowl as they are cooked, and repeat with 2 more tablespoons olive oil and remaining mushrooms.

In same skillet, heat remaining 2 tablespoons olive oil over medium. Sauté leeks until tender, stirring occasionally, 7 to 10 minutes; season with salt. Add garlic; sauté, stirring, until fragrant, about 2 minutes. Add to mushrooms along with chopped parsley; stir to combine. Reserve ⅔ cup mushroom broth; drizzle enough remaining broth over mushroom mixture to keep it moist. Season with salt and pepper. (Mushroom filling and broth can be refrigerated separately in airtight containers up to 1 day.)

Mushroom Béchamel **MAKES 4 CUPS**

Mushroom béchamel can be made one day ahead and stored in an airtight container in the refrigerator.

- 4 tablespoons unsalted butter
- ¼ cup all-purpose flour
- 3 cups milk
- ⅔ cup Mushroom Broth (from recipe above)
- Pinch of freshly grated nutmeg
- Coarse salt and freshly ground white pepper

Melt butter in a saucepan over medium heat. Add flour, and stir constantly until smooth, about 1 minute (it should not take on any color). Whisking constantly, add 1 cup milk, and then the mushroom broth, in a steady stream. Whisk in remaining milk, 1 cup at a time. Simmer béchamel, stirring frequently, until thick enough to coat the back of the spoon, about 3 minutes. Add nutmeg, and season with salt and pepper. Remove from heat and let cool before using or storing.

LEEK *and* PORCINI RISOTTO

SERVES 8 AS A FIRST COURSE *from* **STYLISH DINNER IN THE CLERESTORY**

Reserve the trimmings from the leeks and mushrooms to make the stock. Risotto will continue to thicken off the heat, so be careful not to overcook.

- 3 pounds fresh porcini mushrooms, stems trimmed and peeled (reserve trimmings)
- 4 leeks, white and pale green parts only (reserve trimmings), halved lengthwise, sliced into ⅛-inch-thick half-moons, washed well, and drained
- 3 quarts water
- 3 tablespoons olive oil, plus more if needed
- 1 onion, finely chopped
- 2 cups arborio rice
- ⅔ cup dry white wine
- 4 tablespoons unsalted butter, softened
- ½ cup mascarpone cheese
- 1 cup finely grated Parmigiano-Reggiano cheese (4 ounces)
- Coarse salt and freshly ground pepper

Reserve 4 large porcini; cut the rest into 1-inch pieces. In a medium pot, bring reserved mushroom and leek trimmings and the water to a boil; reduce heat and simmer 45 minutes. Strain mixture through a fine sieve into a bowl, pressing on solids to extract as much liquid as possible; discard solids. You should have 8 cups mushroom broth (add water, if necessary). Pour broth into a saucepan; cover, and heat over lowest setting.

Meanwhile, preheat oven to 200° F. Heat 1 tablespoon olive oil in a large sauté pan. Working in batches (and adding more oil, as needed), cook mushroom pieces until golden brown, stirring often, about 8 minutes. Use a slotted spatula spoon to transfer mushrooms to a paper towel–lined plate, and keep warm in the oven.

Heat remaining 2 tablespoons olive oil in another pot over medium high. Cook onion and leeks until translucent, stirring frequently, about 3 minutes. Add rice, and cook, stirring constantly, until it begins to turn translucent, about 2 minutes. Add wine; cook, stirring, until almost absorbed.

Add the hot broth, ½ cup at a time, stirring until the liquid is almost absorbed before adding more. Repeat until rice is almost completely translucent but still al dente, and mixture is creamy looking, about 25 minutes (you may not need to use all the hot broth). Remove from heat. Stir butter and mascarpone into the risotto until completely incorporated, then fold in Parmesan. Season with salt and pepper.

When risotto is almost finished cooking, season sautéed mushrooms with salt, and thinly slice reserved whole mushrooms. Divide risotto evenly among shallow bowls; garnish with both mushrooms. Serve immediately.

RISOTTO *with* CANTITOE FARM TOMATOES *and* SAUTÉED SHRIMP

SERVES 8 AS A FIRST COURSE *from* **CELEBRATING A MASTER GARDENER**

This late-summer risotto features homegrown tomatoes in a variety of colors. You can use whatever is available at the farmers' market or from your own garden—heirloom varieties, such as Green Zebra, Big Rainbow, and Speckled Roman, are a few beautiful and delicious options.

- 4½ pounds tomatoes, preferably heirloom
- ½ cup plus 2 tablespoons olive oil
- 2 garlic cloves, chopped
  Coarse salt and freshly ground pepper
- 6 cups water or Vegetable Stock (page 421)
- 1 onion, finely chopped
- 2 cups arborio rice
- 4 tablespoons unsalted butter
- ⅔ cup finely grated Parmigiano-Reggiano cheese (3 ounces)
- 16 jumbo shrimp (8 to 10 count), cleaned and deveined
- ¼ cup mixed chopped fresh herbs, such as basil, chervil, rosemary, thyme, and sage, plus sprigs for garnish (optional)

Preheat oven to 220° F. Bring a large pot of water to a boil, and prepare a large ice-water bath. Working in batches (one for each color of tomato), blanch tomatoes until skins are loosened, 5 to 10 seconds, depending on ripeness. Using a slotted spoon or mesh spider, transfer tomatoes to ice bath to stop the cooking. When cool, slip off skins and halve tomatoes crosswise. Working over a bowl to catch the juices, gently squeeze seeds from tomatoes into bowl. Reserve one-quarter tomato halves for purée.

Arrange remaining tomato halves in a single layer on a large rimmed baking sheet. Brush with 2 tablespoons olive oil, sprinkle evenly with the chopped garlic, and season with salt and pepper. Cook 1½ hours, flipping tomatoes every 30 minutes, and opening oven door after 1 hour to allow steam to escape. Remove from oven, and let cool. Cut tomatoes into ½-inch strips, and transfer to a bowl; cover tomato confit to keep warm.

Meanwhile, pass reserved tomato seeds and juice through a fine sieve into another bowl, pressing on solids to extract as much liquid as possible. Discard solids. Purée reserved halved tomatoes in a blender; pour into a fine sieve lined with four layers of cheesecloth. Gather ends of cheesecloth together to form a bundle; press gently to extract as much clear tomato water as possible into bowl with strained reserved juice. Transfer tomato pulp remaining in cheesecloth to a separate bowl; reserve. (Recipe can be prepared up to this point a day ahead; cover and refrigerate all components separately. Before proceeding, bring tomato water and reserved tomato pulp to room temperature and warm tomato confit.)

Bring 6 cups water to a simmer. Heat 2 tablespoons olive oil over medium high in a heavy-bottomed pot. Cook onion until softened but not browned, stirring occasionally, about 4 minutes. Add rice, and cook, stirring constantly, until it begins to turn translucent, about 2 minutes. Add enough reserved tomato water (and heated water, if necessary) to cover rice by ¼ inch; season with salt. Cook, stirring, until liquid is absorbed.

Add any remaining tomato water, and then the hot water, ½ cup at a time, stirring frequently until each addition is absorbed before adding the next. Repeat until rice is almost completely translucent but still al dente, and mixture is creamy-looking, about 25 minutes (you may not need to use all the hot water). Remove from heat. Stir in reserved tomato pulp along with butter, Parmesan, and 2 tablespoons olive oil. Season with salt and pepper.

When risotto is almost finished cooking, heat remaining 2 tablespoons olive oil in a large, heavy skillet over medium high. Sauté shrimp (in batches, if necessary) until bright pink and opaque throughout, about 2 minutes on each side. Transfer to a bowl; season with salt and toss with half the chopped herbs.

Divide risotto evenly among shallow bowls, top each with tomato confit slices and 2 shrimp, and sprinkle with chopped herbs. Garnish with herb sprigs, if desired. Serve immediately.

Main Dishes

BARBECUED BABY-BACK RIBS

SERVES 12 *from* **JULY 4TH BARBECUE**

You can simmer the ribs a day ahead. Let cool completely before wrapping in plastic and refrigerating; bring to room temperature before grilling.

- 6 racks baby-back ribs (each about 1½ pounds and with 10 to 14 ribs)
- 4 celery stalks, coarsely chopped
- 2 carrots, coarsely chopped
- 1 large onion, coarsely chopped
- 1 garlic clove, halved
  Coarse salt and freshly ground pepper
- 2 recipes Pierre's Barbecue Sauce (recipe follows)

Divide ribs between two large pots and add enough water to cover. Bring to a boil, reduce heat, and simmer 3 minutes, skimming foam from surface. Drain; rinse ribs under cold water. Return to pots; cover again with water.

Divide celery, carrots, onion, and garlic between pots; add 1 tablespoon salt to each. Bring to a boil. Reduce to a simmer, and cook until ribs are tender, about 1 hour. Drain; discard vegetables.

Heat grill to medium. (If you are using a charcoal grill, coals are ready when you can hold your hand 5 inches above grates for just 5 to 6 seconds.) Season ribs generously with salt and pepper; brush with barbecue sauce. Grill, turning frequently and brushing with sauce occasionally, until heated through and marked by grill, about 15 minutes. Cut into servings of about three ribs each; brush with more sauce, and serve.

Pierre's Barbecue Sauce MAKES ABOUT 3 CUPS

- ½ cup olive oil
- 4 large onions, coarsely chopped
- 3 garlic cloves, crushed
- 2 red bell peppers, roasted (page 423)
- ½ teaspoon ground chile peppers or chili powder
- ½ teaspoon cayenne
- ¼ teaspoon ground coriander
- ⅔ cup packed dark brown sugar

5½ pounds tomatoes, coarsely chopped
Coarse salt and freshly ground black pepper
⅓ cup white wine vinegar
¼ cup Dijon mustard
2 tablespoons honey
1 tablespoon plus 1 teaspoon Worcestershire sauce
1 tablespoon soy sauce

Heat olive oil in a large pot over medium high. Add onions, garlic, and roasted peppers; sauté, stirring occasionally, until onions are dark golden brown, 8 to 10 minutes. Stir in ground chiles, cayenne, and coriander; cook, stirring, 30 seconds. Add brown sugar; cook, stirring occasionally, 2 minutes. Add tomatoes; season with salt and black pepper. Cook, stirring occasionally, until tomatoes have broken down and are very soft, about 20 minutes. Stir in vinegar, mustard, honey, Worcestershire, and soy sauce.

Strain through a coarse sieve into another saucepan, pressing on solids to remove as much liquid as possible; discard solids. Bring to a boil; reduce heat and simmer rapidly, stirring occasionally, until slightly thickened, 15 to 20 minutes. Adjust seasoning before serving, warm or at room temperature. (Sauce can be made up to 3 days ahead; let cool completely and refrigerate in an airtight container. Reheat over low if desired.)

BARBECUED CHICKEN WINGS

SERVES 12 *from* **JULY 4TH BARBECUE**

You can bake the wings up to a day ahead. Once cooled, refrigerate them in a covered container; bring them to room temperature before grilling.

24 chicken wings
3 tablespoons olive oil
Coarse salt and freshly ground pepper
Pierre's Barbecue Sauce (recipe above)

Preheat oven to 400° F. Arrange wings on two rimmed baking sheets. Drizzle each sheet with the olive oil, dividing evenly. Season with salt and pepper, and toss to combine. Spread in an even layer and bake until cooked through, about 30 minutes.

Heat grill to medium high. (If you are using a charcoal grill, coals are ready when you can hold your hand 5 inches above grates for just 3 to 4 seconds.) Brush wings with barbecue sauce. Grill, turning and brushing with sauce occasionally, until heated through and marked by grill, 6 to 7 minutes. Serve.

SAFFRON *and* ORANGE GLAZED CHICKEN WINGS

SERVES 4 *from* **THE ART OF GRILLING**

1 cup fresh orange juice
2 tablespoons neutral-tasting oil, such as safflower
2 pinches of saffron threads
8 chicken wings
Coarse salt and freshly ground pepper

Whisk together orange juice, oil, and saffron threads. Place chicken wings in a shallow dish or resealable plastic bag and pour marinade over chicken. Cover (or seal bag) and refrigerate at least 4 hours or up to overnight.

Heat grill to medium high. (If using a charcoal grill, coals are ready when you can hold your hand 5 inches above grates for just 3 to 4 seconds.) Remove chicken from marinade, patting off excess, and season with salt and pepper. Discard marinade. Grill chicken on both sides until cooked through, 5 to 7 minutes per side. Serve hot.

BRAISED SHORT RIBS

SERVES 8 *from* **BURGUNDY DINNER**

For the photograph on page 231, the short ribs were cut into three-rib sections, across the bone (as for flanken), with the bones two to three inches long. The ribs can be braised up to two days ahead; let cool completely, then refrigerate with the sauce in an airtight container; reheat before serving. Use a full-bodied red wine, such as Burgundy or Bordeaux, for braising.

8 sections short ribs (each about 1 pound and with 3 ribs)
4 cups dry red wine
6 garlic cloves
2 leeks, white and pale green parts only, cut into 1-inch lengths, washed well and drained
3 carrots, peeled and cut into 3-inch lengths
2 red onions, quartered
2 celery stalks, cut into 3-inch lengths
Coarse salt and freshly ground black pepper
2 tablespoons olive oil
2 cups Beef Stock (page 421) or low-sodium store-bought broth
1 ounce bittersweet chocolate, chopped
2 tablespoons water
1 tablespoon all-purpose flour

Combine ribs, wine, garlic, and vegetables in a large roasting pan. Cover and let marinate in the refrigerator 1 day.

Remove rib sections from marinade and pat dry, then season all over with salt and pepper. With a slotted spoon, transfer vegetables to a colander, and reserve marinade.

Heat olive oil in a large sauté pan over medium high. Sear two rib sections at a time on the meat side until browned, then transfer to a large pot. Once all ribs have been seared, pour off all but 2 tablespoons fat from pan and add vegetables to pan. Sauté until deep golden brown, stirring occasionally, about 8 minutes. Transfer to pot and add reserved marinade and the stock. If necessary, add enough water to just cover ribs and vegetables. Bring to a boil, then reduce heat and simmer, covered, until meat is very tender but is not yet falling apart, about 1½ hours.

Using tongs, transfer ribs to a rimmed baking sheet. Strain liquid through a fine sieve into a saucepan; discard solids. Bring liquid to a simmer; cook, skimming off foam and impurities from the surface, until reduced to 2 cups, about 1 hour. Skim off fat, then stir in chocolate until melted.

In a small bowl, stir together the water and flour, then whisk into sauce. Simmer, whisking, until sauce thickens, about 2 minutes. Strain sauce through a fine sieve into a clean saucepan.

Remove bones and membrane covering underside of ribs. Trim away excess fat. Arrange ribs in a single layer in bottom of pot. Bring sauce to a simmer, then pour over ribs. Bring to a boil. Reduce heat and simmer, covered, until meat is heated through, about 5 minutes. Serve hot.

BRAISED LEG *of* LAMB

SERVES 8 TO 12 *from* **EASTER DINNER**

Ask your butcher to trim the lamb, saving the pelvis bone and trimmings, which will add flavor to the sauce. Look for demi-glace, a classic French reduction used to enrich sauces, at specialty food stores or from online sources.

- 1 leg of lamb (6 to 7 pounds), trimmed and tied (pelvis bone removed and reserved with trimmings)
  Coarse salt and freshly ground pepper
- ⅓ cup olive oil
- 4 celery stalks, halved lengthwise
- 4 large carrots, peeled and cut into large pieces
- 6 shallots, halved
- ½ garlic head, cloves separated (peeled)
- 6 cups Vegetable Stock (page 421) or low-sodium store-bought broth
- 2 cups water
- 3 ounces demi-glace (optional)
  Mint Jelly, for serving (recipe follows)

Preheat oven to 450° F. Pat dry lamb and season all over with salt and pepper. Heat olive oil in a large roasting pan over medium high. Cook lamb, fat side down, until browned, about 5 minutes. Add reserved lamb bone and trimmings, celery, carrots, shallots, and garlic cloves to roasting pan and transfer to oven; roast 30 minutes, turning lamb once.

Combine stock, the water, and demi-glace (if using) in a medium saucepan. Bring to a boil, then remove from heat. Pour enough stock mixture into roasting pan to reach halfway up meat, and cover pan with parchment, then foil. Reserve remaining stock mixture in saucepan. Reduce oven to 350° F and continue to cook until meat is tender and falling off the bone, about 2 to 2½ hours, adding more stock mixture as needed to maintain liquid level.

Transfer lamb to a deep serving dish and cover to keep warm. Discard pelvis bone. Strain liquid in pan through a fine sieve into the saucepan with reserved stock mixture; discard solids. Bring to a boil, skimming off fat that rises to surface, then reduce heat and simmer until sauce is thickened to a syrupy consistency, about 10 minutes. Spoon sauce over lamb. Serve immediately, with mint jelly alongside.

Mint Jelly MAKES 1 CUP

- ¾ teaspoon unflavored powdered gelatin
- ¼ cup cold water
- 1 cup packed fresh mint leaves
- ¾ cup quince or apple jelly

In a cup, sprinkle gelatin over 1 tablespoon water and let soften 5 minutes.

Prepare an ice-water bath. Blanch mint in a pot of simmering water until bright green, about 30 seconds. Transfer to ice bath to stop the cooking. Drain mint, then puree in a blender with remaining 3 tablespoons water.

Heat jelly in a small saucepan until melted, then add softened gelatin, stirring until dissolved. Stir in mint purée and strain through a fine sieve into a bowl, pressing on solids to extract as much liquid as possible (discard solids). Refrigerate, covered tightly, at least 2 hours or up to 2 days.

ROASTED LAMB SADDLE *with* LEMON-THYME JUS

SERVES 8 *from* **VERDANT SPRING DINNER**

If you like, ask your butcher to bone the lamb for you, and reserve the bones for making the sauce. Serve the dish with Fava Bean Ragoût (page 390).

- 2 lamb loins (each 1½ to 2 pounds), boned and tied (reserve bones)
  Coarse salt and freshly ground pepper
- 2 to 3 tablespoons neutral-tasting oil, such as safflower
  Lemon-Thyme Jus, for serving (recipe follows)

Preheat oven to 450° F. Pat dry lamb and season all over with salt and pepper. Heat oil in a large ovenproof skillet until shimmering. Place loins fat side down in pan and sear until golden and crisp, about 8 minutes.

Flip loins and transfer skillet to oven. Roast until an instant-read thermometer inserted in middle of meat registers 145° F for medium rare, 8 to 10 minutes. Transfer lamb to a cutting board; let rest 10 minutes before slicing into thick medallions. Serve with lemon-thyme jus.

Lemon-Thyme Jus MAKES 1 CUP

Lemon thyme looks like the more common variety of the herb, but has a pronounced lemon flavor and aroma. Look for it at farmers' markets and specialty food stores, or substitute regular thyme and add a squeeze of lemon juice along with the olive oil.

- Reserved lamb bones (from Roasted Lamb Saddle, recipe above)
- ¼ cup olive oil, plus more for drizzling
- 2 shallots, chopped
- 1 celery stalk, chopped
- 1 carrot, peeled and chopped
- 2 garlic cloves, finely chopped
- 1 tablespoon tomato paste
- 1 cup dry red wine
  Coarse salt
- 1 tablespoon fresh lemon-thyme leaves

Preheat oven to 400° F. Drizzle bones with olive oil in a roasting pan; toss to coat, then spread in an even layer. Roast until golden brown, 35 to 45 minutes. Let cool slightly. Cut large bones into 6-inch sections (to fit in pot).

Heat 2 tablespoons olive oil in a medium pot over medium. Add shallots, celery, carrot, and garlic; cook, stirring occasionally, until vegetables are softened, about 5 minutes. Increase heat to high, stir in tomato paste, and cook, stirring, 1 minute. Pour in wine and cook until almost evaporated, scraping up any browned bits from bottom of pan with a wooden spoon.

Add roasted bones and enough water to cover (about 6 cups). Bring to a boil, then reduce heat to a gentle simmer. Cook, partially covered, 3 hours, occasionally skimming foam from surface.

Strain stock through a fine sieve into a saucepan; discard solids. Skim off fat from top. Return to a simmer and cook until reduced to about 1 cup. Season with salt, and remove from heat. (Sauce can be prepared to this point up to 3 days ahead; let cool completely before refrigerating in an airtight container, and reheat over medium-low before proceeding.) To serve, whisk in remaining 2 tablespoons olive oil and stir in lemon thyme.

CREAM SCONES HOW-TO

RECIPE PAGE 332 *from* **BREAKFAST ON THE PORCH**

1. Pulse well-chilled butter cubes with half the dry ingredients in a food processor a few times, just to combine and leaving some large butter pieces. Then add to remaining dry ingredients and mix by hand. This two-step process helps evenly work the butter into the flour before blending with the cream and eggs.

2. Turn out dough onto a lightly floured work surface, first patting into a rectangle shape with lightly floured hands. Using a floured rolling pin, gently roll out dough into a rectangle that is about 1 inch thick, being careful not to roll over the edges.

3. Sprinkle dried fruit mixture evenly over dough, leaving a border around the edges; then fold into thirds, like a business letter, starting with a short side. Rotate a quarter-turn, so the flap is on the right (like a book). This is the first "turn."

4. Roll out dough again into a rectangle, using a bench scraper or your hands to lift edges of dough as you work; dust work surface and rolling pin lightly with flour as necessary to prevent dough from sticking. Repeat folding and rotating to complete a second turn.

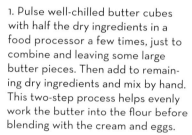   

5. With floured hands, pat dough into a 1¼-inch-thick rectangle. Using a floured 2-inch cutter, cut out rounds as close together as possible to reduce the amount of scraps, which can only be rerolled once. Transfer rounds to a baking sheet as you go, leaving 2 inches between.

6. Brush tops of rounds with egg wash, then sprinkle generously with sanding sugar. During baking, rotate the sheet from front to back halfway through to ensure even cooking.

PASKA DECORATIONS HOW-TO

RECIPE PAGE 335 *from* **EASTER BRUNCH**

 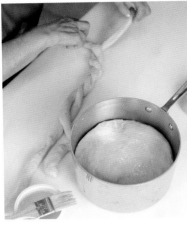  

1. Line a work surface with a large piece of parchment. Divide reserved dough into pieces (one for each rope). Keep the rest covered with plastic wrap while you work. Roll each of two pieces with the palms of your hands into a long, thin strand, about ½ inch in diameter.

2. Starting in the middle and working out toward each end, twist the two strands together. Repeat with two more dough pieces to form another twisted rope. Brush top of paska dough in pan with beaten egg white.

3. Arrange a rope in a circle on dough in pan; trim ends to fit neatly. Cut the other rope in half. Place one half on top of dough in the center; pulling ends out and curling slightly. Press ends gently into dough to adhere. Place other half on top in a crisscross fashion, pressing ends gently to adhere.

4. To form a flower shape (as shown in lower right of step 6), roll a small piece of dough into a long, thin strand with tapered ends. Press ends onto parchment. Use a sharp knife to make even slits on the bias in one side. Roll up strand from one end to the other with the "petals" on top. Attach to top of dough with egg white, pressing gently to adhere.

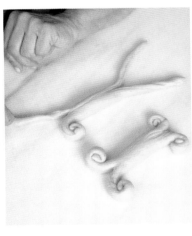  

5. For the decoration shown in far right of step 6, roll each of four dough pieces into a long, thin strand. Arrange two strands side by side; press middle 4 inches together, then angle ends slightly. Roll up each end tightly to resemble a curlicue. Repeat with remaining two strands. Stack in a crisscross fashion. Alternatively, arrange strands on top of each other like a spoke (as shown in bottom right of step 6). Roll up ends so the curlicues are all facing the same direction.

6. If making multiple loaves, form decorations on a baking sheet and brush with egg wash before placing atop dough in pans. To make the braided piece shown in the upper left, roll out three long strands, then braid, trimming and tucking under end pieces. For the piece in the middle, tie a shorter strand into a knot. Brush dough in pan with egg wash just before attaching decorations.

POPPY SEED–CHEESE STRAWS HOW-TO

RECIPE PAGE 340 *from* **HALLOWEEN PUMPKIN BLAZE**

1. With a floured rolling pin, roll out the dough to a 12-by-16-inch-long rectangle. Sprinkle evenly with cheese and poppy seed mixture. Roll over dough again with pin to help mixture adhere.

2. Using a pastry wheel or pizza cutter, trim edges to make even, then cut dough into ½-inch-wide strips.

3. Transfer strips to a baking sheet, about 1 inch apart. Twist each strip from one end to the other, pressing ends gently onto sheet to help straws hold their shape during baking.

ROASTED TOMATO TART HOW-TO

RECIPE PAGE 330 *from* **BREAKFAST ON THE PORCH**

1. Once the tart shell has been baked and allowed to cool, spread mashed roasted garlic in an even layer over the bottom with a flexible spatula.

2. Sprinkle shell evenly with half the cheese, then begin arranging roasted tomato halves on top of cheese, nudging them closely with the spatula.

3. Continue arranging tomato halves in shell until completely covered, then season with salt and pepper. Sprinkle remaining cheese evenly over tomatoes, then drizzle with melted butter before baking.

FRESH PASTA DOUGH HOW-TO

RECIPE PAGE 368 *from* **FRIDAY NIGHT WELCOME DINNER**

1. Measure the ingredients before you begin and clear off enough space on the counter for making dough.

2. Mound the flour in the center of a work surface (or put in a wide, shallow bowl) and make a well in the center. Crack the eggs into the well, sprinkle with salt, and then add the olive oil.

3. Beat the egg mixture with a fork until smooth, then begin to work the flour into the eggs with the fork, gradually incorporating more flour until the wet ingredients are no longer runny.

4. Using a bench scraper and your hands, work the rest of the flour into the eggs, a bit at a time, just until mixture comes together to form a sticky dough. Don't overwork the dough; it's okay if some loose flour remains.

5. Knead dough for about 10 minutes, or until smooth and elastic, scraping up any loose bits of dough with a bench scraper as you work.

6. Divide dough in half, and form each into a rounded mass. Cover dough with plastic wrap (or an inverted bowl) and let rest at room temperature for 1 hour (or overnight in the refrigerator).

7. Transfer dough to a lightly floured work surface and flatten slightly into disks. Divide each half into equal pieces with a bench scraper. At this point, you can roll the pieces through the pasta machine to make lasagna sheets (first cut each half into 6 pieces), as shown opposite, or long strands, such as fettuccine and linguine (cut each half into four pieces).

WILD-MUSHROOM LASAGNA HOW-TO

RECIPE PAGE 368 *from* **FRIDAY NIGHT WELCOME DINNER**

1. Working with one piece at a time (keep remaining pieces covered with a kitchen towel), flatten dough with your hands into an oblong shape somewhat narrower than the pasta machine's opening. Very lightly dust dough with flour and feed through the machine's widest setting.

2. Fold the sheet lengthwise into thirds, like a business letter, and rotate 90 degrees so the flap is open to the right. Repeat sequence two more times at the same setting to smooth the dough and increase its elasticity.

3. Pass dough through increasingly finer settings. If dough tears when passing through machine, sprinkle with a little flour before it's fed; after rolling, remove excess flour with a dry brush. End with second- or third-thinnest setting, until sheet is 1/16 inch thick. Drape sheets over a rack until almost dry, about 20 minutes.

4. Trim pasta sheets to 8-by-4-inch strips, and reserve scraps for filling in gaps. Begin by spreading béchamel in oiled baking dish in an even layer, then layer 4 pasta strips on top, overlapping them slightly, and filling in with any scraps to cover completely. Top with mushroom filling, spreading evenly with the back of a spoon.

5. Spread more béchamel over the mushroom filling, and add another layer of pasta, tucking edges down around side of dish and using scraps as necessary to cover completely. Repeat layering with mushroom filling, béchamel, and pasta strips. Trim edges of pasta as needed with a sharp knife to fit inside dish.

6. Spread remaining béchamel over the last layer of pasta. Sprinkle evenly with Parmesan cheese and season with pepper.

7. Shave well-chilled butter with a vegetable peeler or sharp knife into thin pieces over the top before baking. (Alternatively, cut butter into cubes and dot evenly over top.)

ROASTED TURKEY BREAST HOW-TO

RECIPE PAGE 385 *from* **THANKSGIVING AT BEDFORD**

1. Combine vegetables, herbs, and stock in a vertical roasting pan (or a Bundt pan), distributing evenly and packing gently with a flexible spatula.

2. Loosen skin from turkey breast. Working from the neck end, spread herb butter under skin, patting to distribute evenly. Brush surface of turkey with melted butter, then rub with seasonings. Rest turkey on cone of pan, then place pan on a rimmed baking sheet.

3. Before preheating oven, remove all but lowest rack to allow room for the turkey. Roast until turkey is a deep golden brown and thickest part registers 150°F on an instant-read thermometer, 1 to 1¼ hours. Transfer to a cutting board, and let rest at least 10 minutes before carving.

STUFFED PUMPKIN HOW-TO

RECIPE PAGE 394 *from* **HALLOWEEN PUMPKIN BLAZE**

1. To prepare the pumpkin that will be stuffed, cut out a 5-inch round from the top; reserve top. Scrape out seeds and stringy flesh, and discard. Then prepare the ingredients for the stuffing.

2. Toss the sautéed chestnuts, mushrooms, and vegetables in a bowl with the bread cubes, diced apples, chopped herbs, and olive oil. Season with salt and pepper. Add the eggs, and mix to incorporate.

3. Rub inside of pumpkin shell with olive oil and season with salt and pepper before filling with the stuffing. Replace top, and bake on a rimmed baking sheet until pumpkin is tender (test by piercing the bottom with a sharp paring knife) and stuffing is cooked through.

4. Let cool slightly before transferring to a serving platter. When spooning out the stuffing, be sure to include some of the pumpkin flesh, taking care not to scrape too close to the sides or the shell may split.

APPLE TART HOW-TO

RECIPE PAGE TK *from* **BURGUNDY DINNER**

 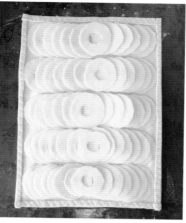  

1. Prepare apples: With a melon baller or a corer, remove core from each apple in one piece. Peel apples with a paring knife, preserving the shape of the fruit. Use a sharp chef's knife to thinly slice crosswise. Brush slices with lemon juice to keep them from browning.

2. Sprinkle chilled tart shell with sugar, then arrange sliced apples on top in neat rows. Start each row at both ends and then continue adding slices in an overlapping manner until you reach the middle, and finish with an apple slice on top.

3. Sprinkle apples evenly with sugar and dot with butter. (To make the variation shown above, an apple-sauce filling is first spread over the tart shell before the apples are added. Start at one end of each row and add more apple slices, overlapping, until you reach the other end.) Brush top of border with beaten egg; do not let it drip down the sides.

4. Bake tart until crust is puffed and deep golden brown; and the apples very tender. Let cool completely before brushing apples with glaze and serving.

BAKED STUFFED APPLES HOW-TO

RECIPE PAGE TK *from* **HALLOWEEN PUMPKIN BLAZE**

1. Core apples with a melon baller or a grapefruit spoon, leaving bottom intact. Fill with stuffing. Bake on a baking sheet until apples are tender (test by piercing the bottoms with a sharp paring knife). The cooking time will depend on size and variety of apple. Let cool on sheet on a wire rack.

2. Spoon vanilla crème anglaise onto each dessert plate, leaving center free. Transfer chocolate crème anglaise to a pastry bag fitted with a fine plain tip. Starting at the outside and working toward the center of the plate, pipe a spiral pattern, leaving about ¼ inch between each curved line.

3. To create the spider-web design, drag the tip of a sharp knife in radiating lines through the chocolate spiral, working from the center of the plate out, and spacing about ½ inch apart.

4. Transfer Swiss meringue to a large pastry bag fitted with a star tip. Pipe a rosette on top of each apple, then lightly brown the edges of the peaks with a small kitchen torch, if desired. Place an apple in the center of each plate just before serving.

PALMIERS HOW-TO

RECIPE PAGE 402   *from* CELEBRATING A MASTER GARDENER

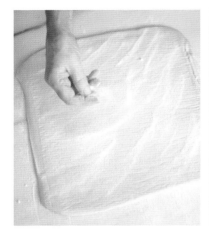   

1. Sprinkle a work surface with sugar. Using a rolling pin, gently roll out dough into a 9½-by-15-inch rectangle, about ⅛ inch thick. Continually coat both sides with sugar as you roll.

2. Using a ruler and sharp knife or a pastry wheel, trim edges to make even. Place dough so that one of the long sides is closest to you. Using your fingers, roll dough lengthwise into a long cylinder as tightly as possible without stretching it, stopping when you reach the middle.

3. Repeat the same rolling procedure with the other long side until you have two tight cylinders that meet in the middle. Transfer to a parchment-lined baking sheet, and chill in the refrigerator at least 1 hour, covered with plastic wrap, before slicing and chilling again for another hour.

4. Bake until beginning to color, 8 to 10 minutes, then remove from oven and flip with an offset spatula. Continue baking until golden brown, 6 to 8 minutes more. Allow palmiers to cool completely on a wire rack before serving.

COOKIE CONE HOW-TO

RECIPE PAGE 409   *from* ICE CREAM SOCIAL

1. To prepare a template, cut a 4¾-inch circle from a piece of plastic, such as a clean lid from a large yogurt or deli container.

2. Place template on a baking sheet. Using a large offset spatula, spread batter in a thin layer over template to form a round. Carefully lift template; repeat to make more rounds. (To make it easier to shape into cones while tuiles are still hot, you may want to bake 3 or 4 total per batch.)

3. Immediately after baking, remove 1 tuile with a small offset spatula; gently wrap around a citrus reamer (or other conical-shaped object). Hold until cone begins to harden, about 10 seconds; transfer to a wire rack, seam side down, to cool completely. Repeat with remaining tuiles.

4. Instead of a wire rack, the cones can be set upright in an egg holder (as shown) or in a flatware caddy or other vessel to help preserve their shape. This also helps hold the cones while filling them with ice cream and serving.

PEACH *and* NECTARINE RICOTTA CROSTATA HOW-TO

RECIPE PAGE 400 *from* **DINNER PARTY DESSERTS**

1. Peel peaches and nectarines (see page 423) and cut into wedges, then toss with brown sugar, cornstarch, salt, and lemon zest.

2. Spoon fruit mixture over chilled dough, covering the ricotta mixture, then begin folding up the edges of the pastry over the fruit, gently pressing the creases as you work.

3. Brush border of pastry with egg wash, which will encourage the crust to brown in the oven.

4. Liberally sprinkle the pastry with coarse sanding sugar; granulated sugar can be used instead.

5. Dot the filling with butter pieces, distributing it evenly, then bake until crust is golden brown and filling is juicy and bubbling, rotating sheet halfway through, about 1 hour. Let cool completely before serving.

MACARONS HOW-TO

RECIPE PAGE 412 *from* **VERDANT SPRING DINNER**

1. Once egg whites and granulated sugar have been beaten to stiff peaks, mix in food coloring, as desired. Sift almond flour and confectioners' sugar into another bowl; fold in whites. Beat batter with spatula just until it no longer holds peaks. (Deflating the whites slightly will ensure the proper outcome.)

2. Fit a large pastry bag with a large, plain tip (cinch the bag just above the tip to prevent the batter from leaking while filling). Fold top of bag over your hand to form a cuff, then fill bag halfway with batter. Fold up bag and twist the top securely to seal.

3. Pipe 1-inch rounds, at least 1 inch apart, onto baking sheets lined with a nonstick baking mat or parchment. (When piping, use one hand to hold bag at the top to exert pressure, and the other to gently guide.) As you release pressure, quickly sweep tip off to one side to avoid forming a peak. Let dry thoroughly before baking.

4. Bake one sheet at a time until cookies are firm to the touch, rotating sheet halfway through to ensure even cooking. Transfer the cookies, still on the mat or parchment, to a wire rack and let cool completely.

5. In preparation for filling, arrange cookies in pairs of similar size, with one facing up and the other facing down. Use your thumb to make a small indentation in center of those cookies with the flat side facing up, to make extra room for the filling.

6. Using a small pastry bag fitted with a small plain tip, pipe desired filling onto indentations in cookies, leaving a ¼-inch border all around.

7. Sandwich paired cookies, gently pressing to adhere (filling should just reach edges). To make more than one color of macaron, divide egg-white mixture into separate bowls, tint as desired, then fold into the almond-flour mixture, which has also been divided accordingly (or tint separate batches). These macarons feature fillings in the same shades as the cookies.

ORANGE EASTER-EGG CAKE DECORATING HOW-TO

RECIPE PAGE 417 *from* **EASTER DINNER**

1. Tuck pieces of parchment under cake to keep platter clean. Prop up cake with a wedge of bread. With a pastry bag fitted with a coupler and a basket-weave tip, pipe adjacent lines of Swiss meringue to cover wedge and back side of egg. Switch to a plain tip; pipe lines across front side of egg, about 1 inch apart.

2. Switch back to basket-weave tip. Starting at center of top line, pipe a short vertical line over one line, then stop at the next; repeat until you reach the bottom. Next, pipe lines adjacent to the first, starting at the second horizontal line; continue until cake is covered, staggering alternating lines for a woven effect.

3. Switch to an open star tip, and pipe a border around the edge of the cake to cover the seams, using a gentle back-and-forth motion to create a ruffled effect.

4. At one of the openings in the basket weave, toward the top of the cake, insert a wooden dowel through the cake and into the wedge. Trim dowel flush with meringue. This will help support the cake until it is served (discard once the cake is sliced).

5. Just before serving, use a small kitchen torch to brown the meringue on the cake, waving the torch quickly back and forth over the surface. If desired, tie a ribbon into a bow and use another dowel to secure it in place at the top of the egg cake.

SPRING GARDEN CAKE MARZIPAN HOW-TO

RECIPE PAGE 418 *from* **EASTER EGG HUNT**

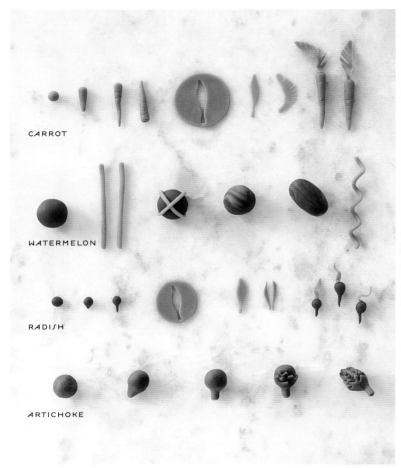

CARROT

WATERMELON

RADISH

ARTICHOKE

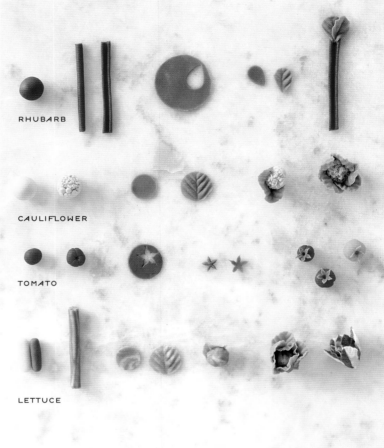

RHUBARB

CAULIFLOWER

TOMATO

LETTUCE

Carrot: Combine orange, tulip red, and a touch of nut-brown gel-paste food colors to achieve the right shade of orange, and tint marzipan. Roll out a pea-size ball of marzipan to the desired length, tapering one end; use a utility knife to etch small grooves along the surface. Using a leaf-shaped cutter or a knife, cut a rolled-out sphere of leaf-green marzipan, then insert into a hole made with a toothpick. (If leaf doesn't stay in place, moisten it with a tiny bit of water and a fine paintbrush before attaching.)

Watermelon: Tint some marzipan dark green and a smaller piece pale green. For each watermelon, work 2 pale-green ropes into a ½-inch ball of dark green marzipan; use a light touch to make the rind's characteristic streaky appearance, without muddying the colors. To create the coiling vines, wrap slender ropes of leaf-green marzipan around a skewer that has been dusted with cornstarch to prevent sticking.

Radish: Tint marzipan with a combination of Christmas red, deep pink, and a bit of violet. Starting with a pea-size ball, pull and pinch while turning to create pointed root end. Top with a single leaf (see instructions for carrot, above).

Artichoke: Combine leaf green with a touch of yellow and nut brown, and use to tint marzipan; roll into ¼-inch balls. Tint a small piece of marzipan brown, and work into the ball to create the artichoke's marbled appearance. Roll out ball, tapering one end, then pinch to shape the stem. Use scissors to create the leaves.

Rhubarb: Tint marzipan with tulip red and a dab of violet. Roll into strings; flatten with your fingertips. Shape stalks by pressing strips around a skewer brushed with cornstarch. Cut out leaves from rolled-out leaf-green dough, adding veins with a leaf veiner, and attach a leaf or two to top of each stalk (see instructions for carrot, left).

Cauliflower: Mix white with a touch of yellow and nut brown; tint marzipan. Roll into tiny balls for florets; press into top of a ¼-inch ball of the same color. For leaves, tint marzipan with leaf green, white, and nut brown; roll out and press small balls into a circle, adding veins with a leaf veiner. Place four leaves around base of ball, bending and shaping around "head."

Tomato: To make red tomatoes, tint marzipan with tulip red, orange, and yellow; for yellow tomatoes, use a mix of yellow and orange. With a toothpick, mark grooves along top of each pea-size ball. Make leaves from rolled-out leaf-green marzipan, using a petal cutter; thin tips with a ball tool, then adhere to tops using a fluted arrow tool. Pinch petals so they won't lie flat.

Lettuce: Tint one batch of marzipan with a blend of green, yellow, and white; tint another batch white. Roll into strings; press together to make one thick strip. Fold in half; roll out again, repeating to achieve a marbled effect. Press pea-size balls into rounds; add veins with a leaf veiner. Place 4 or 5 leaves around base of a ¼-inch ball, bending and shaping for a ruffled look. Use same process for radicchio, using one batch of white marzipan and one tinted with a blend of Christmas red and violet.

ROASTED TURKEY BREAST
with SAGE BUTTER

SERVES 8 TO 12 *from* **THANKSGIVING AT BEDFORD**

This turkey was cooked on a vertical roasting pan, available at specialty cooking stores. You can achieve a similar result by roasting the turkey atop a Bundt pan. Before preheating the oven, place a rack in the lowest position, and remove all others, to allow room for the bird. It's a good idea to measure the space in the oven to make sure the turkey breast will fit in a vertical position; otherwise, cook it on a small roasting pan fitted with a rack on the middle oven rack, and baste once or twice with pan juices. For step-by-step how-to photographs, see page 378.

- 6 tablespoons unsalted butter, softened
- 2 tablespoons minced fresh sage, plus 4 sprigs
  Coarse salt and freshly ground pepper
- 1 turkey breast (6 to 7 pounds)
- 1½ teaspoons crumbled dried sage
- ¼ teaspoon dried thyme
- ¼ teaspoon dried marjoram or savory
- 1 onion, coarsely chopped
- 4 celery stalks, coarsely chopped
- 4 carrots, coarsely chopped
- 6 sprigs thyme
- 2 cups Turkey Stock (recipe follows) or low-sodium store-bought chicken broth

Preheat oven to 400° F, with only one rack in the lowest position. In a small bowl, stir together 4 tablespoons softened butter, the minced fresh sage, and 1 teaspoon salt. Working from the neck end of the turkey breast, loosen skin with your fingers, then spread sage butter under skin, patting to distribute evenly. Melt 2 tablespoons butter and brush onto turkey breast; rub evenly with dried herbs and season with pepper.

Combine vegetables with thyme and sage sprigs in a 10- to 12-inch cast-iron vertical roaster pan (or a 3- to 3½-quart Bundt pan). Pour stock over vegetables, distributing evenly. Arrange turkey breast on cone of pan, then place pan on a rimmed baking sheet or in a roasting pan. Roast until turkey is golden brown and an instant-read thermometer inserted into the thickest part registers 150° F, 1 to 1¼ hours. Transfer turkey to a cutting board (discard vegetables) and let rest 10 minutes before carving.

Turkey Stock MAKES ABOUT 2 QUARTS

- Gizzards and necks from two 16- to 18-pound turkeys
- 2 white onions, quartered (unpeeled)
- 2 heads garlic, halved horizontally
- 2 tablespoons olive oil, plus more for drizzling
- 6 carrots
- 10 sprigs flat-leaf parsley
- 4 pounds wild mushrooms
- 6 fresh sage leaves
- 1 red onion, thinly sliced
- 4 sprigs thyme
  Coarse salt and freshly ground pepper

Preheat oven to 450° F. In a large roasting pan, combine turkey gizzards and neck with white onions and garlic. Drizzle with olive oil and toss to coat. Spread in an even layer and roast until meat and vegetables are very brown, tossing occasionally, about 1 hour.

Transfer contents of roasting pan to a large pot. Add carrots, parsley, mushrooms, sage, and enough water to just cover (2 to 3 quarts). Bring to a boil, then reduce heat and simmer 1 hour. Strain stock through a fine sieve lined with four layers of cheesecloth; discard solids. (At this point, stock can be cooled completely and refrigerated up to 1 week or frozen up to 3 months in an airtight container; thaw in the refrigerator before using.)

Heat olive oil in a saucepan over medium. Sauté red onion until completely soft and caramelized, stirring occasionally, about 12 minutes. Add strained stock and the thyme and cook at a bare simmer 20 minutes. Strain stock again through a fine sieve and discard solids. Season with salt and pepper. (Stock can be allowed to cool and then refrigerated in an airtight container up to 1 day; reheat over medium before serving.)

BRAISED TURKEY LEGS

SERVES 8 TO 12 *from* **THANKSGIVING AT BEDFORD**

To make carving easier, ask your butcher to remove the backbones from the thighs. Reserve the bones to add when braising the turkey legs.

- 2 turkey legs (each 3 to 4 pounds), thighs separated from drumsticks
  Coarse salt and freshly ground pepper
- 2 tablespoons neutral-tasting oil, such as safflower
- 2 large onions, cut into 1-inch chunks
- 2 carrots, peeled and cut into 1-inch chunks
- 1 celery stalk, cut into 1-inch lengths
- 1 garlic head, cloves separated and smashed
- 2½ to 3 quarts Turkey Stock (recipe above) or low-sodium store-bought chicken broth
- 1½ tablespoons all-purpose flour
- 2 tablespoons unsalted butter, softened

Pat dry turkey legs and season with salt and pepper. Heat oil in a large, heavy sauté pan over medium high. Working in two batches, brown turkey legs, turning halfway through, about 7 minutes. Transfer to a large pot.

Add onions, carrots, celery, and garlic to sauté pan. Cook until browned, stirring frequently, about 8 minutes. Transfer vegetables to pot along with enough stock to just cover, and season with salt. Cover pot and bring to a boil, then reduce heat and simmer until turkey is tender, about 1½ hours.

Remove turkey legs from pot and arrange, skin side up, in a single layer in a large roasting pan; tent with foil to keep warm.

Strain braising liquid through a fine sieve into a large saucepan; discard solids. Skim fat from surface. Bring to a simmer; cook until reduced to 3 cups, about 45 minutes. In a small bowl, stir together flour and butter to make a smooth paste. Whisk into simmering liquid and cook until gravy is thickened slightly, about 2 minutes. Remove from heat; cover gravy to keep warm.

Heat broiler, with rack 6 inches from heat source. Remove foil and broil turkey legs until skin is crisp and golden brown, 2 to 3 minutes. Transfer to a cutting board and carve meat from legs. Transfer to a deep platter and serve with gravy.

ROAST TURKEY *with* CORNBREAD STUFFING

SERVES 12 TO 14 *from* **THANKSGIVING AT BEDFORD**

Reserve the giblets and neck for making Turkey Stock (page 385).

- ¾ cup (1½ sticks) tablespoons unsalted butter, melted, plus 4 tablespoons, softened
- 2 cups dry white wine, such as Sauvignon Blanc
- 1 fresh whole turkey (about 26 pounds), rinsed and patted dry, giblets and neck removed
  Coarse salt and freshly ground pepper
  Cornbread Stuffing (page 394)
  Fresh sage or other herbs, for garnish (optional)

Preheat oven to 425° F, with only one rack in the lowest position. Stir together melted butter and wine in a bowl. Fold a very large piece of cheesecloth into quarters so that it is large enough to cover breast and halfway down sides of turkey. Immerse cloth in butter mixture.

Place turkey, breast side up, on a rack in a roasting pan. Fold wing tips under. Season inside turkey with salt and pepper. Loosely fill body and neck cavities with stuffing. Tie legs together with kitchen twine. Fold neck flap under; secure with toothpicks. Rub turkey all over with the 4 tablespoons softened butter; season with salt and pepper.

Remove cheesecloth from butter mixture, squeezing gently into bowl; reserve butter mixture for brushing. Lay cheesecloth over turkey. Place turkey, legs first, into oven. Roast 30 minutes. Brush cheesecloth and exposed turkey with butter mixture. Reduce temperature to 350° F. Roast, brushing with butter mixture every 30 minutes and rotating once, 2½ hours; tent with foil if browning too quickly. Pour ½ cup water into pan if juices are very dark brown.

Discard cheesecloth; rotate pan. Baste turkey with pan juices. Roast, rotating pan halfway through, until skin is golden brown and an instant-read thermometer inserted into thickest part of thigh (and the stuffing) registers 165° F, 1½ to 2 hours more, basting turkey every 30 minutes. Transfer to a platter. Let turkey stand at room temperature 30 minutes, tented with foil, before carving. Garnish with herbs if desired.

PHEASANT POTPIES *with* BLACK TRUFFLES *and* ROOT VEGETABLES

MAKES 8 *from* **CHRISTMAS AT CANTITOE CORNERS**

For the Christmas dinner at Bedford, these potpies were part of a meal that also included Seared Pheasant Breast with Endive Meunière (recipe follows). Each recipe makes good use of different parts of the bird and shares the same truffle sauce. You will need four whole pheasants to make both recipes. Ask your butcher to bone the breasts and remove the legs from the carcass. Reserve the bones for making the stock. You will also need a fresh black truffle (about one ounce) for both pheasant dishes; look for one at specialty food stores or from online sources.

- 8 pheasant legs
  Coarse salt and freshly ground pepper
- ¼ cup plus 3 tablespoons olive oil
- 6 cups Pheasant Stock (recipe follows)

- 1 package (14 ounces) frozen all-butter puff pastry, such as Dufour, thawed in refrigerator
- 2 tablespoons all-purpose flour, plus more for dusting
- 1 can (7 ounces) black truffle peelings in truffle juice or brine (not oil)
- 3 tablespoons water
- 2 large parsnips, peeled and cut into ¼-inch dice
- 1 celery root, peeled and cut into ¼-inch dice
- 5 carrots, peeled and cut into ¼-inch dice
- 6 large leeks, white and pale green parts only, halved lengthwise, cut into 1-inch pieces on the bias, washed well, and drained
- 1 small fresh black truffle (about 1 ounce)
- 1 large egg beaten with 1 tablespoon water, for egg wash

Rinse pheasant legs and pat dry, then season with salt and pepper. Heat 3 tablespoons olive oil in a large, high-sided sauté pan. Sear pheasant, turning occasionally, until brown on all sides, about 10 minutes. Add the stock and simmer, covered, until pheasant is fork-tender, about 1 hour. Transfer pheasant to a platter. Strain braising liquid through a fine sieve into a saucepan; discard solids. When pheasant is cool enough to handle, remove and discard skin and bones. Coarsely chop meat (you should have about 2 cups).

Unfold puff pastry on a lightly floured work surface, and roll out sheet to a 10-by-20-inch rectangle. Using a paring knife or a pastry wheel, cut out eight 5-inch rounds (make sure the rounds are at least ½ inch larger in diameter than the ramekins the potpies will be baked in; use a saucer or inverted bowl as a guide while cutting); place on a parchment-lined baking sheet. Lightly score each round in a crosshatch pattern with the tip of a paring knife, making sure not to cut all the way through. Cover with plastic wrap and refrigerate until thoroughly chilled, at least 30 minutes or up to 3 hours.

To make truffle sauce, add canned truffle peelings with their juice to strained braising liquid, and bring to a boil. Reduce heat; simmer until reduced to 4 cups, about 10 minutes. In a cup, whisk together flour and the water; whisk into liquid. Simmer until thickened slightly, about 5 minutes. Season with salt and pepper. Remove from heat; cover to keep warm.

Preheat oven to 400° F. In a large skillet over medium high, heat remaining ¼ cup olive oil. Add parsnips, celery root, and carrots; cover and cook, stirring occasionally, until beginning to soften, about 5 minutes. Stir in leeks and cook, stirring occasionally, until vegetables are tender, about 5 minutes more. Stir pheasant meat into vegetables and season with salt and pepper.

Divide pheasant mixture among eight 8-ounce ramekins, filling each to ½ inch from the top. Shave six to eight black truffle slices over each serving and drizzle with 3 cups truffle sauce. (Reserve remaining black truffle and 1 cup truffle sauce for the Seared Pheasant Breasts recipe, page 387.)

Brush egg wash around rim of a ramekin and underside of a pastry round; drape pastry over ramekin, lightly pressing edge onto side of dish. Repeat until all ramekins are covered with pastry, then brush pastry with egg wash. Bake on a rimmed baking sheet until crust is golden brown, rotating sheet halfway through, 25 to 30 minutes. Serve immediately.

Pheasant Stock MAKES 6 CUPS

- ¼ cup olive oil
  Reserved breast and rib bones of 4 pheasants, coarsely chopped
- 1 onion, coarsely chopped
- 1 garlic head, cloves separated and smashed (peeled)
- 6 cups Chicken Stock (page 420) or low-sodium store-bought broth

Heat olive oil in a large pot over medium. Add pheasant bones, and cook, stirring, until starting to brown, 2 to 3 minutes. Add onion and garlic; cook until translucent, stirring occasionally, about 6 minutes. Add chicken stock and bring to a boil, then reduce to a bare simmer; cook, skimming off foam occasionally, about 1½ hours. Strain stock through a fine sieve; discard solids. If not using immediately, let cool and refrigerate up to 3 days or freeze up to 1 month in an airtight container; thaw overnight in the refrigerator before using.

SEARED PHEASANT BREASTS *with* ENDIVE MEUNIÈRE

SERVES 8 *from* **CHRISTMAS AT CANTITOE CORNERS**

4 boneless pheasant breasts, skinned and halved
   Reserved fresh black truffle (from Pheasant Potpies recipe, page 386)
   Coarse salt and freshly ground pepper
3 tablespoons olive oil
   Endive Meunière (page 391)
   Reserved truffle sauce (from Pheasant Potpies recipe, page 386)

Rinse pheasant breasts and pat dry. Using a paring knife, cut eight very thin slivers from center of reserved truffle. Make a horizontal slit in the side of each pheasant breast, and insert a truffle sliver in each. Season pheasant all over with salt and pepper.

Heat olive oil in a large sauté pan over medium high. Working in batches, place pheasant breasts in pan, smooth side down. Cook until golden brown, 4 to 5 minutes. Turn breasts with tongs and continue to cook until an instant-read thermometer inserted into thickest part registers 140° F, about 4 minutes. Transfer to a cutting board and let rest 5 minutes before halving each breast and then slicing 1 to 2 inches thick on the bias.

To serve, divide endive among eight plates and arrange half a breast on each. Drizzle with reserved truffle sauce, then shave truffle over the top.

BOILED LOBSTER TAILS *with* ENGLISH SALAD CREAM *and* CILANTRO-PARSLEY PESTO

SERVES 6 *from* **PICNIC AT SEA**

Reserve the meat from the claws to make lobster rolls or to add to salads.

7 quarts water
1 bunch fresh thyme
1 bunch fresh flat-leaf parsley
½ teaspoon black peppercorns
½ teaspoon fennel seeds
3 bay leaves
1 bottle (750 ml) dry white wine
1 leek, white and pale green parts only, cut into ¼-inch-thick rounds, washed well and drained
2 carrots, cut into ¼-inch-thick rounds
1 lemon, cut into ¼-inch-thick rounds
   Coarse salt
6 live lobsters (about 1½ pounds each)
   English Salad Cream, for serving (recipe follows)
   Cilantro-Parsley Pesto, for serving (recipe follows)

Fill a large pot with the water. Make a bouquet garni by placing the herbs, spices, and bay leaves on a square of cheesecloth and tying into a bundle with kitchen twine. Add to pot. Stir in wine, leek, carrots, and lemon slices; season generously with salt. Cover, and bring mixture to a simmer over medium-low heat. Uncover; gently simmer 30 minutes. Strain through a fine sieve into a large bowl; discard solids. (Court-bouillon can be cooled completely and refrigerated in an airtight container up to 1 week or frozen up to 3 months; thaw 1 day in the refrigerator before using.)

Return court-bouillon to clean pot; bring to a boil. Working in batches, plunge lobsters headfirst into pot. Cover; return to a boil. Cook until bright red and cooked through, 7 to 10 minutes. Transfer lobsters to a platter.

Using a kitchen towel to protect your hands, twist off tail and claws of a lobster; discard body. Using kitchen shears, cut along length of tail to make it easier to remove meat. Set tail aside. Separate claws from knuckles; twist and pull off pincers. With back of a knife, crack knuckle end of claw to loosen shell; remove meat. Push knuckle meat out of shell, and reserve for another use. (Refrigerate in an airtight container up to 1 day.) Repeat with remaining lobsters. Refrigerate tails in an airtight container until ready to serve, up to 1 day. Serve with salad cream and pesto.

English Salad Cream MAKES ABOUT 2 CUPS

1 large whole egg plus 2 large egg yolks
½ cup crème fraîche
1 cup milk
¼ cup plus 2 tablespoons white-wine vinegar
1 tablespoon all-purpose flour
½ teaspoon dry mustard
1 teaspoon coarse salt
½ teaspoon freshly ground white pepper

Prepare an ice-water bath. Puree all ingredients in a blender until well combined. Transfer to a heatproof bowl set over a pan of simmering water and cook, whisking, until mixture is thick enough to hold a trail, 4 to 5 minutes. Continue to cook, whisking, 3 minutes more.

Pour mixture into a bowl set in the ice-water bath. Let stand, stirring occasionally, until completely cool. (Salad cream can be refrigerated in an airtight container up to 2 days.)

Note

The eggs in this recipe are not fully cooked, so you may want to use pasteurized eggs when making it, especially if you plan to serve it to young children, the elderly, or anyone else whose health is compromised.

Cilantro-Parsley Pesto MAKES ABOUT ¾ CUP

2 cups loosely packed cilantro sprigs
2 cups loosely packed fresh flat-leaf parsley leaves
1 large garlic clove, minced
   Coarse salt and freshly ground pepper
¼ cup extra-virgin olive oil

Combine herbs and garlic in a food processor, and season with salt and pepper; pulse until finely chopped. With machine running, add the olive oil in a slow, steady stream, and process until combined. (Pesto can be refrigerated in an airtight container up to 2 days.)

LOBSTER SHEPHERD'S PIES

MAKES 8 *from* **BRIDAL SHOWER IN MAINE**

Passing the potatoes through a ricer produces the fluffiest topping, but you can use a masher instead.

- 3 pounds Yukon Gold potatoes, peeled and cut into 2-inch pieces
  Coarse salt and freshly ground pepper
- ¾ cup (1½ sticks) unsalted butter, plus 2 tablespoons, cut into 8 pieces, for topping
- 1 cup milk
- 4 large egg yolks
- 10 large leeks (about 4 pounds), white and pale green parts only, halved lengthwise and thinly sliced, washed well and drained
- ¼ cup plus 1 tablespoon all-purpose flour
- 2 cups shelled fresh peas or frozen peas (do not thaw)
- 3 cups Lobster Stock (recipe follows)
- 6 cups Lobster Meat, plus 8 whole claws reserved for garnish (recipe follows)
- ¼ cup coarsely chopped fresh dill, plus sprigs for garnish

Preheat oven to 400° F. In a medium pot, cover potatoes with water by 1 inch. Bring to a boil, and add salt. Reduce to a simmer and cook until potatoes are very tender, about 20 minutes. Drain well in a colander. While still warm, pass potatoes through a ricer into a bowl. Stir in 5 tablespoons butter until melted and combined. Add milk and season with salt and pepper, stirring to combine. Stir in egg yolks until incorporated.

Wipe pot clean and add 6 tablespoons butter; melt over medium-high heat. Cook leeks, stirring occasionally, 2 minutes. Season with salt and pepper. Cover and cook over medium heat, stirring occasionally, until leeks are tender, about 8 minutes more. Add flour and peas and cook, stirring, 1 minute.

Stir in stock and bring to a boil over high heat, stirring occasionally. Reduce heat and simmer 2 minutes. Add lobster meat (not the claws) and dill, and season with salt. Stir to combine.

Divide lobster filling evenly among eight 10-ounce baking dishes. Transfer potato mixture to a pastry bag fitted with a large French star tip (such as Ateco #863), and pipe mixture around edge of each dish. Arrange dishes on a baking sheet, and top each with one of the butter pieces. Bake until filling is bubbling and top is golden, about 30 minutes. Let stand 15 minutes.

Meanwhile, melt remaining 1 tablespoon butter in a small sauté pan over medium-high heat. Cook reserved lobster claws until bright red, about 2 minutes. Garnish each dish with a lobster claw and dill sprigs.

Lobster Stock and Meat

MAKES 1 QUART STOCK AND 6 CUPS LOBSTER MEAT

If you do not have a large lobster pot, you can cook the lobsters two at a time in an eight- to ten-quart stockpot.

- 6 live lobsters (1½ pounds each)
- 2 tablespoons unsalted butter
- 1 large leek, white and pale green parts only, halved lengthwise and cut into 1-inch pieces, washed well and drained
- 2 carrots, cut into 1-inch pieces
- 2 celery stalks, cut into 1-inch pieces
- ½ cup brandy
- 6 cups water
- 1 can (28 ounces) whole peeled tomatoes
- ¼ teaspoon whole black peppercorns
  Coarse salt

Fill a lobster pot or other large pot two-thirds full with water and bring to a boil. Add lobsters headfirst and cook, covered, until shells are bright red, 5 to 6 minutes. Lobster meat will not be completely cooked.

Transfer lobsters to a colander in the sink. Using kitchen shears, clip the tips of the lobster claws and drain. Let stand until cool enough to handle. Reserve eight claws for garnish, carefully removing large piece of cartilage from each. Remove meat from remaining claws and all the tails, reserving shells. Cut remaining lobster meat into large chunks. Refrigerate all lobster meat (from claws, tails, and body) in an airtight container until ready to use, up to 1 day.

Melt butter in a large pot over medium-high heat. Cut bodies and shells into large pieces. Add leek, carrots, and celery to pot; cook until translucent, stirring often, about 2 minutes. Stir in brandy and cook, stirring, until almost evaporated, about 2 minutes. Add lobster body and shell pieces along with the water, tomatoes, and peppercorns; season with salt. Bring to a boil, then reduce heat and simmer 50 minutes.

Strain stock through a fine sieve into a saucepan; discard solids. Return to a simmer and cook until stock is reduced to 3 cups. (Stock can be cooled completely and refrigerated up to 2 days or frozen up to 1 month in an airtight container; thaw 1 day in the refrigerator before using.)

JOHN DORY *with* RED WINE SAUCE *and* WINTER VEGETABLES

SERVES 8 *from* **STYLISH DINNER AT THE CLERESTORY**

John Dory, also known as St. Pierre (or St. Peter's fish), is prized for its meaty texture and delicate, slightly sweet flavor. Grouper, turbot, and tilapia are good substitutes.

- 1 pound salsify (see headnote on page 392)
- ¼ cup plus 1 tablespoon olive oil
  Coarse salt
- 1 tablespoon unsalted butter
- 1 pint brussels sprouts, trimmed and halved
- 1 small head cauliflower, cut into 1½-inch florets
- ¾ cup water
- 2½ pounds John Dory fillets, cut into 3-by-2-inch diamond shapes
  Red Wine Sauce plus reserved fennel fronds (recipe follows)

Preheat oven to 350° F. Trim ends from salsify, then peel and cut into 3-inch lengths. Place salsify in a bowl of cold water and weight with a plate to keep it submerged until ready to use.

Heat 1 tablespoon olive oil in a large skillet over medium high. Cook salsify, stirring occasionally, until beginning to turn translucent, about 4 minutes. Season with salt and add enough water to come halfway up salsify. Cover and simmer until tender, 8 to 10 minutes. Drain in a colander.

Wipe pan clean. Melt butter over medium-high heat. Add brussels sprouts, cauliflower, and ½ cup of the water. Bring to a simmer, cover, and cook 4 minutes. Uncover and simmer until vegetables are crisp-tender and water evaporates, 3 to 4 minutes more. Remove from heat.

Rub a rimmed baking sheet with 2 tablespoons oil and add the fish in a single layer. Drizzle fish with remaining 2 tablespoons oil, dividing evenly, and season with salt and pepper. Bake just until opaque throughout, 5 to 7 minutes.

Meanwhile, add salsify and remaining ¼ cup water to vegetables in skillet and heat over medium just until warmed through, 3 to 5 minutes. Season with salt.

To serve, spoon 2 to 3 tablespoons warm red wine sauce into each of eight shallow soup bowls. Arrange fish over sauce and spoon vegetables around fish. Garnish with reserved fennel fronds.

Red Wine Sauce MAKES 1½ CUPS

- ¼ cup olive oil
- 1 small fennel bulb, coarsely chopped, feathery fronds reserved for garnish
- 2 celery stalks, coarsely chopped
- 1 carrot, coarsely chopped
- 1 small onion, coarsely chopped
- 4 garlic cloves, smashed
- 1½ cups port wine
- 1 bottle (750 ml) dry red wine
- 5 whole black peppercorns
- 3 sprigs thyme
- 1 tablespoon flour
- 2 tablespoons water

Heat 2 tablespoons olive oil in a heavy, medium saucepan over medium. Cook fennel, celery, carrot, onion, and garlic until translucent, stirring occasionally, about 5 minutes. Add port and simmer, stirring frequently, until reduced to about 3 tablespoons. Add red wine, peppercorns, and thyme; simmer until reduced to about 1½ cups.

Strain through a fine sieve into a small saucepan, pressing on solids with a flexible spatula to extract as much liquid as possible; discard solids. In a small bowl, stir together flour and the water, then whisk into liquid and bring to a simmer, stirring to combine. Simmer, stirring, until sauce thickens, about 2 minutes. Serve immediately.

SAUTÉED DAURADE *with* MEDITERRANEAN VEGETABLES *and* BOUILLABAISSE JUS

SERVES 8 *from* **CELEBRATING A MASTER GARDENER**

Daurade (also spelled Dorade), or sea bream, is from the Mediterranean Sea and is a specialty of France and Italy. Black sea bass or red snapper are good substitutes. If you prefer, ask the fishmonger to clean and fillet the whole fish for you, reserving all the bones and the head of one fish.

for the bouillabaisse jus and fish
- 1 large fennel bulb
- ¼ cup olive oil, plus more if needed
- 1 onion, coarsely chopped
- 2 garlic cloves, coarsely chopped

- 4 daurade (1½ to 2 pounds each), cleaned and boned (to yield 8 skin-on fillets), bones and one head reserved
- ½ star anise or 1½ teaspoons anise or fennel seeds
- 3 tablespoons Pernod or other anise-flavored liqueur
- 2 very ripe tomatoes, chopped
- 2 teaspoons tomato paste
- 3 cups water
- 1 teaspoon saffron threads
  Coarse salt and freshly ground pepper

for the vegetables
- ½ lemon
- 1 celery root
- 2 zucchini
- 2 yellow summer squash
- ½ pound yellow wax beans, trimmed and cut into 2-inch lengths
  Coarse salt
- ¼ cup olive oil
- 1¾ cups water
- 12 baby carrots, halved crosswise

Make the bouillabaisse jus: Remove outer layer from fennel bulb and trim off any stalks, then chop trimmings. Reserve fennel bulb.

Heat 2 tablespoons olive oil in a Dutch oven or medium pot over medium. Add chopped fennel trimmings, onion, and garlic; cook until onion is translucent, stirring frequently, about 3 minutes. Add reserved fish bones and head; cook, stirring, another 3 minutes. Add star anise and Pernod; simmer 1 minute. Stir in chopped tomatoes and cook, stirring occasionally, 5 minutes. Add tomato paste and the water, stirring until tomato paste is incorporated, and simmer 25 minutes.

Strain sauce through a fine sieve into a saucepan, pressing on solids with a flexible spatula to extract as much liquid as possible. Add saffron and simmer over medium heat until reduced to about ¾ cup. Season jus with salt and keep warm.

Prepare the vegetables: Squeeze lemon juice into a bowl of cold water; drop in lemon half. Peel celery root, squaring sides; halve lengthwise, then slice crosswise ⅓ inch thick. Transfer celery root to lemon water. Halve zucchini and yellow squash lengthwise, then cut crosswise 1 inch thick on the bias. Cut reserved fennel bulb in half, then quarter each half.

Blanch wax beans in boiling salted water until crisp-tender, about 4 minutes; drain well.

Heat 1 tablespoon olive oil in a large skillet over medium. Cook fennel until starting to soften, stirring occasionally, about 2 minutes. Add ½ cup water and season with salt. Cook, partially covered, until fennel is just tender and water is almost evaporated, about 4 minutes. Transfer fennel to a platter.

In same pan, heat 1 tablespoon olive oil. Cook drained celery root until beginning to turn tender, stirring occasionally, about 5 minutes. Add ½ cup water and season with salt. Cook, partially covered, until celery root is just tender and water is almost evaporated, about 5 minutes. Transfer to platter with fennel.

Heat 1 tablespoon olive oil in pan. Cook carrots until beginning to turn tender, stirring occasionally, about 3 minutes. Add ½ cup water and season

(RECIPE CONTINUES)

with salt. Cook, partially covered, until carrots are just tender and water is almost evaporated, about 3 minutes. Transfer carrots to platter.

Heat remaining 1 tablespoon olive oil in pan. Cook zucchini and squash until just tender, about 3 minutes. Season with salt and transfer to platter.

Cook the fish: Preheat oven to 375° F, with a rack in the center. Dry fish fillets well with paper towels, then season on both sides with salt and pepper. In a large, heavy sauté pan, heat the remaining 2 tablespoons olive oil over medium high until shimmering. Working in batches, sear the fillets, skin side down, until lightly browned, about 1 minute. Turn fillets and sear on flesh side about 1 minute, then transfer to a rimmed baking sheet. Transfer fish to oven and cook until fillets are just opaque throughout, about 5 minutes.

Return all cooked vegetables to the skillet and add remaining ¼ cup water. Bring to a simmer and cook until vegetables are just heated through and liquid has evaporated, about 3 minutes. To serve, arrange a few vegetables in the center of each plate and top with a fillet. Scatter remaining vegetables around fish; drizzle bouillabaisse jus on top, dividing evenly.

CHOUCROUTE GARNI

SERVES 8 *from* **HALLOWEEN PUMPKIN BLAZE**

Smoked pork chops, such as those by Kasseler Rippchen, and freshly prepared sauerkraut are sold at German food markets and from online sources—such as Schaller & Weber, located in New York's Upper East Side (schallerweber.com). If you prefer, you can pan-sear four lean pork chops and purchase good-quality packaged sauerkraut instead.

1	tablespoon juniper berries
1½	teaspoons cumin seeds
½	teaspoon whole white peppercorns
4	whole cloves
2	bay leaves
2	tablespoons olive oil
2	onions, thinly sliced
½	pound double-smoked slab bacon (in one piece)
½	pound fresh slab bacon (in one piece)
1¼	pounds boneless cooked smoked pork butt
4	pounds sauerkraut (uncooked)
2	cups white wine, preferably Riesling
3	cups Chicken Stock (page 420) or low-sodium store-bought broth
1½	pounds small new potatoes
4	skinless wieners or hot dogs
4	bratwurst sausages
4	andouille sausages
4	smoked pork chops
¼	cup chopped fresh flat-leaf parsley

Preheat oven to 350° F. Make a bouquet garni: Wrap juniper berries, cumin, peppercorns, cloves, and bay leaves in cheesecloth; tie with kitchen string.

Heat olive oil in a large Dutch oven or pot over medium. Cook onions, stirring occasionally, until translucent, about 5 minutes. Add both types of bacon, along with the pork butt and bouquet garni, and top with sauerkraut. Pour in wine and stock and bring to a boil. Remove from heat. Cover and transfer to oven; bake 1 hour.

Meanwhile, cover potatoes with cold water in a saucepan; bring to a boil, then reduce heat and simmer until tender when pierced with a knife, about 15 minutes. Drain; when cool enough to handle, peel potatoes. Add potatoes to pot along with wieners, sausages, and pork chops. Continue to simmer, covered, until potatoes and meat are heated through, 10 to 15 minutes.

Using a slotted spoon, transfer bacon and pork butt to a cutting board; slice. Transfer sauerkraut to a large, deep platter; top with sliced meats, sausages, and potatoes. Discard bouquet garni. Sprinkle with parsley; serve.

Side Dishes

FAVA BEAN RAGOÛT

MAKES 4 CUPS *from* **VERDANT SPRING DINNER**

If you can't find fresh fava beans in the pods, look for frozen shelled favas, or substitute frozen shelled edamame; thaw according to package instructions, and skip the blanching step in the recipe below.

2	cups cherry tomatoes, halved
2	tablespoons extra-virgin olive oil, plus more for drizzling
	Coarse salt and freshly ground pepper
1	tablespoon fresh thyme leaves, preferably lemon thyme
2	red bell peppers, roasted (page 423) and cut into ½-inch strips
1	yellow bell pepper, roasted (page 423) and cut into ½-inch strips
1	pound fingerling potatoes, scrubbed and halved lengthwise
2	cups shelled fava beans (about 2 pounds unshelled)
1	shallot, minced
1	bunch baby carrots, cut into 1½-inch pieces on the bias
1	sprig rosemary

Preheat oven to 400° F. On a rimmed baking sheet, drizzle tomatoes with olive oil, season with salt and pepper, and sprinkle with thyme. Toss to combine, then spread in an even layer. Roast until tomatoes are beginning to burst, about 10 minutes. Transfer tomatoes along with any pan juices to a bowl and add the bell peppers.

Reduce oven to 350° F. On same baking sheet, drizzle potatoes with olive oil; season with salt and pepper. Toss to coat; spread evenly. Roast until tender and golden, about 25 minutes. Let cool, then add to tomato mixture.

While potatoes are cooking, prepare an ice-water bath. Blanch fava beans in a pot of boiling salted water until bright green and tender, about 5 minutes. Transfer to the ice bath to cool, then pop beans out of skins. Add favas to tomato mixture.

In a large sauté pan, heat the olive oil over medium high. Cook shallot until beginning to soften, stirring frequently, about 2 minutes. Add carrots and rosemary, and cook until carrots are tender, stirring occasionally, about 5 minutes. Discard rosemary. Transfer carrots to bowl with fava beans and season ragoût with salt and pepper. Let stand 30 minutes before serving.

ENDIVE MEUNIÈRE

SERVES 8 *from* **CHRISTMAS AT CANTITOE CORNERS**

1 lemon, halved
8 heads endive, outer leaves removed, stem ends trimmed
Coarse salt and freshly ground pepper
3 tablespoons unsalted butter
3 tablespoons all-purpose flour

Squeeze juice from lemon into a pot of water and drop in lemon halves. Add endive and bring to a boil. Season with salt, then reduce heat and simmer, covered, until endive are very tender, about 30 minutes.

Use a slotted spoon to transfer endive to a colander to drain; let cool slightly. On a work surface, flatten endive slightly by pressing gently with the palm of your hand. Arrange in a single layer on a paper towel–lined baking sheet. (Endive can be kept covered at room temperature up to 3 hours.)

Heat butter in large sauté pan over medium. Dredge endive in flour to coat and season with salt and pepper. Sauté endive until golden brown on bottom, 3 to 4 minutes, then turn and cook until other side is golden, about 2 minutes more. Serve immediately.

GRILLED VEGETABLES

SERVES 12 *from* **JULY 4TH BARBECUE**

You can blanch the vegetables a day ahead and refrigerate each type separately in airtight containers.

Coarse salt and freshly ground pepper
12 carrots, preferably thin, trimmed and peeled
2 yellow summer squash, halved lengthwise and sliced into 2-inch pieces on the bias
2 zucchini, halved lengthwise and sliced into 2-inch pieces on the bias
3 small fennel bulbs, trimmed and cut into ¾-inch wedges or ½-inch-thick slices
2 small celery roots, peeled, halved lengthwise, and cut crosswise into ¾-inch-thick pieces
2 tablespoons coarsely chopped fresh thyme
¼ cup packed coarsely chopped fresh basil
2 garlic cloves, finely chopped
1 cup extra-virgin olive oil
3 red or yellow bell peppers, roasted (page 423) and cut into 2-inch pieces
2 heads radicchio, halved through the stem if small and quartered if large, stem end left intact
4 small tomatoes, halved crosswise

Prepare an ice-water bath. Bring a pot of water to a boil; add salt. Blanch carrots until tender, about 5 minutes. Using a slotted spoon, transfer to the ice bath to stop the cooking, then let drain on a kitchen towel or paper towels. Repeat in separate batches with squash, zucchini, fennel, and celery root. Squash and zucchini will take about 5 minutes to become tender, fennel and celery root about 8 minutes.

Heat grill to medium (if you are using a charcoal grill, coals are ready when you can hold your hand 5 inches above grates for just 5 to 6 seconds). Whisk together thyme, basil, garlic, and olive oil; season with salt and pepper.

Brush all of the vegetables with herb oil. Grill roasted bell peppers and blanched vegetables until heated through and marked by grill, about 5 minutes for peppers, 8 to 10 minutes for blanched vegetables, transferring vegetables to serving platters as soon as they are ready. Grill radicchio and tomatoes until cooked through, 7 to 8 minutes for radicchio, 8 to 10 minutes for tomatoes; transfer to platters.

Brush vegetables with remaining herb oil, and season with salt. Serve warm or at room temperature.

TWICE-BAKED POTATOES *with* BROCCOLI

SERVES 12 *from* **JULY 4TH BARBECUE**

Stuffed potatoes can be made a day ahead and refrigerated; bake them for about thirty minutes to heat through.

12 small russet potatoes (about 8 ounces each), pierced with a fork
2 heads broccoli (about 1¼ pounds each), trimmed and cut into florets
Coarse salt and freshly ground pepper
¾ cup (1½ sticks) unsalted butter, softened
¼ cup extra-virgin olive oil

Preheat oven to 400° F. Bake potatoes until tender, about 1 hour. Let cool slightly on a wire rack.

Prepare an ice-water bath. Cook broccoli in a pot of boiling salted water until very tender, about 8 minutes. Transfer to the ice bath to stop the cooking, then drain well.

Slice potatoes lengthwise to remove ½ inch from tops; reserve tops. Holding potatoes with a kitchen towel, scoop out flesh, leaving about a ½-inch-thick shell on skins; discard flesh of two potatoes. Pass remaining flesh through a ricer into a large bowl.

Add broccoli to bowl with potatoes. Using a potato masher or pastry blender, mash broccoli and potatoes together. Add butter and olive oil, and season with salt and pepper; mash until combined. Season potato shells with salt and pepper. Spoon broccoli mixture into shells, and replace reserved tops. Arrange on a rimmed baking sheet and cover with parchment, then foil. Bake until heated through, about 15 minutes. Serve hot.

CELERY ROOT PURÉE

SERVES 8 *from* **BURGUNDY DINNER**

2 celery roots, peeled and cut into 1-inch cubes
3 cups heavy cream
Coarse salt and freshly ground pepper

Bring celery roots and cream to a boil in a large saucepan. Reduce heat; simmer until celery roots are tender, about 30 minutes. Strain through a fine sieve, reserving 2 cups cream. Purée celery roots with reserved cream in a blender until smooth. Season with salt and pepper. Serve immediately.

CHINESE LONG BEANS

SERVES 8 *from* **BURGUNDY DINNER**

As part of a formal dinner, the beans were trimmed to a uniform length and formed into little bundles before cooking, but you could simply spread the beans in an even layer on the baking sheet for a more casual meal.

1½ pounds Chinese long beans, ends trimmed to make uniform
Coarse salt and freshly ground pepper
Best-quality extra-virgin olive oil, for drizzling

Preheat oven to 350° F. Prepare an ice-water bath. Blanch beans in a pot of boiling salted water until just tender, about 4 minutes. Using a slotted spoon, transfer beans to ice bath until cool, then drain and pat dry.

Make bundles by wrapping six or seven beans around your first three fingers. Arrange on a parchment-lined baking sheet. Drizzle with olive oil, and season with salt and pepper. Cook just until heated through, about 10 minutes. Serve warm.

BRAISED SALSIFY

SERVES 8 *from* **BURGUNDY DINNER**

Salsify, a relative of dandelion and chicory, can be found at farmers' markets and some supermarkets in the fall. It has a flavor similar to oysters, and is in fact also known as the "oyster plant." Once you peel away the gnarled exterior, the flesh needs to be kept in cold water to prevent discoloring.

1½ pounds salsify
2 tablespoons extra-virgin olive oil
Coarse salt and freshly ground pepper

Trim ends from salsify, peel, and cut into 3-inch lengths. To prevent browning, soak salsify in a bowl of cold water, weighting with a plate to keep submerged until ready to cook.

Heat olive oil in a large sauté pan over medium high. Cook salsify, stirring occasionally, until beginning to turn translucent, about 4 minutes. Season with salt and add enough water to reach halfway up the sides of salsify. Cover and simmer until tender, 8 to 10 minutes; drain. Serve warm.

ASPARAGUS *with* MUSTARD VINAIGRETTE

SERVES 8 *from* **EASTER DINNER**

If serving the asparagus cold, plunge the spears in an ice-water bath right after blanching; drain and refrigerate in an airtight container, up to 1 day. The asparagus is also delicious drizzled with Hollandaise Sauce (page 423).

2 tablespoons Dijon mustard
⅓ cup champagne or white wine vinegar
Coarse salt and freshly ground pepper
½ cup extra-virgin olive oil
½ cup grapeseed oil
2 bunches large asparagus, trimmed, bottom 2 inches peeled

Whisk together mustard and vinegar in a small bowl; season with salt and pepper. Slowly add olive oil, then grapeseed oil in a steady stream, whisking constantly until emulsified. (Vinaigrette can be refrigerated, covered, up to 1 week; let come to room temperature and whisk to blend before using.)

Blanch asparagus in a pot of boiling salted water until bright green and crisp-tender, 2 to 4 minutes, depending on size. Transfer to a colander to drain. Serve warm, room temperature, or chilled, drizzled with vinaigrette.

RAGOÛT *of* SPRING VEGETABLES

SERVES 8 *from* **EASTER DINNER**

Fresh cranberry beans, also called borlotti, can be found at farmers' markets in the spring, where you will also find fresh fava beans. They are simple to peel, but if you prefer (or can't find them), feel free to substitute thawed frozen shelled edamame, lima beans, or butter beans in place of one or both fresh varieties. Frozen green peas are another convenient alternative, eliminating the need to shell fresh ones.

1 pound baby golden beets, trimmed, greens washed well, drained, and chopped
1 pound baby chioggia beets, trimmed, greens washed well, drained, and chopped
1 pound fresh cranberry beans, shelled
Coarse salt
½ pound sugar-snap peas, trimmed
½ pound snow peas, trimmed
1 pound fresh green peas, shelled (1¼ cups)
1 pound bunch baby carrots, trimmed
1 pound baby turnips, greens and root ends trimmed
1 pound fresh fava beans, shelled (1¼ cups)
3 tablespoons unsalted butter
¾ cup water

In a pot, bring beets and enough water to cover by 1 inch to a boil. Reduce to a simmer, and cook until beets are tender when pierced with the tip of a sharp knife, about 30 minutes. Drain in a colander. When beets are cool enough to handle, rub off skins with paper towels and cut in half lengthwise.

Meanwhile, cook cranberry beans in a pot of simmering salted water until tender, about 20 minutes. Drain and rinse.

Prepare an ice-water bath. Blanch sugar-snap peas in a pot of boiling salted water until bright green and crisp-tender, about 1 minute. With a slotted spoon, transfer snap peas to ice bath to stop the cooking, then drain on a kitchen towel or paper towels. Repeat in separate batches with snow peas, shelled peas, carrots, turnips, and fava beans. Peas will take about 1 minute to become crisp-tender, carrot and turnips 3 to 4 minutes.

Halve or quarter turnips, depending on size. Pop fava beans from their skins. (Vegetables can be prepared to this point up to a day ahead and refrigerated in separate airtight containers or resealable plastic bags.)

In a large sauté pan, bring butter and the water to a simmer. Add vegetables (including beet greens) and cook, tossing occasionally, until water evaporates and vegetables are heated through, about 5 minutes. Season vegetables with salt, and serve warm.

GLAZED CARROTS *and* RED PEARL ONIONS

SERVES 8   *from* **THANKSGIVING AT BEDFORD**

- 4 tablespoons unsalted butter
- 1 bag (10 ounces) red pearl onions, peeled (page 423)
- 1 cup dry red wine
- 2 pounds baby carrots, trimmed
- 1½ cups fresh orange juice (from 4 to 5 oranges)
- ½ teaspoon fresh thyme leaves
- Coarse salt and freshly ground pepper

Melt 2 tablespoons butter in a large saucepan over medium heat. Add pearl onions and wine; cook, stirring occasionally, until onions are tender and most of the liquid has evaporated, about 10 minutes.

Meanwhile, melt remaining 2 tablespoons butter in a large sauté pan over medium heat. Add carrots, orange juice, and thyme; cook, stirring occasionally, until carrots are tender, about 5 minutes.

Combine onion and carrot mixtures in a bowl and season with salt and pepper. Serve warm.

ROOT VEGETABLE BOULANGÈRE

SERVES 8 TO 10   *from* **THANKSGIVING AT BEDFORD**

Potatoes boulangère, a popular dish in France, is similar to a gratin, but without the cream. Here, sweet potatoes and turnips round out the dish, and you could substitute other root vegetables, such as celery root, rutabaga, and parsnips, with equally delicious results. A mandoline makes quick work of slicing the vegetables thin, but a sharp knife or other adjustable-blade slicer can be used instead.

- 2 pounds sweet potatoes
- 2 pounds russet potatoes
- 1 pound turnips
- 1 large onion, halved and cut into ¼-inch-thick slices
- 1 tablespoon olive oil
- Coarse salt and freshly ground pepper
- 1 cup white wine, preferably Riesling
- 1 cup Vegetable Stock (page 421) or low-sodium store-bought broth
- 4 tablespoons unsalted butter, cut into small pieces

Preheat oven to 400° F. Peel sweet potatoes, russet potatoes, and turnips; slice crosswise ⅛ inch thick, and combine in a large bowl with onion slices. Add olive oil, and season with salt; toss to coat.

Arrange vegetables in a shallow 3-quart casserole in overlapping layers. Pour in wine and stock, dot evenly with butter, and season with salt and pepper. Cover with parchment, then foil, and bake until vegetables are tender when pierced with the tip of a sharp knife, about 1 hour. Remove parchment and foil and continue to bake until liquid has evaporated and top is golden, 30 to 45 minutes more. Serve warm.

BABY BRUSSELS SPROUTS *with* WILD RICE *and* PECANS

SERVES 8   *from* **THANKSGIVING AT BEDFORD**

- 2 cups wild rice
- 3 tablespoons unsalted butter
- ¾ cup pecans
- Coarse salt
- 1 cup (5 ounces) red pearl onions, peeled (page 423) and halved through root end
- ½ cup water
- 1 pound baby brussels sprouts
- 2 tablespoons sherry vinegar
- 3 tablespoons pure maple syrup
- 2 teaspoons Dijon mustard

Bring a large saucepan of water to a boil. Stir in wild rice, reduce to a simmer, and cook (uncovered) until tender, about 40 minutes. Drain rice.

Meanwhile, melt 2 tablespoons butter in a large sauté pan over medium heat. Toast pecans, stirring frequently, until fragrant, about 5 minutes. With a slotted spoon, transfer pecans to a plate and season with salt.

Add remaining 1 tablespoon butter, the pearl onions, and the water to pan; simmer until water is evaporated and onions are tender and pale golden, about 10 minutes.

Trim brussels sprouts, then score an X into the bottom of each one. Place in a steaming basket or colander set in a saucepan filled with 1 inch of water. Bring water to a boil, then reduce to a simmer; cover and steam until just tender enough to pierce with the tip of a sharp knife, 6 to 8 minutes.

In a bowl, whisk together sherry vinegar, maple syrup, and mustard. Add rice, brussels sprouts, and onions; toss to coat, and season with salt and pepper. Coarsely chop pecans and add just before serving, warm or at room temperature.

SAUTÉED PORCINI MUSHROOMS *and* CHESTNUTS

SERVES 8   *from* **THANKSGIVING AT BEDFORD**

- 4 tablespoons unsalted butter
- 1 pound fresh porcini mushrooms, trimmed and halved
- 1 pound chestnuts, cooked and peeled (page 423)
- ½ cup Turkey Stock (page 385), Vegetable Stock (page 421), or low-sodium store-bought broth
- ¼ cup finely chopped fresh flat-leaf parsley
- Coarse salt and freshly ground pepper

Melt 2 tablespoons butter in a large sauté pan over medium-high heat. Sauté mushrooms until tender, stirring occasionally, 8 to 10 minutes.

Meanwhile, heat remaining 2 tablespoons butter in another sauté pan. Cook chestnuts until heated through, stirring occasionally, about 5 minutes. Add stock and simmer until almost evaporated, about 5 minutes.

Add mushrooms and parsley to chestnuts and season with salt and pepper, tossing to combine. Serve warm.

CORNBREAD STUFFING

SERVES 8 TO 10 *from* **THANKSGIVING AT BEDFORD**

Follow the recipe for Roast Turkey on page 386 to cook the stuffing in the turkey cavity, or bake it separately as directed below. If you prefer to avoid peeling the chestnuts yourself, buy ones that have been cooked and peeled and are sold in jars or cans. You will need one and a quarter cups.

Cornbread (recipe follows)
½ cup plus 2 tablespoons (1¼ sticks) unsalted butter, plus more, softened, for baking dish
2 cups chestnuts, cooked and peeled (page 423), cut into quarters
2 large onions, finely chopped
1 cup finely chopped celery
½ cup finely chopped shallots
Coarse salt and freshly ground pepper
4 Gala apples, peeled, cored, and cut into ½-inch pieces
½ cup finely chopped fresh flat-leaf parsley
¼ cup finely chopped fresh sage
1 to 1½ cups Turkey Stock (page 385), Chicken Stock (page 420), Vegetable Stock (page 421), or low-sodium store-bought broth

Preheat oven to 375° F. Crumble cornbread into a large bowl. Melt butter in a large skillet over medium heat. Cook chestnuts, stirring occasionally, until they begin to brown, about 8 minutes. With a slotted spoon, transfer chestnuts to bowl, reserving butter in pan.

Add onions, celery, and shallots to pan; season with salt. Cook, stirring occasionally, until they begin to soften, about 5 minutes. Add apples and continue to cook, stirring occasionally, until apples are soft, about 5 minutes more. Transfer to bowl with cornbread mixture. Add parsley, sage, and enough stock to moisten mixture. Toss to combine and season with salt and pepper.

Transfer stuffing to a buttered 3-quart shallow baking dish. (Stuffing can be prepared to this point up to 1 day ahead; cover with plastic wrap and refrigerate. Return to room temperature and uncover before baking.) Bake until heated through and top is lightly browned, about 30 minutes. Serve hot.

Cornbread MAKES ONE 8-INCH SQUARE LOAF

Unsalted butter, softened, for baking pan
1 cup all-purpose flour
1 cup yellow cornmeal
1 tablespoon sugar
1 teaspoon salt
2 teaspoons baking powder
1 cup milk
2 large eggs

Preheat oven to 400° F. Butter an 8-inch-square baking pan. In a bowl, whisk together flour, cornmeal, sugar, salt, and baking powder. In another bowl, whisk together milk and eggs until frothy, then stir into dry ingredients, mixing until just incorporated. Do not overmix; the batter should be lumpy.

Pour batter into prepared pan. Bake until top is golden brown and a cake tester inserted in the center comes out dry, 20 to 25 minutes. Let cool on a wire rack.

STUFFED PUMPKIN

SERVES 8 TO 10 *from* **THANKSGIVING AT BEDFORD**

A cheese pumpkin is the same color as a butternut squash, and it tends to be flatter than the more common sugar pumpkin. The flesh is quite thick and very smooth in texture. If this kind of pumpkin is not available, use what you can find, but check for doneness after seventy-five minutes, as the flesh will most likely not be as thick, and the pumpkin will cook more quickly. For photographs and instructions on preparing this recipe, see page 378.

½ cup plus 2 tablespoons olive oil
1½ cups chestnuts, cooked and peeled (page 423)
1 pound fresh porcini mushrooms, trimmed and cut into ½-inch pieces
1 pound fresh chanterelle mushrooms, trimmed and cut into ½-inch pieces
Coarse salt and freshly ground pepper
1 loaf (1 pound) pullman or other white sandwich bread, cut into ¾-inch cubes
1 pound carrots, peeled and diced
2 large onions, finely chopped
8 celery stalks, diced
1 large sweet potato, peeled, cored, and diced
4 garlic cloves, minced
2 cups Turkey Stock (page 385), Chicken Stock (page 420), Vegetable Stock (page 421), or low-sodium store-bought broth
4 Granny Smith apples, peeled and diced
1 tablespoon fresh thyme leaves
1 tablespoon minced fresh rosemary
1 tablespoon finely chopped fresh sage
½ cup finely chopped fresh flat-leaf parsley
3 large eggs
1 cheese pumpkin (10 to 12 pounds)

Heat 3 tablespoons olive oil in a large sauté pan over medium high until shimmering. Sauté chestnuts, stirring occasionally, until they begin to brown. With a slotted spoon, transfer chestnuts to a plate. Add both mushrooms to skillet and sauté, stirring occasionally, until mushrooms release their juices and begin to turn golden, about 15 minutes. Transfer to a large bowl and season with salt. Add bread cubes, and toss to mix.

Heat 3 tablespoons olive oil in same pan over medium high. Add carrots, onions, celery, sweet potato, and garlic; season with salt and pepper. Cook, stirring occasionally, until vegetables begin to brown, about 10 minutes. Add stock and simmer until vegetables are tender, about 5 minutes. Transfer contents of pan to bread mixture along with the chestnuts. Add apples, herbs, and another 3 tablespoons olive oil. Toss well and season stuffing with salt and pepper, then mix in the eggs.

Preheat oven to 375° F. Remove top of pumpkin by cutting a circle about 5 inches in diameter around stem with a paring knife; reserve top. Scrape out and discard seeds and stringy flesh from pumpkin. Rub inside of pumpkin with remaining 1 tablespoon olive oil and season with salt and pepper. Spoon stuffing into pumpkin and replace top.

Bake stuffed pumpkin on a rimmed baking sheet until pumpkin is tender when pierced with a skewer, 1½ to 2 hours. Do not overcook pumpkin or the side may split. To serve, remove top and scoop out stuffing and some pumpkin flesh with a large spoon.

CRANBERRY-POMEGRANATE GELATIN

SERVES 6 *from* **THANKSGIVING AT BEDFORD**

This gelatin was formed in a turkey-shaped mold, such as one made by Nordic Ware, but any six-cup mold will work. If you prefer, you can prepare two smaller gelatins by dividing the layers between two three-cup molds. To make your own pomegranate juice, see the headnote on page 337; you will need about three pomegranates to yield one and a half cups juice.

for the pomegranate gelatin
2¼ teaspoons unflavored powdered gelatin
1½ cups unsweetened pomegranate juice

for the cranberry gelatin
2 bags (each 12 ounces) fresh or frozen (thawed) cranberries
2½ cups sugar
2 cups cold water
2 teaspoons unflavored powdered gelatin

for assembling
3 clementines

for the cranberry sauce
1 teaspoon unflavored powdered gelatin
1⅓ cups fresh orange juice (from 3 to 4 oranges)
1 cinnamon stick
⅔ cup sugar
1 strip (2 inches long) lemon peel
1 bag (12 ounces) fresh or frozen (thawed) cranberries

Make the pomegranate gelatin: Place a 6-cup mold in the refrigerator to chill. In a saucepan, sprinkle gelatin over ½ cup pomegranate juice, and let soften 5 minutes. Cook over medium-low heat, stirring, just until gelatin is dissolved; do not let boil. Remove from heat and let cool completely. Stir in remaining 1 cup pomegranate juice, then pour into chilled mold. Skim off foam from surface, and refrigerate until partially set, 1 to 1½ hours.

Meanwhile, make the cranberry gelatin: In a saucepan, simmer cranberries, sugar, and 1¾ cups water until berries have burst and mixture has thickened slightly, about 15 minutes. Strain through a fine sieve into a bowl, pressing on solids to extract as much liquid as possible, and scraping pulp from bottom of sieve into liquid. Discard solids. You should have about 1¾ cups liquid.

In a small saucepan, sprinkle gelatin over remaining ¼ cup cold water, and let soften 5 minutes. Add about ½ cup of strained cranberry liquid to softened gelatin, and cook over medium heat, stirring, until gelatin is dissolved; do not let boil. Let cool completely, then stir gelatin mixture into remaining cranberry liquid in a bowl.

To assemble: Cut peel and pith from clementines, then cut segments free from membranes. Gently blot segments dry with paper towels. Press half of clementine segments into pomegranate layer, and gently pour cranberry gelatin on top. Refrigerate until cranberry gelatin is almost set, about 1 hour.

Make the cranberry sauce: In a small bowl, sprinkle gelatin over 3 table-spoons orange juice, and set aside to soften.

Bring remaining orange juice, the cinnamon stick, sugar, and lemon peel to a simmer in a large saucepan. Cook, stirring, until sugar dissolves, about 3 minutes. Add cranberries and cook, stirring occasionally, until berries

have burst and mixture has thickened slightly, about 12 minutes. Remove from heat, and add gelatin mixture, stirring to dissolve. Transfer cranberry sauce to a bowl to cool.

Press remaining clementine segments into cranberry gelatin and gently top with cranberry sauce, spreading evenly in mold. Cover mold and refrigerate 1 day, or up to 3 days.

To serve, dip bottom of mold in a bowl of hot water 10 to 20 seconds, then invert onto a cake stand or serving plate, and carefully remove mold.

Desserts

BLUEBERRY PARFAITS

MAKES 8 *from* **BRIDAL SHOWER IN MAINE**

2 teaspoons unflavored powdered gelatin
½ cup cold water
2 cups Blueberry Purée (page 336)
1 tablespoon fresh lemon juice
2 cups heavy cream
2½ tablespoons confectioners' sugar
1 cup fresh blueberries
Sugared Pansies, for garnish (optional; recipe follows)

In a small saucepan, sprinkle gelatin over the cold water; soften 5 minutes. Cook over medium, stirring, until gelatin is dissolved. Let cool completely.

In a bowl, stir together gelatin, 1½ cups blueberry purée, and the lemon juice. Divide among 8 parfait glasses (6 to 8 ounces) and refrigerate until set, at least 2 hours (or up to 2 days, covered tightly with plastic wrap).

With an electric mixer, whisk cream and confectioners' sugar to stiff peaks. Gently fold in remaining ½ cup blueberry purée until partially blended (mixture should be streaky).

To serve, spoon blueberry cream over gelatin mixture in parfait glasses, dividing evenly. Top each with a few fresh blueberries; garnish with a sugared pansy, if desired.

Sugared Pansies MAKES 8

Be sure to buy only pesticide-free flowers from a reputable source. For the Vanilla Cupcakes on page 415, you will need to coat twenty-four pansies; follow the recipe below, using two large egg whites and one-quarter cup water.

1 large egg white
2 tablespoons water
Fine sanding or superfine sugar
8 pesticide-free pansies

Whisk together egg white and water until smooth and combined, then brush over tops of pansies. Sprinkle with sanding sugar; let dry. (Pansies can be stored in an airtight container at room temperature up to 1 week.)

YOGURT, HONEY, *and* RHUBARB PARFAITS

MAKES 6 *from* **BREAKFAST ON THE PORCH**

Piping the yogurt into the glasses makes for a pretty presentation, but you can simply dollop it with a spoon instead.

- 1¼ pounds rhubarb, trimmed and cut into 1-inch pieces (about 4 cups)
- 1 cup sugar
- 1 cup water
- 4 to 5 cups plain yogurt, preferably Greek-style
  Mild-tasting honey, such as orange-blossom or clover, for drizzling

Stir to combine rhubarb, sugar, and the water in a pot. Bring to a boil, then reduce heat, and simmer until rhubarb is soft and liquid has thickened slightly, about 20 minutes. Remove from heat and let cool completely.

When ready to serve, transfer yogurt to a large pastry bag fitted with a large open-star tip (such as Ateco #826). Dividing evenly, pipe yogurt into 6 glasses (6 to 8 ounces), pulling up as you release pressure to create a peak. Spoon rhubarb compote on top, on one side; drizzle with honey.

RED, WHITE, *and* BLUE PARFAITS

MAKES 12 *from* **JULY 4TH BARBECUE**

for the currant gelatin
- 4½ pounds fresh red currants, stemmed
- 3 cups sugar
- 3 envelopes unflavored powdered gelatin (3 scant tablespoons)
- ⅓ cup cold water

for the panna cotta
- 2 envelopes unflavored powdered gelatin (2 scant tablespoons)
- ⅓ cup cold water
- 3½ cups milk
- 1 cup heavy cream
- ¾ cup sugar

for serving
- 1½ pounds fresh blueberries
- 2 ounces fresh currants on the stem

Make the currant gelatin: Bring currants and sugar to a boil in a large saucepan. Reduce to a simmer, and cook, stirring occasionally, until currants are very soft, about 10 minutes. Remove from heat.

Prepare an ice-water bath. Sprinkle gelatin over the cold water, and let soften 5 minutes. Add to currant mixture; cook over medium-low heat, stirring, until gelatin has dissolved, about 5 minutes. Strain through a fine sieve into a bowl set in the ice bath, gently pressing with a flexible spatula to remove as much liquid as possible; discard solids. Remove bowl and let stand, stirring occasionally, until cool but not set. Spoon 3 to 4 tablespoons currant gelatin into each of 12 parfait glasses (8 to 10 ounces); reserve remaining gelatin at room temperature. Refrigerate glasses until gelatin is completely set, about 1 hour.

Meanwhile, make the panna cotta: Prepare another ice-water bath. Sprinkle gelatin over the cold water and let soften 5 minutes. Bring milk, cream, and sugar almost to a boil in a saucepan; reduce to a simmer. Add softened gelatin; cook, stirring, until gelatin has dissolved, about 5 minutes. Strain through a fine sieve into a bowl set in the ice bath. Remove bowl; let stand, stirring occasionally, until cool but not set. Spoon 3 to 4 tablespoons panna cotta over currant gelatin in each glass; reserve remaining panna cotta at room temperature. Refrigerate until panna cotta is completely set, about 1 hour.

Repeat with another layer each of currant gelatin and panna cotta, chilling each until set. If either mixture becomes too firm to spoon, set over a pot of simmering water until softened. To serve, top each parfait with blueberries and currants.

POMEGRANATE GELATIN *with* FRESH CURRANTS

SERVES 8 *from* **DINNER PARTY DESSERTS**

- 6 envelopes unflavored powdered gelatin (scant ¼ cup plus 2 tablespoons)
- 1½ cups cold water
- 1 cup sugar
- 6 cups unsweetened pomegranate juice
- 3 cups unsweetened white grape juice
  Fresh currants on the stem, for garnish (optional)

Place an 8-cup mold in the refrigerator to chill. In a saucepan, sprinkle gelatin over the cold water, and let soften 5 minutes. Cook over medium-low heat, stirring, just until gelatin is dissolved; do not let boil. Add sugar, and stir gently until dissolved. Remove from heat, and let cool, stirring, about 5 minutes.

Stir in both juices, then pour gelatin mixture into chilled mold, and skim foam from surface. Refrigerate until set, at least 8 hours (or up to 1 day, covered with plastic).

To serve, dip bottom of mold in a bowl of hot water 10 to 20 seconds, then invert onto a cake stand or serving plate, and carefully remove mold. Garnish with fresh currants, if desired.

BAKED LOCAL PLUM *and* NECTARINE "PITHIVIERS"

MAKES 6 *from* **CELEBRATING A MASTER GARDENER**

Pithiviers—named for the French town where it originated—are most often made by encasing a filling of frangipane (an almond cream) between two layers of puff pasty. In these simplified individual versions, baked fruit and ice cream are topped with crisp pastry rounds. Making vanilla sugar is a great way to use leftover vanilla bean pods after the seeds have been scraped out. Tuck the split pods into a container of sugar, seal or cover tightly for at least one week, and use instead of regular sugar for baking or sweetening drinks; it should keep for about three months.

- 2 tablespoons cold unsalted butter, cut into small cubes, plus more, softened, for bowls
- 3 ripe, firm nectarines, halved lengthwise and pitted
- 24 small plums, preferably Italian prune plums, halved lengthwise and pitted
- 2 tablespoons vanilla sugar (see headnote)
  Bourbon Vanilla Ice Cream (recipe follows)
  Crisp Pastry Tops (recipe follows)

Preheat oven to 350° F. Generously butter six 3½-cup ovenproof bowls. Place a nectarine half, cut side down, in center of each bowl. Arrange 8 plum halves, cut sides up, around each nectarine half. Sprinkle with vanilla sugar, and dot with butter, dividing evenly among bowls.

Bake on a parchment-lined baking sheet until fruit is juicy and softened, rotating sheet halfway through, about 30 minutes. Transfer bowls to a wire rack to cool.

To assemble, place a large scoop of ice cream in each bowl, then finish with a pastry top. Serve immediately.

Bourbon Vanilla Ice Cream MAKES ABOUT 6 CUPS

  2   vanilla beans, split lengthwise
  1   quart half-and-half
1¼   cups sugar
  8   large egg yolks
  ¼   cup bourbon

Scrape vanilla seeds into a heavy saucepan, and drop in pods. Whisk in half-and-half and sugar, and cook over medium heat, stirring occasionally, until sugar dissolves and mixture just comes to a simmer.

Lightly beat egg yolks in a large bowl, and gradually whisk in hot half-and-half mixture in a thin stream. Pour mixture back into saucepan, and cook over medium heat, stirring constantly with a wooden spoon, until thick enough to coat the back of the spoon and a candy thermometer registers 160° F, about 10 minutes. Remove from heat, and stir in bourbon. Transfer to a bowl, and let cool completely. Refrigerate, covered, 1 day.

Strain custard through a fine sieve into an ice-cream maker, discarding solids, and freeze according to manufacturer's directions. Transfer ice cream to an airtight container, and freeze until firm, about 2 hours or up to 1 month.

Crisp Pastry Tops MAKES 6

  ¼   cup sugar, plus more for sprinkling
  1   package (14 ounces) frozen all-butter puff pastry, such as Dufour, thawed in the refrigerator
  1   large egg yolk, beaten with 2 tablespoons heavy cream, for egg wash

Preheat oven to 400° F. Sprinkle a clean work surface with sugar. Unfold puff pastry on top of sugar, then sprinkle pastry evenly with sugar. Roll out pastry into a 12-by-14-inch rectangle. Cut out six 4½-inch rounds, and transfer to a large parchment-lined baking sheet.

With a sharp knife, score each pastry round, making curved lines every ½ inch from the center out toward the edges, to resemble a pinwheel. Refrigerate pastry until well chilled, at least 30 minutes, or up to 1 day (covered with plastic wrap).

Brush tops of chilled pastry rounds with egg wash, leaving a ¼-inch border; do not let any drip over cut edges, as it will prevent pastry from rising evenly in the oven. Sprinkle each round with 2 teaspoons sugar. Bake until crisp and caramelized, rotating sheet halfway through, 15 to 18 minutes. Transfer baking sheet to a wire rack, and let tops cool completely.

POACHED PEARS *with* RIESLING
SERVES 12   *from* DINNER PARTY DESSERTS

The best pears for poaching are sweet, juicy varieties such as Comice and Bartlett, which will hold their shape well after cooking. Riesling, available in dry and off-dry (slightly sweet) varieties, has a fruity quality that pairs well with the flavor of pears; Viognier or Chardonnay are other good options.

  12   ripe, firm pears
    1   bottle (750 ml) dry or off-dry Riesling
    ¾   cup packed light brown sugar
    1   vanilla bean, split lengthwise
        Chocolate Mint Leaves, for garnish (optional; recipe follows)

Peel the pears, leaving stems attached, then core them from the bottom, using a small melon baller to scoop out the seeds. Cut a round of parchment to fit inside a large pot (it should be wide enough to hold the pears in one layer). Place pears in pot along with the wine, brown sugar, and enough water to just cover pears (4 to 6 cups). Scrape vanilla bean seeds into pan, then drop in pod. Cover with parchment round.

Bring to a boil, then reduce heat; simmer, turning pears occasionally to coat with liquid, until very tender but not falling apart, 10 to 15 minutes, depending on ripeness and size of pears. Use a slotted spoon to transfer pears to a large bowl. Remove and discard vanilla bean pod. Cover bowl with the parchment round (or cut a new one to fit).

Bring poaching liquid to a boil, and cook until reduced to a thin syrup consistency, about 10 minutes. Pour syrup over pears, and refrigerate, covered with parchment, until cool. Serve pears in shallow bowls or cups; tuck a chocolate mint leaf into stem end of each one, if desired.

Chocolate Mint Leaves MAKES 12

All chocolate is in temper when you buy it: It breaks cleanly, melts smoothly, and has a lovely sheen. But as soon as you melt chocolate, it goes out of temper, so when making leaves or other designs with chocolate, follow these steps to ensure the proper results. Temper only the best-quality brands.

    8   ounces best-quality bittersweet chocolate, finely chopped
  12   large fresh mint leaves, gently cleaned and dried

Reserve ½ cup chopped chocolate; transfer remaining chocolate to a medium heatproof bowl set over (not in) a pan of barely simmering water. Heat, stirring occasionally, until melted and a chocolate or candy thermometer registers 131° F. Remove from heat; stir in reserved ½ cup chocolate until melted. Continue stirring until it cools to 82° F to 84° F. Return to pan of warm water; reheat to 88° F. Use immediately.

Using a small, dry pastry brush, coat underside of each mint leaf with a thick layer of tempered chocolate. (If chocolate drips onto top of leaf, gently wipe it away with your fingertip.) Drape leaves, chocolate sides up, over a large skewer or the handle of a wooden spoon set on a parchment-lined baking sheet. Refrigerate until set, about 10 minutes.

Gently grasp the chocolate layer of each leaf with kitchen tweezers (to prevent melting, don't touch the chocolate with your hands). Holding the stem, peel the leaf away with your fingers. (Chocolate leaves can be refrigerated in a single layer in airtight containers up to 2 days.)

RHUBARB CRUMBLES

MAKES 12 *from* **PEONY GARDEN PARTY**

Allowing the rhubarb-and-sugar mixture to sit overnight in the refrigerator helps keep the rhubarb from breaking down too much once poached. If you like, reserve the poaching liquid for serving over ice cream or making the Rhubarb-Orange Cocktails on page 337.

- 2   pounds rhubarb, trimmed and cut into 1-inch pieces (6 to 7 cups)
- 1   cup sugar
- ¾   cup all-purpose flour
- ¼   cup packed light brown sugar
- ¾   teaspoon ground cinnamon
- ½   teaspoon coarse salt
- 6   tablespoons unsalted butter, softened

Stir together rhubarb and sugar in a large pot, then cover and refrigerate 1 day.

Heat rhubarb mixture over medium high until it just comes to a boil. Remove from heat, cover pot, and let cool to room temperature.

In a bowl, whisk together flour, brown sugar, cinnamon, and salt. Add butter, and stir with a fork until blended. (Topping can be refrigerated in an airtight container up to 1 week.)

Preheat oven to 350° F. Strain rhubarb from syrup, and divide among 12 small (2- to 3-ounce) ovenproof dishes. (Reserve syrup in an airtight container in the refrigerator for another use, if desired.) Sprinkle topping over rhubarb, dividing evenly among dishes.

Place dishes on a rimmed baking sheet. Bake, rotating sheet halfway through, until fruit is bubbling and topping is golden, 20 to 25 minutes. Let cool slightly before serving.

RHUBARB TART

MAKES ONE 9-INCH TART *from* **EASTER DINNER**

- 2   pounds rhubarb, trimmed and cut into 1-inch pieces (6 to 7 cups)
- 1⅔   cups plus 2 tablespoons sugar
  All-purpose flour, for dusting
- ½   recipe Pâte Brisée (page 421)
- 2   large eggs
- ⅔   cup heavy cream
- ⅓   cup milk
- ½   teaspoon pure vanilla extract
- 1   tablespoon cornstarch
- ¼   teaspoon salt

In a large bowl or container, toss rhubarb with 1 cup sugar. Cover, and chill at least 12 and up to 24 hours.

On a lightly floured surface, roll out dough to ⅛ inch thick. Fit into a 9- or 10-inch tart pan with a removable bottom, trimming dough flush with rim. Pierce bottom of dough all over with a fork, and freeze 15 minutes.

Preheat oven to 375° F. Line tart shell with parchment, and fill with pie weights or dried beans. Bake until edges are pale golden, about 20 minutes.

Remove parchment and weights, and continue baking until center is golden, about 10 minutes longer. Transfer to a wire rack, and let cool 15 minutes. Reduce oven to 350° F.

In a bowl, whisk together eggs, cream, milk, ⅔ cup sugar, and the vanilla until combined and sugar has dissolved. Pour custard mixture into cooled tart shell, and bake until barely set in the center, about 10 minutes.

Meanwhile, drain rhubarb, and toss with cornstarch and salt.

Remove tart from oven. Arrange rhubarb over custard, and sprinkle with remaining 2 tablespoons sugar. Bake until rhubarb is tender and browning on tips, about 30 minutes. If edge of tart is becoming too brown, cover loosely with a foil ring. Let tart cool completely on a wire rack before serving.

LEMON TART

MAKES ONE 9-INCH TART *from* **EASTER DINNER**

for the crust
- ⅔   cup all-purpose flour
- ½   teaspoon coarse salt
- ⅓   cup whole blanched almonds
- ½   cup confectioners' sugar
- 6   tablespoons unsalted butter, softened
- 1   teaspoon finely grated lemon zest
- 1   large egg yolk

for the filling
- 3   large eggs
- 1¼   cups granulated sugar
- ¼   cup all-purpose flour
- ½   teaspoon coarse salt
- 2   teaspoons finely grated lemon zest plus ½ cup fresh lemon juice (from 2 to 3 lemons)

for serving
   Confectioners' sugar
   Lemon Chips (recipe follows)

Make the crust: Whisk together flour and salt. In a coffee or spice grinder, grind almonds and confectioners' sugar until fine. With an electric mixer on medium-high speed, cream butter with zest until light. Add almond-sugar mixture, and beat until fluffy, then beat in egg yolk. Add flour mixture, and beat just until combined.

Crumble crust mixture evenly over bottom of a 9- or 10-inch tart pan with a removable bottom, then press evenly onto bottom and up side of pan. Pierce bottom of crust all over with a fork, and freeze until firm, about 15 minutes.

Preheat oven to 375° F. Line chilled tart shell with parchment, and fill with pie weights or dried beans. Bake crust until turning golden around the edges, about 15 minutes. Remove parchment and weights, and continue baking until center is golden, about 10 minutes longer. Transfer to a wire rack, and let cool 20 minutes.

Meanwhile, make the filling: Whisk together eggs, granulated sugar, flour, and salt. Add lemon zest and juice, and whisk until blended. Pour filling into cooled crust. Bake until almost set in center, 20 to 25 minutes (filling will continue to set as it cools). Transfer to a wire rack and let cool completely.

When ready to serve, dust with confectioners' sugar and garnish with lemon chips.

Lemon Chips MAKES ENOUGH FOR 1 TART

Look for a lemon with very thin skin, which will produce more delicate chips.

- 1 lemon, preferably organic
  Confectioners' sugar

Preheat oven to 250° F. Slice lemon as thin as possible with a very sharp knife. Remove and discard seeds. Arrange lemon slices in a single layer on a baking sheet lined with a nonstick baking mat, and dust evenly with confectioners' sugar. Bake until sugar dissolves, about 45 minutes. Flip lemon slices, and dust second sides with sugar. Bake until golden and crisp, 1 to 1½ hours more, depending on thickness of skin. Let cool completely. (Chips can be stored in an airtight container, between layers of parchment, at room temperature up to 1 day.)

BLUEBERRY JAM TARTLETS

MAKES 12 *from* PICNIC AT SEA

- ¼ cup all-purpose flour, plus more for work surface
  Almond Shortcrust Pastry (recipe follows)
- 2 large eggs
- ½ cup sugar, plus more for sprinkling
- 3 tablespoons whole blanched almonds, toasted (page 423) and finely ground
- ¼ teaspoon salt
- ⅓ cup plus 2 teaspoons blueberry jam
- ½ cup small fresh blueberries, preferably wild
- 2 tablespoons sliced blanched almonds

On a lightly floured work surface, roll out pastry dough to ⅛ inch thick. Cut out twelve 4½-inch rounds, rerolling scraps, if needed. Fit each pastry round into a 3- or 3¼-inch tartlet pan, pressing it into bottom and up sides; trim edge flush with rim. Divide shells between two baking sheets. Pierce bottom of dough all over with a fork, and freeze 15 minutes.

Preheat oven to 375° F. Line each tartlet shell with parchment, and fill with pie weights or dried beans. Bake until crust is starting to dry and is light golden, about 15 minutes. Remove parchment and weights. Let cool completely on wire racks.

Meanwhile, with an electric mixer, whisk eggs and sugar on medium speed until pale and fluffy, then fold in flour, ground almonds, and salt.

Spread about 1½ teaspoons jam into each tartlet shell. Add blueberries, dividing evenly. Press lightly with a fork. Top each with 2 tablespoons batter, and sprinkle with sugar and sliced almonds. Bake until tops have risen and are golden, 16 to 18 minutes. Let cool completely on wire racks. (Tartlets can be stored in airtight containers at room temperature up to 1 day.)

Almond Shortcrust Pastry

MAKES ENOUGH FOR 12 TARTLETS

- ⅓ cup whole blanched almonds
- 1½ cups all-purpose flour
- 1 tablespoon sugar
- ½ teaspoon salt
- ½ cup (1 stick) cold unsalted butter, cut into small pieces
- 1 large egg yolk
- 1 to 2 tablespoons ice water

Finely grind almonds in a food processor. Add flour, sugar, and salt; pulse to combine. Add butter; pulse until mixture resembles coarse meal. Add yolk and 1 tablespoon ice water; pulse until dough just comes together, adding up to 1 tablespoon more water, if needed. Turn out dough onto plastic wrap and shape into a disk. Wrap well, and chill at least 30 minutes. (Pastry can be refrigerated up to 3 days or frozen up to 1 month; thaw 1 day in the refrigerator before using.)

DOUBLE-CRUST APPLE PIE

MAKES ONE 9-INCH DOUBLE-CRUST PIE *from* THANKSGIVING AT BEDFORD

- ½ to ¾ cup granulated sugar
- ¼ cup all-purpose flour, plus more for dusting
- ¾ teaspoon ground cinnamon
- ¼ teaspoon ground ginger
- ½ teaspoon coarse salt
- 3 pounds assorted baking apples, such as Granny Smith, Rome, Cortland, Mutsu, Golden Russet, and Empire
- 1 tablespoon fresh lemon juice
  Pâte Brisée (page 421)
- 2 tablespoons unsalted butter, cut into pieces
- 1 large egg yolk beaten with 1 tablespoon heavy cream, for egg wash
  Fine sanding sugar, for sprinkling

Preheat oven to 400° F. Stir together granulated sugar, flour, cinnamon, ginger, and salt in a bowl. Peel, quarter, and core apples, then cut into ½-inch slices. In a large bowl, toss apple slices with lemon juice, then add sugar mixture, and toss to distribute evenly.

On a lightly floured surface, roll out one disk of dough into a 13-inch round. Fit dough into a 9-inch glass pie plate, gently pressing into plate. Trim edge to a ½ inch overhang, then fill with apple mixture and dot with butter. Roll out the remaining disk of dough in the same manner, and drape over the filling. Use kitchen shears to trim overhang to 1 inch. Fold edges of top and bottom dough under, gently pressing to seal, on top of rim.

Brush egg wash over top crust, and sprinkle with sanding sugar. Cut five or six slits in top crust to allow steam to escape. Bake 10 minutes, then reduce oven to 375° F and continue baking until crust is golden brown and juices are bubbling, 60 to 75 minutes more. Let cool completely on a wire rack before serving.

APPLE TART

MAKES ONE 14-INCH TART *from* **BURGUNDY DINNER**

This tart is best served the day it is baked. For step-by-step how-to photographs, see page 379.

- 1 package (14 ounces) frozen all-butter puff pastry, such as Dufour, thawed in the refrigerator
  All-purpose flour, for dusting
- 2¼ pounds small tart apples, such as Granny Smith (about 6)
- 1 tablespoon fresh lemon juice
- ¼ cup plus 2 tablespoons sugar
- 2 tablespoons unsalted butter, cut into pieces
- 1 large egg, lightly beaten

for finishing tart
- ¼ cup quince or apple jelly
- 1 teaspoon Cognac

Preheat oven to 425° F, with rack in the center. Unfold puff pastry on a lightly floured surface. Roll out dough to a 15-inch square. Chill pastry on a large parchment-lined baking sheet until firm, 15 to 20 minutes.

Meanwhile, core apples, then peel with a paring knife. Using a sharp chef's knife, slice each apple crosswise ⅛ inch thick. Brush with lemon juice to prevent browning.

Transfer puff pastry (still on the parchment) to a work surface, and cut a ½-inch strip from each side of square; lightly score top of strips in a zigzag fashion with a paring knife. Return pastry (without the parchment) to the baking sheet. Lightly brush water over edges to make a ½-inch border, and top with scored pastry strips, overlapping corners and trimming to fit.

Sprinkle ¼ cup sugar evenly over tart, then arrange apple slices on top in rows (see the how-to photographs on page 379), pressing gently on each to flatten slightly. Sprinkle apples with remaining 2 tablespoons sugar and dot with butter, dividing evenly. Brush top of border with beaten egg (do not let it drip down sides, as it will inhibit rising).

Bake tart 10 minutes. Reduce oven to 375° F, and continue to bake until crust is puffed and deep golden brown and apples are tender, 20 to 30 minutes longer. If dough under apples begins to rise, slit puffed part with the tip of a sharp knife to allow air to escape. Transfer baking sheet to a wire rack, and let tart cool completely.

Finish the tart: Heat jelly with Cognac in a small saucepan until melted, stirring until smooth. Brush glaze over apples. Serve the tart at room temperature.

PEACH *and* NECTARINE RICOTTA CROSTATA

MAKES ONE 12-INCH TART *from* **DINNER PARTY DESSERTS**

The method for making the pastry dough (called fraisage in French), whereby you smear smaller portions of dough on a work surface before gathering them together in a ball, ensures that the fat (butter and shortening) is evenly distributed for the most tender results. Preheating the baking sheet helps the crust cook at the same rate as the filling. For step-by-step how-to photographs, see page 381.

for the crust
- 2 cups all-purpose flour, plus more for dusting
- 1 teaspoon coarse salt
- ½ cup vegetable shortening, chilled
- 5 tablespoons cold unsalted butter, cut into ½-inch dice
- ¼ cup ice water, plus more as needed

for the filling
- ⅔ cup ricotta cheese, preferably fresh
- 2 ounces cream cheese, softened
- 1 large egg
  Finely grated zest of 1 lemon plus juice of ½ lemon
- ½ cup plus 2 tablespoons packed light brown sugar
- 3 tablespoons cornstarch
- ¼ teaspoon coarse salt
- 1½ pounds yellow peaches (about 6)
- 1½ pounds white nectarines (about 6)

for finishing tart
- 1 large egg yolk beaten with 1 tablespoon heavy cream, for egg wash
- 2 tablespoons coarse sanding sugar
- 2 tablespoons unsalted butter, cut into small pieces

Make the crust: Whisk together flour and salt in a bowl. With a pastry blender or two knives, cut shortening and butter into flour until there are only pea-size lumps remaining. Working quickly with fingertips, rub lumps of fat to flatten. Add the ice water and toss with a fork until incorporated. Squeeze a pinch of dough; if it does not hold together, add up to 3 tablespoons more ice water, 1 tablespoon at a time, tossing to incorporate.

Gather dough into a ball and turn out onto a clean work surface. Working with about ¼ cup of dough at a time, and using the heel of your hand, smear dough forward, flattening any remaining pieces of fat and further blending pastry dough. Gather dough into a ball again; flatten into a disk. Wrap with plastic; refrigerate until chilled, at least 2 hours or up to 2 days.

Prepare the filling: Preheat oven to 375° F, with a (rimless) baking sheet on center rack. In a small bowl, mash together ricotta and cream cheese. Stir in egg, half the lemon zest, and 2 tablespoons brown sugar.

On a lightly floured work surface, roll out dough to a 16-inch round. Spread ricotta mixture in a 9-inch round in the middle of dough. Transfer to a parchment-lined (rimless) baking sheet and refrigerate.

In a small bowl, stir together remaining ½ cup brown sugar, the cornstarch, salt, and remaining lemon zest. Peel peaches and nectarines (page 423) and cut into ¾-inch wedges. In a large bowl, toss fruit with sugar mixture and lemon juice. Remove dough from refrigerator, and spoon fruit mixture evenly over ricotta in a 10-inch round. Fold surrounding pastry up over fruit (tart will spread to 12 inches during baking).

Finish the tart: Brush pastry with egg wash, and sprinkle with sanding sugar. Dot fruit with butter. Carefully slide tart and parchment onto preheated baking sheet, and bake until crust is deep golden brown and juices are bubbling, rotating sheet halfway through, about 1 hour. Transfer sheet to a wire rack, and let tart cool completely before serving.

PEAR CROSTATA

MAKES ONE 14-INCH TART *from* **PÂTÉ CAMPAGNARD LUNCH**

3   pounds ripe, firm pears (about 10), peeled, cored, and sliced ½ inch thick
¼   cup granulated sugar
1   tablespoon cornstarch
    All-purpose flour, for dusting
    Tart Dough (page 422)
1   large egg yolk beaten with 1 teaspoon water, for egg wash
¼   cup sanding sugar

Toss fruit with granulated sugar and cornstarch in a bowl, and set aside to macerate.

Preheat oven to 375° F. Flour a large (at least 18 inches long) piece of parchment. Place dough on parchment. Using your knuckles, press edges of dough so it doesn't crack during rolling. Lightly flour top of dough to prevent sticking; roll into an 18-inch round, about ⅛ inch thick. Transfer dough (still on parchment) to a large baking sheet.

Mound fruit in the center of dough, leaving a 2-inch border all around. Fold dough over fruit, pleating it as you go. Brush the exposed dough with the egg wash and sprinkle with sanding sugar.

Bake until crust is golden brown and filling is bubbling in the center, 45 to 50 minutes. Transfer sheet to a wire rack, and let tart cool completely.

MAPLE-PUMPKIN PIE

MAKES ONE 9- TO 10-INCH SINGLE-CRUST PIE
from **THANKSGIVING AT BEDFORD**

    All-purpose flour, for dusting
½   recipe Pâte Brisée (page 421)
¾   cup pure maple syrup
2   star anise
1   cinnamon stick
8   whole cloves
2¼   cups canned unsweetened pumpkin purée
3   large eggs
2   cups milk
1   teaspoon ground cinnamon
½   teaspoon grated, peeled fresh ginger
¼   teaspoon freshly grated nutmeg
    Pinch of mace
1   teaspoon salt

Preheat oven to 400° F. On a lightly floured surface, roll out dough into a 14-inch round. Fit dough into a 9-inch deep-dish pie plate (or a regular 10-inch pie plate), gently pressing into plate. Trim to a ½-inch overhang, and fold edge under, gently pressing to seal, on top of rim. Crimp as desired. Pierce bottom of dough all over with a fork, and refrigerate while preparing filling.

In a small saucepan, heat maple syrup, star anise, cinnamon stick, and cloves over medium just to boiling. Remove from heat, cover, and let steep 15 minutes.

Combine pumpkin purée, eggs, milk, ground cinnamon, ginger, nutmeg, mace, and salt in a large bowl. Strain maple-syrup mixture through a fine sieve into bowl (discard solids), and whisk to fully blend.

Pour filling into pie shell. Bake 35 minutes, then reduce oven to 375° F and continue to bake until filling is almost set in the center, 25 to 30 minutes longer (filling will continue to set as it cools). Let cool completely on a wire rack before serving.

PECAN-CARAMEL TART

MAKES ONE 10-INCH TART *from* **THANKSGIVING AT BEDFORD**

    All-purpose flour, for dusting
½   recipe Pâte Sucrée (page 421)
½   cup water
2   cups raw sugar, such as turbinado, or lightly packed light brown sugar
¼   cup light corn syrup
½   cup (1 stick) unsalted butter, cut into small pieces
¾   cup heavy cream
2½   cups pecans (10 ounces)

Preheat oven to 400° F. On a lightly floured surface, roll out dough to a 13-inch round. Fit into a 10-inch tart pan with a removable bottom, pressing into bottom and up sides. Trim to a 1-inch overhang and fold in edge, pressing gently against side of pan. Pierce bottom of tart shell all over with a fork.

Line tart shell with parchment, and fill with pie weights or dried beans. Bake until edges are pale golden, about 20 minutes. Remove parchment and weights. Reduce oven to 375° F, and continue baking until center is golden, about 10 minutes more. Let cool on a wire rack.

In a medium saucepan, bring the water, sugar, and corn syrup to a boil, stirring to dissolve sugar. Wash down sides of pan with a pastry brush dipped in water to prevent crystals from forming. Continue to cook without stirring until caramel is a deep golden brown, swirling pan occasionally to color evenly, 10 to 15 minutes. Remove from heat, and whisk in butter, a few pieces at a time, until combined. Pour in cream, and whisk gently to combine, then stir in pecans.

Pour filling into tart shell, and let cool completely. (Tart can be stored, covered, up to 2 days at room temperature.)

FIG CROSTATA

MAKES ONE 14-INCH TART *from* **PÂTÉ CAMPAGNARD LUNCH**

2¾   pounds fresh Black Mission figs (3 containers), stemmed and halved
¼   cup granulated sugar
     Juice of 1 lemon
     Pinch of coarse salt
     All-purpose flour, for dusting
     Tart Dough (page 422)
1   large egg yolk beaten with 1 teaspoon water, for egg wash
¼   cup sanding sugar

Toss figs with granulated sugar, lemon juice, and salt; let macerate.

Preheat oven to 375° F. Flour a large (at least 18 inches long) piece of parchment. Place dough on parchment. Using your knuckles, press edges of dough so it doesn't crack during rolling. Lightly flour top of dough to prevent sticking; roll into an 18-inch round, about ⅛ inch thick. Transfer dough (still on parchment) to a large baking sheet.

Mound figs in the center of dough, leaving a 2-inch border all around. Fold the border over the fruit, pleating it as you go. Brush the exposed dough with the egg wash, and sprinkle with sanding sugar.

Bake until crust is golden brown and filling is bubbling in the center, 45 to 50 minutes. Transfer sheet to a wire rack, and let tart cool completely.

PALMIERS

MAKES 2½ DOZEN *from* **CELEBRATING A MASTER GARDENER**

Serve these flaky pastries the same day they are baked. When making them, refer to the step-by-step how-to photographs on page 380. For a savory version, see the recipe for Gorgonzola Palmiers (page 340).

¾   cup sugar
1   package (14 ounces) frozen all-butter puff pastry dough, such as Dufour, thawed in refrigerator

Sprinkle half the sugar on a work surface. Unfold dough onto sugar and sprinkle evenly with remaining sugar. Gently roll out dough into a 9½-by-15-inch rectangle, about ⅛ inch thick, being careful not to press too hard around the edges. Gently turn over dough once or twice during rolling to ensure an even coating of sugar.

Trim edges of dough with a pastry wheel or paring knife. Arrange dough with a long side facing you. Using your fingers, roll up dough lengthwise as tightly as possible without stretching into a cylinder, stopping when you reach the middle. Repeat rolling procedure with the other long side until you have two tight cylinders that meet in the middle. Wrap in plastic; chill at least 1 hour or up to 1 day.

Transfer dough to a cutting board. Using a sharp knife, slice dough crosswise ½ inch thick. Place on parchment-lined baking sheets, spacing ½ inch apart. Firmly flatten each with the palm of your hand. Chill 1 hour.

Preheat oven to 400° F. Bake palmiers until they begin to darken, 8 to 10 minutes. Remove from oven, and quickly flip each one using an offset spatula. Return to oven, and continue to bake until pastry is deep golden brown and well caramelized, 6 to 8 minutes more. Transfer palmiers to a wire rack to cool completely before serving.

CREAM PUFFS *with* WARM CHOCOLATE SAUCE

SERVES 8 TO 12 *from* **CHRISTMAS DINNER AT CANITOE CORNERS**

The puffs can be filled and refrigerated up to three hours before serving. Whip the heavy cream and fold into the pastry cream just prior to piping.

1   cup heavy cream
2   recipes Vanilla-Bean Pastry Cream (page 422)
    Pâte à Choux Puffs (recipe follows)
    Warm Chocolate Sauce (recipe follows)

Whip heavy cream to soft peaks. In a large bowl, whisk pastry cream briefly until smooth, then gently but thoroughly fold in whipped cream. Transfer lightened pastry cream to a pastry bag fitted with a plain ¼-inch tip (such as #3 or #4). Insert tip of bag into bottom of a puff, and squeeze gently, taking care not to overfill. Repeat with remaining puffs.

Arrange a layer of puffs in a circle on a rimmed serving platter, then stack puffs to form a pyramid. Drizzle chocolate sauce over the top at the table. Alternatively, arrange three or four puffs on individual plates, and drizzle with chocolate sauce.

Pâte à Choux Puffs MAKES ABOUT 3 DOZEN

Do not use extra-large eggs or the dough will become too runny and will not puff when baked. If making the Croquembouche (right), do not sprinkle puffs with sanding sugar.

1   cup water
½   cup (1 stick) unsalted butter
1   teaspoon granulated sugar
    Pinch of salt
1¼   cups all-purpose flour
5   large eggs, plus 1 large egg beaten with 1 tablespoon water, for egg wash
1   tablespoon pearl sugar, for sprinkling (optional)

Preheat oven to 325° F, with racks in upper and lower thirds. In a heavy saucepan, bring the water, butter, granulated sugar, and salt to a boil over medium-high heat. Remove from heat, and add flour all at once, stirring vigorously until dough forms a ball and pulls away from the side of the pan.

Transfer mixture to a mixing bowl, and beat with an electric mixer on low speed until it is slightly cooled, about 2 minutes. With mixer on medium speed, add 4 eggs, one at a time, beating until incorporated after each addition. Test the batter by touching it with your finger and lifting to form a string. If a string does not form, the batter needs more egg. Lightly beat another egg, and add a little at a time, just until batter forms a string.

Transfer batter to a pastry bag fitted with a plain ½-inch tip (such as Ateco #806). Pipe 1½-inch rounds, 1 inch apart, onto parchment-lined baking sheets. Brush egg wash over puffs, and sprinkle evenly with pearl sugar, if desired.

Place in oven and immediately raise heat to 375° F. Bake until puffed and deep golden brown, rotating sheets from top to bottom and front to back halfway through, 20 to 25 minutes. Transfer to a wire rack, and let cool completely. (Puffs can be stored in airtight containers at room temperature up to 1 day, or frozen up to 1 month.)

Warm Chocolate Sauce MAKES ABOUT 1 CUP

- 1½ tablespoons unsalted butter
- ½ cup sugar
- ¼ cup light cream
- ½ cup light corn syrup
- ⅛ teaspoon salt
- ½ teaspoon pure vanilla extract
- ¼ cup unsweetened cocoa powder

Combine all ingredients except cocoa in a saucepan, and bring to a boil over medium heat, stirring constantly with a wooden spoon, until butter is melted and sugar is dissolved. Stir in cocoa, and cook, stirring constantly, until mixture is thick enough to coat the back of the spoon, 2 to 3 minutes. Serve warm. (Once cooled, the sauce can be refrigerated in an airtight container up to 3 days. Reheat over low before serving, stirring until smooth.)

CROQUEMBOUCHE

SERVES 32 *from* **DINNER PARTY DESSERTS**

Croquembouche molds come in a range of sizes; the one used here is about twenty inches high. The metal molds are available at baking supply stores or online. Although there are several components to the recipe, each can be made in advance and assembled just before serving. You may need to make several batches of caramel because it hardens quickly.

- 8 recipes Vanilla-Bean Pastry Cream (page 422)
- 4 recipes Pâte à Choux Puffs (page 402)
- 1 cup sugar
  Pinch of cream of tartar
- ¼ cup water
  Vegetable oil, for mold
  Spun Sugar (recipe follows)

Working in batches, transfer pastry cream to a pastry bag fitted with a plain ¼-inch tip (such as #3 or #4). Insert tip of bag into bottom of a puff, and squeeze gently, taking care not to overfill. Repeat with remaining puffs. Arrange filled puffs on a baking sheet, and refrigerate until ready to use.

Prepare an ice-water bath. In a small saucepan, combine sugar, cream of tartar, and the water; bring to a boil over medium heat, stirring to dissolve sugar. Wash down sides of pan with a pastry brush dipped in water to prevent crystals from forming. Continue cooking, without stirring, until sugar has dissolved, 5 to 6 minutes. Raise heat to high, and cook until syrup is amber in color, about 5 minutes, swirling pan to color evenly. Remove from heat, and dip bottom of pan in the ice bath for 3 seconds.

While caramel is cooking, oil the inside of croquembouche mold, coating evenly and thoroughly.

Using tongs, carefully dip a filled puff into caramel to coat completely, letting excess drip back into pan. Place in mold, at the tip. Repeat dipping and placing more puffs, arranging them in concentric rings as you work. Make sure the puffs are touching and adhere to one another. Once all sides are covered with puffs, repeat with more rings of puffs to fill the middle of the mold. If at any point the caramel begins to harden in the pan, warm briefly over low heat. Let stand until caramel is set in mold, about 15 minutes. To unmold, invert mold onto serving platter or cake stand. Tap

on sides several times with a wooden spoon, then gently press on sides of mold to release. Carefully lift mold to remove. Decorate with spun sugar. (Once assembled, croquembouche can be kept at room temperature until ready to serve, up to 5 hours.)

Spun Sugar MAKES ENOUGH FOR 1 CROQUEMBOUCHE

The beeswax keeps the spun-sugar strands pliable; look for it at specialty baking or craft supply stores, or from online sources. Spun sugar is best made in a cool, dry work area up to one hour before serving.

-   Vegetable oil
- 1 cup sugar
- ⅔ cup light corn syrup
- 2 teaspoons grated beeswax

Lightly oil a wooden laundry rack (or two wooden spoons securely taped to your work surface with the handles extending off the counter). Cover the floor underneath with newspaper or parchment.

In a small saucepan, bring sugar and corn syrup to a boil, and continue to boil until mixture is pale amber and reaches 265° F on a candy thermometer. Remove from heat, and let cool 2 minutes. Stir in the beeswax.

Cool the mixture, stirring occasionally, until it reaches 150° F. Test by dipping a fork into the caramel and holding it over the pan; the caramel should fall back into pan in long golden threads. Dip a handheld whisk with the top cut off (or two forks, side by side) into the caramel, and wave the caramel back and forth over the drying rack, allowing the strands to fall in long, thin threads. Wrap the strands around the croquembouche as soon as possible.

BAKED MERINGUE CUPS *with* RASPBERRIES *and* PASTRY CREAM

MAKES ABOUT 36 *from* **PEONY GARDEN PARTY**

-   Swiss Meringue for Cups (recipe follows)
- 1 cup Vanilla-Bean Pastry Cream (page 422)
- 36 small fresh raspberries
- 36 small fresh mint leaves
  Confectioners' sugar, for dusting

Preheat oven to 200° F. Line two baking sheets with parchment, adhering paper to sheet in each corner with a small dab of meringue. Transfer meringue to a pastry bag fitted with a plain ¼-inch tip (such as #3 or #4). Pipe a 1-inch-diameter round base about ¾ inch in height. Pipe a circle on the perimeter of the base, then pipe another circle on top (for the sides). Repeat with remaining meringue, spacing cups 1 inch apart.

Bake meringues until they are nearly crisp but still white, 45 to 60 minutes. Reduce oven to 175° F if meringue starts to take on color. Turn off oven and let meringues cool completely in oven, preferably 1 day. (Store in a dry, dark area at room temperature in an airtight container up to 1 week.)

To assemble, briefly whisk chilled pastry cream until smooth, then transfer to a pastry bag fitted with a plain ½-inch tip (such as Ateco #806; or use a small, sturdy resealable plastic bag with the corner snipped off). Pipe pastry cream into meringue cups. Top each with a raspberry, then tuck a mint leaf alongside. Dust tops with confectioners' sugar, and serve immediately.

Swiss Meringue for Cups
MAKES ENOUGH FOR ABOUT 36 CUPS

- 2 large egg whites
  Pinch of cream of tartar
- ¼ cup superfine sugar
- ¼ cup confectioners' sugar, sifted
- ½ teaspoon pure vanilla extract

In a metal mixing bowl, whisk egg whites and cream of tartar to break up egg whites. Set bowl over (not in) a pan of simmering water (do not let bottom of bowl touch water, or eggs may begin to cook). Whisk until whites are foamy. Gradually whisk in both sugars; continue whisking until mixture is completely smooth (test by rubbing some between your fingertips).

Attach bowl to a standing mixer, and whisk on low speed 5 minutes. Increase speed to high, and whisk until meringue is stiff and glossy, about 5 minutes more. Mix in vanilla, and use immediately.

VACHERIN
SERVES 10 *from* **DINNER PARTY DESSERTS**

- 6 large egg whites, room temperature
- 1½ cups granulated sugar
- 2 teaspoons pure vanilla extract
- 1½ cups heavy cream
- 2 tablespoons confectioners' sugar, plus more for dusting
- 12 ounces fresh raspberries, preferably a mixture of red and gold (about 3 cups)

Preheat oven to 200° F, with racks in upper and lower thirds. Using an inverted 9-inch round cake pan as a guide, trace a 9-inch circle on each of two pieces of parchment. Place each sheet, marking side down, on a baking sheet.

With an electric mixer on medium-high speed, whisk egg whites to soft peaks. Reduce speed to medium, and add ¼ cup granulated sugar, mixing to combine, then gradually add remaining 1¼ cups granulated sugar, 1 tablespoon at a time, and mix until whites are very stiff and glossy. Add 1 teaspoon vanilla; mix just until combined.

Divide batter between traced circles, and use an offset spatula to spread evenly to the edges. Bake meringues until dried and crisp on the outside but still white, about 3½ hours, rotating sheets from top to bottom and front to back every 30 minutes. Reduce oven to 175° F if meringue starts to brown. Transfer sheets to wire racks, and let cool completely.

Combine cream, remaining 1 teaspoon vanilla, and the confectioners' sugar in a chilled metal bowl; whip until stiff peaks form. Cover with plastic wrap, and refrigerate until ready to use.

To assemble vacherin, place one meringue circle on a serving plate, and spread half of the whipped cream over it. Sprinkle with two-thirds of the berries. Place remaining meringue circle on top, spread whipped cream in the middle, then sprinkle with remaining berries. Serve immediately, cutting into wedges with a serrated knife.

ÎLE FLOTTANTE
SERVES 8 TO 10 *from* **DINNER PARTY DESSERTS**

This "floating island" is a large meringue baked in a Bundt pan and then generously drizzled with caramel. Slices of the meringue are served atop crème anglaise drizzled with more caramel.

for the meringue
- 9 large egg whites, room temperature (reserve 4 yolks for crème anglaise)
- ¼ teaspoon coarse salt
- 1 teaspoon cream of tartar
- 1 cup plus 2 tablespoons superfine sugar
- 2 teaspoons pure vanilla extract
  Vegetable oil cooking spray

for the caramel
- 1 cup granulated sugar
- ½ cup heavy cream

for serving
  Crème Anglaise (page 422)

Prepare the meringue: Preheat oven to 375° F. Bring a kettle of water to a boil. Coat a 10- to 12-cup Bundt pan with cooking spray and invert onto a paper towel to allow excess to drain.

With an electric mixer on medium speed, whisk egg whites, salt, and cream of tartar until foamy. With mixer running, add superfine sugar, 1 tablespoon at a time, gradually increasing the speed to high. Whisk until meringue is very stiff and glossy but not dry, 3 to 4 minutes more. Reduce speed to low, and mix in vanilla.

Spoon meringue into prepared pan, pressing to ensure there are no air bubbles or pockets. Smooth the surface of the meringue with a small offset spatula. Place the Bundt pan in a roasting pan, and transfer to oven. Add boiling water to the roasting pan so that it reaches 2 inches up the sides of the Bundt pan. Bake meringue until well risen and lightly browned on top, about 20 minutes. Remove Bundt pan from water bath, and let cool on a wire rack.

Make the caramel: Prepare an ice-water bath. Heat granulated sugar in a saucepan over medium until dark amber, swirling pan occasionally to color evenly. Carefully stir in cream (it will spatter); continue cooking, swirling pan, until a candy thermometer registers 230° F. Immediately dip bottom of pan in ice bath for 3 seconds to stop the cooking. Let caramel cool completely.

To serve: Unmold meringue onto a platter (it should have a lip around edge to hold the caramel and be slightly larger than the meringue). Pour cooled caramel over top of meringue, allowing it to drip over the side and pool in the middle. Slice meringue into wedges.

Spoon crème anglaise onto individual plates, and place a meringue wedge on each. Drizzle with more caramel, and serve immediately.

MERINGUE *with* QUINCE SORBET *and* CRÈME ANGLAISE

SERVES 8 *from* **THANKSGIVING AT BEDFORD**

To form sorbet into quenelles, you will need two wet soup spoons: Use one spoon to scoop up a tablespoon of sorbet. With one spoon in each hand, and with spoons pointing toward each other, scrape sorbet back and forth from one spoon to the other a few times, forming it into a small, slightly pointed egg shape. Or you can form perfect balls of sorbet with a small ice cream scoop.

- 12 large egg whites
- ¾ teaspoon salt
- ¾ teaspoon cream of tartar
  Finely grated zest of 1 lemon plus 1 tablespoon fresh lemon juice
- 1½ teaspoons pure vanilla extract
- 3 cups sugar
  Crème Anglaise, for serving (page 422)
  Quince Sorbet, for serving (recipe follows)

Preheat oven to 200° F. With an electric mixer on medium speed, whisk egg whites to soft peaks. Beat in salt, cream of tartar, lemon zest and juice, and vanilla. With mixer running, gradually beat in sugar, then continue beating until meringue holds stiff peaks.

Cut a piece of parchment to fit a large baking sheet. Draw a 10- to 11-inch-long oval in middle of parchment. Turn parchment over, and use it to line the baking sheet, securing corners to sheet with small dabs of meringue. Spoon meringue onto parchment, using the marking as a guide.

Bake 30 minutes, then reduce oven to 175° F and continue to bake until meringue is crisp and dry on the outside but still white, about 4½ hours more. Turn off oven, and let meringue cool completely in oven, preferably 1 day.

When ready to serve, cut meringue into eight pieces with a serrated knife (or break into uneven pieces). Spoon crème anglaise on one side of 8 dessert plates, and top each with meringue. Arrange two quenelles (see headnote) of sorbet alongside.

Quince Sorbet MAKES ABOUT 1½ QUARTS

- 4 quince (about 2 pounds), peeled, cored, and cut into 2-inch pieces
- 1¼ cups sugar
- 8 cups water
- 1 tablespoon fresh lemon juice

In a heavy pot, bring quince, sugar, and the water to a boil, then reduce heat. Simmer until quince is tender, about 1 hour. Let cool slightly. Working in batches, purée mixture in a blender until smooth, being careful not to fill jar more than halfway each time. Strain through a fine sieve into a bowl. Stir in lemon juice, then cover and refrigerate overnight.

Pour mixture into an ice cream maker, and freeze according to manufacturer's instructions. Transfer sorbet to an airtight container, and freeze until firm, about 2 hours or up to 1 week.

ICE CREAM

MAKES 1 QUART *from* **ICE CREAM SOCIAL**

- 1 pint fresh strawberries, rinsed and hulled
- ¾ cup sugar
- 2 cups milk
- ½ cup heavy cream
- ½ teaspoon fresh lemon juice

Place strawberries in a large bowl, and sprinkle with sugar. Using a potato masher or wooden spoon, crush strawberries until they are broken into pieces (about ½ inch). Cover, and refrigerate until sugar dissolves, about 1 hour. Whisk in remaining ingredients, then cover and refrigerate at least 2 hours or up to 1 day.

Pour mixture into an ice cream maker and freeze according to manufacturer's instructions. Transfer ice cream to an airtight container, and freeze until firm, about 2 hours or up to 1 month.

ICE CREAM BOMBE

SERVES 8 *from* **DINNER PARTY DESSERTS**

The ice cream bombe shown on page 280 was formed in an antique copper mold, one of a vast collection. Any type of metal mold will do, or you can use cake pans, including loaf pans and springform pans, or even large bowls, which are admittedly easier to fill (no nooks and crannies) and to unmold. This recipe was just right for filling an eight-cup mold. To determine the volume of yours, fill it with water, then pour the water into a liquid measuring cup. The amount of water will show how much ice cream you need for that mold. Feel free to substitute good-quality store-bought ice cream and sorbet.

- 1 quart Pistachio Ice Cream (recipe follows)
- 1 pint Black-Currant Sorbet (recipe follows)
- 1 pint Strawberry Sorbet (recipe follows, strawberry-lavender variation)
  Fresh strawberries, for garnish (optional)
  Warm Chocolate Sauce, for serving (page 403)

With an electric mixer, beat pistachio ice cream until soft but still holding its shape, 1 to 2 minutes. Using a spoon or flexible spatula, place about two-thirds of the ice cream in bottom of an 8-cup mold, creating a thick layer about one-third the height of the mold; spread ice cream into any details of mold and press firmly to make sure there are no gaps or air bubbles. Use the remaining pistachio ice cream to spread a layer of even thickness up the sides of the mold, all the way to the rim, leaving the middle free. Freeze until firm, about 2 hours.

Soften black-currant sorbet with mixer, as above. Remove mold from freezer and spoon sorbet in a layer over pistachio ice cream, filling the next third of the mold in the middle. Return to freezer for another 2 hours.

Soften sorbet, as above. With an offset spatula, spread in a smooth layer on top, filling in the middle. Cover with plastic wrap and freeze 1 day.

To unmold, dip the bottom of the mold in hot water for a few seconds, then invert onto a serving plate, and carefully lift off mold. If desired, garnish with strawberries. To serve, spoon chocolate sauce onto 8 plates, dividing evenly. Cut bombe into wedges with a sharp knife dipped in hot water, and place a wedge on top of sauce on each plate.

Pistachio Ice Cream MAKES 1½ QUARTS

Look for pistachio paste at baking supply shops and specialty stores or from online resources.

- 2½ cups heavy cream
- 2 cups milk
- 8 large egg yolks
- ¾ cup sugar
- ¼ teaspoon salt
- ¼ cup pistachio paste

Bring cream and milk to a simmer in a large saucepan. Remove from heat; cover to keep warm.

With an electric mixer, beat yolks, sugar, and salt on high speed until mixture has tripled in volume and can hold a ribbon on surface for 2 seconds when beater is lifted. Reduce speed to medium. Using a measuring cup or a ladle, slowly pour 1 cup warm cream mixture into yolk mixture, then add another 1 cup cream mixture, beating to combine.

Prepare an ice-water bath. Pour custard into saucepan with cream mixture. Cook over medium-high heat, stirring constantly with a wooden spoon, until thick enough to coat the back of the spoon, and an instant-read thermometer registers 180° F, 5 to 7 minutes. Stir in pistachio paste until combined. Strain custard through a medium-mesh sieve into a bowl set in the ice bath. Let cool completely, stirring often. Refrigerate, covered, at least 2 hours or up to 1 day.

Pour custard into an ice cream maker, and freeze according to manufacturer's instructions. Transfer to an airtight container, and freeze until firm, about 2 hours or up to 1 month.

Black-Currant Sorbet MAKES 1 QUART

Crème de cassis is a black-currant-flavored liqueur available at most wine shops. If fresh currants are not available, look for frozen black-currant purée at specialty shops or from online retailers. You will need one pound of purée; omit the water and stir in thawed purée with the other ingredients.

- 1¼ pounds fresh black currants
- ½ cup water
- 1¼ cups plus 2 tablespoons Simple Syrup (page 422)
- 3 tablespoons crème de cassis

In a saucepan, bring currants and the water to a boil. Remove from heat, and strain mixture through a fine sieve into a bowl, pressing gently on solids with a flexible spatula to remove as much liquid as possible. Discard solids. Let purée cool slightly, then transfer to a bowl, and stir in simple syrup and crème de cassis. Refrigerate, covered, at least 2 hours or up to 1 day.

Pour mixture into an ice cream maker, and freeze according to manufacturer's instructions. Transfer sorbet to an airtight container and freeze until firm, about 2 hours or up to 1 week.

Strawberry Sorbet MAKES 1 QUART

Make the variation that follows for the Ice Cream Bombe on page 405; be sure to look for lavender that is free of pesticides.

- 4 cups water
- 3 cups sugar
- ¾ cup light corn syrup
- 3 pounds fresh strawberries, rinsed, hulled, and quartered
- ¼ cup fresh lemon juice

Heat the water, sugar, and corn syrup in a saucepan over medium, stirring occasionally, until sugar is dissolved. Let cool slightly. Purée in a blender with strawberries until smooth (work in batches, if necessary, to avoid filling jar more than halfway). Transfer to a bowl, stir in lemon juice, then cover and refrigerate at least 2 hours or up to 1 day.

Pour mixture into an ice cream maker, and freeze according to manufacturer's instructions. Transfer sorbet to an airtight container, and freeze until firm, about 2 hours or up to 1 week.

-Lavender Variation
After heating the water, sugar, and corn syrup mixture, add a few sprigs of fresh lavender; cover, and let steep while mixture cools, about 30 minutes, then remove and discard lavender. Proceed with recipe.

RHUBARB *and* RASPBERRY SORBETS *with* FRUIT COMPOTE

SERVES 8 *from* VERDANT SPRING DINNER

- 2 cups sugar
- 2 cups water
- 3 or 4 sprigs lemon thyme
- 1 cinnamon stick
- ¼ teaspoon coarse salt
- 1 vanilla bean, split lengthwise
- 3 pounds rhubarb, trimmed and cut into 2-inch pieces (about 9 cups)
  Raspberry Sorbet (recipe follows)
  Whipped cream (unsweetened), for serving
- 8 mint sprigs

Stir together sugar and the water in a saucepan. Add lemon thyme, cinnamon stick, and salt; scrape in vanilla seeds and add the pod. Bring to a boil, stirring, until sugar is dissolved. Add rhubarb. Reduce heat, and partially cover pan. Simmer, stirring occasionally, until rhubarb is just beginning to break down, about 5 minutes. Remove from heat.

Using a slotted spoon, transfer poached rhubarb to a bowl. Strain cooking liquid through a sieve into another bowl; discard solids. Let syrup and compote cool completely, then cover and refrigerate at least 2 hours or up to 1 day.

Pour rhubarb syrup into an ice cream maker, and freeze according to manufacturer's instructions. Transfer sorbet to a large airtight container, and freeze until firm, about 2 hours or up to 1 week.

When ready to serve, spoon a small amount of rhubarb compote onto each dessert plate, dividing evenly, then add a scoop each of rhubarb and raspberry sorbets. Spoon whipped cream on top, and garnish with a mint sprig.

Raspberry Sorbet MAKES 1 QUART

- 1⅔ pounds fresh raspberries
- ¾ cup water
- 1¾ cups Simple Syrup (page 422)

Pulse raspberries and the water in a food processor until smooth. Strain through a fine sieve into a bowl, pressing gently with a flexible spatula to remove as much liquid as possible; discard solids. (You should have about 2 cups raspberry purée.) Add simple syrup, and stir until well combined. Refrigerate, covered, at least 2 hours or up to 1 day.

Pour mixture into an ice cream maker, and freeze according to manufacturer's instructions. Transfer sorbet to a large airtight container, and freeze until firm, about 2 hours or up to 1 week.

ICED COFFEE *with* ESPRESSO ICE CREAM

MAKES 4   *from* ICE CREAM SOCIAL

- 1 cup heavy cream
- 2 teaspoons sugar
- 1 vanilla bean, split lengthwise and seeds scraped (pod reserved for another use)
  Espresso Ice Cream (recipe follows)
- 1½ cups prepared coffee, chilled

With an electric mixer, whisk the heavy cream, sugar, and vanilla seeds to medium-stiff peaks. Place a large dollop of whipped cream in each of 4 soda glasses, then top with 3 medium scoops of espresso ice cream. Pour in the chilled coffee until it just covers the ice cream, then top with another dollop of whipped cream. Serve immediately with a straw.

Espresso Ice Cream MAKES 1½ QUARTS

- 2 cups skim milk
- 2 cups heavy cream
- ½ cup crushed espresso beans
- 8 large egg yolks
- 1 cup sugar
- ¼ teaspoon coarse salt

Bring milk and cream just to a simmer in a saucepan. Add espresso beans and remove from heat; cover and let steep 10 minutes. Strain through a fine sieve into a bowl; discard solids.

In a clean saucepan, whisk together egg yolks, sugar, and salt until blended. Gradually whisk in milk mixture. Cook over medium, stirring constantly with a wooden spoon, until custard thickens slightly and evenly coats back of spoon (it should hold a line drawn by your finger), 10 to 12 minutes.

Prepare an ice-water bath. Strain custard through a fine sieve into a bowl set in the ice bath and let cool completely, stirring often. Refrigerate, covered, at least 2 hours or up to 1 day.

Pour custard into an ice cream maker, and freeze according to manufacturer's instructions. Transfer ice cream to an airtight container, and freeze until firm, about 2 hours or up to 1 month.

CHERRY CHOCOLATE-CHUNK ICE CREAM *with* HOT FUDGE SAUCE

SERVES 10; MAKES 1½ QUARTS ICE CREAM   *from* ICE CREAM SOCIAL

- ¾ cup sugar
- 6 large egg yolks
- 2 cups milk
  Pinch of salt
- 1 vanilla bean, split lengthwise
- 1 cup heavy cream
- 1 cup fresh cherries, pitted
- 2 tablespoons white rum
- 1 cup coarsely chopped bittersweet chocolate
  Hot Fudge Sauce, for serving (recipe follows)

In a bowl, whisk together ½ cup sugar and the yolks. Combine milk, salt, and remaining ¼ cup sugar in a saucepan; scrape in vanilla seeds and add the pod. Bring to a simmer, and cook, stirring, until sugar is dissolved; remove from heat. Remove and discard vanilla bean.

Using a measuring cup or a ladle, slowly pour about ½ cup hot milk mixture into the egg-yolk mixture, whisking constantly. Continue adding milk mixture, ½ cup at a time, whisking until combined. Pour mixture back into saucepan, and cook over low heat, stirring constantly with a wooden spoon, until thick enough to coat the back of the spoon (it should hold a line drawn by your finger), 10 to 12 minutes.

Prepare an ice-water bath. Strain custard through a fine sieve into a bowl; stir in cream. Set bowl in ice bath and let cool completely, stirring often. Refrigerate, covered, at least 2 hours and up to 1 day.

Place cherries in a small bowl, and cover with rum. Pour custard into an ice cream maker, and freeze according to manufacturer's instructions. During the last minute of churning, add cherries and their liquid, along with the chocolate. Continue churning until set but not hard. Transfer to an airtight container, and freeze until firm, about 2 hours or up to 1 month.

To serve, place one large scoop of ice cream in each shallow bowl and drizzle with hot fudge sauce.

Hot Fudge Sauce MAKES 2 CUPS

- 1 cup heavy cream
- ½ cup light corn syrup
- 12 ounces semisweet chocolate, finely chopped

Combine cream and corn syrup in a saucepan. Cook over medium heat, stirring frequently, until bubbles barely break the surface. Remove from heat. Add chocolate, and whisk until melted. Serve hot.

ROOT BEER FLOATS

MAKES 4 *from* **ICE CREAM SOCIAL**

1 quart Vanilla-Bean Ice Cream (recipe follows)
3 bottles best-quality root beer

Divide ice cream among 4 soda glasses, using an ice cream scoop. Dividing evenly, slowly pour the root beer into the glasses until it just covers the ice cream and forms a foamy head. Serve immediately.

Vanilla-Bean Ice Cream MAKES 1½ QUARTS

8 large egg yolks
1 cup sugar
¼ teaspoon coarse salt
2 cups milk
2 vanilla beans, split lengthwise (or 2 teaspoons pure vanilla extract)
2 cups heavy cream

In a saucepan, whisk together egg yolks, sugar, and salt until blended. Gradually whisk in milk. Cook over medium heat, stirring constantly with a wooden spoon, until custard thickens slightly and evenly coats the back of the spoon (it should hold a line drawn by your finger), 10 to 12 minutes.

Scrape vanilla seeds into pan, then drop in pod; cover, and let steep 30 minutes. (If using vanilla extract, there is no need to let the mixture steep.)

Prepare an ice-water bath. Strain custard through a fine sieve into a bowl, then stir in cream. Set bowl in ice bath and let cool completely, stirring often. Refrigerate, covered, at least 2 hours or up to 1 day.

Pour mixture into an ice cream maker, and freeze according to manufacturer's instructions. Transfer ice cream to an airtight container, and freeze until firm, about 2 hours or up to 1 month.

LEMON-BUTTERMILK ICE CREAM

MAKES 1 QUART *from* **ICE CREAM SOCIAL**

2 lemons, preferably organic
1⅓ cups sugar
¼ teaspoon salt
1⅓ cups buttermilk
Candied lemon peel, for garnish (optional)

Wash the lemons in warm water, then slice off the ends and discard. Very thinly slice the lemons, removing all seeds. There should be about 1⅓ cups slices. Place in a bowl, and toss with the sugar. Cover, and refrigerate 1 day.

Transfer mixture to a blender, and add the salt and buttermilk. Purée until almost smooth but leaving some larger pieces. Pour into a bowl, then cover and refrigerate at least 2 hours or up to 1 day.

Pour mixture into an ice cream maker, and freeze according to manufacturer's instructions. Transfer ice cream to an airtight container, and freeze until firm, about 2 hours or up to 1 month. Garnish with peel, if desired.

CHOCOLATE HONEY ICE CREAM *with* BUTTERSCOTCH SAUCE

SERVES 8; MAKES 1 QUART ICE CREAM *from* **ICE CREAM SOCIAL**

6 ounces bittersweet chocolate chips
5 large egg yolks
2 tablespoons sugar
2 cups milk
½ cup honey
Butterscotch Sauce, for serving (recipe follows)

Place chocolate chips in a large heatproof bowl. In another heatproof bowl, whisk together egg yolks and sugar.

Bring milk and honey just to a boil in a large saucepan, then immediately reduce heat to low. Whisking constantly, slowly strain the hot milk mixture through a fine sieve into the egg mixture. Pour mixture back into saucepan, and cook over medium heat, stirring constantly with a wooden spoon, until thick enough to coat the back of the spoon (it should hold a line drawn by your finger), 10 to 12 minutes.

Prepare an ice-water bath. Strain the custard into the bowl of chocolate chips, and stir until chocolate is melted and mixture is smooth. Set bowl in ice bath and let cool completely, stirring often. Refrigerate, covered, at least 2 hours or up to 1 day.

Pour custard into an ice cream maker, and freeze according to manufacturer's instructions. Transfer ice cream to an airtight container, and freeze until firm, about 2 hours or up to 1 month.

To serve, place one large scoop of ice cream in each shallow bowl, and drizzle with butterscotch sauce.

Butterscotch Sauce MAKES 2 CUPS

1 cup heavy cream
6 tablespoons unsalted butter
⅓ cup packed light brown sugar
3 tablespoons light corn syrup

Bring cream, butter, brown sugar, and corn syrup to a boil over high heat in a saucepan; cook, stirring occasionally, until sugar has dissolved, 2 to 3 minutes. (Sauce can be refrigerated, covered, up to 1 week; cool completely before storing.) Serve warm (reheat over low) or at room temperature.

MINT–CHOCOLATE CHIP ICE CREAM

MAKES ABOUT 1½ QUARTS *from* **ICE CREAM SOCIAL**

2 cups heavy cream
2 cups milk
Pinch of salt
2 bunches fresh mint
1 cup sugar
8 large egg yolks
3 ounces bittersweet chocolate, chopped

Bring cream, milk, and salt to a simmer in a saucepan. Add the mint. Remove from heat, and let steep at least 1 hour (or up to 1 day, covered, in the refrigerator). Strain through a fine sieve into a clean saucepan, gently pressing on mint to remove liquid; discard solids.

In a bowl, whisk together sugar and yolks. Bring the milk mixture just to a simmer. Using a measuring cup or a ladle, slowly pour about ½ cup of the hot milk mixture into the egg-yolk mixture, whisking constantly. Continue adding milk mixture, ½ cup at a time, whisking until combined. Pour mixture back into saucepan, and cook over low heat, stirring constantly with a wooden spoon, until mixture is thick enough to coat the back of the spoon (it should hold a line drawn with your finger), 10 to 12 minutes.

Prepare an ice-water bath. Strain custard through a fine sieve into a bowl set in the ice bath, and let cool completely, stirring often. Refrigerate, covered, at least 2 hours or up to 1 day.

Pour custard into an ice cream maker, and freeze until the consistency of soft-serve according to manufacturer's instructions; add chocolate, and continue churning until set but not hard. Transfer to an airtight container, and freeze until firm, about 4 hours or up to 1 month.

COOKIE CONES

MAKES 8 TO 10   *from* **ICE CREAM SOCIAL**

These simple cones are nothing more than tuiles that have been baked as rounds and then curled into a cone shape while cooling. Use the lid of a plastic storage container for making the template, and a conical-shaped object, such as a citrus reamer or a parchment cornet, to shape the tuiles. See page 380 for the how-to photographs.

- 1 cup sugar
- 1 cup all-purpose flour
-    Pinch of salt
- 4 large egg whites, room temperature
- 5 tablespoons unsalted butter, melted and cooled
- ¾ teaspoon pure vanilla extract

In a blender or food processor, pulse to combine sugar, flour, and salt. Add egg whites, melted butter, and vanilla; process until completely combined. Refrigerate batter, covered, at least 2 hours or up to 1 day.

Preheat oven to 350° F, with a rack in the center. Prepare a template by cutting out a 4¾-inch circle from sturdy plastic (such as the lid of a storage container). Place the template on top of a baking sheet (line with a nonstick baking mat for easier removal after baking). Use an offset spatula to spread a very thin layer of batter over the template to form a round, then lift template and repeat to make more rounds, spacing 1 inch apart.

Bake until golden, rotating sheet halfway through, about 6 minutes. Transfer sheet to a wire rack. Working quickly, remove one tuile with an offset spatula, and wrap around a conical-shaped object to form a cone. Hold until tuile begins to harden, about 10 seconds, then transfer to a wire rack, seam side down, to cool completely. Repeat with remaining tuiles. If tuiles become too cool to shape, return to oven for 30 seconds. Repeat with remaining batter. (Cones are best the same day, but can be stored in an airtight container at room temperature up to 3 days.)

CHEWY CHOCOLATE GINGERBREAD COOKIES

MAKES 2 DOZEN   *from* **PICNIC AT SEA**

- 1½ cups plus 1 tablespoon all-purpose flour
- 1¼ teaspoons ground ginger
- 1 teaspoon ground cinnamon
- ¼ teaspoon ground cloves
- ¼ teaspoon freshly grated nutmeg
- 1 tablespoon unsweetened Dutch-process cocoa powder
- ½ cup (1 stick) unsalted butter, softened
- 1 tablespoon finely grated peeled fresh ginger
- ½ cup packed dark brown sugar
- ¼ cup unsulfured molasses
- 1 teaspoon baking soda
- 1½ teaspoons boiling water
- 7 ounces best-quality semi-sweet chocolate, cut into ¼-inch chunks
- ¼ cup granulated sugar

Sift together flour, ground ginger, cinnamon, cloves, nutmeg, and cocoa into a medium bowl. With an electric mixer, beat butter and fresh ginger on medium speed until lightened. Add brown sugar; beat until combined. Add molasses and beat until combined.

In a small bowl, dissolve baking soda in the boiling water. Beat half of flour mixture into butter mixture. Beat in baking soda mixture, then remaining half of flour mixture. Mix in chocolate. Turn out dough onto a large piece of plastic wrap. Pat out to a 1-inch thickness; wrap in plastic. Refrigerate until firm, at least 2 hours or up to 1 day.

Preheat oven to 325° F. Roll dough into 1½-inch balls; place 2 inches apart on parchment-lined baking sheets. Refrigerate 20 minutes, then roll balls in granulated sugar. Bake until surfaces just begin to crack, 10 to 12 minutes, rotating halfway through. Let cool on sheets on a wire rack 5 minutes, then transfer cookies to rack and cool completely. (Cookies are best the same day they are made, but can be stored in airtight containers at room temperature up to 5 days.)

LEMON MELTAWAYS

MAKES ABOUT 5 DOZEN   *from* **TEA IN THE AFTERNOON**

Lime zest and juice can be used instead of the lemon in this recipe.

- 1¾ cups plus 2 tablespoons all-purpose flour
- 2 tablespoons cornstarch
- ¼ teaspoon coarse salt
- ¾ cup (1½ sticks) unsalted butter, softened
- 1 cup confectioners' sugar, sifted
-    Finely grated zest of 2 lemons plus 2 tablespoons fresh lemon juice
- 1 tablespoon pure vanilla extract

Whisk together flour, cornstarch, and salt in a bowl. With an electric mixer, cream butter and ⅓ cup confectioners' sugar until light and fluffy. Add lemon zest and juice and vanilla, and mix until fluffy. Add flour mixture, and mix on low speed just until combined. **(RECIPE CONTINUES)**

Divide dough in half and shape each into a log about 1¼ inches in diameter. Wrap each in plastic; refrigerate logs until firm, at least 1 hour or up to 1 day.

Preheat oven to 350° F. Cut logs into ¼-inch-thick rounds. Place rounds on parchment-lined baking sheets, spacing about 1 inch apart. Bake cookies until pale golden, about 13 minutes, rotating sheets halfway through. Transfer cookies to wire racks to cool slightly. While still warm, toss cookies with remaining ⅔ cup sugar in a resealable plastic bag. Let cool completely. (Cookies can be refrigerated in an airtight container up to 2 weeks.)

CHOCOLATE CHIP COOKIES

MAKES 20 *from* **PICNIC AT SEA**

2¾ cups all-purpose flour
1¼ teaspoons salt
1 teaspoon baking powder
1 teaspoon baking soda
2½ sticks unsalted butter, softened
1¼ cups packed dark brown sugar
¾ cup granulated sugar
2 large eggs
1 teaspoon pure vanilla extract
1½ cups semisweet chocolate chips

Preheat oven to 350° F. Sift together flour, salt, baking powder, and baking soda into a medium bowl. With an electric mixer on medium-high speed, cream butter and both sugars until fluffy. Beat in eggs, one at a time, scraping down sides of bowl as needed. Beat in vanilla. Reduce speed to low. Add flour mixture; beat until combined. Mix in chocolate chips.

Using a 2¼-inch ice cream scoop (about 3 tablespoons), drop dough onto parchment-lined baking sheets, spacing about 2 inches apart. Bake until golden around edges but soft in the middle, rotating sheets halfway through, about 15 minutes. Let cool on sheets on a wire rack 5 minutes, then transfer cookies to rack and let cool completely. (Cookies can be stored in airtight containers at room temperature up to 1 week.)

MADELEINES

MAKES ABOUT 2 DOZEN *from* **BRIDAL SHOWER IN MAINE**

½ cup (1 stick) unsalted butter, melted and cooled, plus more for pans
4 large eggs
⅔ cup granulated sugar
¼ teaspoon salt
1 teaspoon pure vanilla extract
Finely grated zest of 1 lemon
1 scant cup finely sifted all-purpose flour
Lemon Glaze (recipe follows)
Purple Luster Dust (optional)

Preheat oven to 350° F. Brush madeleine pans or small molds with butter. With an electric mixer, beat eggs, granulated sugar, salt, vanilla, and zest on medium-high speed until pale and thickened. Mix in melted butter. Using a spatula, fold in flour in batches (to prevent lumps).

Spoon batter into each mold, filling each about three-quarters full. Bake until firm in the center, about 10 minutes, rotating pans halfway through. Immediately turn out onto a wire rack and let cool completely.

Brush glaze on madeleines. Let set until glaze dries completely, then use a dry pastry brush to apply luster dust. (Cookies can be stored in a single layer in airtight containers at room temperature up to 1 day.)

Lemon Glaze MAKES ABOUT 1 CUP

1½ cups confectioners' sugar, sifted
¼ teaspoon finely grated lemon zest plus 3 tablespoons fresh lemon juice

Stir together confectioners' sugar, lemon zest, and juice until glaze is smooth, thick, and opaque. Use immediately.

CITRUS-CORNMEAL SHORTBREAD

MAKES ABOUT 3 DOZEN *from* **EASTER EGG HUNT**

1 cup (2 sticks) unsalted butter, softened
¾ cup confectioners' sugar, sifted
2 teaspoons pure vanilla extract
1½ teaspoons finely grated orange zest
2 cups all-purpose flour
¼ cup plus 2 tablespoons yellow cornmeal
1 teaspoon coarse salt

With an electric mixer, cream butter and confectioners' sugar until pale and fluffy. Add vanilla and zest, and mix until combined, scraping down sides of bowl as necessary. Reduce speed to low. Add flour, 2 tablespoons cornmeal, and the salt; mix until well combined.

Divide dough in half; shape each into a log about 1½ inches in diameter. Wrap each in plastic, and refrigerate until firm, at least 1 hour or up to 1 day.

Preheat oven to 350° F. Place remaining ¼ cup cornmeal on a piece of parchment. Roll logs in cornmeal to coat. Cut logs into ¼-inch-thick rounds, and place rounds on parchment-lined baking sheets, spacing about 1 inch apart. Bake cookies until pale golden, 25 to 30 minutes, rotating sheets halfway through. Transfer sheets to a wire rack to cool completely. (Cookies can be stored in an airtight container at room temperature up to 1 week.)

SHORTBREAD *with* LEMON CURD *and* MERINGUE

MAKES ABOUT 3 DOZEN *from* **PEONY GARDEN PARTY**

Lemon Curd (recipe follows)
Swiss Meringue (page 422)
Citrus-Cornmeal Shortbread (recipe above)

Fit each of two pastry bags with a plain ½-inch tip (such as Ateco #806). Fill one bag with lemon curd and the other with meringue. Pipe a small dollop of curd on each cookie, then pipe meringue on top of curd, swirling tip slightly and pulling up while releasing to form a peak. Use a small kitchen torch to lightly brown the tops of each meringue. (Alternatively, place cookies on a baking sheet, and broil until tops are lightly browned, watching carefully to avoid burning.) Serve immediately.

Lemon Curd MAKES 2 CUPS

8 large egg yolks
  Finely grated zest of 2 lemons plus ½ cup plus 2 tablespoons fresh lemon juice (from 3 to 4 lemons)
1 cup sugar
⅛ teaspoon salt
½ cup plus 2 tablespoons (1¼ sticks) cold unsalted butter, cut into pieces

Whisk together yolks, lemon zest and juice, and sugar in a heavy-bottomed saucepan. Cook over medium heat, stirring constantly and scraping bottom and side of pan with a wooden spoon, until thick enough to coat the back of the spoon and a candy thermometer registers 170° F, 8 to 10 minutes.

Remove from heat. Whisk in salt and then butter, one piece at a time, whisking until smooth after each addition. Strain through a fine sieve into a bowl, and let cool. Cover with plastic wrap, pressing it directly onto surface to prevent a skin from forming. Refrigerate until chilled and set, about 2 hours or up to 3 days.

SPRITZ COOKIES

MAKES 2 TO 3 DOZEN *from* **HOLIDAY OPEN HOUSE BRUNCH**

1½ cups (3 sticks) unsalted butter, softened
1 cup granulated sugar
2 large egg yolks
3¾ cups sifted all-purpose flour
¼ teaspoon salt
1 tablespoon pure vanilla extract
  Fine sanding sugar, for sprinkling (optional)

Preheat oven to 350° F, with rack in upper and lower thirds. With an electric mixer, cream butter and granulated sugar until light and fluffy. Add egg yolks, flour, salt, and vanilla; mix well to combine.

Transfer dough to a cookie press, and press out desired shapes onto two parchment-lined baking sheets, spacing 1 to 2 inches apart. Sprinkle with sanding sugar, if desired.

Bake until cookies are pale golden around the edges, 7 to 10 minutes, rotating baking sheets from top to bottom and front to back halfway through. Transfer cookies to a wire rack to cool completely. (Cookies can be stored in an airtight container at room temperature up to 1 week.)

NOAH'S ARK COOKIE CUTOUTS

MAKES ABOUT 2 DOZEN 4-INCH COOKIES
from **HOLIDAY OPEN HOUSE BRUNCH**

4 cups sifted all-purpose flour, plus more for dusting
1 teaspoon baking powder
½ teaspoon salt
1 cup (2 sticks) unsalted butter, softened
2 cups granulated sugar
2 large eggs
2 teaspoons pure vanilla extract
  Royal Icing (recipe follows)
  Fine sanding sugar, for decorating (optional)

Whisk together flour, baking powder, and salt in a bowl. With an electric mixer, cream butter and granulated sugar until light and fluffy. Mix in eggs and vanilla. Reduce speed to low. Gradually mix in flour mixture. Divide dough in half; flatten each half into a disk, and wrap in plastic. Refrigerate until firm, at least 1 hour or up to 1 day.

Let one disk of dough stand at room temperature just until soft enough to roll, about 10 minutes. Roll out dough on a lightly floured work surface to just under ¼ inch thick, adding more flour as needed to keep dough from sticking. Cut out shapes with 4- or 5-inch cookie cutters, transferring to parchment-lined baking sheets as you work, and spacing about 1 inch apart. Reroll scraps, and cut out more shapes. Repeat with remaining disk of dough. Chill cookies in freezer until very firm, about 15 minutes.

Preheat oven to 325° F, with racks in upper and lower thirds. Bake, rotating sheets from top to bottom and front to back halfway through, until edges just turn golden, 15 to 18 minutes. Let cool on sheets on wire racks.

To decorate, transfer icing to a pastry bag fitted with a plain ⅛- to ¼-inch tip (such as #2 or #3). Flood cookies with icing: Pipe to outline cookies, then pipe more icing inside outline; spread to fill in gaps with a skewer or small offset spatula. While icing is still wet, pipe polka dots on top, using icing in contrasting colors (and separate pastry bags); stretch dots into flourishes with the tip of a toothpick or wooden skewer for a marbleized look. Flock, or sprinkle, wet icing with sanding sugar, if desired. Let set 1 day at room temperature. (Decorated cookies can be stored between layers of parchment in an airtight container at room temperature up to 1 week.)

Royal Icing MAKES ABOUT 2½ CUPS

You can tint the icing any color you wish. To make the colors shown on page 39, mix true red food coloring with black for silver, and mix ivory with egg yellow for gold. If using the icing for "flooding," or covering the tops of the cookies, you may need to thin it with a little water.

¼ cup plus 1 tablespoon meringue powder
1 pound confectioners' sugar, sifted
⅓ cup water
  Gel-paste food coloring

With an electric mixer on low speed, mix meringue powder, confectioners' sugar, and the water until combined. If tinting, divide among bowls, and tint with food coloring as desired. If not using immediately, cover and refrigerate up to 1 week; stir until smooth before using.

FUDGY BROWNIES

MAKES 12 TO 16 *from* **PICNIC AT SEA**

- 1 cup (2 sticks) unsalted butter, cut into pieces, plus more, melted, for baking dish
- ⅔ cup all-purpose flour, plus more for dish
- ½ teaspoon salt
- 12 ounces good-quality semisweet chocolate, coarsely chopped
- 1¼ cups packed light brown sugar
- 4 large eggs
- 1 teaspoon pure vanilla extract

Preheat oven to 375° F. Brush a 9-by-13-inch baking dish with melted butter. Dust with flour, and tap out excess. Whisk together flour and salt in a small bowl. Melt chocolate and butter in a heatproof bowl set over (not in) a pan of simmering water, stirring constantly. Let cool completely.

With an electric mixer on high, whisk brown sugar and eggs until fluffy. Reduce speed to low. Beat in chocolate mixture and vanilla. Add flour mixture, and beat until just combined. Spread batter evenly in prepared dish.

Bake until top has cracked, center is just firm to the touch, and a cake tester inserted into center comes out with only a few moist crumbs attached, 25 to 30 minutes. Transfer to a wire rack, and let cool completely in dish. Cut into squares. (Brownies can be stored in an airtight container at room temperature up to 2 days.)

CHOCOLATE BROWNIES *with* GANACHE TOPPING

MAKES 48 *from* **PEONY GARDEN PARTY**

- 1 cup plus 6 tablespoons (2¾ sticks) unsalted butter, cut into pieces, plus more, melted, for baking dish
- 7 ounces bittersweet chocolate (preferably 70% cacao), finely chopped
- 4 large eggs
- 1½ cups packed light brown sugar
- 1 cup all-purpose flour
  Pinch of salt
  Ganache Topping (recipe follows)
  Confectioners' sugar, for dusting

Preheat oven to 350° F. Brush a 9-by-13-inch baking dish with melted butter. Line with parchment, allowing a 2-inch overhang on long sides, and butter parchment. Melt chocolate and butter in a heatproof bowl set over (not in) a pot of simmering water, stirring constantly. Let cool slightly.

With an electric mixer, beat eggs and brown sugar until fluffy. Fold in chocolate mixture, then fold in flour and salt until combined. Pour batter into prepared dish, and smooth top with a spatula. Bake until a cake tester inserted into center comes out with only a few moist crumbs attached, 20 to 25 minutes. Transfer to a wire rack, and let cool in pan. Using parchment, lift brownies from pan, and let cool completely on rack. (Brownies can be stored in an airtight container at room temperature up to 2 days.)

Cut brownies into 1½-inch squares. Fill a pastry bag fitted with an open star tip (such as #18) with ganache, and pipe a rosette on each brownie. Dust with confectioners' sugar just before serving.

Ganache Topping MAKES ABOUT ¾ CUPS

- 4 ounces bittersweet chocolate, finely chopped
- ½ cup heavy cream
- 1 tablespoon milk
- 1 teaspoon light corn syrup
- 1 teaspoon unsalted butter

Place chocolate in a heatproof bowl. In a heavy saucepan, bring cream, milk, corn syrup, and butter to a simmer over medium heat, stirring occasionally to combine. Pour cream mixture over chocolate and let stand 5 minutes, then stir until chocolate is melted and mixture is smooth. Let cool completely, stirring occasionally. Ganache will thicken as it cools.

MACARONS

MAKES ABOUT 4 DOZEN *from* **VERDANT SPRING DINNER**

The recipe for French macarons is simple and basic. However, there are a few steps to pay particular attention to if you have not made these cookies before; for step-by-step instructions, see the how-to photographs on page 382. Also, be sure to allow the cookies to dry completely before baking, which will help produce the characteristic "foot." If they have not dried long enough, the tops of the cookies may crack during baking. This recipe is adapted from one by Alexandre Talpaert, pastry chef at Benoit, in Manhattan.

- 1¼ cups almond flour or finely ground blanched almonds
- 1¾ cups confectioners' sugar
- 4 large egg whites
- ½ cup granulated sugar
  Gel-paste food coloring in yellow, light green, brown, or pink (depending on desired filling)
  Lemon Cream, Pistachio Ganache, Chocolate Ganache, or Raspberry Jam fillings (recipes follow)

Whisk together almond flour and confectioners' sugar, then sift into a large bowl. With an electric mixer on medium speed, whisk egg whites until foamy. With the mixer running, gradually add granulated sugar, beating to combine. Increase mixer speed to medium high, and beat until whites are stiff and glossy. Add food coloring, and mix until blended.

Fold the whites into the almond-flour mixture, then beat vigorously with the spatula just until batter slowly sinks into a smooth mass when the spatula is lifted. Transfer to a large pastry bag fitted with a plain ⅜- to ½-inch tip (such as Ateco #806). Pipe 1-inch rounds, about 1 inch apart, onto two baking sheets lined with nonstick baking mats or parchment. Let rounds dry until a crust forms on the top of the cookie, 30 minutes to 1¼ hours, depending on the texture of the batter and the level of humidity.

Preheat oven to 350° F. Bake cookies, one sheet at a time, until cookies are firm, about 18 minutes, rotating sheet halfway through. Remove from oven, and immediately slide the cookies (still on mat or parchment) onto a wire rack and let cool completely.

Using a small offset spatula, gently lift off cookies; arrange side by side, in pairs of similar size, with one facing up and the other facing down. With your thumb, make a small indentation in the flat side of the macarons that are upside down.

Transfer desired filling to a small pastry bag fitted with a plain ¼-inch tip (such as #3 or #4). Pipe onto indentations on macarons. Sandwich the pairs together, pressing gently to adhere. (Macarons can be refrigerated in an airtight container up to 5 days; let sit at room temperature about 15 minutes before serving.)

Lemon Cream MAKES 1½ CUPS

½ teaspoon unflavored powdered gelatin
1½ teaspoons cold water
2 large eggs
¼ cup sugar
½ teaspoon finely grated lemon zest plus ¼ cup fresh lemon juice (from 1 to 2 lemons)
5½ tablespoons unsalted butter, cut into small pieces

In a bowl, sprinkle the gelatin over the cold water, and let soften 5 minutes.

Lightly beat eggs in another bowl. In a small saucepan, stir together sugar and lemon zest and juice; bring to a boil over medium heat. Whisking constantly, pour some lemon mixture into the eggs to temper, then pour mixture back into saucepan, and cook, whisking constantly, until mixture thickens, about 2 minutes. Remove pan from heat, and whisk in softened gelatin, whisking until gelatin is dissolved.

Strain custard through a fine sieve into a clean bowl. Let cool 5 minutes, then whisk in butter, a few pieces at a time, until incorporated. Cover the cream with plastic wrap, pressing it onto surface to prevent a skin from forming, and refrigerate until ready to use, up to 3 days.

Pistachio Ganache MAKES ABOUT ¾ CUP

4 ounces white chocolate, finely chopped
½ cup heavy cream
1 tablespoon pistachio paste (available online or at baking supply stores)

Place white chocolate in a heatproof bowl. In a heavy saucepan, bring the cream and pistachio paste to a boil, whisking until blended. Pour hot cream mixture over chopped chocolate; cover, and let stand 5 minutes before whisking until smooth. Keep at room temperature until firm. (Ganache can be refrigerated in an airtight container up to 2 weeks; return to room temperature before piping.)

Chocolate Ganache MAKES ABOUT ¾ CUP

4 ounces bittersweet chocolate, finely chopped
¼ cup heavy cream
5 tablespoons unsalted butter, cut into small pieces, softened

Place chocolate in a heatproof bowl. In a heavy saucepan, bring cream to a boil, then pour over chocolate; cover, and let stand 5 minutes before

whisking until smooth. Whisk in butter, a few pieces at a time, until incorporated. Keep at room temperature until firm. (Ganache can be refrigerated in an airtight container up to 2 weeks; return to room temperature before piping.)

Raspberry Jam MAKES ABOUT 1 CUP

12 ounces fresh raspberries (about 2¼ cups)
1 cup plus 2 tablespoons sugar
1⅛ teaspoons fresh lemon juice
Pinch of coarse salt
½ teaspoon finely grated orange zest

Place a few small plates in the freezer. Stir berries, sugar, lemon juice, salt, and half the orange zest in a large, heavy pot. Bring to a boil, stirring to dissolve sugar and mashing lightly with a potato masher. Skim foam from surface. Cook, stirring more frequently as jam thickens, until it has the consistency of very loose jelly, 8 to 9 minutes. Remove from heat.

Remove a plate from freezer; drop a spoonful of jam on it. Return to freezer for 1 to 2 minutes; nudge edge of jam with a finger. It should hold its shape. If jam is too thin and spreads, return it to a boil, testing every minute, until jam holds its shape on plate.

Strain about half of the jam through a fine sieve into a bowl; discard seeds. Return strained jam to pot; stir in remaining zest. Return to a boil, then remove from heat. Let cool before using or storing. (Jam will keep in an airtight container in the refrigerator up to 1 month.)

S'MORES

MAKES 8, WITH EXTRAS *from* **FRIDAY NIGHT WELCOME DINNER**

You can, of course, opt for store-bought graham crackers (and marshmallows) when making s'mores, but these tree-shaped versions are utterly charming and worth the extra effort. We used a plastic faux bois texture mat to create a woodgrain pattern before baking the grahams; you can find these food-safe mats at chineseclayart.com. Choose whichever type of chocolate—milk, semisweet, or bittersweet—you like best.

16 Graham Crackers (recipe follows)
1 bar (4 ounces) chocolate, snapped or cut into 8 pieces
16 Marshmallows (recipe follows)

Heat a grill to medium. (If you are using a charcoal grill, coals are ready when you can hold your hand 5 inches above grates for just 5 to 6 seconds.) Place a graham cracker, flat side up, on each serving plate, then top with a piece of chocolate.

Press each marshmallow onto the tip of a skewer. Cook marshmallows, turning occasionally, until toasted to desired doneness. Using a fork, push each marshmallow onto a chocolate-covered graham cracker. Sandwich with remaining graham crackers. Serve immediately.

Graham Crackers MAKES 16 TO 20

¾   cup all-purpose flour, plus more for dusting
¾   cup graham or whole-wheat flour
½   teaspoon baking soda
¼   teaspoon baking powder
¼   teaspoon coarse salt
½   teaspoon ground cinnamon
6   tablespoons unsalted butter, softened
⅓   cup packed light brown sugar
1   tablespoon honey
1   large egg

In a bowl, whisk together both flours, baking soda, baking powder, salt, and cinnamon. With an electric mixer, cream butter, brown sugar, and honey until fluffy. Scrape down sides of bowl. With mixer on low speed, add egg, and mix until combined. Add flour mixture, and mix until combined.

Turn out dough onto a lightly floured surface; divide in half. Roll each piece of dough between two sheets of parchment to a ⅛-inch thickness. Remove top parchment and place a lightly floured faux bois mat (see headnote, page 413) on dough, pattern side down. With a rolling pin, lightly roll over mat to imprint dough. Carefully remove mat. Transfer dough on parchment to a baking sheet and chill 15 minutes. Using a 3-inch tree-shaped cutter, cut out as many cookies as possible. Transfer shapes to a parchment-lined baking sheet (reserving scraps), spacing about 1 inch apart, and refrigerate until firm, about 10 minutes. Meanwhile, repeat with remaining half of dough. Gather together all scraps, chill, and cut out more shapes.

Preheat oven to 350°F, with racks in upper and lower thirds. Bake graham crackers until golden brown, rotating sheets from top to bottom and front to back halfway through, about 10 minutes. Transfer cookies to a wire rack to cool completely. (Graham crackers can be stored in an airtight container at room temperature up to 1 week.)

Marshmallows MAKES 16

2   envelopes unflavored powdered gelatin (2 scant tablespoons)
1⅓   cups cold water
1½   cups granulated sugar
⅓   cup light corn syrup
⅛   teaspoon coarse salt
1   teaspoon pure vanilla extract
    Confectioners' sugar, sifted, for coating
    Vegetable oil cooking spray

Coat an 8-inch square cake pan with cooking spray, and line with parchment, then spray parchment. In a mixing bowl, sprinkle gelatin over ⅔ cup cold water, and let soften 5 minutes. Bring granulated sugar, corn syrup, salt, and remaining ⅔ cup water to a simmer in a heavy saucepan, stirring to dissolve sugar. Continue to simmer until a candy thermometer reaches 238°F, about 5 minutes.

Attach bowl to standing mixer; with mixer on low speed, slowly pour syrup in a steady stream down side of bowl into softened gelatin. Continue beating, gradually increasing speed to high, until mixture is thick and almost tripled in volume, about 8 minutes. Mix in vanilla.

Transfer mixture to prepared pan, and smooth evenly with an offset spatula. Let stand at room temperature until set, at least 3 hours, or up to 1 day covered with plastic wrap.

Transfer to a cutting board. Cut into 1-inch squares using a sharp knife dipped in hot water. Roll marshmallows in confectioners' sugar to coat. (Marshmallows can be kept at room temperature in an airtight container up to 4 days.)

BAKED STUFFED APPLES

MAKES 8   *from* HALLOWEEN PUMPKIN BLAZE

What makes these stuffed apples appropriate for a Halloween celebration is the spiderweb pattern—created with two flavors of crème anglaise—on the plates on which they are served. See page 379 for the step-by-step how-to photographs.

2   oranges, zested and juiced
1   teaspoon finely grated lemon zest
½   cup raisins, chopped
¼   cup Cognac or other brandy
⅓   cup coarsely chopped pecans
⅓   cup coarsely chopped walnuts
¼   cup coarsely chopped shelled pistachios
½   cup packed light brown sugar
    Pinch of ground cinnamon
    Pinch of ground mace
8   apples (about 3 pounds), preferably Northern Spy
    Swiss Meringue (page 422; use 3 egg whites and ¾ cup sugar)
    Crème Anglaise, with chocolate variation (page 422)

In a bowl, stir together both zests, orange juice, raisins, and Cognac; cover, and let stand at room temperature 8 hours, or up to 1 day.

Preheat oven to 325°F, with a rack in the center. Stir nuts, brown sugar, cinnamon, and mace into raisin mixture. With a small melon baller, core apples, starting at stem end and leaving blossom end intact. Stand cored apples on a baking sheet lined with a nonstick baking mat, and fill each one with raisin mixture, dividing evenly. Bake until base of an apple is tender when pierced with the tip of a sharp knife, 25 to 45 minutes, depending on size and variety. Cool apples on baking sheet on a wire rack.

Fit a large pastry bag with an open-star tip (such as #18) and fill with Swiss meringue. Pipe a rosette on top of each apple. Using a small kitchen torch, carefully brown the edges of the meringue. (Alternatively, place meringue-topped apples under the broiler until golden, 1 to 2 minutes, watching carefully to avoid burning.)

Spoon about 3 tablespoons crème anglaise onto each of 8 dessert plates. Transfer chocolate crème anglaise to a small pastry bag fitted with a plain fine tip (or place in a small sturdy plastic bag and snip off corner). Starting at the outside and working toward the center of the plate, pipe a spiral pattern as shown in the how-to photographs on page 379. Create a spiderweb design by dragging a knife in radiating lines through the chocolate spiral, starting from the center of the plate and working toward the border. Place a meringue-topped apple in the center of each plate, and serve immediately.

PUMPKIN MOUSSE

SERVES 8 TO 10 *from* **THANKSGIVING AT BEDFORD**

---

 1 envelope unflavored powdered gelatin (1 scant tablespoon)
 ¼ cup cold water
 ½ cup plus 2 tablespoons canned unsweetened pumpkin purée
 4 large eggs, separated
 ¼ cup plus 2 tablespoons pure maple syrup
    Pinch of freshly grated nutmeg
 ½ teaspoon pure vanilla extract
 ½ teaspoon ground ginger
 ½ teaspoon ground allspice
 ¼ teaspoon salt
    Pinch of freshly ground white pepper
 2 tablespoons dark rum
 ¼ cup sugar
 1 cup heavy cream
    Sweetened whipped cream, for serving (optional)
    Pastry Leaves, for garnish (optional; see Pâte Brisée note, page 421)

In a small saucepan, sprinkle gelatin over the cold water, and let soften 5 minutes. Cook softened gelatin over medium heat, swirling pan, just until gelatin is dissolved; do not let boil. Let cool completely.

Place pumpkin purée in a large bowl. Stir in softened gelatin, then add egg yolks, maple syrup, nutmeg, vanilla, ginger, allspice, salt, white pepper, and rum. Whisk until fully blended.

With an electric mixer on medium speed, whisk egg whites and the sugar to soft peaks. Gently fold egg-white mixture into pumpkin mixture to combine. Whip heavy cream on medium high to stiff peaks, then gently but thoroughly fold into pumpkin mixture.

Divide mousse among 8 to 10 glasses; refrigerate until set, at least 2 hours, or up to 1 day covered with plastic wrap. If desired, top each with a dollop of sweetened whipped cream and a pastry leaf before serving.

MINI TIRAMISÙ

MAKES 12 *from* **PEONY GARDEN PARTY**

 ⅓ cup freshly brewed espresso
 ¼ cups Kahlúa or other coffee-flavored liqueur
 ¼ cup plus 3 tablespoons sugar
 3 large egg yolks
 ⅓ cup mascarpone cheese
 1¼ cups heavy cream
 1½ teaspoons instant espresso powder
 ½ teaspoon unsweetened cocoa powder
 8 ladyfingers, each broken into thirds
    Bittersweet chocolate shavings, for serving

Stir together brewed espresso, liqueur, and ¼ cup sugar until sugar is dissolved. Set aside to cool. With an electric mixer on medium speed, beat egg yolks until smooth. Gradually beat in remaining 3 tablespoons sugar, then continue to beat until light and fluffy. In a small bowl, stir 2 tablespoons egg yolk mixture into mascarpone to lighten it, then gently fold into

whipped yolk mixture. Whip 1 cup heavy cream on medium speed to soft peaks, then fold into mascarpone mixture in two additions.

In another bowl, stir together 1 tablespoon brewed-espresso mixture, the espresso powder, and cocoa powder until powders are dissolved. Gently fold in half the mascarpone mixture, until blended.

Dip a ladyfinger piece into the remaining brewed-espresso mixture to moisten, then place in bottom of a 2- to 3-ounce glass. Repeat with 11 more pieces, placing one in each glass. Add a dollop of plain mascarpone mixture to each glass, dividing evenly. Dip remaining ladyfinger pieces in the brewed-espresso mixture, and layer 1 in each glass. Divide the flavored mascarpone mixture among glasses, spooning over ladyfingers. Cover tops of glasses with plastic, and refrigerate until cold, about 1 hour, or up to 2 days.

Just before serving, whip remaining ¼ cup heavy cream into soft peaks. Transfer to a pastry bag fitted with a plain ½-inch tip (such as Ateco #806). Pipe decorative swirls on top of desserts, and sprinkle with chocolate shavings.

Note

The eggs in this recipe are not fully cooked; it should not be prepared for pregnant women, babies, young children, the elderly, or anyone else whose health is compromised.

VANILLA CUPCAKES
with SUGARED PANSIES

MAKES 24 *from* **BRIDAL SHOWER IN MAINE**

---

 3 cups cake flour (not self-rising), sifted
 2 teaspoons baking powder
 1 teaspoon coarse salt
 1 cup (2 sticks) unsalted butter, softened
 2 vanilla beans, split lengthwise and seeds scraped
    (pods reserved for another use)
 1¾ cups sugar
 1 cup milk
 8 large egg whites, room temperature
    Vanilla Frosting (recipe follows)
    Sugared Pansies, for garnish (optional; page 395)

Preheat oven to 325°F, with racks in center and lower positions. Line two standard 12-cup muffin tins with papers. In a bowl, whisk together flour, baking powder, and salt. With an electric mixer on medium speed, cream butter, vanilla seeds, and 1½ cups sugar until light and fluffy. Scrape down sides of bowl. With mixer on low speed, add flour mixture in three batches, alternating with two additions of milk, and scraping sides of bowl as needed.

In a clean mixing bowl, whisk egg whites on high speed to soft peaks. Gradually add remaining ¼ cup sugar, beating to stiff glossy peaks. Fold one-third of the whites into the batter, then carefully fold in remaining whites. Divide batter evenly among prepared muffin cups, filling each about three-quarters full.

Bake until a cupcake springs back gently when touched, rotating tins halfway through, about 25 minutes. Let cool in tins on a wire rack 10 minutes, then turn out onto rack to cool completely. (Cupcakes can be refrigerated in an airtight container up to 3 days.) When ready to serve, spread with frosting, and garnish with pansies, if desired.

Vanilla Frosting MAKES 4 CUPS

1½ cups (3 sticks) unsalted butter, softened
1 pound (4 cups) confectioners' sugar, sifted
½ teaspoon pure vanilla extract

With an electric mixer on medium-high speed, cream butter until pale and creamy. Reduce speed to medium and add confectioners' sugar, ½ cup at a time, beating well after each addition, and scraping down sides of bowl as needed; after every two additions, raise speed back to high, and beat 10 seconds to aerate frosting, then return to medium. Frosting will be very pale and fluffy. Add vanilla, and beat until frosting is smooth. (Frosting can be refrigerated up to 1 week in an airtight container. Before using, bring to room temperature, and beat on low speed until smooth, about 5 minutes.)

SEMOLINA CAKE

SERVES 8 *from* **DINNER PARTY DESSERTS**

For the cake shown on page 285, the batter was baked in a six-cup copper pomme anna mold. You can use an eight-inch round cake pan that is at least two inches deep in place of the mold.

1 cup plus ¾ cup sugar
½ cup plus 2 tablespoons water
3½ cups milk
½ cup heavy cream
½ vanilla bean, split lengthwise
¼ teaspoon coarse salt
¾ cup plus 1 tablespoon fine semolina
2 large whole eggs, plus 1 large egg yolk, lightly beaten
1 teaspoon baking soda
1 cup raisins
¼ teaspoon freshly grated nutmeg
¼ teaspoon ground cinnamon
   Crème Anglaise (page 422)

Cook 1 cup sugar and 2 tablespoons water in a small skillet over medium-high heat, swirling pan occasionally, until caramel is a deep golden brown, about 4 minutes. Pour in remaining ½ cup water, and cook, swirling pan, just until water is incorporated. Pour half the caramel into an 8-inch heavy round cake pan at least 2 inches deep, and immediately swirl to coat bottom and halfway up the sides. Reserve remaining caramel.

Combine milk, cream, and remaining ¾ cup sugar in a large saucepan. Scrape in vanilla seeds, then drop in pod, and whisk to combine. Heat over medium until mixture bubbles at the edges, about 15 minutes. Remove from heat and let steep, covered, 30 minutes. Remove and discard vanilla pod.

Preheat oven to 350° F. Return pan to medium heat, and cook until bubbles form around the edge, about 8 minutes. Add salt, and sprinkle in semolina, whisking constantly. Reduce heat to medium low and simmer gently until thickened, stirring frequently with a wooden spoon to prevent sticking, about 5 minutes. Remove from heat. Whisk ½ cup hot-milk mixture into beaten eggs, then pour back into pan and whisk until combined. Stir in baking soda, raisins, nutmeg, and cinnamon. Pour into prepared pan, and smooth top with an offset spatula.

Bake 15 minutes. Reduce oven to 300° F, and continue baking until top is puffed and golden and a cake tester inserted in the center comes out clean, about 45 minutes more. Tent with foil if the top begins to brown too much during baking. Transfer to a wire rack, and let cool 15 minutes before turning out onto a cake stand or platter. Pour reserved caramel over the top, then cut into slices and serve with crème anglaise.

MINI HONEY FRUITCAKES

MAKES 12 *from* **HOLIDAY OPEN HOUSE BRUNCH**

1¾ cups all-purpose flour
2 teaspoons baking powder
1 teaspoon coarse salt
¾ cup (1½ sticks) unsalted butter
½ cup sugar
⅓ cup honey
2 large eggs
1 cup fresh ricotta cheese or ¾ cup milk
1 cup pecans or blanched almonds, toasted (page 423) and finely ground (about 1 cup)
1 cup dried apricots, diced, plus more for garnish
1 cup dried cranberries or cherries, finely diced, plus more for garnish
   Honey Glaze (recipe follows)
   Mixed Citrus Sauce, for serving (recipe follows)
   Mixed Citrus Curd, for serving (recipe follows)

Preheat oven to 325° F. Cut out 12 squares (each about 5½ inches) of parchment, and press a square into each cup of a standard muffin tin, creasing to fit (or line with cupcake liners). Whisk together flour, baking powder, and salt.

With an electric mixer on medium speed, cream butter and sugar until light and fluffy. Add honey, and beat on medium-high speed until combined, scraping down sides of bowl as necessary. Beat in eggs until combined. Add flour mixture in three batches, alternating with the ricotta and beginning and ending with flour; beat until combined after each. Mix in nuts and dried fruits.

Divide batter evenly among prepared cups, and bake until a cake tester inserted in center of a cake comes out clean, about 40 minutes, rotating tin halfway through. Let cool in tin 10 minutes, then brush with honey glaze and garnish with a few dried fruits. Brush with more glaze, then remove from tin and let cool completely on a wire rack. Serve on plates, with citrus sauce and curd alongside.

Honey Glaze MAKES ½ CUP

½ cup honey
   Pinch of salt
2 tablespoons fresh lemon juice

Bring honey to a boil in a small saucepan, and continue to boil 3 minutes. Stir in salt and lemon juice to combine. Let cool before using.

Mixed Citrus Sauce MAKES ABOUT 2½ CUPS

1¼ cups sugar
3 tablespoons cornstarch
¼ teaspoon salt
2 cups hot water
½ cup (1 stick) unsalted butter, cut into pieces
  Finely grated zest of 2 lemons plus ½ cup fresh
  lemon juice (from 2 to 3 lemons)
¼ cup fresh blood-orange juice or lime juice (from 1 to 2
  blood oranges or limes), or a combination

In a saucepan, whisk to combine sugar, cornstarch, and salt, then whisk in the hot water. Bring to a boil, whisking constantly; continue to boil, whisking, until mixture thickens, about 6 minutes more.

Stir in butter, lemon zest, and all juices. Cook, stirring, until smooth and clear, 2 to 3 minutes. Remove from heat. Serve warm or room temperature. (Once cooled, sauce can be refrigerated in an airtight container up to 2 weeks; before serving, reheat over medium low, if desired.)

Mixed Citrus Curd MAKES 1½ CUPS

4 large whole eggs plus 6 large egg yolks
1 cup sugar
  Finely grated zest of 2 lemons plus ½ cup fresh lemon juice
  (from 2 to 3 lemons)
½ cup fresh orange juice (from 1 to 2 oranges), lime juice
  (from 3 to 4 limes), or tangerine juice (from 2 to 3 tangerines)
6 tablespoons unsalted butter, cut into pieces

In a saucepan, whisk together whole eggs and yolks. Add sugar, lemon zest and juice, and ¼ cup orange juice. Cook over low heat, stirring constantly with a wooden spoon, until thick enough to coat the back of the spoon (it should hold a line drawn by your finger), 8 to 10 minutes.

Remove from heat, and add butter, a piece at a time, stirring until smooth after each addition. Stir in remaining ¼ cup orange juice. Strain through a fine sieve into a bowl. Cover with plastic wrap, pressing it directly onto the surface of the curd to prevent a skin from forming. Refrigerate until cold and set, at least 2 hours or up to 1 day. Whisk until smooth before using.

ORANGE EASTER-EGG CAKE
with TINY MERINGUE NESTS

SERVES 10   *from* EASTER DINNER

You will need an egg-shaped mold to bake the cake, a three-inch wedge of sturdy rustic bread to prop up the cake for decorating and displaying, and two quarter-inch wooden dowels for securing the cake and ribbon. Look for egg-shaped molds, such as those made by Wilton, at specialty baking stores or from online resources. For photographs and instructions on assembling and piping the meringue on the cake, see the how-to on page 383.

1 cup (2 sticks) unsalted butter, melted and cooled,
  plus more, softened, for mold
1½ cups sifted cake flour (not self-rising), plus more for mold
1 cup plus 3 tablespoons sugar

6 large eggs, separated
  Finely grated zest of 2 blood oranges plus ⅔ cup strained
  fresh blood-orange juice (from 4 to 5 oranges)
½ teaspoon pure almond extract
1½ cups almond flour or finely ground blanched almonds
½ teaspoon salt
⅓ cup heavy cream
½ cup Blood-Orange Curd (recipe follows)
  Toasted slivered almonds, for decorating platter (optional; page 423)
  Wedge of rustic bread (3 inches), for supporting cake
  Swiss Meringue (page 422)
  Orange jelly beans, for decorating platter (optional)
  Tiny Meringue Nests (recipe follows)

Preheat oven to 350° F. Butter both halves of an egg-shaped cake mold (about 9 by 4 by 3 inches). Dust with cake flour, and tap out excess. With an electric mixer on medium speed, beat 1 cup sugar with the egg yolks until pale. Add blood-orange zest and juice and almond extract, beating well to combine. Beat in almond flour.

Whisk the egg whites in a clean bowl on medium speed to soft peaks. Add salt and remaining 3 tablespoons sugar, and continue beating to stiff, glossy peaks. Fold melted butter into yolk mixture. Whisk in one-third of whites, then gently but thoroughly fold in remaining whites.

Divide batter between mold sections and place on a baking sheet; tuck pieces of crumpled foil under mold to prevent it from tipping, if necessary. Bake until a cake tester inserted in center comes out clean, 30 to 40 minutes. Transfer to a wire rack, and let cool 15 minutes. To unmold, run a paring knife around edges, and turn out cakes onto racks to cool completely. (Cakes can be wrapped in plastic and refrigerated, up to 1 day.)

Trim flat sides of cakes with a serrated knife to make level. In a chilled bowl, whip cream to soft peaks. Beat curd until smooth, then fold in whipped cream. Spread curd mixture over flat side of one cake, then attach other cake. Wrap in plastic, and refrigerate until chilled, at least 3 hours or up to 1 day.

Spread slivered almonds on a serving platter. Spread sloped side of a 3-inch wedge of bread with some Swiss meringue, then prop up cake on wedge in center of platter. Tuck parchment around edges of cake. Transfer remaining Swiss meringue to a pastry bag fitted with a coupler, and use a basket-weave tip (such as Wilton 1D) and a large plain tip (such as Ateco #7) to pipe meringue over cake (and wedge) in a basket-weave fashion as instructed on page 383. Switch to an open-star tip (such as Ateco #18), and pipe a border to cover the seams. Secure cake with a 12-inch wooden dowel, trimming flush with surface.

Arrange jelly beans around edge of platter, then nestle meringue nests in jelly beans and fill nests with more jelly beans. Use a small kitchen torch to lightly brown the meringue on the cake. If desired, use a dowel to attach a ribbon tied into a bow to top of cake. Serve immediately.

Blood-Orange Curd MAKES 1½ CUPS

- 1 teaspoon unflavored powdered gelatin
- 2 tablespoons cold water
- 4 large whole eggs plus 6 large egg yolks
- 1 cup sugar
  Finely grated zest of 2 blood oranges plus ½ cup fresh blood-orange juice (from 3 to 4 oranges)
- ¼ cup fresh lemon juice (from 1 to 2 lemons)
- ¼ teaspoon salt
- 6 tablespoons unsalted butter, cut into small pieces

Sprinkle gelatin over the cold water in a bowl; let soften, about 5 minutes.

In a small, heavy saucepan, whisk together whole eggs and the yolks. Add sugar, zest, juices, and salt. Cook over low heat, stirring constantly with a wooden spoon, until mixture is thick enough to coat the back of the spoon (it should hold a line drawn by your finger), 8 to 10 minutes.

Remove from heat, and add the softened gelatin, stirring until dissolved. Add butter, one piece at a time, stirring until smooth after each addition. Strain curd through a fine sieve into a bowl. Cover with plastic wrap, pressing it directly onto surface to prevent a skin from forming. Refrigerate until cold and set, at least 2 hours or up to 1 day. Whisk until smooth before using.

Tiny Meringue Nests MAKES 8

- 3 large egg whites
- ¾ cup sugar

Preheat oven to 200° F. Combine egg whites and sugar in the heatproof bowl of an electric mixer set over (not in) a pan of simmering water. Whisk until mixture is hot to the touch and sugar is dissolved (test by rubbing some between your fingers), about 3 minutes. Attach bowl to standing mixer; whisk mixture on medium-high speed until completely cooled (test by feeling the bottom of the bowl) and stiff peaks form, about 10 minutes.

Immediately transfer meringue to a pastry bag fitted with an open-star tip (such as Ateco #18). Pipe nests, about 1¼ inches in diameter, on parchment-lined baking sheets, spacing 1 inch apart. Bake until dry and crisp on the outside but still white, about 1 hour. Reduce oven to 175° F if meringue starts to brown. Let cool completely. (Meringue nests can be stored in airtight containers at room temperature up to 1 week.)

SPRING GARDEN CAKE

SERVES 40 TO 50 *from* **EASTER EGG HUNT**

See page 384 for step-by-step instructions and photographs on making the marzipan vegetables that adorn this showstopping cake.

- Brownie Cakes (recipe follows)
- 3 recipes Vanilla Swiss Meringue Buttercream (recipe follows)
- Carrot-Orange Cakes (recipe follows)
- 20 chocolate wafer cookies, finely ground
- 1 pound green sprinkles
- Marzipan Vegetables (recipe follows)
- Pastillage Fence (recipe follows)
- Candy pebbles, for garnish

Use a serrated knife to trim cake layers to make level. Arrange two of the four brownie layers on a ¼-inch piece of foam board with the long sides touching. Spread top with about 3 cups buttercream. Place a carrot cake layer on each brownie layer. Spread top and sides with about 5 cups buttercream. Top with remaining brownie layers. Chill until frosting is firm, about 15 minutes. Spread entire cake with remaining buttercream, and chill until firm, about 30 minutes or up to 1 day.

Using a paring knife or skewer, mark off "garden plots" in the buttercream. Fold foil into long sections to form barriers; place them on the plot marks to keep plots separate from paths. Sprinkle ¼ cup ground cookies into each plot and green sprinkles onto the paths. Remove and discard foil. Arrange marzipan vegetables in plots. Press pastillage fence onto sides of cake (keep bottoms flush with cake bottom), about ½ inch apart, preserving the curve shape at top of each section. Leave an opening at one side as a garden's entrance. Garnish platter with candy pebbles.

Brownie Cakes MAKES FOUR 9-BY-13-INCH LAYERS

- 1 pound (4 sticks) unsalted butter, cut into small pieces, plus more for pans
- 8 ounces good-quality unsweetened chocolate, coarsely chopped
- 1 pound good-quality semisweet chocolate, coarsely chopped
- 2¾ cups all-purpose flour
- 2 teaspoons baking powder
- 1 teaspoon salt
- 3 cups sugar
- 12 large eggs
- 2 tablespoons pure vanilla extract

Preheat oven to 325° F, with racks in upper and lower thirds. Line four 9-by-13-inch baking pans with parchment, leaving a 2-inch overhang on long sides. (If you don't have four baking pans, you can bake two layers at a time.) Butter paper (excluding overhang). Heat butter and both chocolates in a large heatproof bowl set over (not in) a pan of simmering water, stirring until melted. Remove from heat and let cool slightly.

Whisk together flour, baking powder, and salt in another bowl. Whisk sugar into chocolate mixture to combine, then add eggs, and whisk until mixture is smooth. Stir in vanilla. Add flour mixture; stir until just incorporated.

Divide batter evenly among prepared pans, and spread evenly with an offset spatula. Bake, rotating sheets from top to bottom and front to back halfway through, until a cake tester inserted into a cake (avoid center and edges) comes out with a few moist crumbs attached, about 30 minutes. Transfer pans to wire racks to cool 15 minutes, then lift out cakes (with parchment overhang) and let cool completely on racks. (Cake layers can be wrapped tightly in plastic and refrigerated up to 1 day or frozen up to 1 month; thaw in refrigerator before using.)

Carrot-Orange Cakes MAKES TWO 9-BY-13-INCH LAYERS

- 2½ cups neutral-tasting oil, such as safflower, plus more for pans
- 4 cups all-purpose flour
- 1 tablespoon ground cinnamon
- 2 teaspoons baking powder
- 2 teaspoons salt
- 4 cups sugar
- 8 large eggs, lightly beaten
- 8 cups finely grated carrots (about 2 pounds)
  Finely grated zest of 2 oranges
- 2 cups walnuts (about 9 ounces), toasted (page 423) and coarsely chopped

Lightly oil two 9-by-13-inch baking pans, and line with parchment. Into a bowl, sift together flour, cinnamon, baking powder, and salt. With an electric mixer on medium speed, beat oil and sugar to combine. With mixer on low speed, slowly add half the flour mixture; mix until blended. Add remaining flour mixture in three additions, alternating with the eggs, and ending with flour; scrape down sides of bowl as needed. Mix until combined, about 1 minute. Stir in carrots, zest, and nuts.

Divide batter between prepared pans and bake cakes until tops are golden and firm, about 1 hour. Let cool completely in pans on a wire rack. (Cakes can be wrapped tightly in plastic and refrigerated up to 1 day or frozen up to 1 month; thaw in refrigerator overnight before using.)

Vanilla Swiss Meringue Buttercream

MAKES 5 CUPS

- 5 large egg whites
- 1 cup plus 2 tablespoons sugar
- 1 pound (4 sticks) unsalted butter, cut into small pieces, softened
- 1 vanilla bean, split lengthwise and seeds scraped (reserve pods for another use)

Whisk egg whites and sugar in the heatproof bowl of an electric mixer set over (not in) a pan of simmering water until sugar has dissolved and an instant-read thermometer registers 160° F, 2 to 3 minutes.

Attach bowl to standing mixer; whisk on high speed until fluffy and cooled, about 10 minutes. Reduce speed to medium low; add butter, several pieces at a time, beating well after each addition. Don't worry if mixture appears curdled; it will become smooth again with continued beating. Beat in vanilla seeds. Reduce speed to low; beat until smooth. (Buttercream can be refrigerated, covered, up to 3 days; before using, bring to room temperature, and beat on low until smooth.)

Marzipan Vegetables

MAKES ENOUGH TO DECORATE SPRING GARDEN CAKE

- 8 ounces almond paste
- 2 cups confectioners' sugar, sifted
- ¼ cup plus 2 tablespoons light corn syrup
  Gel-paste food colors, for tinting

Pulse almond paste and confectioners' sugar in a food processor until combined. Add the corn syrup, and pulse until combined. Mixture should hold together when pressed. Transfer to a clean work surface; knead until a smooth dough is formed. Wrap in plastic, and keep at room temperature until ready to use. (Marzipan is best used the day it is made; wrap tightly in plastic to prevent it from drying out.) To tint, divide into pieces and add food coloring with a toothpick, kneading until fully distributed before adding more. Form marzipan into vegetables according to instructions on page 384.

Pastillage Fence

MAKES ENOUGH TO DECORATE SPRING GARDEN CAKE

- 5 cups plus 3 tablespoons confectioners' sugar, plus more if needed
- ¼ cup plus 2 tablespoons cornstarch, plus more for dusting
- 2 teaspoons unflavored powdered gelatin
- ¼ cup plus 3 tablespoons cold water
- 1 large egg white
  Juice of ½ lemon

Sift confectioners' sugar and cornstarch into the bowl of an electric mixer fitted with the paddle attachment. In a separate bowl, sprinkle gelatin over ¼ cup plus 2 tablespoons cold water. Let soften 5 minutes.

In a heatproof bowl, combine egg white and remaining 1 tablespoon cold water. Set bowl over (not in) a pan of gently simmering water; stir until warm to the touch, about 2 minutes. Remove from heat; add softened gelatin, and stir until dissolved. (If gelatin does not dissolve completely, return mixture to pan of simmering water; stir until completely dissolved.)

Add gelatin mixture to cornstarch mixture. Add lemon juice, and mix on low speed until mixture comes together. Do not overmix. If it appears too dry, add a few drops of lukewarm water; if it appears too wet, sprinkle in more confectioners' sugar. Transfer pastillage to a clean work surface dusted with cornstarch. Knead until smooth, two to three times. Wrap in plastic wrap and chill up to 24 hours; bring to r-oom temperature before using.

Pinch off a small piece of pastillage (keep the rest wrapped); place on a clean work surface dusted with cornstarch. Roll out to a 5-by-6-inch rough rectangle, about ⅛ inch thick. Using a ruler (or other straight edge) and a pastry wheel or paring knife, trim to a 4½-by-5-inch rectangle. With a short side facing you, cut a half-moon shape from top edge of rectangle, using an inverted 10-inch bowl as a guide. (The shortest point in the middle should be about 4½ inches.) Cut lengthwise into eight ½-inch-wide strips. With a spatula, transfer pickets to a parchment-lined baking sheet to dry at least 6 hours or up to 1 day. Repeat steps to roll pastillage and form pickets ten times.

INDIVIDUAL DIABLO CAKES

MAKES 8 *from* **STYLISH DINNER IN THE CLERESTORY**

These cakes were decorated with pink macarons around the sides and garnished with sugared grapes and figs, but they are also delightful when simply glazed. For the macarons, follow the recipe on page 412, tinting the cookie batter pale pink with gel-paste food coloring and filling with raspberry jam. The raisins need to soak at least one day, so plan accordingly.

- ¼ cup raisins
- ¼ cup Scotch whiskey or rum
- ½ cup (1 stick) unsalted butter, cut into tablespoons and softened, plus more, melted, for ramekins
- ¼ cup plus 1 tablespoon cake flour (not self-rising), plus more for ramekins
- 1 cup semisweet chocolate morsels
- 2 tablespoons water
- 3 large eggs, separated
- ⅔ cup sugar
- ⅔ cup almond flour or finely ground blanched almonds
- ¼ teaspoon salt
  Chocolate Glaze (recipe follows)
  Macarons, for decorating (optional; page 412)
  Sugared Fruit, for garnish (optional; recipe follows)

Soak raisins 1 to 2 days in whiskey.

Preheat oven to 350° F. Brush eight 6-ounce ramekins or custard cups with melted butter, then line bottoms with parchment rounds. Butter parchment and dust ramekins with flour, tapping out excess. Place ramekins on a rimmed baking sheet.

In a heatproof bowl set over (not in) a pan of simmering water, melt chocolate with the water. Stir in butter, 1 tablespoon at a time, and then whisk until smooth. Remove from heat.

With an electric mixer on medium speed, beat egg yolks and sugar until creamy, about 8 minutes. Add the chocolate mixture, and mix until combined. Add the flour and ground almonds; mix on low speed just until combined. Gently stir in the raisins and whiskey.

In another mixing bowl, whisk egg whites and salt until stiff but not dry, about 3 minutes. Fold the egg-white mixture into the chocolate mixture in three additions.

Divide batter evenly among prepared ramekins. Bake until a cake tester inserted in the center of a cake comes out clean and the cakes begin to shrink away from the sides of the pan, about 25 minutes, rotating sheet halfway through. Let cool in ramekins 20 minutes, then turn out onto a wire rack to cool completely. Using a serrated knife, trim tops of cakes to make level; sweep away any crumbs with a pastry brush.

Return to baking sheet and spread each cake with cooled glaze, using an offset spatula to create a smooth coat. Chill until glaze is set, about 25 minutes. Transfer chilled cakes to a rack on a parchment-lined rimmed baking sheet. Pour the warm glaze slowly over top of cakes; use an offset spatula to smooth the top and sides. Let glaze set, about 15 minutes, attaching macarons to sides of cake after about 5 minutes, if desired.

To serve, place a cake on each dessert plate, and garnish with sugared fruit.

Chocolate Glaze MAKES 2½ CUPS

- 12 ounces bittersweet chocolate (preferably 70% cocoa), finely chopped
- 1¼ cups heavy cream

Prepare an ice-water bath. Place chocolate in a heatproof bowl. Bring cream to a boil in a heavy saucepan. Pour cream over chocolate; let stand 5 minutes, then stir until chocolate is melted and mixture is smooth. Transfer 1 cup glaze to a small bowl set in the ice bath, stirring until thick before spreading over cakes. Set remaining glaze over (not in) a pan of barely simmering water, and keep warm until ready to pour over cake.

Sugared Fruit MAKES ENOUGH TO GARNISH 8 CAKES

- 4 large egg whites (or ½ cup powdered egg whites or meringue powder)
- ½ cup warm water
- ½ cup superfine sugar
- 1 bunch red Champagne grapes, preferably organic, cut into small clusters
- 1 pint fresh Black Mission figs, halved lengthwise

In a small bowl, beat egg whites (or powdered egg whites) and the warm water until frothy. Put superfine sugar in another bowl.

Working with one at a time, dip grape clusters into egg whites, and shake off excess; roll in sugar to coat. Transfer to a parchment-lined baking sheet. Use a small pastry brush to coat fig halves with egg whites; shake off excess. Roll in sugar, then transfer to baking sheet. Let set at room temperature, uncovered, up to 1 day.

Basics

CHICKEN STOCK

MAKES 2½ QUARTS

- 5 pounds assorted chicken parts (backs, necks, and wings)
- 2 carrots, cut into 1- to 2-inch lengths
- 2 celery stalks, cut into 1- to 2-inch lengths
- 2 onions, cut into eighths
- 1 bay leaf
- 1 teaspoon whole black peppercorns

Place chicken parts in a large pot and add enough water to cover by 1 inch (about 3 quarts). Bring to a boil, skimming foam from surface. Add remaining ingredients. Reduce heat to a bare simmer and cook, skimming frequently, 1 hour.

Strain stock through a fine sieve lined with cheesecloth into a large heatproof measuring cup or another pot (do not press on solids). Discard solids. Skim off fat if using immediately, or let cool completely before transferring to airtight containers. Refrigerate at least 8 hours to allow the fat to accumulate at the top; lift off and discard fat before using or storing stock. (The stock can be refrigerated up to 3 days or frozen up to 3 months; thaw overnight in the refrigerator before using.)

VEGETABLE STOCK

MAKES 3 CUPS

2 large horseradish roots (about 12 ounces each), scrubbed and cut into 1½-inch pieces
2 celery stalks, cut into 1-inch pieces
1 large onion, coarsely chopped
1 quart water

Combine all ingredients in a medium pot and bring to a boil. Reduce heat, cover, and simmer 45 minutes. Strain stock through a fine sieve into a bowl (do not press on solids); discard solids. Let cool completely before transferring to an airtight container. (The stock can be refrigerated up to 3 days or frozen up to 3 months; thaw overnight in the refrigerator before using.)

BEEF STOCK

MAKES 6 QUARTS

8 sprigs flat-leaf parsley
6 sprigs thyme
4 sprigs rosemary
2 bay leaves
1 tablespoon whole black peppercorns
1 pound beef stew meat, cubed
5 pounds veal bones, cut into small pieces
1 large onion, unpeeled and quartered
2 large carrots, cut into thirds
2 celery stalks, cut into thirds
2 cups dry red wine

Preheat oven to 400° F. Tie parsley, thyme, rosemary, bay leaves, and peppercorns in a piece of cheesecloth to make a bouquet garni.

Arrange the meat, bones, onion, carrots, and celery in an even layer in a heavy roasting pan. Roast, turning every 20 minutes, until vegetables and bones are deep brown, about 1½ hours. Transfer meat, bones, and vegetables to a large pot.

Pour off fat from roasting pan, and discard. Place the pan over high heat. Add wine, and stir, using a wooden spoon to loosen any browned bits from the bottom of the pan; boil until the wine is reduced by half, about 5 minutes. Pour the mixture into the pot.

Add enough water to just cover bones (about 6 quarts) and bring to a boil, then reduce heat to a bare simmer. Skim foam from surface. Add bouquet garni and continue to simmer over lowest possible heat for 3 hours, skimming surface as needed. If at any time liquid level drops below the bones, add more water.

Strain stock through a fine sieve lined with cheesecloth into a large heat-proof measuring cup or another pot (do not press on solids). Discard solids.

Skim off fat if using immediately, or let cool completely before transferring to airtight containers. Refrigerate at least 8 hours to allow the fat to accumulate at the top; lift off and discard fat before using or storing stock. (The stock can be refrigerated up to 3 days or frozen up to 3 months; thaw completely in the refrigerator before using.)

PÂTE BRISÉE

MAKES ENOUGH FOR ONE 9-INCH DOUBLE-CRUST PIE OR TWO 9- TO 10-INCH TARTS OR SINGLE-CRUST PIES

When using the pastry dough in savory recipes, omit the sugar.

2½ cups all-purpose flour, plus more for dusting
1 teaspoon salt
1 teaspoon sugar
1 cup (2 sticks) cold unsalted butter, cut into small pieces
¼ to ½ cup ice water

Pulse flour, salt, and sugar in a food processor to combine. Add butter, and pulse until mixture resembles coarse crumbs with some larger pieces remaining. Evenly drizzle ¼ cup ice water over mixture. Pulse until dough is crumbly but holds together when squeezed. If dough is too dry, add up to ¼ cup more water, 1 tablespoon at a time, and pulse to combine.

Turn out dough onto a floured surface and divide dough in half, then shape into disks. Wrap each half in plastic and refrigerate until firm, about 1 hour or up to 1 day. (Dough can be frozen up to 1 month; thaw overnight in refrigerator before using.)

Note
Save the dough scraps for making pastry cutouts such as the sweet maple leaves that garnish the Pumpkin Mousse on page 415: Reroll dough once, then use a floured leaf cutter to cut out as many leaves as possible. Place on a baking sheet and bake at 350° F until light golden and crisp, rotating sheet halfway through, about 12 minutes. Cool completely before using or storing in an airtight container at room temperature, up to 3 days.

PÂTE SUCRÉE

MAKES ENOUGH FOR ONE 9- TO 14-INCH TART

1¼ cups all-purpose flour, plus more for dusting
1 tablespoon plus 1½ teaspoons sugar
½ teaspoon salt
½ cup (1 stick) cold unsalted butter, cut into small pieces
1 large egg yolk, lightly beaten
2 to 4 tablespoons ice water

Pulse flour, sugar, and salt in a food processor to combine. Add butter; process until mixture resembles coarse crumbs with some larger pieces remaining. Add egg yolk; pulse to combine. Evenly drizzle 2 tablespoons ice water over mixture and pulse until dough just begins to come together. If dough is too dry, add up to 2 tablespoons more water, 1 tablespoon at a time, and pulse to combine.

Turn out onto a floured work surface and shape into a disk. Wrap in plastic and refrigerate until firm, about 1 hour or up to overnight. (Dough can be frozen up to 1 month; thaw before using.)

THE RECIPES

TART DOUGH

MAKES ENOUGH FOR ONE 14-INCH TART

- 2 cups all-purpose flour
- ½ cup fine yellow cornmeal
- 1 teaspoon sugar
- 1 teaspoon salt
- 1 cup (2 sticks) very cold unsalted butter, cut into small cubes
- ¼ cup plus 1 tablespoon ice water, plus more if needed

Pulse flour, cornmeal, sugar, and salt in a food processor to combine. Add butter, and pulse until mixture resembles coarse crumbs with some larger pieces remaining. Evenly drizzle ¼ cup plus 1 tablespoon ice water over mixture. Pulse until dough is crumbly but holds together when squeezed. If dough is too dry, add more water, 1 tablespoon at a time, and pulse to combine.

Turn out dough onto a work surface and knead once or twice, then shape into a disk. Wrap in plastic and refrigerate until firm, about 1 hour or up to overnight. (Dough can be frozen up to 1 month; thaw overnight in refrigerator before using.)

SWISS MERINGUE

MAKES 4 CUPS

Even the tiniest amount of yolk in your egg whites will prevent them from whipping. Be sure your hands and all equipment are clean, dry, and oil-free.

- 4 large egg whites
  Pinch of cream of tartar
- 1 cup sugar
- 1 teaspoon pure vanilla extract

In a metal mixing bowl, whisk egg whites and cream of tartar to break up egg whites. Set bowl over (not in) a pan of simmering water (do not let bottom of bowl touch water, or eggs may begin to set). Whisk until whites are foamy, then gradually whisk in sugar, and continue whisking until mixture is completely smooth (test by rubbing some between your fingertips).

Attach bowl to a standing mixer and whisk on low speed 5 minutes. Increase speed to high, and whisk until meringue is stiff and glossy, about 5 minutes more. Mix in vanilla and use immediately.

SIMPLE SYRUP

MAKES ABOUT 2 CUPS

Follow the recipe to make as much syrup as desired, using equal parts sugar and water. You can also add flavorings, such as fresh herbs, sliced fresh ginger, pounded lemongrass stalks, or citrus peel, to the prepared syrup; let them steep while syrup cools. Discard before using or storing.

- 1¼ cups sugar
- 1¼ cups water

Bring sugar and the water to a boil in a saucepan, stirring to dissolve sugar. Remove from heat; let cool to room temperature before using or storing. (Syrup can be refrigerated, covered, up to 6 months.)

VANILLA-BEAN PASTRY CREAM

MAKES ABOUT 1 CUP

- ¼ cup sugar
- 2 tablespoons cornstarch
- 1 cup milk
- 1 vanilla bean, split lengthwise
- 2 large egg yolks
- 1 tablespoon unsalted butter, cut into small pieces
  Pinch of salt

In a saucepan, whisk together sugar and cornstarch until blended; stir in milk. Scrape vanilla seeds into milk mixture, then add the pod. Whisking constantly, bring to a simmer over medium heat.

Whisk egg yolks until blended in a bowl. While whisking, slowly add about half the hot milk mixture to temper the egg yolks, then pour back into pan with remaining milk mixture. Bring to a simmer over medium-high heat, whisking constantly. Reduce heat and simmer, stirring constantly, until thick enough to hold its shape when lifted with the spoon, about 3 minutes. Remove from heat.

Strain through a fine sieve into a bowl, pressing with a flexible spatula to extract as much liquid as possible; discard solids. Stir butter and salt into warm pastry cream until incorporated. Let cool slightly, then cover with plastic wrap, pressing it directly onto the surface to prevent a skin from forming. Refrigerate until chilled, at least 2 hours or up to 2 days.

CRÈME ANGLAISE

MAKES ABOUT 2 CUPS

1¼ cups milk
¾ cup heavy cream
½ vanilla bean, split lengthwise
4 large egg yolks
3 tablespoons sugar
   Pinch of salt

Combine milk and cream in a saucepan. Scrape in vanilla bean seeds and add the pod. Bring to a simmer over medium heat.

Whisk together egg yolks, sugar, and salt in a bowl. While whisking, slowly add about half the hot milk mixture into the yolk mixture to temper, then pour mixture back into pan with remaining milk mixture. Cook over medium heat, stirring constantly, until mixture is thick enough to coat the back of the spoon, about 5 minutes.

Strain through a fine sieve into a bowl, pressing with a flexible spatula to extract as much liquid as possible; discard solids. Cover with plastic wrap and refrigerate until chilled, at least 2 hours or up to 2 days.

Chocolate Variation
Transfer ½ cup crème anglaise to a small bowl and stir in 2 ounces finely chopped bittersweet chocolate; let stand 3 minutes, then stir until chocolate is melted and mixture is smooth.

HOLLANDAISE SAUCE

MAKES ABOUT 1 CUP

3 large egg yolks, room temperature
4½ teaspoons fresh lemon juice
¾ cup (1½ sticks) unsalted butter, melted and cooled
   Coarse salt

Whisk yolks in a large heatproof glass bowl until they begin to turn pale, about 1 minute. Whisk in 4½ teaspoons warm water. Set bowl over a pan of barely simmering water; heat yolk mixture, whisking vigorously, until thickened, 2 to 3 minutes (do not overcook). Remove bowl from pan. Whisk in lemon juice.

Whisking constantly, pour in melted butter, one drop at a time at first, leaving milky solids behind; whisk until thickened. Season with salt. If not serving immediately, pour hot water from pan into a separate (cool) pan; set bowl on top. Keep sauce warm, whisking occasionally, up to 30 minutes. If sauce becomes too thick, whisk in warm water, 1 teaspoon at a time, to thin.

Basic Techniques

Toasting Nuts: Spread nuts on a rimmed baking sheet and toast in a 350° F oven until fragrant and darkened slightly, 7 to 10 minutes, tossing occasionally. Transfer to a plate to cool.

Hard-Cooking Eggs: Place eggs in a deep saucepan and cover with cold water by 1 inch. Bring to a boil, then immediately remove from heat. Cover and let stand 13 minutes. Use a slotted spoon to transfer eggs to an ice-water bath to stop the cooking and cool completely. Unpeeled eggs can be refrigerated up to 1 week. To peel, roll the hard-cooked egg under your palm on a work surface to crack the shell, then hold the egg under cold running water while peeling.

Roasting Peppers: Roast peppers over a gas flame or under the broiler, turning as each side blackens, until charred all over. Let cool in a covered bowl, then rub off skins with paper towels. Do not rinse. Remove and discard core and seeds.

Peeling Pearl Onions: Blanch onions in a pot of boiling water for 30 seconds. Use a slotted spoon to transfer onions to an ice-water bath to stop the cooking. When cool enough to handle, cut off the root end with a paring knife and pop the onions from the skins.

Peeling Tomatoes: Using a paring knife, lightly score bottom of tomatoes with an X. Blanch tomatoes in a pot of boiling water until skins are loosened, 5 to 30 seconds depending on ripeness. Use a slotted spoon to transfer tomatoes to an ice-water bath to stop the cooking. When cool enough to handle, peel tomatoes and cut each into quarters, then scoop out and discard seeds and pulp.

Peeling Peaches and Nectarines: Blanch fruit in a pot of boiling water until skins are loosened, 10 to 30 seconds depending on ripeness. Use a slotted spoon to transfer fruit to an ice-water bath to stop the cooking. When cool enough to handle, gently remove skins with your fingers; remove any tough spots with a paring knife.

Peeling Chestnuts: Cut a slit in each chestnut with scissors or a paring knife. Cook chestnuts in a pot of boiling water for 20 minutes, then drain in a colander. When cool enough to handle, peel off and discard shells and inner brown skins.

Grilling Tips

- Chicken should be started skin side down, basting frequently. Once the first side has browned, turn it over and grill to finish.

- Chicken wings should be marinated and basted often so the tips do not burn.

- Kebabs should be cooked slowly and turned frequently.

- Hamburgers should be plump and not too large; grill slowly until medium-rare, then top with cheese, not before. Take care not to overcook burgers, and to grill the bun or roll for serving.

- Shrimp and seafood take very little time to grill; marinate or brush with a mix of oil and herbs, or any other flavorful marinade. Turn frequently, brushing lightly with the herbed oil or marinade.

- Ribs should be precooked, then grilled very slowly until well done.

Acknowledgments

A book of this scope and size requires the help and involvement of many people. I have been working on the subject matter for this book—entertaining—since I published my very first book, on the same subject, in 1982. Recipes were tried, and those that were good were collected in files. Parties were planned, tables were set, flower arrangements devised, themes created, and decorations invented. Over the years the best of those myriad ideas were photographed and assembled into this volume, and I lovingly sat down to write when the book was designed and the pages set. I had a very good time creating this book amidst the other work I do on a daily basis and with my many friends and colleagues, employees and suppliers who worked so hard.

Helping me with the parties, the food, the planning, the styling of the photos, and the actual photography were the following:

Pierre Schaedelin

Frédéric Lagrange

Kevin Sharkey

Ayesha Patel

Laura Acuna

Peggy Knox

Sanu Sherpa

Cheryl Dulong

Claire Sasner

Lily Pei

Maria Galvez

Julia Eisemann

Erica Einfeldt

Kate Shillo

Tom Borgese

Susie Ercole

Eliad Laskin

Michael Fiore

Gretchen Sweet

Bryan Dow

Designing and laying out the thousands of photographs, and editing my text:

Eric A. Pike

Ellen Morrissey

William van Roden

Evelyn Battaglia

Jessi Blackham

Testing the recipes prepared by me and Pierre were the following food editors:

Christine Albano

Shira Bocar

Monita Buchwald

Sarah Carey

Elizabeth Vought Greene

Anna Kovel

Heather Meldrom

Lesley Stockton

Others at MSLO helped put the book together, inluding maintaining schedules, coordinating and cataloging the photographs, and providing other invaluable support:

Leigh Ann Boutwell

Denise Clappi

Amy Conway

Alison Vanek Devine

Erin Fagerland

Stephanie Fletcher

Catherine Gilbert

Heloise Goodman

Fritz Karch

Marcie McGoldrick

Hannah Milman

Matthew Papa

Amy Vreeland

And as always, we are grateful for our longtime publishing partners at Clarkson Potter:

Rica Allannic

Amy Boorstein

Angelin Borsics

Doris Cooper

Derek Gullino

Maya Mavjee

Mark McCauslin

Marysarah Quinn

Lauren Shakely

Jane Treuhaft

Kate Tyler

General Index

Recipe Index

Note: Page references in *italics* refer to photographs.

Photograph Credits

All photographs by Frédéric Lagrange except on the following pages:

Simon Watson: 11 (left), 70–71, 104, 106 (top two and bottom left), 107, 109–11

Anna Williams: 11 (right), 34–40, 42, 116, 118–19, 121–33

Joel Meyerowitz: 24 (left), 218 (right)

John Kernick: 62 (left), 220–25, 236–49

Hugh Stewart: 134–35, 137–43

Helen Norman: 153 (left)

Christopher Baker: 159, 161 (left 3), 163–64

Ditte Isager: 193, 194–97, 24–25, 80 (right), 81, 270, 272, 302–8, 310